Sentencing Advocacy

Sentencing Advocacy

Principles and Strategy

C.J. Williams

McFarland & Company, Inc., Publishers
Jefferson, North Carolina

This book has undergone peer review.

ISBN (print) 978-1-4766-8754-4
ISBN (ebook) 978-1-4766-4747-0

Library of Congress and British Library
cataloguing data are available

Library of Congress Control Number 2022042905

Printed in the United States of America

McFarland & Company, Inc., Publishers
Box 611, Jefferson, North Carolina 28640
www.mcfarlandpub.com

To all the men and women
who have dedicated their careers
to the criminal justice system.

Acknowledgments

I owe a debt of gratitude to those who read early manuscripts of this book, in whole or in part. These include my longtime friend and former colleague Sean Berry, Assistant Federal Public Defender Chris Nathan, who now teaches a course with Sean and me on sentencing advocacy, John Zielke, Jill Bushaw, and Daren Schumaker, all of the United States Probation Office for the Northern District of Iowa. Each of them provided me with valuable feedback and suggestions that have made this book significantly better than what I started with. Any errors that remain are mine and mine alone. I also am indebted to all of the prosecutors, defense attorneys, and probation officers with whom I have worked over the past decades in my capacity as defense attorney, prosecutor, and judge. What I know about sentencing advocacy is largely the product of that experience and what I have learned from others. Finally, I wish to thank my editors at McFarland who saw promise in this topic and helped me navigate the manuscript through the editorial process to successful publication.

Table of Contents

Preface

This book addresses effective sentencing advocacy at every stage of a criminal case, from investigation through pretrial, plea, trial, sentencing hearings, and post-sentencing proceedings. It also addressed all aspects of sentencing, including not only terms of imprisonment or probation, but fines, forfeiture, and collateral consequences of criminal sentences. This book emphasizes the need to approach sentencing advocacy holistically, as a critical aspect of attorney advocacy in every criminal case.

The need for a book on this topic is great. Fewer and fewer cases are proceeding to trial for many reasons, thus shifting the focus of effective advocacy in criminal cases away from trial advocacy. The reality is that the vast majority of criminal charges result in convictions, either by way of a guilty plea or trial. Each of the offenders in these cases will be sentenced. Sentencing advocacy therefore needs to be central in the minds of prosecutors and defense attorneys alike, not an afterthought as it all too often is. Further, far too little attention is paid or training provided to law students and attorneys on effective sentencing advocacy. The fact that there are so few books and articles on the topic shows the neglect it has received. What few books exist on the topic of sentencing focus more on the law of certain sentencing issues, such as restitution or forfeiture, and little if any attention is devoted to the role of advocacy in sentencing.

This book is directed at a wide audience, as there appears to be no comprehensive book in publication on the topic. Thus, the book covers some aspects of sentencing advocacy that may appear fundamental to an experienced practitioner. And yet, it delves into some detail on some aspects of sentencing advocacy that may appear too complex to a novice in the practice of criminal law. Importantly, this is not a book on the law of sentencing issues. In other words, although the book addresses legal issues involved in sentencing advocacy, it does not purport to be a book setting out the law on current sentencing issues. Rather, the focus is on how attorneys can use advocacy at every stage of a criminal case to advance the interests of their clients in achieving the best sentence for their clients, whether they represent the government or offenders.

I based this book on research of primary sources, such as statutes, judicial decisions, and sentencing Guidelines, on secondary sources such as law review articles, and on my personal experience and observations after more than three decades as a criminal defense attorney, federal prosecutor, and federal judge.

1

The Importance of Effective Sentencing Advocacy

"[N]o more difficult task confronts judges than the determination of punishment not fixed by statute."[1]

Of all the hearings that take place in a courtroom, none is more important, more emotional, and more impactful than sentencing hearings. The sentencing of a criminal offender is the culmination of a criminal investigation and prosecution. It is the time when the government punishes the offender for criminally violating societal norms. For law enforcement officers who investigated the case, a sentencing hearing may feel like the ultimate vindication of their hard work and dedication. For crime victims, sentencing hearings can encompass great emotional turmoil and drama. Criminal offenders' family and loved ones tensely await the outcome as they witness the sentencing proceeding that may separate them from the person they love and change their lives forever. And, of course, for criminal offenders a sentencing hearing is often the most important and traumatic event in their lives, when they suffer shame and embarrassment, guilt and regret, and apprehension and fear about their future. A sentencing hearing is the climax in the drama of a criminal case, with all the pathos of the most emotional Hollywood production.

The sentence a judge ultimately imposes could place the offender behind bars for months, years, or even life. The sentence can financially ruin the offender and potentially his family as well, while in some cases it may also simultaneously provide hope of restitution to victims of financial crimes. A criminal sentence can have a tremendous ripple effect on the offender and others through a myriad of collateral consequences, such as deportation, loss of a professional license, and sex offender registration requirement, all of which can have a life-time effect, regardless of the length of any sentence of incarceration.

Sentencing hearings also constitute proceedings in which judges have the widest discretion to rule. Indeterminate sentencing provides judges almost unfettered discretion to impose sentences anywhere within the statutory ranges, between the mandatory minimum and the maximum sentence the legislature established. This range is often measured in decades. And in exercising that discretion, judges are permitted to consider almost anything, including not only the nature and circumstances of the criminal offense, but everything about the history and characteristics of the offender, the impact on victims, and the goals of sentencing. In doing so, judges are free from the restraints of evidence rules designed to ensure factfinders consider only reliable evidence. Rather, in sentencing hearings judges are free to consider any evidence that has a "sufficient indicia of reliability to support its probable accuracy."[2] Further, unlike in many other contexts in which district judges enter rulings, in sentencing hearings judges are largely unbound by precedent on the ultimate sentence to be imposed.

Advocacy at a sentencing hearing by both prosecutors and defense attorneys is crucial. Sentencing Guidelines may provide a template for judges in determining appropriate sentences, but Guidelines are just that—guidelines—and are not binding. Instead, a lone judge has ultimately to consider all the facts, factors, and goals of sentencing, and then mentally and sometimes emotionally struggle to arrive at a sentence that the judge deems appropriate. Attorneys have an important calling to use the art of persuasion to influence sentencing judges' decisions. Effective advocacy at sentencing has perhaps a greater chance to influence the outcome of the hearing than in nearly any other type of hearing. As important, effective representation before the sentencing hearing, and indeed even before any determination of guilt, can significantly impact the judge's sentencing options and define the scope of the punishment that may be imposed at the time of sentencing. In short, effective sentencing advocacy starts long before the sentencing hearing.

It is surprising, then, that so little has been written on effective sentencing advocacy. To be sure, there are numerous volumes extant about the law of sentencing. Similarly, many books advise attorneys on how to be effective advocates in jury trials, while many others provide guidance on effective appellate advocacy. Very little has been written, however, on how attorneys can or should be effective advocates at a sentencing hearing. Likewise, almost nothing has been written about effective sentencing advocacy during the pendency of the criminal case and before the sentencing hearing. This volume is intended to fill that gap in part.

The need for attention to sentencing advocacy is great. Some attorneys treat sentencing as an afterthought, and it has been described as the most neglected part of a criminal case.[3] In the federal system, attorney neglect of sentencing advocacy may be, in part, a product of several decades of a mandatory-guideline system when judges had very little discretion at sentencing. As one commentator has noted, it appears that in the federal system, attorneys' sentencing advocacy skills have atrophied during the decades of the mandatory sentencing Guidelines and determinant sentencing regimes adopted in the 1980s.[4] After *United States v. Booker*, 543 U.S. 320 (2005), and its progeny, however, the United States Federal Sentencing Guidelines are no longer mandatory—they are just guidelines. Except for mandatory minimum sentences, the federal sentencing scheme has largely returned to a form of indeterminant sentencing. Yet, the prosecutors and defense attorneys practicing law today cut their teeth on and grew of age during a time of a form of determinant sentencing, when judges had very little discretion at sentencing. There was correspondingly little need for effective sentencing advocacy. An entire generation of attorneys are consequently untrained in the art of effective sentencing advocacy in federal court. Thus, effective sentencing advocacy has never been more important in the federal system. Not only do sentencing judges again have broad discretion to impose sentences, the long-ago elimination of parole in the federal system means that the sentences judges impose will be the sentences the offenders actually serve. No longer does a parole board parole an offender after serving only part of the sentence imposed.

Yet, the problem of attorneys failing to devote sufficient attention to sentencing as a critical and essential stage in a criminal case is not limited to attorneys practicing in federal court. Sentencing advocacy is at least equally neglected in the state systems. Indeed, in state courts, sometimes prosecutors do not even appear at sentencing hearings and stand-in defense attorneys often represent offenders at sentencing hearings.[5]

Effective representation of clients in criminal cases, whether the clients are governments or offenders, demands effective sentencing advocacy. Attorneys cannot effectively represent their clients if the focus of their efforts remains only on the determination of guilt. To be sure, preparing for trial and trying criminal cases remains an essential part of all attorneys' duties. But attorneys should simultaneously recognize that less than ten percent of all criminal cases result in jury trials; more than 90 percent of the offenders will plead guilty. Of those criminal cases that go to trial, based on past statistics, the government will win more than 90 percent of them. Thus, the vast majority of offenders represented by defense attorneys will be sentenced. Ignoring that fact until the day of reckoning by focusing only on trials and treating sentencing as an afterthought is a tremendous disservice to offenders.

Effective sentencing advocacy not only serves the clients—the offender and the government—but it also serves the community at large. Sentences that are carefully tailored to advance the goals of sentencing generate trust in the criminal justice system, protect the public, helps reform offenders, and minimize the adverse consequences to victims and the public. Poorly structured sentences resulting from ineffective sentencing advocacy can cause more systemic problems than they solve. We trust the adversarial justice system to arrive at the truth; the truth in a sentencing hearing includes arriving at a sentence that is sufficient, but not greater than necessary, to achieve the goals of sentencing. 18 U.S.C. § 3553(a). The adversary system only works, however, if the advocates for both sides are effective and zealous.

This book on sentencing advocacy discusses the topic primarily in the context of federal sentencing. It does so for two very practical reasons. First, it is what I know. I served as a law clerk for a federal judge. I was a federal prosecutor for more than 20 years. And even when I was in civil private practice for five years in a large Kansas City law firm, the limited white-collar criminal defense work I performed was in federal court. And now I have been a federal judge for about four years and have sentenced hundreds of offenders. People write about what they know, and if I know anything, I know federal criminal practice. Second, the differences and nuances of sentencing practices and procedures in the 50 states are too many and too varied, from my brief survey, to be easily addressed in a single volume.

That is not to say that this book entirely ignores state court sentencing advocacy.

At appropriate places, I point out and discuss how state sentencing procedures may differ from the federal system. Regardless, the points I make in this book about effective sentencing advocacy largely apply to state prosecutors and defense attorneys. Although my discussion of sentencing advocacy is placed in the context of federal statutes, guidelines, rules, and procedures, the principles of effective sentencing advocacy discussed are easily transferrable to the context of any state practice. The federal system is simply the backdrop against which I illustrate methods of effective sentencing advocacy. Change the context, and the methods remain largely still applicable.

This is not a book on the law of sentencing, although I do discuss the law of sentencing to the extent it impacts the scope and nature of effective sentencing advocacy. For example, effective advocacy depends upon understanding the decision-maker's views, limitations, and restrictions. It follows, then, that effective sentencing advocacy requires attorneys to have an understanding of how judges view sentencing, their focus on the goals of sentencing, and how their decision-making authority is restricted and structured by the governing statutory and procedural sentencing scheme. Similarly, in considering whether to advocate that judges depart or vary from sentencing Guidelines ranges of imprisonment, it is important that attorneys have some understanding of the general law applying to judges' discretion to depart or vary. On the other hand, because the focus of this book is on effective sentencing advocacy, I will not delve into any detail into the significant amount of case law addressing each of the many grounds for departures or variances from sentencing Guidelines, or summarize the legion of cases ruling on whether sentencing judges abused their discretion when imposing fines, ordering forfeiture of property, or imposing conditions of supervised release or probation.

As a final caveat, this book does not explore sentencing advocacy in capital cases. Having tried two capital cases and worked on many more as a prosecutor, I am all too aware that sentencings in capital cases bear no resemblance to sentencings in non-capital cases. As capital litigators know, "Death is different."[6] Whether the capital case is in state or federal court, the sentencing portion of a capital case is combined with and integrated into the trial on the merits in one form or another. The nature of the evidence admitted and legally admissible in the sentencing phase of a capital case differs dramatically from that in a noncapital case. And in the federal system, and in most state courts, a jury, not a judge, determines whether the offender should die, whereas just the opposite is true in noncapital cases.[7] Thus, the actual so-called sentencing hearing that follows the jury's verdict in a capital case is little more than a formality, especially when, as in the federal system, the judge is bound by the jury's sentencing verdict. Although perhaps someone should write a book on sentencing advocacy in capital cases, this is not that book.

In this book, I set out to provide guidance to both prosecutors and defense attorneys on how to be effective advocates in non-capital sentencing hearings with federal court as the context for the discussion. The beginning chapters address big-picture issues including sentencing advocacy skills, sentencing advocacy before guilt, and the statutory and Guidelines sentencing schemes. The next section covers sentencing advocacy between guilt and the sentencing hearing, such as preparing for and objecting to the presentence investigation report and drafting sentencing memoranda. Several chapters then address the sentencing hearing itself, while another half-dozen chapters separately address the various sentencing sanctions, including incarceration, fines, etc. The final few chapters discuss post-sentencing advocacy including appeals and supervised release revocation hearings. The concluding chapter contains final observations about sentencing advocacy.

This book is written for a wide audience, from law student to experienced attorney, from probation officer to prosecutor to defense attorney. As a result, the individual reader may find some chapters more relevant and applicable than others. A reader may also find some portions of the book too basic, while other portions too in-depth. I have attempted to find a middle ground with the goal of providing a one-volume book addressing sentencing advocacy in general. Readers looking for more in-depth analysis of specific sentencing issues will have to search out more narrowly-tailored books, if there are any, or conduct their own research.

It is my hope that the reader will emerge from this book with a better understanding of how to effectively advocate at each step of the sentencing process. Cases can vary significantly in terms of the seriousness of the offense and the harshness of possible punishment. Not every case will call upon attorneys to exercise all the methods, tasks, and skills discussed in this book. Nevertheless, many cases will justify the greatest effort by attorneys for both the government and the offender. The goal is to equip both sides with instruction on how to be more skillful in advocacy at sentencing. I trust that the adversarial system will best serve justice when both prosecutors and defense attorneys fully and zealously represent their clients to the best of their abilities in a sentencing hearing. My goal is to serve justice by enhancing attorneys' effectiveness in sentencing advocacy.

2

Principles of Judicial Advocacy

Before examining sentencing advocacy in particular, it is advisable to first consider "judicial advocacy" more generally. By judicial advocacy, I mean advocating to a judge as opposed to a jury or to a panel of appellate judges.[1] As will be explained in following chapters, effective sentencing advocacy involves far more than the written and oral presentations made to the sentencing judge. Nevertheless, ultimately and most importantly, effective sentencing advocacy requires attorneys to persuade a single sentencing judge who alone is responsible for determining the offender's fate. The sentencing hearing is the culmination of all the other work lawyers do to prepare for sentencing. Although that preparation work is an essential part of sentencing advocacy, in the end, attorneys and the offender face a judge who will decide the sentence. Thus, at every step of sentencing advocacy, attorneys should consider how the decisions they make may impact their ability to persuade the judge at the sentencing hearing to impose the sentence they desire. Before turning to anything else then, it is important first to understand how to persuade sentencing judges.

As I will explain in this chapter, persuading a judge is different from persuading a jury and is different from persuading a group of judges. Advocacy is the art of persuasion.[2] Law schools and other organizations teach skills associated with trial advocacy, with a presumption that the decision-maker is a jury.[3] Law schools also teach appellate advocacy, with a focus on arguing fine legal points in a formal setting within time limits to a panel of judges.[4] Educators and professional trainers have devoted little time or attention, however, to teaching the skills involved with advocacy to a district judge—judicial advocacy, in other words. The skills taught in trial advocacy and appellate advocacy classes have limited application to advocating to district court judges, particularly when they are serving in a fact-finding capacity, as is often the case in sentencing hearings. There are significant differences between jury advocacy, appellate advocacy, and judicial advocacy in the context in which arguments are made and the nature of the decision-makers whom the advocates are attempting to persuade. Thus, the skills learned in jury trial advocacy focused on persuading a jury, and the skills taught in appellate advocacy focused on persuading an appellate panel of judges, are not wholly transferable to persuading district judges. Indeed, some jury advocacy methods may be not only inappropriate or inapplicable but may also be ineffective or counterproductive when trying to advocate to a judge.

There are many differences in advocating to juries, courts of appeal, and judges, but such differences generally fall into two broad categories: context and the decision-maker. Within the context category, there are differences in whether: (1) advocacy is written and oral, or only oral; (2) facts are in dispute; and (3) evidence rules apply. Within the decision-maker category, there are differences in whether: (1) group decision-making occurs; (2) there are collateral pressures on the decision-maker; (3) the decision-maker is legally trained; (4) the decision-maker is knowable; (5) the advocate will reappear before the decision-maker; and (6) the advocate and decision-maker can converse. Charting out these differences helps illustrate them.

Factor	*Jury*	*Appeal Courts*	*District Courts*
Written & oral advocacy	No	Yes	Yes
Facts in dispute	Yes	No	Often
Rules of evidence apply	Yes	No	Sometimes
Group decision-making	Yes	Yes	No
Collateral pressures on decision-maker	No	No	Yes
Decision-maker knowable	Limited	Yes	Yes
Decision-maker trained in legal reasoning	No	Yes	Yes
Reappear before decision-maker	No	Maybe	Yes
Conversation possible	No	Limited	Yes

I will discuss each of these differences in more detail below with a focus in particular on how they are manifested in sentencing hearings.

A. Differences in Context

1. Whether Advocacy Is Written, Oral, or Both

When attorneys advocate to judges, they can and often do so using both written and oral advocacy. Unlike jurors, judges make decisions based not just on what is presented in the courtroom, in evidence or oral argument, but also based on the written submissions of the parties in the form of motions, responses, and sometimes proposed findings of fact, and conclusions of law. Attorneys file briefs or memoranda summarizing the relevant facts, setting out the legal standards, and arguing why their client's position should prevail. When attorneys advocate to appellate courts, they always do so in writing and sometimes (but decreasingly) advocate orally. Frequently, if not always, both district judges or appellate judges have reviewed the attorneys' briefs before oral argument, and if they have not, they do so after oral argument. Unlike jurors, judges may begin to form their views and opinions about cases as a result of reading written submissions by the parties before the attorneys make any courtroom presentation. Indeed, when judges read the briefs in advance of argument, they may enter the hearings or oral arguments already having a fair idea of how they will likely rule.

Contrast this process to jury trials. Juries do not have the benefit of written briefs summarizing the facts, stating the law, and stating the parties' arguments.

They learn the facts and hear the arguments for the first time only through oral presentation at the trial. Although judges instruct juries on the law, instructions are a neutral statement of the law and not a form of attorney advocacy.

Consider how this difference can affect sentencing advocacy. It is well-known that people, including judges, comprehend and remember better when provided both written and oral explanations.[5] This means repetition may be a more important part of advocacy to jurors and much less necessary when judges are the decision-makers. Judges can be presumed to have read sentencing memoranda in advance of the sentencing hearing. This fact should allow attorneys to narrow the focus at sentencing hearings to emphasize important points or tease out the nuances of the issue in a manner that would be difficult to do in writing.

On the other hand, when attorneys advocate with both the written word and orally, it requires them to determine the best way to weave those methods together. Attorneys who merely repeat in oral argument at a sentencing hearing what they wrote in their sentencing memorandum are ineffective.[6] When sentencing hearings involve evidentiary disputes that the judge will have to resolve, however, attorneys have an opportunity in a sentencing memorandum to provide the judge with a summary of the evidence the attorneys anticipate will be presented at the sentencing hearing. When done well, these summaries will prepare the judge to receive the evidence in the best light and be viewed from the perspective most advantageous to an attorney's client.

Attorneys should also consider the possibility that the judges may have already largely made up their minds from the sentencing memorandum and presentence report about the sentence they are likely to impose. With this in mind, it should emphasize how critical it is for attorneys to devote considerable effort toward writing effective and persuasive sentencing memoranda and ensuring the presentence reports are comprehensive and correct. It may also be advantageous for attorneys to encourage judges to suspend drawing conclusions until the sentencing hearing, suggesting in the attorneys' sentencing memoranda that what the judge hears at the hearing may paint a different picture of the offense or the offender than appears from reading the presentence report and sentencing memoranda. Knowing, though, that judges are sure to formulate at least some idea of the appropriate sentence as a result of reading the presentence report and sentencing memoranda, attorneys need to learn the skill of discerning what judges are thinking and how to persuade judges to change their minds.

2. Whether the Facts Are in Dispute

The content and nature of an attorney's advocacy depends significantly on whether the decision maker is also a factfinder. Juries are always factfinders, and district judges often take on a fact-finder role as well. Appellate court judges, in contrast, never serve as factfinders.

There is a fundamental difference in advocacy when facts are in dispute versus when the facts are fixed in a cold record. When attorneys are advocating that a decision-maker find certain facts, it calls upon all the skills of rhetoric, using pathos, ethos, and logos.[7] Effective advocates either intentionally or intuitively incorporate all three elements to some degree when striving to persuade a factfinder.[8] The most talented attorneys, however, recognize that the focus and emphasis on the elements should vary, depending on the nature of the case. In some cases, logic is the most compelling aspect of the argument, while in others an appeal to emotion is more likely to succeed. Hence the familiar saying: "If the facts are against you, argue the law. If the law is against you, argue the facts. If the law and the facts are against you, pound the table and yell like hell."[9] Attorneys must persuade the factfinder to find the facts favorable to their party, and then explain how those facts support their legal positions. Sometimes attorneys need to use their rhetorical and reasoning skills to persuade factfinders that they should prevail, even when factfinders do not find the facts to be as claimed.

When, on the other hand, attorneys argue to a court of appeals on a cold record,[10] it calls upon very different advocacy skills.[11] Sometimes attorneys need to use their rhetorical skills to bring the cold record to life, while most often attorneys focus on the logos part of rhetoric to persuade appellate courts that they should prevail as a matter of legal reasoning based on the facts developed below. Even when facts are in dispute, how attorneys advocate should change depending on whether the factfinder is a jury or is a judge.

3. Whether the Rules of Evidence Apply

Although both jurors and judges serve as factfinders, they do so with different restrictions. When jurors serve as factfinders, the rules of evidence apply. Indeed, the very purpose of evidence rules is to protect jurors from unreliable evidence.[12] This purpose is reflected in Federal Rule of Evidence 104(c), which requires judges to conduct hearings on the admissibility of evidence "so that the jury cannot hear it" under certain circumstances or when "justice so requires."[13] Thus, effective advocacy to juries requires presenting evidence that is admissible under the rules and objecting to inadmissible evidence.

In stark contrast, when judges serve as factfinders, the rules of evidence often do not apply at all, and even when they do apply, they apply in a "relaxed" manner.[14] When it is understood that the Federal Rules of Evidence were designed to protect unsophisticated jurors from unreliable evidence and the chicanery of clever counsel, it is not surprising that the Federal Rules of Evidence would not generally apply when judges serve as fact finders. In theory, trained judges are experienced in analyzing evidence and familiar with the chicanery of counsel, and thus do not need the protection that evidence rules provide to laypersons. So, it makes sense, for instance, that in making evidentiary rulings, judges are not bound by any of the Federal Rules of Evidence "except those on privilege."[15]

Importantly for purposes of this book, rules of evidence do not apply in sentencing hearings. Thus, attorneys advocating to judges in sentencing hearings when the rules of evidence do not apply should consider the implications. Evidence that would not be admissible under the rules is admissible when the rules do not apply. Attorneys cannot object to the admission of evidence at sentencing hearings by invoking evidence rules that do not apply. In a later chapter, I will discuss at length effective advocacy in a sentencing when the rules of evidence do not apply.

B. The Decision-Maker

1. Whether Group Decision-Making Occurs

As decision-makers, individual judges differ much more significantly from juries than they do from individual jurors. As individuals, judges comprehend and retain information in the same manner as individual jurors. Judges and jurors both learn and comprehend information from hearing and seeing, in response to aural and visual stimuli. In short, individual judges employ similar cognitive processes as jurors, subject to the same limitations as any other human.[16]

Jurors reach decisions, however, through a group process to arrive at a verdict on behalf of the jury as a body. The process of arriving at a verdict on behalf of the group requires jurors to talk among themselves, debate the issues, and consider other jurors' perspectives and opinions. Jurors may persuade other jurors and change their minds to reach a verdict. Jurors may also reach compromises to reach a verdict. By discussing the evidence among themselves, jurors as a group may gain perspectives and see solutions that would not have occurred had any single juror been acting alone. On the other hand, a strong, though misguided, juror may sway other jurors through pressure or charisma to reach a decision that, left alone, an individual juror may not otherwise have made.

Unlike district judges, but like juries, appellate judges engage in a form of group decision-making. Appellate judges discuss and debate cases before them and are influenced positively and negatively by the input of their fellow judges.[17] Like district judges, but unlike juries, however, appellate judges ultimately reach individual decisions and are not bound to reach a unanimous decision. An appellate judge may always issue a concurring or dissenting opinion; jurors cannot.

In sentencing hearings, though, district judges are juries of one. Gone are both the negative and positive attributes of group decision-making.[18] The danger of groupthink is absent. District judges do not face peer pressure influencing their sentencing decisions during the judge's internal mental deliberations. Also missing, however, are the advantages of the exchange of multiple points of view and the pooling of memories, dynamics that occur in group decision-making.[19] The benefits of sounding out ideas, bouncing around possible solutions, debating points, and brainstorming are not available when a district judge must reach a sentencing decision alone.[20] In sentencing hearings, judges do not have the benefit of the advice of other judges in determining the appropriate sentence.

For purposes of effective sentencing advocacy, this means that attorneys should recognize that the sentencing judge alone is making the decision. There is one person, and one person only, that the attorney must persuade. The ultimate judgment is left to a lone judge's judgment. Therefore, attorneys should consider what factors besides the law and the facts present in a particular case may influence the judge's decision making. These other factors may include collateral pressures on the judge and the judge's background and experience.

2. Whether There Are Collateral Pressures on the Decision-Maker

Judges also have significant responsibilities that come with their power, and those responsibilities can influence how they make decisions. Many of these responsibilities are unique to district judges and are not present with appellate judges. While listening to testimony, considering evidence, and hearing attorneys' arguments at sentencing hearings, district judges are also responsible to ensure that witnesses are treated with respect and not harassed, and that attorneys conduct themselves in a professional and ethical manner.[21] While a district judge may be trying to concentrate on the case at hand, the judge is simultaneously watching the clock and thinking of other cases and other litigants, always mindful of limited judicial resources. District judges struggle to find the proper balance between permitting the parties the full benefit of having their day in court against the need to allow time for every other litigant to have their day in court as well. District judges are aware that additional briefing, more evidence, and additional argument will cost the parties more in resources, including attorneys' fees and expenses. Judges recognize they need to reach reasoned and thoughtful decisions but also feel the pressure of the need for a speedy resolution of every case, knowing that parties need and deserve timely decisions.[22] All these practical considerations that are a product of district judges' responsibilities affect the manner in which judges consider and decide cases.

Jurors, in contrast, generally do not consider any of these practical and collateral matters when they are asked to reach decisions. Nor do appellate judges face these issues when, on appeal, time constraints are largely absent. There are no equivalent statutes or rules that compel or urge appellate judges to reach speedy resolutions of appeals.

The presence of collateral pressures can impact effective sentencing advocacy. Attorneys should be alert to whether collateral pressures are affecting a judge's ability to concentrate on the evidence or argument. For example, a judge may not be able to give a complex sentencing hearing the attention it deserves if the judge is also presiding over a complex jury trial the same week as the sentencing hearing. It may be better for an attorney to seek a continuance of a sentencing hearing if it becomes apparent that other job pressures could prevent the judge from giving full time and attention to a case. Attorneys should also endeavor to be more concise with judges than they are with jurors. Attorneys need to ensure they are timely with written pleadings, knowing that delays in filing may impact the judge's ability to focus and give sufficient time to the matter. It is also important that attorneys accurately estimate the amount of time that may be required for a sentencing hearing and to work with the court's staff to schedule the hearing for enough time that the judge does not feel rushed to conclude the hearing or make a sentencing decision because other litigants are waiting.

3. Whether the Decision-Maker Is Knowable

The most fundamental tenet of effective public speaking is to know one's audience. There is a tremendous difference between what attorneys can know about jurors and what attorneys can know about sentencing judges. Voir dire enables attorneys to learn some limited information about prospective jurors in order for attorneys to make more informed for-cause challenges and to exercise peremptory strikes.[23] Juror questionnaires,[24] private investigation of prospective jurors,[25] and jury consultants[26] can supplement voir dire to provide attorneys with more information about prospective jurors. In the end, however, the information trial attorneys have about individual jurors is limited and imperfect, restricted by access, time, and money.

Judges, on the other hand, are more of an open book. Judges are public officials about whom much is known and with a little effort, attorneys can learn even more about them. There is a treasure trove of information about judges in the public domain, particularly about federal judges whose lengthy and detailed Senate Judicial Questionnaires are publicly filed. Many judges also provide information about their preferences and practices on court websites. Judges often speak publicly at conferences about their preferences and practices or publish articles in bar journals or law reviews. Sentencing hearings take place in open court, so any attorney striving to learn how to most effectively advocate to a judge in a sentencing hearing can observe the judge's practices and procedures in other sentencing hearings. Finally, other attorneys who have appeared before a judge are available sources of information about the judge's past practices and procedures.

Of course, the important thing is what attorneys do with the information they have about decision-makers. All too often, trial attorneys use the limited information they have about prospective jurors only to decide whom to challenge for cause or remove using a peremptory strike. Trial attorneys often fail to consider juror information in tailoring the presentation of their cases to the jurors. Instead of adjusting and modifying the presentation of the evidence and their arguments to better appeal to the background, abilities, and views of the jurors, trial attorneys simply present their cases as if all jurors and juries are the same. Similarly, all too often, attorneys present their cases to judges in sentencing hearings as if all judges were alike.

To be most effective, attorneys should prepare their case and tailor their sentencing arguments to the judges before them. For example, it may be apparent through research that a particular sentencing judge is most troubled by violence in offenders' criminal histories, while another judge is particularly receptive to arguments for more lenient sentences for offenders who have suffered abuse as children. Knowing these predispositions about the sentencing judges, attorneys can work to develop the record so that the relevant facts are fully developed or explained in the presentence report, thoroughly addressed in sentencing memoranda, supported when necessary by additional evidence at the sentencing hearing, persuasively addressed by the attorneys in argument, and potentially even discussed by the offender during allocution.

4. Whether the Decision-Maker Is Legally Trained

Judges, like jurors, are human. Judges also have emotions (perhaps some more than others) and thus can have emotional responses to evidence. Judges also have their fair share of biases, prejudices, preconceptions, and presumptions as a result of their backgrounds, histories, and experiences. Judges are different from jurors, however, because of their legal training.

In law school, judges learned deductive reasoning. Through their experience as attorneys, they honed their analytic skills and disciplined their minds to focus only on material facts and issues. While in their capacity as attorneys, judges developed the ability to wall themselves off emotionally from cases, as doctors do, to approach cases with something akin to clinical detachment.[27] While they are attorneys, and even more so once they gain the bench, judges focus on facts that have legal significance and disregard facts that do not. Judges are also members of the same social and professional class as attorneys, sharing the same language, having similar formative experiences, and being bound by the same core rules of ethics and values.[28] When attorneys are talking to judges, then, they are talking to one of their own. This is very dissimilar to attorneys talking to jurors.

Because judges are legally trained and mentally disciplined to make dispassionate decisions based on reason and logic, any appeals to emotion, the pathos part of classical rhetoric, not only find little purchase with judges but may be seen as insulting by suggesting that judges would make a decision based on emotion.[29] Conversely, when jurors are factfinders, attorneys may want to emphasize the emotional appeal of their position over a merely logical argument. Thus, when arguing to judges, attorneys should focus on the law and the facts. At sentencing hearings, although attorneys should be emphatic on important points, they generally should save drama and theatrics for juries. Judges are not persuaded by such displays; indeed, vociferous oral advocacy may have just the opposite effect.[30] Judges expect attorneys to speak to them at an intellectual level, with an emphasis on reasoning and common sense rather than emotions. In short, attorneys should emphasize logos over pathos in sentencing hearings.

5. Whether the Advocate Will Reappear Before the Decision-Maker

Juries are comprised of a group of individuals randomly gathered together and selected through an empanelment process that results in each jury being unique from every other jury. Thus, attorneys will never appear again before the same jury. Indeed, most courts excuse jurors from further service for some period of time once they have served, so it is highly likely that attorneys will never see an individual juror again.

Appellate panels are somewhat similar in that they are typically comprised of three appellate judges randomly assigned to the case. It is possible, depending on the nature of an attorney's practice and the frequency of appearing in the court of appeals, that an attorney could appear before the same three-judge panel more than once on different cases. It is likely that any attorney with a regular appellate practice will appear before the same appellate judges repeatedly, albeit on different panels.

Except in the largest districts with scores of judges, in contrast, attorneys will regularly appear before the same district judges over and over again at sentencing hearings. Whether an attorney will frequently reappear before a decision-maker may affect advocacy. Attorneys need not worry about future consequences with juries. Attorneys can take inconsistent positions from one jury to the next. They can engage in sharp practices before a jury without worrying about how it may affect them in the future on other cases; they can exaggerate and bluff without being concerned that it could affect their future credibility. Not so with judges, whether they be district or appellate judges. Attorneys should always consider the reputation they form with judges before whom they may or will reappear.[31] This is particularly true in sentencing hearings as attorneys are likely to repeatedly appear in front of the same judge; although the offenders will change, the judges will often remain the same. Attorneys are also bound by ethical rules to be candid with the court.[32] And judges have power over attorneys, who are officers of the court and answerable to judges for misconduct. Judges and attorneys both recognize that what judges say and how judges render their decisions can, in some cases, impact attorneys' careers for better or worse.

6. Whether the Advocate and Decision-Maker Can Converse

Judges differ significantly from juries as decision-makers because judges have the ability to, and often do, ask questions of witnesses and attorneys. Jurors cannot ask questions of attorneys and in most cases, jurors remain mute observers of the proceedings.[33] This difference significantly alters how attorneys advocate to jurors and how they can advocate to judges. Attorneys and judges can have a conversation and through that conversation achieve a level of understanding that cannot occur when attorneys are talking at jurors. Attorneys can ask judges if their arguments are understood and inquire of judges about what questions or concerns judges have about the evidence or argument. Although a judge may ultimately disagree with an attorney's position, through conversation it can at least be certain that the judge understands that position.

The opportunity for a true conversation is greater with district judges that it is in an appellate setting. Appellate arguments are rigid and timed with even the longest of them seldom exceeding a half-hour per side (and most often are limited to ten or fifteen minutes per side). Appellate arguments have the tone and appearance of formal debates. To the extent there is an exchange, it resembles much more an interrogation than a conversation, with only one side asking questions.[34] Although district judges have time pressures different from appellate judges, most district judges do not impose arbitrary and short deadlines to arguments in sentencing hearings. Thus, with district judges there is a real opportunity for a more informal and lengthy exchange to take place. Sentencing advocacy to a district judge, then, assumes a very different tone and can become much more conversational than in a formal appellate presentation.

In sentencing hearings then, attorneys should attempt to develop a conversation with the judge. Attorneys should welcome questions by the judge of their witnesses and help further develop the record through additional questions on any topic the judge has addressed through questions of the witness. Some judges may also be receptive to direct inquiries by attorneys about the issues. With these judges, attorneys may feel at liberty to ask what concerns the judge most about the offender's history or where the judge believes the evidence is weakest on a sentencing enhancement or reduction argument, for example. Attorneys should strive to develop an exchange of information, a conversation, with sentencing judges so that the attorneys can fully and effectively communicate and address the sentencing judges' concerns.

C. Practical Advice for Effective Judicial Advocacy in Sentencing

In summary, there are important differences in effective advocacy to judges, juries, and appellate courts. In this part, I have only touched upon the most obvious and significant differences to highlight the need for attorneys to recognize that all advocacy is not the same. Attorneys should keep these differences in mind when considering every other aspect of sentencing advocacy. Throughout the remainder of this book, I will return periodically to emphasize the principles of effective judicial advocacy as they apply at various stages of sentencing procedures and hearings. Here, though, is some practical advice for effective judicial advocacy as applied in the context of criminal sentencing.

First, attorneys should recognize that, unlike juries, judges can review exhibits in advance of sentencing hearings. In jury trials, jurors see exhibits only after the judge admits the exhibits and a party presents the exhibit at trial. When judges must serve as factfinders in contested sentencing hearings, attorneys can, and should, provide the judges with exhibits in advance of the sentencing hearing. Advance review of the exhibits aids judges in understanding testimony and allows time for the judge to fully review exhibits. This is particularly true with video or audio exhibits or lengthy written exhibits. Doing so allows them to review the exhibits when it best fits in the judges' schedules and shortens the length of the sentencing hearings. An attorney should provide the judge with exhibits in advance of a sentencing hearing even if the opposing party has an evidentiary objection to the exhibits. The judge must necessarily see the disputed exhibit to rule on its admissibility in any event, so it is best to allow the judge time to review it in detail and thereby more likely make a correct ruling.

Second, attorneys should tailor witness questions for presentation to a judge by omitting unnecessary background questions that attorneys may otherwise think necessary in front of jurors to educate the jury or personalize the witness. Judges have a base of knowledge lacking with jurors. Judges know common terms used in drug trafficking, for example, and do not require witnesses to explain them. Judges are also much more focused the essential facts and are less likely to be influenced by peripheral facts about witnesses such as whether they are married and have children.

That said, attorneys should nevertheless remember the need to make a good appellate record. If a particular fact is important to the case, such as firearms being tools of the drug trade, then the attorneys need to elicit those facts even if it is obvious the judge already knows that fact from other cases. Similarly, if an attorney believes that personalizing a witness by eliciting background facts might indeed influence the judge's perception of the witness (the ethos part of classical rhetoric), then the attorney should elicit the background facts.

Third, attorneys need to work with witnesses to ensure the evidence is presented to the judge as factfinder. In other words, it is important that exhibits are displayed or explained in ways that the judge can see them. The judge is the sole decision-maker at a sentencing hearing. All efforts should be made to ensure the judge can fully see and comprehend the evidence. Attorneys should instruct witnesses to have eye contact with the judge and understand the need to communicate to the judge. Attorneys should also prepare witnesses to expect and welcome questions from judges in sentencing hearings.

Attorneys need to recognize that evidence rules do not apply in sentencing hearings. Attorneys are trained from law school to think of admissible evidence and may by habit unconsciously limit the scope of what they present at sentencing hearings even when the rules do not apply. In sentencing hearings, judges may consider almost anything in arriving at a sentence that is sufficient but not greater than necessary to achieve the goals of sentencing.[35] The proponent of evidence should recognize the expanded and essentially limitless scope of information that can be presented to a judge in sentencing hearings.

Opposing counsel should recognize the inapplicability of the rules of evidence but be prepared to argue why the reasons underlying the inapplicable rules should still cause the judge to give the evidence little weight. It is important for attorneys to recognize the values underlying the rules of evidence in determining what and how to present such information to a judge, even when the rules of evidence do not apply. Judges remain free to afford the information whatever weight the judge deems appropriate. The closer the evidence hews to that which would be admissible under the evidence rules, the more likely it is that the judge will afford it greater weight. Common sense should tell attorneys that a judge is unlikely to afford much weight to uncorroborated triple hearsay, for example.

When presenting information in sentencing hearings, attorneys should nevertheless still attempt to present evidence that would be admissible under the rules whenever possible. When they cannot do so, attorneys should recognize why the evidence would be inadmissible under the rules, that is, identify what makes the evidence unreliable, and attempt to address that weakness through corroborating circumstances or other evidence to enhance its trustworthiness.

As noted, attorneys can know far more about judges than they can of jurors. Attorneys should adjust their presentations based on the judge's experience and familiarity with the facts and procedural history of the case. Attorneys should adjust their presentations based on the sentencing judge's experience and familiarity with the facts and procedural history of the case.[36] To be effective sentencing advocates, attorneys should find out what the judge knows about the subject matter and the legal issues involved in the sentencing hearing. Attorneys should research to find out if the judge has ruled on or issued opinions about the sentencing issues present in the attorney's case. How an attorney advocates can be affected by how familiar the judge is with the case as a result of handling prior issues in the case.

Judges are trained to think analytically. They focus on facts that are material to the legal test or framework at issue. Effective sentencing advocacy, then, emphasizes logic, facts, and law in both written and oral advocacy and eschew appeals to judges' emotions.

Written advocacy in sentencing is directed to a judge who not only completed law school but also practiced law in some capacity before taking the bench. This background means that the sentencing judge will apply critical thinking to any written argument. Attorneys should assume judges will detect exaggerations of the factual record or inaccurate descriptions of case holdings. When attorneys engage in such practices, they risk the loss of credibility with judges. Once lost, credibility is difficult to restore. Apart from accuracy, effective written sentencing advocacy requires organization, efficiency, and precision. Judges have intense demands on their limited time. Judges preside over many hearings on a daily basis. When judges are not in their courtrooms, they are in their chambers reading. The sentencing memorandum an attorney submits to the judge is almost certainly not the only document the judge will read that day. As with any form of communication, knowing the audience and tailoring the message to that audience then is imperative. Among other things, this means eliminating unnecessary boilerplate sections, keeping pathos-based arguments to a minimum unless they are clearly appropriate, avoiding personal attacks on opposing counsel, and being as brief as possible.

Attorneys should also be careful not to offend judges. Attorneys sometimes make statements or arguments intended for the benefit of their clients, quasi clients (e.g., crime victims), the press, or other third parties. In an effort to curry favor with or favorable appearances before others, some attorneys will try to shift blame onto judges. For example, defense attorneys will sometimes argue that if the judge imposes a particular sentence, then the judge will be responsible for tearing the offender from his family or depriving the offender's family of a parent or financial support. Judges are understandably offended by such comments for it is the offender, not the judge, who jeopardized everything and caused collateral damage to others. Similarly, prosecutors may argue that failing to impose a particular sentence on an offender would constitute a miscarriage of justice for crime victims or society as a whole. Judges are equally offended by such comments because the government has the burden of proof in criminal cases.

As I will discuss in more detail in a later chapter, I recognize that the judge is not the only member of the audience to whom an attorney's oral comments are addressed. Attorneys legitimately need to consider the effect their comments may have on their clients and others. Nevertheless, attorneys should understand that when they tailor their comments to appeal to another member of the audience, they may adversely affect the effectiveness of their advocacy to the judge. Because the judge is the sole decision-maker at a sentencing hearing, attorneys have to recognize that tension may exist and weigh which is more important: persuading the judge or mollifying or impressing other audience members.

Attorneys should invite questions and receive them with enthusiasm. Questions from the bench can be annoying, as they interrupt the attorney's flow and may raise issues the attorney wished to avoid or intended to address later in the presentation. If annoyed, attorneys should keep it to themselves. Questions are the judge's opportunity to zero in on the issues the judge finds to be most relevant or troubling. Attorneys should not, then, treat questions as intrusions or interruptions.[37] Nor should they respond by stating that they will get to that issue later.[38] Attorneys should just answer the questions enthusiastically and directly and move on.

Finally, attorneys should be flexible and tune into the judge's verbal and non-verbal cues. Although every judge is different, most will make it clear when it is time to move on or to be finished. These can range from the subtle, such as looks of boredom or annoyance, to the direct: "Move on, counsel." Although there are other audience members at a sentencing hearing to whom an attorney's statements may be directed or intended, attorneys should keep in mind that the sentencing judge is the primary audience and, ultimately, the person the attorneys are attempting to persuade. If the judge makes it clear that an attorney has made the point, the attorneys should move on.

3

The Goals of Sentencing

Before turning to any other aspect of effective sentencing advocacy, it is imperative first to identify the goals of sentencing. When imposing sentences, judges properly focus on the goals of sentencing. In the federal system, judges are mandated by statute explicitly to consider the goals of sentencing. Even without such an explicit directive, as a practical matter sentencing judges always have the goals of sentencing in mind when struggling to arrive at an appropriate sentence. Knowing this, effective sentencing advocacy requires that attorneys likewise focus their attention on the goals of sentencing throughout their sentencing advocacy efforts.

There is more than one perspective of what is meant when referring to the goals of sentencing. At a sentencing hearing, the government's goal may be to impose the most severe sentence of incarceration available under the statute or some other period of incarceration deemed appropriate, along with the maximum fine, full restitution, and imposition of all other collateral consequences that could apply. The goal for an offender, on the other hand, is invariably to seek the least amount of time behind bars, the lowest fine, and the least onerous collateral punishments possible. The offender's family members likely share the offender's goals of the lightest sentence possible, but not always. Crime victims likely share many of the prosecutor's goals, but sometimes want harsher or more lenient punishment than the prosecutor believes appropriate.

Here, when speaking of the goals of sentencing, I am not talking about the goals of the parties and other various interested stakeholders in a given sentencing hearing. Rather, I am here referencing the societal and penological goals of sentencing. These are the goals that judges are charged with considering when determining offenders' sentences. These are, then, the goals that advocates should always keep in mind when formulating their arguments to judges who always have these goals in mind.

The goals of sentencing have changed only marginally over time, and not at all in the last century. As stated in *United States v. Scroggins*, 880 F.2d 1204, 1206 (11th Cir. 1989),

> Prior to the American Revolution, colonial courts fashioned sentences with three basic purposes in mind: to punish the offender for his crime, thereby satisfying society's desire for retribution ("punishment"); to deter others from committing the same crime by demonstrating its disadvantageous consequences ("general deterrence"); and to incapacitate the wrongdoer, so as to protect society from further criminal activity ("specific deterrence" or "incapacitation").

In the 1800s, authorities added rehabilitation as a fourth basic goal of sentencing.[1] In the federal system, Congress codified these goals in Title 18, United States Code, Section 3553(a).[2]

As part of the Sentencing Reform Act of 1984,[3] Congress charged federal judges with the responsibility of arriving at a sentence that is sufficient, but not greater than necessary, to achieve the goals listed in that section. *United States v. Irey*, 612 F.3d 1160, 1238 (11th Cir. 2010) notes, "Thus, although all the sentencing factors identified in § 3553(a) must be considered, the heart of the inquiry is the district court's assessment of the four traditional purposes of sentencing § 3553(a)(2) has codified." (Tjoflat, J., concurring in part and dissenting in part.) Hence, any attorney wishing to effectively advocate for a sentence in federal court should have these goals in mind at all times and structure their arguments around these goals.

As codified in the federal statute 18 U.S.C. § 3553(a)(2), Congress articulated the goals of sentencing as follows:

(A) to reflect the seriousness of the offense, to promote respect for the law, and to provide just punishment for the offense;
(B) to afford adequate deterrence to criminal conduct;
(C) to protect the public from further crimes of the defendant; and
(D) to provide the defendant with needed educational or vocational training, medical care, or other correctional treatment in the most effective manner.

Each of these goals deserve some elaboration.

Congress seemingly listed three goals under subsection (A), but they are all inter-related aspects of a single goal. That goal is imposing a sentence that is severe enough, but not too severe; lenient enough, but not too lenient. It is a little like Goldilocks finding the porridge with the perfect temperature. Imposing a sentence that reflects the seriousness of the offense speaks to a level of proportionality.[4] The notion that the punishment should fit the crime is one of the most basic and fundamental of tenets of a fair criminal justice system.[5] This is sometimes referred to as "just desserts."[6] This is the embodiment of the goal of retribution.

Promoting respect for the law can be complicated, for a sentence either too lenient or too severe can jeopardize respect for the law. When offenders are perceived to receive a "slap on the wrist" as a criminal sentence, it can cause the public to question the justice system and tempt some people to take justice into their own hands. Conversely, a sentence that the public perceives as unduly harsh can cause the public to rebel against what it believes to be a heavy-handed government. This tenet of just punishment is, to some degree, reflected in the Eighth Amendment's prohibition against cruel and unusual punishment. The public places a high priority on having a sentence fit the crime.[7]

And finally, the goal of achieving a just sentence is the embodiment of a system of justice that is fair and incorporates concepts of both proportionality and equality. As the sponsors of the United States Senate Report accompanying the Sentencing Reform Act explained in 34 S. Rep. 98–225, 1984 U.S.C.C.A.N. 3182, 3258–59:

> [Just punishment]—essentially the "just deserts" [sic] concept—should be reflected clearly in all sentences; it is another way of saying that the sentence should reflect the gravity of the defendant's conduct. From the public's standpoint, the sentence should be of a type and length that will adequately reflect, among other things, the harm done or threatened by the offense, and the public interest in preventing recurrence of the offense. From the defendant's standpoint the sentence should not be unreasonably harsh under all the circumstances of the case and should not differ substantially from the sentence given to another similarly situated defendant convicted of a similar offense under similar circumstances.

Thus, as one federal judge described it in *United States v. Wilson*, 350 F. Supp. 2d 910, 917, "[t]he concept of 'just punishment' requires the court to consider society's views as to appropriate penalties, not just a judge's own personal instincts." (D. Utah 2005).

In short, seeking proportionality, respect for the law, and just punishment are all related. Proportionality is focused on the impact on the offender. In other words, the goal is to impose a sentence on the offender reflective of the seriousness of the crime the offender committed. Respect for the law, on the other hand, is more generally directed at the public's perception of the sentence. In other words, a disproportionate sentence may cause the public to lose respect for the law and thereby jeopardize the criminal justice system as a whole, regardless of the impact on the individual offender. And seeking a just punishment embodies a global sense of fundamental fairness, both to the individual offender being sentenced, to others similarly situated, and to others affected by the crime, including society as a whole and any crime victims.

The second factor under Section 3553(a)(2) is deterrence. The concept of deterrence incorporates two types of deterrence: specific deterrence and general deterrence. Specific deterrence refers to imposing a sentence sufficiently severe to deter the offender being sentenced from committing a similar crime in the future.[8] General deterrence refers to imposing a sentence sufficiently severe to discourage others from committing a similar crime.[9] Deterrence as a sentencing goal is the often subject to criticism and skepticism. It is arguable whether a longer prison sentence would deter some offenders from reoffending any more than would a shorter sentence. For example, drug addicts who sell drugs to support their addiction will likely be little deterred from returning to the same conduct, regardless of the length of sentence imposed, as long as they remain addicted. On the other hand, some white-collar offenders might be highly susceptible to specific deterrence as a result of the risk of loss of their professional positions, licenses, or reputations after conviction.

The effectiveness of general deterrence is even more subject to conjecture. Although one can measure the effectiveness of specific deterrence to some extent by studying the degree of recidivism by offenders depending on the severity of their sentences, it is nearly impossible to realistically measure the extent to which any sentence achieves the goal of general deterrence. At best, one can look at broad criminal justice statistics over time compared to changes in punishment severity during the same time period and draw conclusions from any correlation that appears. The problem, of course, is that a decrease in crime rates during a time period of increasingly harsh sentences could be causal related or it could be the result of any number of other societal influences.

The goal of protecting the public from the offender, the third factor listed under Section3553(a)(2), encompasses the concept of incapacitation. Under this factor, a sentencing judge is charged with considering the nature and seriousness of the danger the offender poses to society, weighing evidence of recidivism, and arriving at a sentence that will adequately protect the public. For violent offenders with long criminal records of committing serious offenses, despite being repeatedly punished, the only way to protect society may be to send the offender to prison for a significant period of time. A long sentence removes the offender's capacity to commit more crimes by removing that offender from society. At least during the time of incarceration, that offender no longer poses a danger to society (though, to be sure, the offender may still pose a danger to other inmates and correctional staff).

The final goal under Section 3553(a)(2), imposing a sentence that "provide[s] the defendant with needed educational or vocational training, medical care, or other correctional treatment in the most effective manner," incorporates the sentencing goal of rehabilitation. This goal is focused on the offender and requires a sentencing judge to look carefully at the offender's history and characteristics. Judges are to consider the likelihood the offender could be rehabilitated and consider options, other than or in addition to, periods of incarceration to help rehabilitate the offender. Judges may not, however, increase an offender's sentence to ensure the offender would have access to certain opportunities in prison. For example, an offender may greatly benefit from drug treatment. The Federal Bureau of Prison's residential drug treatment program, which has a high success rate, is a limited resource and so offenders sentenced to less than two years in prison will often not be eligible to participate in the program. A judge cannot sentence an offender to more than two years solely for the purpose of ensuring the offender has access to the program.

Effective sentencing advocacy requires attorneys for both sides to consider these goals of sentencing in representing their clients. At each step of the process, from the investigation to the offender's allocution, attorneys should focus on how their decisions and arguments address the goals of sentencing. With these goals in mind, then, I will turn to providing a tutorial about federal statutory and guideline sentencing provisions that attorneys should first understand to be effective sentencing advocates.

4

Statutory and Guidelines Provisions

I have stated that this is not a book on the law of sentencing. Yet, to place discussions about effective sentencing advocacy in the proper context and for the reader to fully comprehend the material, it is necessary to provide a condensed explanation of statutory and guideline sentencing provisions. This substantive law provides the legal framework within which attorneys must work and the structure in which they exercise their advocacy skills to achieve sentences that further the goals of sentencing. In this chapter, I will explain the federal statutory and Guidelines sentencing scheme for the practical reasons articulated in Chapter 1. Nevertheless, state sentencing schemes are usually very similar in their broad application to the federal scheme.

A. *Indeterminate Sentencing, Determinate Sentencing, and Advisory Guidelines*

Generally speaking, sentencing schemes fall into one of two categories: indeterminate sentencing and determinate sentencing. An indeterminant sentencing scheme is one in which the legislature sets a maximum sentence (and sometimes minimum sentence) and leaves it to the discretion of the sentencing judge to determine the appropriate sentence within the statutory range established by the legislature. An indeterminant sentencing scheme may also involve a shared responsibility among the branches of government for determining the length of sentence an offender may serve. In many indeterminant sentencing schemes, particularly in many states, the legislature establishes the minimum and maximum sentencing range, a judge imposes a sentence within that statutory range, and the executive branch decides through a parole board how much of the sentence the judge imposed the offender actually must serve.

A determinate sentencing scheme is one when the legislature enacts laws that either completely or substantially eliminate sentencing judges' discretion by setting the punishment directly in statutes or through an administrative process. A determinate sentence is one that parties can largely calculate, based on statutory provisions, in advance of the hearing. In determinate sentencing schemes, judges impose specific sentences—not a range of months or years. Moreover, under true determinate sentencing schemes, there is no parole. The sentence imposed is the sentence served, absent perhaps time off for good behavior. In a completely determinate sentencing scheme, there is no provision for the executive branch, through a board of parole, to change the sentence the court imposed.

The federal government and many state governments have alternatively employed various forms of determinate and indeterminate sentencing schemes over the course of the last several hundred years. Today, almost all states employ primarily indeterminate sentencing schemes in which all three branches of government are involved in determining the sentence an offender actually serves. The federal system has employed both indeterminate and determinate forms of sentencing schemes at times. The federal government once employed an indeterminant sentencing scheme essentially identical to that employed in most states. Then, for a period of a couple of decades, the federal sentencing scheme was essentially a determinant scheme under which Congress eliminated most judicial sentencing discretion and removed the executive branch from controlling the actual length of the sentence served by eliminating parole. Now the federal sentencing scheme involves a form of indeterminant sentencing. Under this system, Congress establishes mandatory minimums and maximums of statutory ranges, judges have wide discretion imposing sentences within those statutory ranges, and the executive branch remains unable to adjust the sentence served through the granting of parole. To fully understand the role of and need for effective sentencing advocacy in the present sentencing federal sentencing scheme, it is instructive to have some familiarity with the evolution of the federal sentencing system.

Before 1984, the federal system used an indeterminate sentencing scheme that involved all three branches of government in determining the sentence an offender would ultimately serve. Congress set maximum and some minimum sentences by statute. Judges then had the discretion, within the statutory range Congress established, to sentence an offender to whatever sentence the judge found appropriate. Then the executive branch, through the parole board, determined through parole hearings how much of the sentence the judge imposed the offender would actually serve. In that system, sentencing advocacy at the sentencing hearing stage was important because the judge had wide discretion in determining the sentence.

In the Sentencing Reform Act of 1984, however, Congress adopted a largely determinant sentencing scheme. The Act was the product of a concern over rising crime rates and a perception that the indeterminant sentencing scheme was unfair, sometimes resulting in significant disparities in sentences based on race, ethnicity, and other factors unrelated to the seriousness of the crime or the history and characteristics of the offender. At the same time, there was dissatisfaction with the parole system in that there was a perception that there was no truth in sentencing. Although a judge might sentence an offender to ten years in prison, a parole board may release the offender after serving only a small fraction of the sentence the judge imposed.

The Sentencing Reform Act of 1984 ushered in a system involving mandatory sentencing Guidelines and eliminated parole with the twin goals of reducing sentencing disparity and achieving truth in sentencing. Congress formed a sentencing commission charged with formulating sentencing Guidelines that provided a narrow range of months of incarceration for every federal offense based on two factors: the nature of the offense and the offender's criminal history. For each offense, the Guidelines provided a base offense level—a number—that could then be increased or decreased based on offense conduct characteristics and offender characteristics. The Guidelines provided a means of calculating another number for an offender based on the nature and the offender's criminal history. Using a grid in which the offense level score appears on the vertical axis and the criminal history score on the horizontal access, the intersection of the offender's two scores corresponded to a range of months. The greater the offender's offense conduct score, the lower on the grid the offender's range would be found and the greater the resulting sentence. Similarly, the greater the offender's criminal history score, the farther to the right on the grid the offender's range would appear and the greater the sentence would be.

Offenders with lowest offense conduct scores and lowest criminal history scores would have a sentencing range of zero to six months. Offenders with the top offense conduct score and the top criminal history score would end up with a sentencing range of life in prison, without the possibility of parole. Between those two extremes were ranges with the low end of one to seven months and other ranges with the top range of 360 months to life in prison. Each range within the grid was rather narrow, generally only a matter of a few months to a few years.[1]

Under the mandatory sentencing Guidelines scheme, the sentencing judge was essentially required to sentence an offender within the narrow range established by the Guidelines calculation. The Guidelines contained some provisions that allowed a judge to "depart" from the Guidelines range under certain circumstances. The Guidelines indicated that some grounds for departure were valid if it took the case outside the heartland of the type of cases contemplated by the Guidelines. The most important of these grounds for departure was if an offender provided substantial assistance to the government by cooperating in the investigation or prosecution of another. On the other hand, the Guidelines also prohibited a judge from departing from the Guidelines on certain grounds. Drug addiction is an example of one such ground that could not support a departure even if an offender's drug addiction was severe and might explain why the offender engaged in the criminal conduct. If a court was authorized to depart under the Guidelines, then the scheme reverted to a form of an indeterminate sentencing scheme when the judge had the discretion to sentence an offender anywhere within the statutory range established by Congress. A court of appeals was empowered, however, to reverse such a sentence if the appellate court found that the extent of the departure was unreasonable because the judge departed too far.

In arriving at offense levels, the Sentencing Commission strove to peg offense levels to a term of months that was consistent with the number of months offenders actually spent in prison, based on an exhaustive study of past prison sentences under the former indeterminate sentencing scheme. For example, under the indeterminate sentencing scheme, an offender convicted of being a felon in possession of a firearm could be sentenced up to ten years in prison, receive a five-year sentence by the judge, and get out in two years after making parole. If, on average, that was typical for offenders convicted of that offense, the Sentencing Commission adopted a base offense level that, when applied to the sentencing table, would result in a two-year sentence. Because the Sentencing Reform Act eliminated parole, an offender receiving a two-year sentence would actually serve the full two years.

When Congress eliminated parole in the Sentencing Reform Act of 1984 to achieve a degree of truth in sentencing, it instituted two other mechanisms that furthered some of the benefits that parole formerly performed. First, it provided that offenders could earn a small reduction in their sentence, less than 15 percent, for good behavior in prison. Before, in the indeterminate sentencing scheme, offenders had a motivation to behave in prison because it increased their chances of parole. Without some benefit for behaving, an offender may have little practical motive to behave in prison. Using our example, then, an offender sentenced to two years in prison might, if the offender behaved in prison, receive a three and a half-month reduction in the offender's 24-month sentence.

Second, Congress created a program of supervised release. Depending on the severity classification of the crime of conviction (i.e., Class A Felony, Class B Felony, etc.), the judge could impose a term of supervised release within a range of years provided by statute. While on supervised release, the offender would be subject to certain terms and conditions governing their conduct. United States Probation Officers would monitor the offender on supervised release in much the same way parole officers monitored parolees under the former system.

Supervised release is considered part of the punishment for the original offense of conviction. If an offender violates the conditions of supervised release, a judge can revoke the offender's supervised release and send the offender back to prison for any time the offender would otherwise have been on supervised release. This system of supervised release serves the function of assisting in the offender's rehabilitation that parole formerly served in the indeterminate sentencing scheme.

The federal courts operated under this mandatory guideline form of a determinate sentencing scheme for about twenty years, from 1984 to 2005. In this system of mandatory guidelines, advocacy at the time of the sentencing hearing played a much less important role. Advocacy in plea negotiations and interaction with the probation officer calculating the offender's sentencing Gidelines scores became much more vital. At sentencing hearings, advocacy took a more technical turn in which attorneys litigated the intricacies of the various Guidelines provisions and fought over whether enhancements and reductions did or did not apply. Once the judge determined the Guidelines score, then the judge had so little discretion in the ultimate sentence, hemmed in by the narrow range that the Guidelines applied, that little effort was placed on persuading the sentencing judge about the ultimate sentence to impose. Efforts to personalize the sentence to the specific offender, to explain mitigating factors that may exist outside the Guidelines' factors, even pleas for mercy, were largely wasted and inapplicable. Hence, attorneys' sentencing advocacy skills atrophied.

Under the mandatory sentencing Guidelines system, a dramatic power shift occurred. The judicial branch was stripped of much of its power to determine an offender's sentence. That power was effectively transferred to the executive branch. The charges prosecutors chose to bring and, through plea negotiations insist on pleas to, largely and directly dictated the Guidelines sentence that would apply. Thus, prosecutors possessed significant power to significantly determine the sentences offenders would serve. The elimination of parole, however, removed the executive branch's ability to control the length of sentence the offender actually served. The sentence dictated by the Guidelines became the actual sentence served, less only any time the offender earned in good behavior time reductions.

All that changed in 2005 when the United States Supreme Court found the mandatory nature of the sentencing Guidelines constituted an unconstitutional delegation of powers by Congress to an agency, the United States Sentencing Commission. In *United States v. Booker*, 543 U.S. 320 (2005), the Supreme Court held that the Guidelines were just that—guidelines. In subsequent cases, the Supreme Court clarified the role of the Guidelines under a system in which they are advisory. *Gall v. United States*, 552 U.S. 38, 49 (2007) states, "[A] district court should begin all sentencing proceedings by correctly calculating the applicable Guidelines range. As a matter of administration and to secure nationwide consistency, the Guidelines should be the starting point and the initial benchmark" (citation omitted). This includes determining any Guidelines departures from the advisory Guidelines sentencing range. A sentencing judge "may not presume that the Guidelines range is reasonable." *Id.* at 50. After determining the advisory Guidelines sentence, the sentencing judge must then consider the arguments of the parties and the factors set forth in Title 18, United States Code, Section 3553(a). *Gall*, 552 U.S. at 49–50. A sentencing judge can "vary" from the advisory Guideline range based on any of the factors identified in Section 3553(a). A judge may also vary from the Guidelines based on a disagreement with the Guidelines. *Pepper v. United States*, 562 U.S. 476, 515 (2011). In every case, the district court must explain the basis for its chosen sentence on the record. *Gall*, 552 U.S. at 50. Appellate courts retain the power to reverse a sentence if they find the extent of a variance to be unreasonable. *Id.* at 51.

The factors in Section 3553(a) are very broad and, essentially, provide judges significant discretion to sentence offenders anywhere within the Congressionally determined statutory range. The factors include the Guidelines, and they include the goals of sentencing discussed in Chapter 2. The factors in Section 3553(a) are:

(1) the nature and circumstances of the offense and the history and characteristics of the defendant;
(2) the need for the sentence imposed—
  (A) to reflect the seriousness of the offense, to promote respect for the law, and to provide just punishment for the offense;
  (B) to afford adequate deterrence to criminal conduct;
  (C) to protect the public from further crimes of the defendant; and
  (D) to provide the defendant with needed educational or vocational training, medical care, or other correctional treatment in the most effective manner;

(3) the kinds of sentences available;
(4) the kinds of sentence and the sentencing range established for—
 (A) the applicable category of offense committed by the applicable category of defendant as set forth in the Guidelines—
  (i) issued by the Sentencing Commission pursuant to section 994(a)(1) of title 28, United States Code, subject to any amendments made to such guidelines by act of Congress (regardless of whether such amendments have yet to be incorporated by the Sentencing Commission into amendments issued under section 994[p] of title 28); and
  (ii) that, except as provided in section 3742(g), are in effect on the date the defendant is sentenced; or
 (B) in the case of a violation of probation or supervised release, the applicable guidelines or policy statements issued by the Sentencing Commission pursuant to section 994(a)(3) of title 28, United States Code, taking into account any amendments made to such guidelines or policy statements by act of Congress (regardless of whether such amendments have yet to be incorporated by the Sentencing Commission into amendments issued under section 994[p] of title 28);
(5) any pertinent policy statement—
 (A) issued by the Sentencing Commission pursuant to section 994(a)(2) of title 28, United States Code, subject to any amendments made to such policy statement by act of Congress (regardless of whether such amendments have yet to be incorporated by the Sentencing Commission into amendments issued under section 994[p] of title 28); and
 (B) that, except as provided in section 3742(g), is in effect on the date the defendant is sentenced.
(6) the need to avoid unwarranted sentence disparities among defendants with similar records who have been found guilty of similar conduct; and
(7) the need to provide restitution to any victims of the offense.

18 U.S.C. § 3553(a). In a later chapter I will address in detail each of these factors and discuss how attorneys can and should structure their sentencing arguments around these factors.

Effective sentencing advocacy has never been as important as it is now. It is even more important now in the federal system than it was before the period of mandatory sentencing Guidelines. Before 1984, judges had a lot of discretion in determining the sentence, but the sentence offenders actually served were often very different from the sentence imposed because of parole. Now, not only do sentencing judges again have tremendous discretion in determining an offender's sentence, that sentence is now the sentence that the offender will in fact serve because there is no parole in the federal system. In short, federal judges now have more power to determine an offender's sentence than ever before in history. Thus, learning how to be an effective sentencing advocate before a federal judge has never been more important.

B. The Interaction Between Statutory and Guidelines Provisions

Before I summarize the nature of federal statutory sentencing provisions and Sentencing Guidelines provisions, it is important to say a few words about the intersection between the two sets of provisions. In short, statutes trump Guidelines. No matter what the Guidelines may recommend a sentence should be, in any conflict between the Guidelines and a statute, the court must follow the statute. There are times, for instance, that based on the offense conduct, a Guidelines calculation may suggest a twenty-year sentence, but if the crime of conviction carries only a ten-year maximum sentence, then the court cannot sentence an offender to more than ten years. Likewise, if the statute provides a mandatory minimum sentence, say 25 years, then the sentencing judge cannot sentence an offender to less than the statutory minimum sentence, even if the Guidelines recommend a 20-year sentence. Understanding this basic concept is important because it is not uncommon for the Guidelines and statutory provisions to conflict. Attorneys who make charging decisions or enter into plea negotiations without keeping an eye on the interplay between statutory and Guidelines sentencing provisions may very well be unhappy with the sentencing result.

C. Federal Statutory Sentencing Provisions

In the federal system, statutory sentencing provisions assume several forms. First, every criminal offense contains a statutory provision establishing a maximum sentence.[2] Many of them also contain mandatory minimum sentences. Mandatory minimum sentences appear primarily in drug trafficking, firearms, child exploitation, and child pornography statutes, but they also pop up in a variety of other criminal statutes. The nature of the offense conduct generally determines the applicability of mandatory minimum and maximum sentences. For example, in drug trafficking cases, the quantity of drugs involved can trigger mandatory minimum sentences with the greater the quantity of drugs, the greater the possible maximum sentence. In some firearms cases, the nature of the firearm and how it was used can make the difference between whether the offense of conviction carries a mandatory minimum sentence and the maximum sentence that will apply. These statutes also often set maximum fines and sometimes minimum fines, and sometimes set minimum terms of supervised release.

Second, Congress has also enacted several recidivist sentencing statutes intended to ensure lengthy sentences for repeat offenders. Some of the recidivist statutes are mandatory, while the application of others is left within the discretion of prosecutors. One of the most frequently invoked mandatory recidivist sentencing statutes is the Armed Career Criminal Act, Title 18 United States Code, Section

924(e). An offender convicted of being a prohibited person (a felon, for example) in possession of a firearm, in violation of Title 18, United States Code, Section 922(g), normally faces a maximum term of imprisonment of ten years. 18 U.S.C. § 924(a)(2). If, however, the offender has previously been convicted of three or more felony offenses involving crimes of violence or drug trafficking, then the offender faces a mandatory minimum sentence of 15 years in prison and can be sentenced up to life in prison without the possibility of parole. 18 U.S.C. § 924(e). This sentencing enhancement applies regardless of whether the government sought the enhanced penalty and regardless of whether the government gives notice that the penalty will apply. Importantly, sometimes whether an offender qualifies as an Armed Career Criminal is not apparent until the probation office has completed an examination of the offender's criminal history and produces a presentence report.

Prosecutors have the discretion, in other instances, to invoke recidivist sentencing provisions. The drug trafficking statutes contain provisions that allow for enhanced mandatory minimum sentences and increased maximum sentences, including mandatory life in prison without the possibility of parole, when the offender has previously been convicted of felony drug trafficking offenses. These provisions do not automatically apply, however; they are only triggered if the government chooses to invoke them and provides the offender with notice of that invocation before trial or a guilty plea, under Title 21, United States Code, Section 851. The government retains the discretion at any time up until sentencing to withdraw such a notice and not pursue an enhanced sentence. If the government pursues the enhanced sentence, the court is bound to sentence the offender accordingly, regardless of how the Guidelines come out and regardless of whether the offender resists.

Finally, before we leave the statutory provisions, it is important to discuss supervised release statutory provisions. As previously noted, supervised release is part of the punishment imposed for the crime of conviction. If a judge revokes an offender's supervised release and returns the offender to prison, it is not as punishment for the violation but, rather, is in part punishment for the original offense.[3] Thus, any discussion of sentencing advocacy must include a discussion of supervised release as part of sentencing.

Under 18 U.S.C. § 3583 and Guidelines §5D1.1, an offender sentenced to prison for a felony or misdemeanor may also be sentenced to a term of supervised release. The length of the term of supervised release is linked to the severity of the crime:

> Except as otherwise provided, the authorized terms of supervised release are—
> (1) for a Class A or Class B felony, not more than five years;
> (2) for a Class C or Class D felony, not more than three years; and
> (3) for a Class E felony, or for a misdemeanor (other than a petty offense), not more than one year.

18 U.S.C. § 3583(b). Congress has, however, enacted laws that impose mandatory minimum periods of supervised release and other laws that increase the range of supervised release beyond those listed in Section 3583(b). For example, for offenses involving a minor victim, such as child exploitation, Congress imposed a mandatory

minimum term of supervised release of five years and increased the maximum period of supervised release to life. 18 U.S.C. § 3583(k). Similarly, in the drug trafficking statutes, Congress provided for increased mandatory minimum terms of supervised release for repeat offenders and increased the maximum term of supervised release to life. 21 U.S.C. § 841(b). As with statutory provisions imposing terms of incarceration, statutory provisions imposing terms of supervised release trump any Guidelines provisions.

D. Federal Sentencing Guidelines Provisions

There are many books published on the United States Sentencing Guidelines that delve into the intricacies and substantive law of the Guidelines. I do not intend to replicate such works here. Rather, I will generally describe the structure of the Guidelines with a focus on the aspects important for purposes of sentencing advocacy. The reason for reviewing the United States Sentencing Guidelines here is to provide the reader with a general overview of the Guidelines to place in context later references to them when discussing methods of effective sentencing advocacy. In any given case, an attorney will want to conduct thorough research of the Guidelines provisions applicable to that case, based on the charges and facts unique to that case.

For sentencing advocacy, the most important thing about a review of the United States Sentencing Guidelines is for attorneys who practice in both federal and state courts to understand the reasoning underlying Guidelines provisions. In federal courts, judges now impose sentences based on all the factors in Section 3553(a), of which calculating the advisory Guidelines is only one. Good sentencing advocates emphasize the reasoning behind the Guidelines to persuade judges to impose appropriate sentences. Attorneys practicing in federal court are far more effective basing arguments on the reasoning behind the Guidelines than they are when they simply apply them in rote fashion. Attorneys practicing in state court should similarly use the reasoning underlying the Guidelines to structure arguments in state court even though the United States Sentencing Guidelines obviously do not apply in state courts. A significant amount of time and study, thought and analysis have gone into the creation of the Guidelines. The reasoning behind Guidelines provisions provide a logical basis upon which attorneys can base broader arguments.

As noted before, the Guidelines are based on concept that an offender's sentence should be based on two governing factors: offense and criminal history. Certain Guidelines provisions (primarily in Chapters 2 and 3) determine a score representing the seriousness of the offense conduct. Other Guidelines provisions (Chapter 4) determine a score representing the seriousness of the offender's criminal history. Using a chart in which the offense level score is located on the vertical axis and the criminal history score is located on the horizontal axis, the recommended range of imprisonment is determined by the intersection of the two scores.

Sentencing Table
(in months of imprisonment)

	Offense Level	*Criminal History Category (Criminal History Points)* *I* *(0 or 1)*	*II* *(2 or 3)*	*III* *(4, 5, 6)*	*IV* *(7, 8, 9)*	*V* *(10, 11, 12)*	*VI* *(13 or more)*
Zone A	**1**	0–6	0–6	0–6	0–6	0–6	0–6
	2	0–6	0–6	0–6	0–6	0–6	1–7
	3	0–6	0–6	0–6	0–6	2–8	3–9
	4	0–6	0–6	0–6	2–8	4–10	6–12
	5	0–6	0–6	1–7	4–10	6–12	9–15
	6	0–6	1–7	2–8	6–12	9–15	12–18
	7	0–6	2–8	4–10	8–14	12–18	15–21
	8	0–6	4–10	6–12	10–16	15–21	18–24
Zone B	**9**	4–10	6–12	8–14	12–18	18–24	21–27
	10	6–12	8–14	10–16	15–21	21–27	24–30
	11	8–14	10–16	12–18	18–24	24–30	27–33
Zone C	**12**	10–16	12–18	15–21	21–27	27–33	30–37
	13	12–18	15–21	18–24	24–30	30–37	33–41
Zone D	**14**	15–21	18–24	21–27	27–33	33–41	37–46
	15	18–24	21–27	24–30	30–37	37–46	41–51
	16	21–27	24–30	27–33	33–41	41–51	46–57
	17	24–30	27–33	30–37	37–46	46–57	51–63
	18	27–33	30–37	33–41	41–51	51–63	57–71
	19	30–37	33–41	37–46	46–57	57–71	63–78
	20	33–41	37–46	41–51	51–63	63–78	70–87
	21	37–46	41–51	46–57	57–71	70–87	77–96
	22	41–51	46–57	51–63	63–78	77–96	84–105
	23	46–57	51–63	57–71	70–87	84–105	92–115
	24	51–63	57–71	63–78	77–96	92–115	100–125
	25	57–71	63–78	70–87	84–105	100–125	110–137
	26	63–78	70–87	78–97	92–115	110–137	120–150
	27	70–87	78–97	87–108	100–125	120–150	130–162
	28	78–97	87–108	97–121	110–137	130–162	140–175
	29	87–108	97–121	108–135	121–151	140–175	151–188
	30	97–121	108–135	121–151	135–168	151–188	168–210
	31	108–135	121–151	135–168	151–188	168–210	188–235
	32	121–151	135–168	151–188	168–210	188–235	210–262
	33	135–168	151–188	168–210	188–235	210–262	235–293
	34	151–188	168–210	188–235	210–262	235–293	262–327
	35	168–210	188–235	210–262	235–293	262–327	292–365
	36	188–235	210–262	235–293	262–327	292–365	324–405
	37	210–262	235–293	262–327	292–365	324–405	360–life
	38	235–293	262–327	292–365	324–405	360–life	360–life

	Criminal History Category (Criminal History Points)					
Offense Level	***I (0 or 1)***	***II (2 or 3)***	***III (4, 5, 6)***	***IV (7, 8, 9)***	***V (10, 11, 12)***	***VI (13 or more)***
39	262–327	292–365	324–405	360–life	360–life	360–life
40	292–365	324–405	360–life	360–life	360–life	360–life
41	324–405	360–life	360–life	360–life	360–life	360–life
42	360–life	360–life	360–life	360–life	360–life	360–life
43	life	life	life	life	life	life

The United States Sentencing Guidelines are structured in a logical and sequential manner. When applying the Guidelines, one starts with Chapter 1 and then proceeds in sequence through the following chapters, as applicable. Each chapter contains sections. Many sections contain subsections. Many also contain definitions. And almost all of them contain commentary. The commentary typically includes Application Notes. These notes reflect the Sentencing Commission's interpretation of the Guidelines and instruct the court about how the Commission believes the court should apply the Guidelines provisions. The commentary is generally binding on the court on the proper interpretation of the Guidelines.[4]

Chapter 1 provides basic definition of terms and general application principles governing all subsequent chapters. It is important for attorneys to frequently reference the Chapter 1 definitions when applying the other Guidelines provisions. It is also important to understand that other definitions are contained elsewhere in the Guidelines under specific sections. Definitions, wherever found, can significantly affect the application of the Guidelines, and attorneys who lose sight of these definitions run the risk that the Guidelines will be misapplied to the case.

Chapter 2 is the offense conduct chapter. It is the longest chapter, containing key Guidelines provisions that largely determine the placement of an offender on the vertical axis of the sentencing chart. Every federal offense is assigned an offense level in Chapter 2, with adjustments up and down based on specific offense characteristics. Appendix A to the Guidelines is a table listing by statute nearly every federal criminal offense in the code[5] with a cross reference to the Chapter 2 Guidelines provision that applies to the commission of that offense. Specific offense characteristics encompass facts about a particular crime that may make it more, or less, serious in nature. Specific offense characteristics of a bank robbery, for example, would include the amount of money taken or the use of a firearm, dangerous weapon, or violence. It is important for attorneys to note that some of the Chapter 2 sections provide cross-references, directing the court to apply a different Chapter 2 section than would otherwise apply if certain facts are present. For example, if an offender commits the crime of bank robbery in violation of Title 18, United States Code, Section 2113, Appendix A states that the applicable Chapter 2 Guidelines section is 2B3.1. But, Section 2B3.1(c) provides that "[i]f a victim was killed under circumstances that would constitute murder under 18 U.S.C. § 1111 had such killing taken place within the territorial or maritime jurisdiction of the United States, apply §2A1.1 (First Degree Murder)." USSG §2B3.1. Thus, a court would, under the cross reference, sentence a bank robber who killed a teller during commission of the offense under the murder Guidelines provisions.

Once the offense level is determined through application of Chapter 2, then it is subject to adjustments in Chapter 3. The adjustments in Chapter 3 are based on factors potentially applicable to all crimes, in contrast to the Chapter 2 adjustments that are often applicable only to particular types of criminal conduct. Chapter 3 adjustments focus more on the nature of the offender or victims and contemplate facts that suggest that the crime or the criminal is more or less reprehensible. There are five parts within Chapter 3: Part A addresses victim-related adjustments; Part B addresses role-in-the-offense adjustments; Part C contains adjustments for obstructive conduct; Part D deals with adjustments when offenders are convicted of multiple offenses; and Part E provides adjustments for acceptance of responsibility.

Chapters 2 and 3 together determine an offender's offense level, the placement of the offender on the vertical axis of the sentencing chart.

Chapter 4 determines an offender's placement on the horizontal axis, an offender's criminal history category. There are six criminal history categories, labeled I through VI. In Chapter 4, a court applies zero to three points to an offender's prior convictions based on the age and seriousness of the prior convictions. The seriousness of a prior conviction is determined by the length of the sentence the court imposed for that conviction with the thought that it best reflects the seriousness of the offense. Chapter 4 contains provisions that exempt certain convictions from scoring any criminal history points. If a conviction is more than ten years old or is of a type that is deemed petty, for example, it will receive no points. Similarly, convictions that score one point will be counted only up to four points, no matter how many "one-pointers" an offender may have. Importantly, Chapter 4 also contains provisions for determining if an offender is deemed a career offender based on a combination of the offender's age (i.e., over 18), the nature of the offense of conviction (e.g., violent crime or serious drug offense), and the offender's criminal history (i.e., two or more prior felony convictions involving violence or serious drug offenses). An offender deemed a career offender will automatically be placed in Criminal History Category VI, regardless of how the offender's criminal history would otherwise score under the Chapter 4 provisions.

Chapter 5 is entitled "Determining the Sentence," and has multiple parts. Part A contains the sentencing table. Part B addresses terms and conditions of probation. Part C addresses terms of imprisonment and in particular the zones. The sentencing table is divided into three sentencing "zones," labeled A, B, and C. Sentencing options differ depending on the zone. Under Zone A, a term of incarceration is not generally required, and the court can impose probation. Under Zone B, some term of incarceration is required, but the minimum term can be satisfied through various means, including home confinement. Under Zone C, incarceration is required. Part D sets out the rules of imposition of terms of supervised release. Part E addresses restitution, fines, assessments, and forfeitures. Part F deals with sentencing options, such as community confinement, community service, victim notice, and other collateral restrictions and impositions on the offender. Part G takes on the complicated ramifications of multiple convictions and overlapping terms of imprisonment as a result of either multiple federal convictions or a combination of federal and state convictions when terms of imprisonment have been, are, or could be served consecutively or concurrently. Not all these provisions apply in every case but several will, and have varying levels of importance to the attorneys and offender depending on the specific facts of the case and the offender.

Chapter 5, Parts H and K (there are no Parts I & J) are devoted to departures from the Guidelines. These parts identify both grounds that could provide sentencing judges with a basis to depart from the Guidelines range and with grounds that sentencing judges generally should not use as a basis to depart.[6] For example, Section 5H1.5 instructs that an offender's employment record "is not ordinarily relevant in determining whether a departure is warranted." USSG §5H1.5. On the other hand, Section 5K2.1 provides that if a death resulted from the offense, "the court may increase the sentence above the authorized guideline range." USSG §5K2.1.

The most frequently invoked departure ground is for substantial assistance, under Section 5K1.1. If an offender cooperates with the government, and the prosecutor believes the offender has provided "substantial assistance in the investigation or prosecution of another person who has committed an offense," then the government (and only the government) can move for a downward departure from the Guidelines range to reward the offender for that cooperation. Section 5K1.1 sets out five factors the court is to consider in determining whether to grant the motion and the extent of the departure. It is important for defense counsel to recognize the need to advocate for their clients when the government makes motions under Section 5K1.1 to ensure that the description and significance of cooperation is portrayed to the court in the light most favorable to their clients. All too often the government alone describes the nature and extent of cooperation and, although it may be perfectly accurate, it may not be described in a way that fully benefits the offender. As will be mentioned again later, defense counsel should also recall that if an offender cooperated, but the government does not make a motion under Section 5K1.1 because the cooperation did not reach the level of being deemed "substantial," a court can still vary downward from the Guidelines sentence under the Section 3553(a) factors because the attempted cooperation arguably reflects a high degree of acceptance of responsibility.

Finally, it should be noted that not all grounds for departures are neatly cabined in Chapter 5, Sections H and K. Chapters 2, 3, and 4 also occasionally contain provisions suggesting grounds for departures when facts exist of an extraordinary nature not accounted for in the Guidelines provision. For example, under the firearms provisions, Section 2K2.1, comment 11 notes that "[a]n upward departure may be warranted in any of the following circumstances: (A) the number of firearms substantially exceeded 200; (B) the offense involved multiple National Firearms Act weapons (e.g., machine guns, destructive devices), military type assault rifles, non-detectable ('plastic') firearms … (C) the offense involved large quantities of armor-piercing ammunition … or (D) the offense posed a substantial risk of death or bodily injury to multiple individuals[.]" USSG §2K2.1, cmt. n.11. Likewise, Section 3A1.2, which provides enhancements when the victim of a crime is government official, contains an application note indicating that an upward departure may be appropriate "[i]f the official victim is an exceptionally high-level official, such as the President or the Vice President of the United States." USSG §3A1.2, cmt. n.5. As a final example, Guidelines Section 4A1.3 articulates grounds for upward and downward departures from the Guidelines range when "reliable information indicates that the offender's criminal history category substantially" over- or under-represents "the seriousness of the defendant's criminal history or the likelihood that the offender will commit other crimes." USSG §4A1.3(a) & (b).

Chapter 6 of the United States Sentencing Guidelines addresses sentencing procedures, plea agreements, and crime victims' rights. Chapter 7 applies to the sentencing of an offender whose supervised release or probation has been revoked due to violations. And Chapter 8 applies to the sentencing of corporations. I address Chapter 7 and revocations of supervised release and probation in the antepenultimate and penultimate chapters of this book. I discuss the sentencing of corporations in a later chapter as well, but suffice it to say that there is a significant role for pre-charge and pre-sentencing sentencing advocacy for corporations because Chapter 8 contains provisions that decrease a corporation's sentence based on the corporation's pre-sentencing conduct directed at detecting, addressing, and working to prevent criminal violations by its officers and employees.

E. Burdens of Proof in Sentencing

The burden of proof at a sentencing hearing, no matter the issue, is by a preponderance of the evidence. The party who bears the burden of proof differs on the issue. Generally speaking, the burden is on the government to prove any fact the existence of which will increase an offender's sentence or impinge on an offender's liberty or property interest. Conversely, an offender bears the burden to prove any fact the existence of which would result in a decrease in the offender's sentence.[7] In federal court, this also means that whichever party is asking the court to depart or vary from the advisory Guidelines bears the burden of proof.[8]

It follows, then, that the government bears the burden of proof to establish offenders' base offense levels and any Guidelines enhancement that would increase offenders' offense levels, any facts supporting upward departures from the Guidelines, and any prior convictions that would increase offenders' criminal history scores. Under the Section 3553(a) analysis, the government bears the burden to prove any facts it is relying on in advocating for upward variances from the advisory Guidelines range. Likewise, the government bears the burden of proving facts showing that the offenders' conduct caused losses to victims and to prove the amount of restitution owed to victims. Similarly, the government must prove by a preponderance of the evidence any facts that would form a basis for imposition of special terms of supervised release not dictated by statute. Lastly, the government bears the burden to prove facts in connection to forfeiture, including that the property to be forfeited constituted proceeds or was used to facilitate the commission of the offense.

Conversely, offenders have the burden to prove by a preponderance of the evidence any facts that would decrease Guidelines offense levels, such as specific offense characteristics that result in a decrease in base offense levels. This means, for example, that offenders bear the burden to prove that they have clearly accepted responsibility under Section 3E1.1. Similarly, offenders bear the burden to prove facts justifying a downward departure or downward variance from the advisory Guidelines range. Because the Guidelines require the court to impose a fine unless offenders are indigent, offenders bear the burden of proving by a preponderance of the evidence that they are indigent.

It must be noted, however, that the Ninth Circuit Court of Appeals has adopted a requirement that the government's burden of proof increases to the higher standard of "clear and convincing evidence—in cases where there is 'an extremely disproportionate impact on the sentence.'" *United States v. Valle*, 940 F.3d 473, 479 (9th Cir. 2019) (quoting *United States v. Jordan*, 256 F.3d 922, 930 [9th Cir. 2001]). Other circuit courts of appeal have rejected this heightened burden of proof requirement in sentencing hearings.[9]

F. Summary

This chapter only serves to highlight the principal aspects of the federal sentencing statutes and Guidelines to provide a context and foster a better understanding in the following chapters about how attorneys can be effective in advocating within the sentencing scheme. The more familiar attorneys become with the Guidelines and the case law and the more experience they gain, the better they will become at sentencing advocacy. State statutory and guidelines schemes will differ to some degree from the federal statutes and Guidelines, but these differences are more in nuance than in nature. Much of the sentencing advocacy techniques and methods discussed in this book, as applied within the context of federal statutes and the United States Sentencing Guidelines, can be directly applied within the state court systems. In other instances, the techniques and methods may need to be adjusted to adapt to the nuanced differences in the wording of the state statutes and guidelines.

5

Scope of a Criminal Sentence

A criminal sentence is more than simply the number of months or years that offenders will spend behind bars, although that is understandably often the primary focus and of utmost importance to offenders. Criminal sentences will always include at least some additional forms of punishment or result in adverse collateral consequences. In every sentencing hearing, a judge will also decide whether to impose a fine and the size of that fine and, in the federal system, whether to impose a term of supervised release or probation (along with the conditions of any supervised release or probation that is imposed). In many sentencing hearings, there are a host of other adverse collateral consequences for offenders, including deportation, restitution, forfeiture, loss of professional licensure, debarment, and registration as a sex offender, among others. It is fitting then, before we move on to examine methods of effective advocacy, to take stock of the scope of a criminal sentence.

In most cases in the federal system, the primary penalty is the deprivation of liberty. This most often involves a period of incarceration in some form. Federal sentencing judges have no control over the type of penal institution where offenders will be housed; that is left to the discretion of the Federal Bureau of Prisons. Judges can only make a recommendation to the Federal Bureau of Prisons as to the facility where the offender is to serve time. Nevertheless, it is important that attorneys understand that the length of sentence, the nature of the offense, and other characteristics about the crime and the offender will have an impact on the type of institution where the offender will be housed. The Federal Bureau of Prisons will assign a security classification to the offender based on a formula that includes the length of the sentence and the nature of the crime (e.g., whether it involves violence). The security classification will also depend on other facts included in the offender's presentence report, regardless of whether the facts are directly tied to the offense of conviction or even the offender's United States Sentencing Guidelines calculation. For example, indications in the presentence report that the offense or other conduct involved violence or firearms will result in a higher security classification. Likewise, the nature and extent of the offender's criminal history, evidence of prior escapes, witness tampering, gang affiliation, and the like may also affect an offender's security classification. Years of incarnation aside, the type of institution where an offender serves those years of incarceration will significantly impact the nature of that incarceration and the offender's daily quality of life while incarcerated. Thus, as

I will discuss in a later chapter, it is essential that attorneys ensure that an offender's presentence report is complete and accurate.

Sentences can include a period of probation instead of a term of incarceration. Although probation is qualitatively better for an offender than a period of incarceration, it is important that attorneys recognize that probation is a significant punishment. As the United States Supreme Court explained:

> We recognize that custodial sentences are qualitatively more severe than probationary sentences of equivalent terms. Offenders on probation are nonetheless subject to several standard conditions that substantially restrict their liberty. Probationers may not leave the judicial district, move, or change jobs without notifying, and in some cases receiving permission from, their probation officer or the court. They must report regularly to their probation officer, permit unannounced visits to their homes, refrain from associating with any person convicted of a felony, and refrain from excessive drinking. Most probationers are also subject to individual "special conditions" imposed by the court.

Gall v. United States, 552 U.S. 38, 48 (2007) (internal citations omitted).[1] Offenders sentenced to terms of probation typically have travel restrictions limiting their movement to the district of conviction. Offenders under probation are also often barred from changing jobs without notifying and sometimes getting permission from their probation officers. Effective sentencing advocacy requires attorneys to carefully consider, then, the length and conditions of any term of probation imposed in lieu of incarceration with the same level of attention attorneys pay to length of periods of incarceration.

When, in the federal system, courts impose periods of incarceration, they almost invariably also impose a term of supervised release to follow. Like probation, "supervised release is itself a serious sanction that imposes significant limitations on a defendant's liberty." *United States v. Book*, 889 F.3d 95, 101 (2d Cir. 2018). Sentencing judges have significant discretion in imposing supervised release and determining the terms of supervise release. Nevertheless, judges may only impose conditions of supervised release that are reasonably related to factors enumerated in Title 18, United States Code, Section 3553(a). Those conditions must "involve no greater deprivation of liberty than is reasonably necessary" for the purposes of the Section 3553(a) factors, and must be "consistent with any pertinent policy statements issued by the Sentencing Commission." 18 U.S.C. § 3583(d). This requires sentencing judges to make an individualized inquiry into the facts and circumstances underlying the specific case and offender to ensure that the conditions of supervised release satisfy those statutory requirements. Effective sentencing advocacy requires attorneys to devote careful attention to the terms and conditions of supervised release and, when appropriate, litigate those matters.

For every federal offense, sentencing judges may also impose a fine. There are several factors for courts to consider in determining whether to impose a fine and the amount of fine to be imposed. First, the Eighth Amendment to the Constitution contains an Excessive Fines Clause. *See* U.S. Const. amend. VIII: "Excessive bail shall not be required, nor excessive fines imposed, nor cruel and unusual punishments inflicted." Second, federal statutes establish sentencing ranges for specific offenses. Finally, two United States Sentencing Guidelines provision address fines:

the general fines guideline, USSG §5E1.2, and the guideline for the particular substantive offense at issue. The Guidelines direct that "[t]he court shall impose a fine in all cases, except where the defendant establishes that he is unable to pay and is not likely to become able to pay any fine." USSG §5E1.2(a). The burden is on offenders at sentencing to show that they cannot pay fines. Effective sentencing advocacy requires careful consideration of fines as part of offenders' sentences. In some cases, a criminal fine may promote the goals of sentencing more effectively than a period of incarceration, particularly when the motive for and harm caused by the crime was monetary in nature. A criminal fine, particularly a significant fine, may also have a devastating impact on an offender and the offender's family, even when it does not rise to the level of an excessive fine under the Eighth Amendment. Finally, it must be noted that when corporations are offenders, criminal fines are the principal, albeit not the sole means, of punishment.

In the federal system, judges must also impose special assessments on every offender as part of the sentence, regardless of the ability to pay.[2] Congress enacted the special assessment requirement as a form of punishment and for the primary purpose of providing funds to support the Crime Victims Fund.[3] Under Title 18, United States Code, Section 3013, the sentencing court must impose a special assessment ranging from $5 to $100 for individuals, and $400 for corporations, for every count of conviction. Although at first blush a special assessment may not seem to be a serious consequence of sentencing, it can seriously affect indigent offenders. The Federal Bureau of Prisons will take a portion of any funds offenders earn out of their pay and out of their commissary funds until the special assessment is paid in full. Offenders may be barred from participating in certain programing while incarcerated when any portion of their special assessments remain unpaid. More significantly, courts must impose an additional $5,000 special assessment on offenders for every count of conviction for certain offenses related to sexually exploiting children.[4] *See* Justice for Victims of Trafficking Act of 2015, 18 U.S.C. §§ 3013(a)(2)(A), 3014(a)(3). Unlike the Special Assessments under Section 3013, however, a sentencing court may decline to impose this additional special assessment for indigent offenders.

When crimes involve victims, restitution will be a sentencing issue. Federal law mandates the imposition of restitution for certain offenses. The Victims of Trafficking and Violence Protection Act (VTVPA) and the Mandatory Victims Restitution Act (MVRA) require restitution for the violation of specifically identified statutes. 18 U.S.C. § 1593(a). In other cases, judges have the discretion to order restitution. The parties may, as part of a plea agreement, also agree that offenders will pay restitution even when no statute would necessarily mandate that the offenders pay restitution. Unless an offender agrees to more in a plea agreement, restitution can be imposed only for victims of the crime of conviction. Restitution typically consists of "the full amount of the victim's losses," including medical services, therapy and rehabilitation, transportation, housing, childcare, and "any other losses suffered by the victim as a proximate result of the offense." 18 U.S.C. § 1593(b)(3) (citing § 2259[c][2]). The government bears the burden of proving the restitution amount owed by a preponderance of the evidence. As will be discussed later, this requires prosecutors to work with victims to effectively advocate on behalf of victims to obtain full restitution. It is important to note that restitution represents the real loss to victims, which is often different from and less than the "intended loss" or the loss amount calculated under the Guidelines.

The government may also seek to forfeit property as part of a criminal sentence. The government can forfeit real or personal property, including tangible and intangible property (such as intellectual property), if it represents the proceeds of, or it was used to facilitate the commission of, the crime of conviction. The Excessive Fines Clause of the Eighth Amendment bars forfeitures that are grossly disproportionate or excessive in relation to the offense committed. *United States v. Bajakajian*, 524 U.S. 321, 324 (1998) (prohibiting forfeitures that are "grossly disproportional to the gravity of a defendant's offense"). "The touchstone of the constitutional inquiry under the Excessive Fines Clause is the principle of proportionality: The amount of the forfeiture must bear some relationship to the gravity of the offense that it is designed to punish." *Id.* The government has the burden of showing a direct factual nexus between the crime of conviction and the asset that it seeks to forfeit. The asset must be the fruit of the crime of conviction or have been used to facilitate the crime. The offender has the burden of showing that forfeiture of the asset would be disproportionate to the crime of conviction.

The Supreme Court has declined to establish a test for determining whether a forfeiture is constitutionally "excessive."[5] Generally, courts look for forfeitures that are "grossly disproportional"—an inherently imprecise term—to the underlying conduct.[6] Ultimately, proportionality is a fact-specific inquiry that might provide opportunity for attorneys to use advocacy skills at sentencing.

Finally, it is important for attorneys to consider the collateral sentencing consequences that may arise from sentences in particular cases. Sex offenses will often carry a collateral consequence of requiring the offender to register as a sex offender, sometimes for life. This collateral consequence can be a more long-lasting and serious restriction on an offender's liberty interest than the term of incarceration. Convictions under other statutes may allow federal agencies to bar the offender from participating in federal programs or from receiving federal funds. For example, a fraud conviction for a crime involving Medicare funds may subject the offender to being barred from participating in any program involving Medicare funds. If the offender is a health care provider, this may spell the end of the offender's medical career. Similarly, convictions for violations of certain types of offenses can have significant collateral immigration consequences. For example, convictions for violent crimes or those involving dishonesty may bar an offender from ever being able to become a United States citizen, while convictions for other offenses may not. It is important for defense attorneys to work with or consult immigration attorneys in these cases to fully and accurately advise clients about these collateral sentencing ramifications.

The point here is that it is of paramount importance that attorneys fully recognize and comprehend all the collateral sentencing consequences to a conviction, particularly in connection with plea negotiations. A plea to a violation of one statute may require sex offender registration or result in debarment from federal programs, while a plea to a violation of another statute may not. If attorneys are not fully cognizant of these sentencing ramifications during charging decisions and plea negotiations, they may result in unintended sentencing consequences. As I will discuss in the next chapter, effective sentencing advocacy begins long before the finding of an offender's guilt.

In short, effective sentencing advocacy requires attorneys to look beyond just the term of incarceration. Criminal sentences are comprised of much more than the number of months or years behind bars. Although the deprivation of liberty through incarceration deserves attorneys' primary attention, attorneys should always consider all the other components of a criminal sentence.

6

Sentencing Advocacy Before Guilt Determination

Effective sentencing advocacy begins long before an offender has pleaded guilty or is found guilty. Although the focus of this book will be on sentencing advocacy that occurs after guilt has been established, it is crucial that attorneys understand that decisions made, steps taken, and omissions occurring long before the offender has been found guilty have a tremendous impact on sentencing.[1] Decisions prosecutors and defense attorneys make at every stage of a case, from investigation through guilty plea or trial, will affect the nature of the final sentence. Investigation and charging decisions can affect mandatory minimums and maximum sentencing ranges. Charging decisions can also impact how sentencing Guidelines apply. Defense team investigations into the offense conduct and the offender's history and characteristics can inform the defense attorney about how the United States Sentencing Guidelines may apply to the case and what options are available for departure and variance motions. Effective advocacy in motions hearings can affect what charges remain pending at sentencing. Plea bargaining advocacy can shape the nature of the sentencing issues and define the scope of sentencing options. In short, attorneys should make decisions throughout the life of a criminal case always conscious of the sentencing ramifications.

There are many decisions at various stages of a criminal case that can impact sentences. A detailed and lengthy analysis of these stages of a criminal case, and all the decisions and factors that could have an impact on an offender's sentence, however, is beyond the scope of this book. Interested readers can find other sources in the bibliography that address these stages of a criminal case in more detail. Here, the objective is to point out to attorneys some of the key decisions before determination of guilt that can affect an offender's sentence so as to emphasize the need for attorneys to think holistically about and plan comprehensively for sentencing throughout the life of a criminal case.

A. *Prosecution Investigations and Charging Decisions*

When prosecutors are working with law enforcement officers to investigate crimes, they should keep an eye on how decisions made during the investigation can impact sentencing options down the road. The evidence found and not found (or looked for) during an investigation can obviously affect the prosecutor's charging options. But those charging decisions can in turn, of course, greatly influence the possible sentencing options. Good prosecutors lead law enforcement officers in conducting criminal investigations because officers are not in the same position as prosecutors to understand or appreciate the need for evidence for purposes of persuasion. This is particularly true with sentencing issues.

Officers will be familiar with the elements of many criminal offenses, but for prosecutors to prevail in all aspects of a prosecution, including sentencing, there is often a need for evidence far beyond the bare minimum necessary to prove the elements of an offense. Officers may or may not be aware of facts that, if proven, could impact the statutory parameters of sentencing, such as triggering mandatory minimum sentences or increasing the maximum sentencing range. Officers may not recognize that the prosecutor could bring other charges that carry different sentencing options if certain facts were found. Rather, law enforcement officers often are focused on the most obvious offense that the target appears to have commited. Many officers will likely be unfamiliar with the complex guideline and statutory factors that can affect an offender's sentence. Without guidance from the prosecutor, officers generally will not know what they do not know, and thus will not know to look for and secure evidence that could directly impact sentencing options.

For example, in a drug trafficking investigation, prosecutors and law enforcement officers may have various investigation operational options to exercise. Officers may be able to make one or more controlled buys of drugs from the target and have some ability to influence the quantity of drugs purchased. Officers may also be able to communicate with the target of the investigation in person or over a telephone. If prosecutors make officers aware that it is important, officers may be able to investigate and find out what the target drug dealer is doing with the proceeds from his drug sales. Each of these things can impact the sentencing options available to the prosecutor down the road. Federal drug sentences are often driven by drug quantity calculations under the Guidelines. Drug quantities can also trigger mandatory minimum sentences. A charge of using a telephone to conduct a drug transaction, on the other hand, has no mandatory minimum sentences and a lower maximum sentence than a distribution charge. The spending of drug proceeds can sometimes support money laundering charges, which can provide other sentencing options and guideline enhancements.

Based what the prosecutor knows about the target and the evidence uncovered, the prosecutor may decide to pursue different charging options. Considering the goals of sentencing, if the prosecutor believes the target is dangerous and incapacitation may be necessary, perhaps the prosecutor believes it would be important to conduct more controlled buys for larger quantities so as to trigger mandatory minimum sentences or higher guideline levels. On the other hand, if the target is a low-level person in the drug organization with an addiction problem and the prosecutor hopes to use the target as a means to get at people higher in the organization, then it may be important to ensure that a controlled buy is arranged by telephone so as to give the prosecutor that option for a charge that carries a lesser sentence. Similarly, a prosecutor may determine that a money laundering charge would more accurately reflect the target's role and criminal culpability or would open up other sentencing options, such as fine amounts and forfeiture. Again, prosecutors will know what facts would support various charges and sentencing options far better than the officers. Thus, prosecutors should help guide the officers' investigations so the prosecutor has the maximum number of charging, and hence sentencing, options available.

The evidence obtained during an investigation can also impact sentencing options irrespective of the impact the evidence may have on charging decisions. The United States Sentencing Guidelines include enhancements and reductions based on offense characteristics. Whether those Guidelines adjustments apply depends on whether there is evidence to support them. For example, assume the target of a criminal investigation was a felon who was believed to be in possession of a firearm. Assume further that law enforcement officers executed a search warrant of the target's house and found him there in possession of a firearm. If the firearm was stolen, then there is a sentencing enhancement under the Guidelines regardless of whether the offender knew the firearm is stolen. If the offender possessed the firearm only for collection or sporting purposes, on the other hand, there would be a sentencing Guidelines reduction in the offense level. If officers are aware that these facts can affect sentencing, they can conduct the investigation in a manner to discover the existence of evidence that would support or not support Guidelines enhancements and reductions. For example, as to the purpose for which the offender possessed the firearm, officers can investigate this by asking the target why he possesses the gun, using leading or nonleading questions, or officers can look for circumstantial evidence that would shed light on the issue, such as where the firearm was located (near drugs or under the pillow). If law enforcement officers are unaware of how these facts can influence the sentence, though, they will not know to look for them. It is the prosecutor's job to work with officers to make sure they understand the sentencing issues and encourage them to look for evidence important for sentencing.

Finally, as mentioned in the introduction, a criminal sentence is much more than only the period of incarceration. It can include restitution, forfeiture, victim impact, and many other collateral consequences depending on the crime and the offender. Prosecutors should work closely with law enforcement officers during the investigation to ensure that steps are taken to obtain the evidence and information that may be important for these sentencing issues. For example, if the crime is a financial crime with many victims, the criminal investigation needs to include identifying, locating, and potentially seizing the offender's assets so that they will be available for restitution. Failing to do this in a timely manner may allow the offender to dissipate those assets and deprive the government of the ability to obtain restitution for the victims.

B. Defense Investigations

Just as investigative steps taken by the government can affect sentencing advocacy options in the future, so too can defense attorneys affect sentencing advocacy options by conducting a timely investigation focused on sentencing factors. In all likelihood, defense attorneys will not learn of or be involved in a criminal case until the government brings charges. That is not always the case, however, particularly in white collar cases. Often white-collar targets will learn that they are under investigation when they or their companies receive grand jury subpoenas. The targets may include corporations, which can be charged with criminal offenses. The United States Sentencing Guidelines provide for potential reductions in corporate sentences (usually imposed by way of financial penalties) when the corporation conducts its own investigation and aids the government in the investigation of criminal activities by corporate employees and others. With human targets of white collar investigations, early investigation by defense attorneys may provide opportunities to mitigate the ultimate sentence by discovering ways to mitigate the damage to victims, provide cooperation to the government, show extraordinary acceptance of responsibility by confessing or paying restitution before the court has ordered it, or by generally engaging in early negotiations with the government before the government has expended more resources running up the costs of prosecution. In short, when they are aware of a criminal investigation before the government brings charges, defense attorneys have an opportunity to quickly investigate the case and search for ways to mitigate the sentencing ramifications. It can also be a time when defense attorneys can tease as much information as possible out of the prosecution so as to better prepare a defense and portray the target in the most favorable light to place him in a better position for future plea and sentencing negotiations.

In most cases, though, defense attorneys begin their representation way behind the prosecution. By the time they become involved, their clients have been charged and the speedy trial clock is ticking. At that point, defense attorneys must learn the facts quickly, evaluate the possibility of legal challenges to the evidence and charges, assess whether the case is triable, and work with their clients to reach decisions about pleading guilty or contesting the case at trial. At the same time, defense attorneys should also always keep sentencing issues in mind and investigate the facts as they might bear on sentencing as well as on guilt. Defense attorneys may look into whether, for example, their clients know information that could be helpful to the government's investigation of others, opening up the possibility for a sentencing reduction for cooperation. Similarly, if an offender is charged with being a prohibited person in possession of a firearm, the defense attorneys should investigate whether evidence exists to show that the offender possessed the firearm solely for a lawful collection or sporting purpose, opening up the possibility for a sentencing reduction under the sentencing Guidelines. Ultimately, good sentencing advocacy means that defense attorneys should not be solely focused the question of guilt in their investigation into the facts of the case but should also consider facts that could affect the offender's sentence. Defense attorneys should also not assume that the government has investigated and uncovered all facts that would be relevant and helpful to the offender in sentencing. It stands to reason that the government's investigation would be focused on uncovering facts that could increase the offender's sentence. A defense investigation focused on mitigation may uncover additional facts leading to a lower sentence.

Defense attorneys can use various methods to investigate cases as part of their sentencing advocacy efforts. Defense attorneys can, with leave of court under Rule 17 of the Federal Rules of Criminal Procedure, issue subpoenas for production of documents. For example, if an incarcerated government cooperator has claimed the defendant was responsible for a greater drug weight than the evidence may otherwise show, a defense attorney may seek to subpoena the jail calls for the cooperator, anticipating that the cooperator likely said something over those calls the defense attorney could use to impeach the cooperator. The government sometimes moves to quash such subpoenas in some cases when issued to government entities when there are grounds to do so or the defense attorney has not complied with applicable regulations, but subpoenas issued to non-government third parties are usually successful.

When possible, defense attorneys should use staff or private investigators to conduct other investigations, such as witness interviews or inspections of crime scenes so that, if necessary, the defense attorneys will be able to call the investigators as witnesses later. Sometimes, however, defense attorneys just have to get out to do their own investigation. Just as prosecutors should, for example, always visit the scene of the crime personally so they can fully comprehend the facts, so too should defense attorneys visit the scene of the crime. When defense attorneys have difficulty securing the assistance of investigators or can justify limited expenses for such investigators, it is sometimes necessary for defense attorneys to do more of the initial leg work of investigations themselves. The defense attorneys may later hire investigators to follow up only on the limited areas the defense attorneys found fruitful and for which they need a witness they can call at a sentencing hearing.

C. Pretrial Detention or Release

It may surprise most attorneys that pretrial detention decisions should be considered part of sentencing advocacy, but the truth is that they should. No one wants to be incarcerated. It is not surprising, then, that when offenders are arrested, they want to be released pending trial. In many if not most cases, release is appropriate and has many benefits not only for the offender personally but also for the case and sentence. It is far easier for defense attorneys to work with offenders, negotiate pleas, and prepare for trial when offenders are released and can meet with attorneys in their offices instead of having to do so in the local jail. If offenders cooperate with the government, it is far easier for that cooperation to occur, and there are more cooperation options, when offenders are not incarcerated. For purposes of this book, however, it is also important that defense attorneys in particular consider the sentencing ramifications of pretrial release/detention decisions.

After the Bail Reform Act of 1984, offenders in the federal system are generally released under supervision or detained pending trial in cases involving crimes against children, some violent crimes, and drug trafficking offenses. Bail is used much less in the federal system than in the state system. When federal courts impose bail obligations, they are typically in amounts that offenders can afford to post but cannot afford to lose by fleeing. When the court releases offenders pending trial, the offenders are often under close supervision. In appropriate cases, this close supervision includes regular drug testing. In most state systems, the amount of bail determines whether offenders are released. If released, state offenders are subject to varying degrees of oversight, but nothing like in the federal system. Release pending trial and sentencing can impact sentencing both positively and negatively.

In the federal system, an offender released pending trial and, in particular, released pending sentencing, receives a lower security classification rating from the Bureau of Prisons. The security rating dictates the security level of the institution where offenders serve their sentences. Offenders allowed to be on pretrial release, and to remain on release after guilty pleas or findings of guilt and sentencing, will receive the lowest security classification rating. This is particularly true if they are also allowed to self-surrender to the prison. Low security ratings open the possibility of offenders serving time in a prison camp instead of a penitentiary. Offenders' quality of life while serving a sentence is significantly different in a low-security versus a high-security facility. Thus, generally speaking, it is in most offenders' best interests, for purposes of sentencing ramifications, to be released pending trial and sentencing and to self-surrender to the penal institution.

On the other hand, offenders should be cautious about what they ask for. All too many offenders have serious addiction problems. Others have anger-management issues. Still others are unrepentant recidivists. Offenders who may win the battle of pretrial detention may lose the war of sentencing if, while on release, they violate the terms and conditions of release. Offenders who use drugs or commit other crimes while on release may not only face the possibility of additional charges, but their poor conduct on release will most certainly impact the sentence that the judge imposes for the underlying offense. An offender may forfeit any reduction in his sentence for acceptance of responsibility, for example, by engaging in continued criminal conduct while on release. Defense attorneys should warn offenders about the danger posed by their associates; offenders need to be mindful of who their real friends are and to disassociate from those who may expose them to drugs or other criminal conduct while the offender is on pretrial release. These false friends only expose offenders to temptations and the risks of being present in the midst of criminal activity. Thus, in some cases, it may be in offenders' best interest not to be released pending trial if there is a high likelihood that the offenders will be unable or unwilling to abide by the terms of release. Pretrial release may, in some cases, only be giving ropes to offenders with which to hang themselves.

To be sure, it is a tough sell to persuade offenders on the idea that it is in their best interest to remain in jail pending the outcome of their cases. Nevertheless, good sentencing advocacy may call upon defense attorneys to explain the risks of release, especially on the potential sentence, so that offenders can at least make a fully informed decision. In one example, a defense attorney shared that he successfully litigated continued pretrial release for his client, despite a violation, only to have the client continue to violate pretrial release, leading to a more severe sentence in the end. Defense attorneys can emphasize the severe sentencing ramifications should the offender violate conditions of release and have a candid conversation with the offender about the severity of their addiction or other problems. When, however, an offender insists on trying to be released from custody pending trial or sentencing, then the defense attorney must zealously represent the offender. This may include instructing the offender on the need to abide by all terms and conditions of release and explaining the adverse consequences that may result if the offender violates those terms and conditions of release. Even though it might be in their client's best interest to remain detained, however, defense attorneys are ethically obliged to advocate for what their clients want when liberty is at stake.

D. Post-Offense, Presentence Conduct

The period between an initial appearance on charges and the sentencing hearing, and in particular between a finding of guilt (by plea or verdict) and the sentencing hearing, can be a critical stage when an offender's conduct could impact the sentence positively or negatively. As part of sentencing advocacy, a defense attorney should explain to an offender the consequences that the offender's conduct during this interval can have on the offender's ultimate sentence. Good defense attorneys will maintain contact with their clients during this period, even when there are not necessarily any motions pending, and the probation officer has not yet completed the draft presentence report. It is a mistake for defense attorneys to disengage from their clients during this critical stage. Offenders are more likely to misbehave during this period, or have second thoughts about the plea agreement or decision to plead guilty and contemplate moving to withdraw their plea, jeopardizing a sentencing reduction for acceptance of responsibility. When defense attorneys keep engaged with their clients during this period, they can often prevent the offender from engaging in misconduct and effectively address the offender's second thoughts and concerns.

Some post-guilt/presentence conduct can clearly harm an offender at sentencing. As discussed above, drug use while on pretrial release shows contempt for the court and a degree of recidivism that could increase an offender's sentence. Similarly, criminal conduct during this interval, whether the offender is incarcerated or is on release, may adversely impact the offender's sentence. If an offender assaults another inmate while awaiting sentencing, threatens or tampers with witnesses, or possesses drugs in jail, it may very well result in sentencing enhancements for obstruction of justice or forfeiture of any reduction for acceptance of responsibility, culminating in a longer prison term. Defense attorneys should explain this to offenders and advise them against engaging in any such conduct.[2]

On the other hand, some offender conduct during this period can substantially help an offender at the time of sentencing. If an offender takes advantage of drug treatment or other programming focused on rehabilitation, whether the offender is in or out of jail pending sentencing, it can paint the offender in a more positive light at the time of sentencing. Similarly, when the offender's crime harmed others, efforts to take responsibility by paying restitution to victims can show extraordinary acceptance of responsibility. Again, defense attorneys should explain all this to offenders, explore options with them, and attempt to aid the offenders in taking advantage of these opportunities.[3]

Defense attorneys also often encounter offenders with mental illnesses and diagnosed addiction issues. When they do, defense attorneys should do more than use words to aid their clients. It is sometimes necessary for defense attorneys to take action by connecting the offender to a social worker or getting the offender signed up for Alcohol Anonymous or Narcotics Anonymous classes, and if necessary driving them there.

When restitution will be an issue at sentencing, defense attorneys sometimes need to actively assist their clients in addressing this issue. Defense attorneys should review offenders' financial condition in detail so as to identify any assets that offenders could liquidate to pay off restitution. It is also important that defense attorneys monitor the offenders' finances to ward off attempts to hide or move assets in a way that could come back to hurt the offender at sentencing. Defense attorneys may also consider seeking continuances of sentencing hearings if doing so may buy offenders more time to scrape together some money for making restitution payments before sentencing.

When offenders have the ability to take steps showing acceptance of responsibility but decline to do so, it can adversely impact an offender's sentence. I am frequently surprised in victim cases when an offender has pleaded guilty to the crime, does not contest that the offender owes restitution or the amount of restitution owed, and has income or other assets, making monthly payments for cable television and other luxuries. Yet by the time of the sentencing hearing, the offender has not made any effort whatsoever to pay any portion of the restitution. Even an effort to pay a small amount of money toward restitution pending the sentencing hearing would show true acceptance of responsibility. The failure to make even this token effort calls into question, in my mind, the degree to which the offender truly accepts responsibility for harming others.

E. Motions Practice

In criminal cases, pretrial motions are brought almost solely by offenders. Prosecutors seldom file pretrial motions except for motions in limine to address anticipated evidentiary issues at trial. Defense motions are, appropriately, usually focused on the issue of guilt. A court order suppressing some or all the evidence or dismissing some or all the charges will have an obvious impact on the government's ability to convict the offender. Motions practice may, however, also significantly impact sentencing advocacy options. Success in removing some evidence or charges from the guilt phase of a trial can, for example, affect what, if any, mandatory sentencing provisions will apply at sentencing.

On the other hand, defense attorneys should also keep in mind that sentencing judges can almost always consider suppressed evidence and criminal conduct that did not result in convictions, and even conduct of which an offender was acquitted, in arriving at a sentence. Thus, in considering whether to bring motions, defense attorneys should at least consider whether winning the motion will have any impact at all on the ultimate sentence. If not, they may want to consider whether it is worth bringing the motion when it is clear that an offender will be pleading guilty. Filing motions that will have no practical effect on guilt or the sentence, but only create more work for the government, may with some prosecutors impact the defense attorneys' ability to negotiate a favorable plea deal for their clients.

F. Plea Bargaining

The reality is that an overwhelming majority of criminal cases are resolved by way of guilty pleas. Plea bargaining can have the greatest impact on an offender's sentence. Thus, effective sentencing advocacy requires attorneys to enter into plea bargaining only after careful consideration of all the possible sentencing ramifications. Most attorneys, and most offenders for that matter, are primarily focused on plea bargaining on the statutory minimum and maximum sentences and the Guidelines implications on the length of the term of incarceration. This is as it probably should be. An offender's liberty should almost always be the primary consideration.

Nevertheless, plea negotiations focused on the length of the likely term of incarceration is not always as straightforward as it may seem. In contemplating plea options, the parties should carefully consider the interplay between sentencing Guidelines and statutory provisions. Regardless of what the Guidelines advise, an offender can only be sentenced to the extent of the maximum statutory penalty. For example, if an offender's offense conduct and criminal history support a Guidelines sentence of 135 to 168 months, but the offender pleads to a charge with a maximum ten-year sentence, then the effective Guidelines range is 120 months. Similarly, regardless of what the Guidelines advise, an offender cannot be sentenced any lower than an applicable statutory mandatory minimum sentence. So, in our example, if the statutory mandatory minimum sentence is 240 months, then that becomes the effective Guidelines sentence. The difficulty is that the attorneys may not be fully aware of all the facts that will influence the Guidelines sentence. Often offenders' criminal histories can be difficult to uncover or verify, and it is frequently complicated to calculate criminal history scores. Nevertheless, almost everything about criminal cases is available online these days and, with enough effort, criminal history scores can be calculated with relative certainty. Probation officers are often willing to discuss and sometimes provide some preliminary estimates of criminal history scoring to both prosecutors and defense attorneys. This information may be of great assistance, even before an offender has been found or pleaded guilty, in plea negotiations. When prior convictions may be critical in determining mandatory minimum sentences or criminal history categories, it is worth the costs for defense attorneys to get copies of the actual court documents. In the end, both prosecutors and defense attorneys should enter plea negotiations doing the best they can to predict how the Guidelines will apply to an offender's case.

The interplay between the United States Sentencing Guidelines and statutory penalties can impact whether the parties see any benefit from a plea deal. If a statutory minimum or maximum sentence will determine an offender's sentence and deprive the offender of any actual benefit in a Guidelines reduction for acceptance of responsibility, and even foreclose an opportunity to try to persuade a judge into imposing a lesser sentence by way of a downward variance motion, then the offender may see no downside to going to trial. Similarly, if a prosecutor believes the Guidelines would exceed the statutory maximum sentence if the offender pleaded guilty to a single count in the indictment, and the prosecutor believes a Guidelines sentence is appropriate considering all the goals of sentencing, then the prosecutor may insist on a plea to multiple counts so that the court can stack the maximum penalties to make it possible for the court to sentence the offender within the Guidelines range. If an offender is unwilling to do so, then the prosecutor may determine that it would be better to go to trial than enter into a plea agreement.

The crime or crimes of conviction can also affect the application of the United States Sentencing Guidelines in ways that may not be obvious. The "crime of conviction" is a term of art in the Guidelines, and the application of Guidelines provisions often depend on the crime of conviction, regardless of the relevant criminal conduct. The crime of conviction will have the obvious impact of determining which Chapter 2 section of the United States Sentencing Guidelines apply. Beyond that, however, the crime of conviction may impact the application of other Guidelines provisions in Chapters 2, 3, and 4. Some specific offense characteristics under Chapter 2 provisions apply, or do not apply, based on the crime of conviction. Whether certain Chapter 3 provisions apply may also depend upon the crime of conviction. Finally, the crime of conviction can sometimes even influence an offender's criminal history score. If the offense conduct giving rise to a prior conviction is also offense conduct involved in the crime of conviction, then the prior conviction may not score any criminal history points. Even more importantly, the significant sentencing enhancements for career offenders and armed career criminals are triggered by the nature of the crime of conviction, such as whether it is a serious drug offense or a crime of violence. There has been significant litigation and several United States Supreme Court cases over what crimes of conviction qualify to trigger these sentencing enhancements, especially over the term "crimes of violence." The same offense conduct charged two different ways may result in a career offender calculation for one charge but not the other. This book is not the place to take a deep dive into that evolving body of law, but it is a place to emphasize the need for attorneys to recognize at the time of plea negotiations the importance of an offenders' criminal history in determining a sentence.

In negotiating pleas, attorneys should also consider all the other sentencing ramifications beyond the period of incarceration. There are many. The crime of conviction will establish both the statutory and Guidelines fine ranges. Offenders convicted of some child exploitation offenses must pay a $5,000 special assessment, unless the court finds them to be indigent. The crime of conviction is a key factor in determining whether restitution is mandatory or even possible. The government can recover costs of prosecution when an offender is convicted of certain offenses but not others. Whether a crime victim has a statutory right to address the court may depend on the charge to which the offender pleads guilty. There are, similarly, significant immigration ramifications for noncitizens that can affect whether they are deported, whether they could ever apply for citizenship, and the offenses and sentences that may apply were the offender caught illegally re-entering the United States, just to name a few. Finally, guilty pleas to certain charges may trigger obligations by an offender to register as a sex offender, while others do not.

Attorneys can seek sentencing concessions during plea negotiations, regardless of how the Guidelines might apply and sometimes regardless of statutory provisions. In other words, as part of plea negotiations, the parties can stipulate to how they believe the Guidelines should apply. Typically, these agreements are binding on the parties but not the sentencing judge. On the other hand, if the parties enter into a plea agreement under Federal Rule of Criminal Procedure 11(c)(1)(C) and stipulate to a Guidelines application or even the ultimate sentence, and the sentencing judge accepts the plea agreement, then the plea deal is equally binding on the sentencing judge. Parties may also agree to seek or not seek application of certain Guidelines provisions within their control. For example, whether an offender is eligible for a third level off for acceptance of responsibility under Section 3E1.1(b) depends on the government's willingness to make a motion for the reduction. Other Guidelines applications may depend on the government producing evidence at the time of sentencing to trigger the enhancement. If the government does not present the evidence, then the Guidelines provision will not apply, even if the facts would otherwise support it. In some cases, the parties can reach agreements to sentencing ramifications that, absent an agreement, would not be available under the law. For example, if an offender pleads guilty to an offense that does not require or even provide an option for restitution to victims, the offender can nevertheless agree to pay restitution as part of a negotiated plea deal.

In short, when negotiating a plea agreement, both defense attorneys and prosecutors should very carefully consider all the many statutory and Guidelines sentencing ramifications, both as they affect the term of incarceration but also all the other sentencing components and collateral consequences.

G. Organizations

When offenders are corporations or other organizations, presentencing planning takes on a different form than when offenders are human beings. Here, defense attorneys are not concerned with their clients going to jail. To be sure, there may be directors, officers, and employees also subject to criminal charges and sentencing, but when defense attorneys represent organizations, their clients are really the owners and shareholders. What matters to owners and shareholders is maintaining the viability of the organization as a going concern and minimizing any decrease in the organization's value.

Prosecution of an organization almost always involves a negotiated plea, and negotiations can be complicated for several reasons. Organizations act through officers, and defense attorneys thus communicate with officers when representing organizations, yet the officers are not the client. Defense attorneys should be ever conscious to negotiate an outcome that has the best sentencing ramifications for the organization, regardless of what impact it may have on any director, officer, or employee. Negotiations will also often involve a request for the organization to share with the government the results of any internal investigation. This may require the organization to consider whether to waive attorney-client and attorney work product privileges tied to internal investigations. Generally, prosecutors cannot ask for corporations to waive the attorney client privilege though; this decision is for the corporation to make based on its own assessment of the costs and benefits.

Under the United States Sentencing Guidelines, a corporation's sentence may be impacted by its "culpability score." Some of the factors comprising the score are outside the defense attorney's control, such as the size of the organization, who in the hierarchy of the organization was involved or condoned the criminal activity, and whether the organization had previous convictions for violations. How an organization responds to discovery of criminal conduct by its agents, however, can also impact the sentence, and this is when there is a place for defense attorneys to exercise effective sentencing advocacy skills. If an organization unreasonably delays disclosure of the crime to law enforcement officers after discovery, it can increase the organization's sentence. On the other hand, if the organization promptly reports the crime, it can decrease the organization's offense level. Similarly, if the organization cooperates with the government's investigation of the criminal conduct, it can further reduce the corporation's offense level. Defense attorneys have a sentencing advocacy role, then, to influence the timing of the organization's disclosure and the degree of the organization's cooperation, from the moment the organization hires the defense attorney to represent it in relation to the criminal investigation. In other words, a defense attorney cannot solely focus on determining whether the organization committed a crime and who within the organization may be subject to criminal charges. The defense attorney should also be ever cognizant that as the clock ticks, it may impact the organization's sentence.

Fines are the principal form of punishment for organizations. In determining the amount of the fine, the sentencing judge must consider numerous factors. Here, again, is an area where effective sentencing advocacy can come into play. The collateral consequences of the fine on the organization and its ability to do business, the consequences it may have on subsidiary organizations not involved in the criminal conduct, and the impact on the ability of the organization to pay restitution, among other things, can impact the amount of the fine that the court should impose. To be effective sentencing advocates, attorneys on both sides of the aisle should investigate these matters long before the sentencing hearing.

As with individuals, a criminal conviction and sentence can have collateral consequences for organizations as well. A significant concern for organizations is disbarment, that is being barred from doing business with the federal government. Government agencies control this decision, but as part of a plea or sentencing agreement, the parties can sometimes work with the agency at issue to reach a global resolution addressing disbarment as part of the ultimate disposition of the case. An organization may agree to pay a larger fine, for example, in exchange for an agreement that the agency will not bar the organization from future business relationships with the federal government. The significance of disbarment will depend on the percentage of an organization's business tied to government contracts or funding, but in some instances, it can make the difference in whether the organization can survive.

7

Stages in the Sentencing Process

After a guilty verdict is announced, or the offender utters the words "guilty" in a plea hearing, what are the steps that follow culminating in the pronouncement of sentence? This short chapter answers that question, identifying the stages in federal criminal cases that take place after a guilty plea or finding of guilt leading up to and through the sentencing hearing. In doing so, it simultaneously lays out the structure for most of the remaining chapters in this book, as the following chapters will be devoted to fleshing out more detail on each of these steps. Here, I will only briefly identify and describe what occurs at each stage. The subsequent chapters will delve into greater detail about each stage and, more importantly, examine what attorneys can do at each stage to be effective sentencing advocates.

The order in the stages of sentencing is largely flexible and left to the discretion of the judge, although some stages must occur before others. Preparation of a presentence report, also referred to as a PSR, necessarily comes first, and the pronouncement of sentence must always come at the end. Between those two bookends, the rest is somewhat flexible. Here, I have laid out the stages of the process in the order that I proceed in my courtroom. I will mention in later chapters how attorneys' sentencing advocacy may be impacted when judges use different orders.

The first stage in the federal sentencing process involves the probation officer drafting the presentence report. Chapter 8 in this book addresses this stage, and includes not only the role of attorneys in connection with the probation officer's investigation and drafting of a presentence report, but also attorneys' responsibility in reviewing and objecting to such reports. In almost all federal districts, probation officers conduct their own independent review of the government's evidence to draft the offense conduct section of a presentence report, the section describing the criminal conduct. In a few districts the parties are required by local rule or practice to submit a joint factual stipulation either before or at a guilty plea hearing, and probation officers will typically incorporate this stipulation into the offense conduct section of the presentence report. When parties enter into a plea agreement and the plea agreement contains a factual stipulation, probation officers will similarly incorporate those factual stipulations into the offense conduct section of the presentence report. As for other portions of the presentence report, such as the offender's criminal and personal history, probation officers will rely on information obtained directly from the offender during an interview and through the probation officer's own investigation. Probation officers will strive to obtain documentation about everything in the offender's background, including education, medical and mental health treatment, and employment history. Verifying background information about an offender is especially important for purposes of motions to vary from the Guidelines. For that reason, probation officers will often note in the presentence reports whether such information is verified. The preparation of a presentence report takes time. Some take longer than others. There is no maximum period set by law or rule for probation officers to produce presentence reports, but officers must produce the original report to the parties 35 days in advance of the sentencing hearing and the final report to the court and the parties at least seven days before the sentencing hearing. FED. R. CRIM. P. 32(e)(2) and (g).

Once a probation officer drafts a presentence report, the officer will send a draft of the report to the parties. The parties are given fourteen days to lodge objections to the draft presentence report. FED. R. CRIM. P. 32(f)(1). Generally, a sentencing judge may rely on any uncontested portions of a presentence report in imposing sentence. Thus, this is a vital stage in the sentencing process when attorneys should carefully review every portion of the presentence report and lodge objections or make corrections when appropriate. The probation officer will consider the parties' objections and either accept or reject their objections. The probation officer will then produce a final presentence report that notes the parties' objections and the probation officer's response to the objections.

Once the probation officer has issued the final presentence report, then the attorneys will have an opportunity to file sentencing memoranda. This stage is the subject of Chapter 9 in this book. Sentencing briefs should address any legal sentencing issues, such as the application of disputed statutory and Guidelines provisions. Sentencing briefs may also include motions for upward or downward departures or variances from the advisory Guidelines sentence. Some judges require departure or variance motions to be filed as separate pleadings. Depending on the case, sentencing briefs may also address other disputed issues such as fines, restitution, victim issues, and other collateral issues. Every federal sentence brief should address the sentencing factors at Title 18, United States Code, Section 3553(a).

After or in conjunction with briefing the sentencing issues, attorneys should turn next to preparing for the sentencing hearing. Chapter 10 in this book discusses the tasks attorneys should take in preparing for sentencing hearings. The nature and scope of preparation for a sentencing hearing differs tremendously depending on whether there are factual disputes that require findings by the sentencing judge, legal disputes that the sentencing judge must resolve, both, or neither. Sometimes the only decision for the sentencing judge to make at the hearing is the ultimate sentence to be imposed. In other cases, there are so many factual and legal issues in dispute that a sentencing hearing requires attorneys to gather evidence and mark exhibits, prepare witnesses, and make notes for legal arguments similar to preparing for a trial and closing argument.

The sentencing hearing itself is, of course, the culmination of the sentencing process. Chapter 11 examines sentencing hearings in general, and Chapters 12 through 23 cover each part of a sentencing hearing in detail. In federal court, a sentencing hearing must include certain things, regardless of whether and the extent to which the sentencing issues are disputed. The sentencing judge must calculate the advisory Guidelines sentence. The judge must give the parties an opportunity to be heard. The judge must consider all the factors in Title 18, United States Code, Section 3553(a). The judge must provide the offender an opportunity to make a statement. Then the court must pronounce sentence. In some cases, though, the court will also hear testimony and take evidence. Sentencing hearings can take on the appearance of minitrials; indeed, some sentencing hearings take longer than many trials. And if there are complex legal issues involved, then the sentencing hearing can also take on the appearance of an appellate argument to a panel of one judge. In these fact-intensive, legal issue–filled sentencing hearings, skillful advocacy is crucial.

The final stage is the judge's actual imposition of the sentence at the conclusion of the sentencing hearing and the filing of the judgment and committal order afterwards. This stage of sentencing is the topic of Chapter 24. As I emphasize and explain in detail in that chapter, there is a role for sentencing advocacy here as well. It is incumbent upon attorneys to ensure that the oral pronouncement of sentence is complete and accurate. Attorneys should also review the written judgment to ensure that it is consistent with the oral pronouncement of sentence and to ensure that it, too, is complete and accurate.

I will turn now to take up each of these sentencing stages in more detail and to examine how attorneys can be effective advocates at each stage.

8

Drafting of and Objecting to Presentence Investigation Reports

The drafting of the presentence report is a crucial stage in the sentencing process. The presentence report sets the bar and frames the scope of the issues for the court to address at the sentencing hearing. Although probation officers draft the presentence report, attorneys have an advocacy role to play in helping to shape the final product to ensure that it is complete and correct. That role begins during the probation officer's investigation of the case. By submissions to the probation officer, attorneys can assist the officer in the drafting of the report itself. Attorneys' advocacy continues with a careful and critical review of the draft presentence report. Finally, effective sentencing advocacy requires attorneys to submit complete, clear, and precise objections to any errors they find upon their review of the draft presentence report.

It is hard to overemphasize the importance of effective sentencing advocacy at this stage of the process. When attorneys neglect their responsibility to ensure that the presentence investigation report is complete and accurate, adverse consequences can follow. Judges may lash out at attorneys for failing to ensure the presentence report is accurate, clients and family members may be upset when the presentence report fails to include all of the important and material information about an offender, and ultimately courts of appeal may reverse a sentence and remand the case for resentencing. As the presentence report is the single most important document in any sentencing hearing, both the prosecutor and defense attorney should be heavily invested in ensuring that it is the best that it can be.

A. *The Probation Officer's Presentence Investigation*

Most state courts, and all federal courts, require a presentence investigation and the generation of a presentence report. In federal court, Federal Rule of Criminal Procedure 32(c) identifies a probation officer's obligations for conducting a presentence investigation. Rule 32(c) provides:

(1) **Required Investigation.**

(A) **In General.** The probation officer must conduct a presentence investigation and submit a report to the court before it imposes sentence unless:

(i) 18 U.S.C. 3593(c) or another statute requires otherwise; or

(ii) the court finds that the information in the record enables it to meaningfully exercise its sentencing authority under 18 U.S.C. § 3553, and the court explains its finding on the record.

(B) **Restitution.** If the law permits restitution, the probation officer must conduct an investigation and submit a report that contains sufficient information for the court to order restitution.

(C) **Interviewing the Defendant.** The probation officer who interviews a defendant as part of a presentence investigation must, on request, give the defendant's attorney notice and a reasonable opportunity to attend the interview.

FED. R. CRIM. P. 32(c).

Although Rule 32(c)(1)(A)(ii) authorizes judges to dispense with the preparation of a presentence report, this is seldom done for the obvious reason that judges need and want as much information as possible to determine appropriate sentences.[1] Judges rely heavily on presentence reports to provide that information. When Congress amended Rule 32 in 1974, it understandably explained "that such a report ought to be routinely required except in cases where there is a reason for not doing so." FED. R. CRIM. P. 32(c)(1), 1974 Amendment Notes. Choosing not to order a presentence report is a matter of judicial discretion; thus, appellate courts will overturn a district court judge's decision to dispense with the preparation of a presentence report only when it constitutes an abuse of discretion.[2] Under Rule 32(c), a court abuses its discretion when it lacks information to "meaningfully exercise its sentencing authority." *See* FED. R. CRIM. P. 32(c)(1)(A).[3] There is no provision in Rule 32 allowing parties to waive preparation of a presentence report or stipulate to not having the probation office prepare a presentence report. Similarly, under the Guidelines, an offender "may not waive preparation of the presentence report." USSG §6A1.1(b).

Only in rare occasions should parties advocate for the court to dispense with a presentence report. One such occasion may be when an offender is facing a time-served sentence and is in custody. Preparing a presentence report takes time, and the offender may have an interest in dispensing with a presentence report so as to get out of custody. As noted, offenders cannot waive preparation of a presentence report, but they can move the court to exercise its authority under Rule 32(c)(1)(A)(ii) to dispense with a presentence report. Another, and probably better, alternative when time may be of the essence in the preparation of a presentence report is for offenders to move the court to order the expedited preparation of a presentence report. Probation offices are very busy and already work hard to triage preparation of presentence reports to expedite those when the offender may face a time-served sentence. Nevertheless, the court can order the probation office to expedite preparation of a particular presentence report if there is any concern that the normal process would not give the case adequate priority.

From a sentencing advocacy point of view, both offenders and the government benefit from presentence reports. As will be discussed in more detail, presentence reports contain a wealth of information for both parties. The presentence report identifies contested matters, defines the disputed issues, and narrows the focus of the sentencing hearing. The uncontested parts of the presentence report provide facts upon which the parties may rely in advocating for certain sentencing positions.

Probation officers often start their investigation by obtaining from the government a copy of the government's discovery file. Prosecutors should facilitate this process immediately after the finding of an offender's guilt by working with staff to generate a digital copy of the discovery file. In some cases, it may assist the probation officer for the prosecutor to explain how the file is organized or how to search through the file for information. It is not helpful to probation officers for prosecutors to provide the officers with data dumps of large volumes of discovery with no guidance or assistance in sorting through or understanding the evidence. Prosecutors should not do this. Here is an opportunity for prosecutors to assist the probation officer in processing and understanding the evidence so that the draft presentence report is complete and accurate and truly reflects the offense conduct. It also helps speed up the drafting process. From the government's (and victim's perspective), justice delayed is justice denied. To be effective advocates, prosecutors should do what they can to assist probation officers' work through the government's discovery file.

Prosecutors should also continue to conduct the criminal investigation, when necessary, to supplement the government's file with evidence that may not have been necessary for the guilt stage of the criminal case but will be important for purposes of sentencing. For instance, a prosecutor may not have found it proper to expend limited investigative resources before the finding of guilt on issues such as restitution or the offender's ability to pay a fine. But these are important issues for sentencing. After the offender's guilt has been determined, prosecutors may conclude that it is appropriate to direct law enforcement officers to conduct investigations into these areas and in turn provide that information to the probation officer. It is in the government's best interest that the probation officer can timely and accurately investigate the offense conduct, and as the government's attorney, prosecutors should endeavor to assist the probation officer to conduct the investigation in any way possible.

Defense attorneys need not sit on their hands at this stage of the sentencing process. The presentence report certainly will contain a section on the offense conduct as reflected in the government's discovery file and as supplemented by the prosecutor between the determination of guilt and the drafting of the presentence report. But defense attorneys may also have information not in the government's file that bears on the offense conduct. More often, defense attorneys have access to other information that will be important to populate other portions of the presentence report. Indeed, defense attorneys may be in the best position and possibly the only ones who can provide the probation officers with information about offenders' history and characteristics. When applicable, defense attorneys should provide or facilitate the probation officer's access to educational, medical, and psychological records. Defense attorneys should work with an offenders' family members to provide the probation officer with family history information. It will be important for offenders to have sentencing judges focus more on offenders' history and characteristic and not solely on the offense conduct. Thus, to be effective sentencing advocates, defense attorneys should strive to provide probation officers with as much information about offenders' history and characteristics as possible so that portion of the presentence report is complete, robust, and accurate. Indeed, defense attorneys may find it appropriate in some cases to provide the probation officer with their own offense conduct statement that addresses Guidelines reductions, such as when there is an argument that an offender's base offense level for illegal possession of a firearm should be reduced because the offender possessed the firearm only for lawful sporting or collection purposes.

Rule 32(c) requires probation officers to interview offenders as part of the presentence investigation. Defense attorneys should be present with offenders during these interviews. Unfortunately, some defense attorneys neglect to attend these interviews. This is a mistake. Defense attorneys can and should facilitate the interview and help the probation officer flesh out information that will be helpful to the offender. At the same time, defense attorneys may advise clients in certain circumstances not to answer some of the probation officer's questions if doing so may incriminate offenders or harm them in sentencing. Defense attorneys should not inhibit the probation officer in conducting the interview, but defense attorneys must zealously represent their client's interest. Defense attorneys should be cautious when advising clients not to answer questions to make sure that it will not hurt the offender at sentencing and in rehabilitation. For example, if an offender refuses to answer questions about the offender's prior drug use, it may prevent the offender from being eligible for drug treatment while incarcerated. Such treatment may help the offender and reduce time spent in custody. It may also prevent the defense attorney from seeking a downward variance on the ground that the offender's drug addiction drove his offense conduct.

On the other hand, there are some nuances in the United States Sentencing Guidelines calculations, particularly with firearms violations, when disclosing drug use could conceivably increase an offender's Guidelines offense level. The point here is that defense attorneys should very carefully consider the pros and cons of having offenders disclose information to probation officers and help offenders make informed decisions. Defense attorneys should not adopt blanket practices of either having offenders refuse to provide information, or tell everything, to probation officers.

B. Drafting of the Presentence Investigation Report

Upon completion of the presentence investigation, the probation officer writes a draft presentence report. Federal Rule of Criminal Procedure 32(d) prescribes the general requirements for the broad contents of that report. Rule 32(d) provides:

> (1) **Applying the Advisory Sentencing Guidelines.** The presentence report must:
> (A) identify all applicable guidelines and policy statements of the Sentencing Commission;
> (B) calculate the defendant's offense level and criminal history category;
> (C) state the resulting sentencing range and kinds of sentences available;
> (D) identify any factor relevant to:
> (i) the appropriate kind of sentence, or
> (ii) the appropriate sentence within the applicable sentencing range; and
> (E) identify any basis for departing from the applicable sentencing range.
> (2) **Additional Information.** The presentence report must also contain the following:
> (A) the defendant's history and characteristics, including:
> (i) any prior criminal record;
> (ii) the defendant's financial condition; and
> (iii) any circumstances affecting the defendant's behavior that may be helpful in imposing sentence or in correctional treatment;
> (B) information that assesses any financial, social, psychological, and medical impact on any victim;
> (C) when appropriate, the nature and extent of nonprison programs and resources available to the defendant;
> (D) when the law provides for restitution, information sufficient for a restitution order;
> (E) if the court orders a study under 18 U.S.C. § 3552(b), any resulting report and recommendation;
> (F) a statement of whether the government seeks forfeiture under Rule 32.2 and any other law; and
> (G) any other information that the court requires, including information relevant to the factors under 18 U.S.C. § 3553(a).
> (3) **Exclusions.** The presentence report must exclude the following:
> (A) any diagnoses that, if disclosed, might seriously disrupt a rehabilitation program;
> (B) any sources of information obtained upon a promise of confidentiality; and
> (C) any other information that, if disclosed, might result in physical or other harm to the defendant or others.

FED. R. CRIM. P. 32(d).

It is here that effective sentencing advocacy calls upon attorneys to make written submissions to probation officers to influence the content of the written report. The government sometimes does so; for whatever reason, defense attorneys seldom do. Both sides should.[4] This is an opportunity to advocate to probation officers who draft presentence reports, the single most important document judges rely on in determining offenders' sentences. Attorneys should not pass up this opportunity to provide input to the probation officer. When attorneys pass up the opportunity to provide input to the probation officer, they are foregoing an opportunity to advocate for their client. Effective sentencing advocacy demands that attorneys assist probation officers in their investigation to ensure the presentence report is complete and accurate.

Some defense counsel may hesitate to provide information to probation officers under the impression that probation officers are only concerned about public safety and are institutionally biased against offenders. These defense attorneys may believe that it would be a waste of time to provide information to probation officers if that is the case. It is my impression, however, that probation officers strive to remain neutral and provide sentencing judges with all relevant information regardless of whom it favors. Regardless, defense attorneys are advocates. They are trained in advocacy. Part of sentencing advocacy may be to persuade probation officers just as it is to persuade judges. Defense attorneys who feel probation officers have an anti-defendant bent should face the challenge of trying to bring those probation officers around to the defense perspective using their advocacy skills rather than throwing up their hands in defeat without trying.

Probation officers have no first-hand knowledge of the case, but the attorneys know it intimately. The attorneys are in an ideal position then to provide assistance to probation officers in drafting the presentence report. This is particularly true when an offender is found guilty after a trial. The evidence that came out at trial may be different in material respects from the evidence contained in the government's discovery file. The evidence at trial will also obviously be focused on the elements of the offenses of conviction, not on the factors that may be important under the sentencing Gidelines or other sentencing factors. Without input from the parties about the evidence that was actually admitted at trial, the probation officer is in a very poor position to draft an accurate presentence report. Even when offenders plead guilty, simply providing probation officers with stipulations of fact, perhaps from plea agreements, is wholly inadequate. These factual stipulations are often bare-bone recitals of the essential facts necessary to satisfy the elements of the offense because the stipulations are the result of negotiation, not advocacy. There are often many additional facts that one party may believe are important in determining the offender's sentence, but that the other party dispute or are at least unwilling to admit in a stipulated factual statement. It is not surprising then that probation officers report that these factual stipulations are typically inadequate.[5]

The practice of attorneys providing information to probation officers to aid their presentence investigation is so varied that there is no consensus on the name for these submissions. In the Northern District of Iowa, where I served as a prosecutor and where I now serve as a judge, the submissions are referred to as "offense conduct statements." This is a misnomer, though, because they included far more than simply a description of the offense conduct. These statements include Guidelines calculations and criminal history information, and address other sentencing issues as well, such as restitution, fines, and forfeiture. Other districts refer to these written submissions as the "government's versions of the offense," "statements of offense," "proffers of facts," or "offense summaries." These terms are equally inadequate and inaccurate as the term "offense conduct statement" to describe what is typically is, or what should be, included in such written submissions. Absent an adequately descriptive label for these submissions, I will coin one here: Presentence Investigation Statement. Both sides should submit them: a Government's Presentence Investigation Statement and an Offender's Presentence Investigation Statement.

First, Presentence Investigation Statements should describe in detail the pertinent facts constituting the offense conduct and brief any legal or Guidelines issues implicated by the offense conduct. In doing this, attorneys should be careful never to misstate the facts or the law. Good attorneys will provide Presentence Investigation Statements that are drafted in a sufficiently neutral and factual manner that the probation officer feels comfortable adopting it as written. Indeed, attorneys should provide Presentence Investigation Statements to probation officers electronically so that probation officers can cut and paste them directly into the draft presentence report.

The primary function of a Presentence Investigation Statement is to describe for the probation officer the facts surrounding the criminal conduct. Good Presentence Investigation Statements should, however, do much more. Thorough Presentence Investigation Statements should also identify the statutory penalties, including terms of incarceration, fines, special assessments, and the terms of supervised release or probation the parties believe appropriate. They also describe any likely collateral consequences, such as restitution and forfeiture, that will be part of the offender's sentence.

When attorneys summarize the offense conduct in Presentence Investigation Statements, or frankly when they describe any information contained in the discovery file, it is helpful to provide the probation officer with a specific reference citation, so the officer can easily find the source document. With the advent of digital discovery, this should be easy as most documents in discovery are marked with unique "Bates" numbers. The easier attorneys make it for probation officers to check the source documents, the more likely it is that probation officers will adopt the attorney's submission and accurately describe the information.

Presentence Investigation Statements should also contain the attorney's calculation of how the sentencing Guidelines apply to the offender.[6] Attorneys should calculate the Guidelines thoroughly and carefully, making sure to consider all possible offense characteristics, grounds for cross-references, and departures. When an offense characteristic results in an adjustment to the Guidelines, attorneys should provide citations to the discovery file again so that the probation officer can verify the information easily and accurately. For example, if the prosecutor believes that a drug trafficking offender should be held responsible for a given quantity of controlled substances, it is incumbent upon the prosecutor to explain precisely how the prosecutor arrived at that drug quantity and to provide precise citation to the source for the quantity in the discovery file. Attorneys should also identify and acknowledge possible areas of dispute and provide authority for the attorney's position on any Guidelines provisions the attorney believes may be debatable or in dispute.

In Presentence Investigation Statements, attorneys should also provide probation officers with any information they have about offenders' criminal history. The government will typically have included some criminal history information in the discovery file. Whenever an offender's criminal history is essential to the calculation of the offense conduct level, such as when the offender may qualify as a career offender, the attorneys should try to obtain and send to the probation officer copies of the key pleadings from the pertinent prior convictions. When the government is relying upon prior convictions to trigger Guidelines enhancements, prosecutors should identify them for the probation officer. The reality is that no one is better at obtaining source documents, and getting clear and accurate information about offenders' criminal histories, than probation officers. I worked as a prosecutor for more than two decades, and despite my government position, neither I nor the law enforcement officers working with me could always obtain cooperation from some jurisdictions in getting copies of pleadings, particularly from state courts. Probation officers, however, work together nationwide. Probation officers help each other because they know they may need to call upon a colleague in another jurisdiction for the same information. Thus, probation officers are very effective in obtaining complete and accurate criminal history information on offenders.

Each side should provide probation officers with as much collateral information as possible in their Presentence Investigation Statements about an offender's history and characteristics. Typically, defense attorneys will have much greater access to this type of information. Prosecutors will seldom have much access to information about offenders' personal lives. Nevertheless, when prosecutors believe there is something in an offender's personal history that may be particularly important for purposes of sentencing, they may consider directing law enforcement resources toward investigating this information.

Attorneys should also be careful not to neglect addressing the applicable fine range, offenders' ability to pay fines when their ability to do so may be at issue, and all other collateral issues, such as restitution, forfeiture, sex offender registration, and the like. When crimes involve victims, prosecutors should work with their victim coordinators to solicit victim impact statements and submit them to the probation office. Some probation officers include the victim impact statements in an appendix to the presentence report. When restitution is an issue, prosecutors should work with their victim coordinators to solicit documentation from victims to support the restitution claims. It is the government's burden to prove that a victim was proximately harmed by the offender's conduct and to prove that the amount of restitution claimed is supported by sufficient evidence. Sometimes, though, prosecutors neglect this issue until shortly before the sentencing hearing. By then it may too late for victims to gather the necessary documentation to support their restitution claims. Likewise, defense attorneys sometimes make the same mistake of not talking with their clients and investigating restitution claims in advance of sentencing hearings.

C. Reviewing the Draft Presentence Report

After a probation officer completes a presentence investigation, the officer will draft a presentence report. The officer then discloses the report to the parties. In the federal system, the disclosure requirements are governed by Rule 32(e), which provides:

> (e) **Disclosing the Report and Recommendation**
> (1) **Time to Disclose.** Unless the defendant has consented in writing, the probation officer must not submit a presentence report to the court or disclose its contents to anyone until the defendant has pleaded guilty or nolo contendere, or has been found guilty.
> (2) **Minimum Required Notice.** The probation officer must give the presentence report to the defendant, the defendant's attorney, and an attorney for the government at least 35 days before sentencing unless the defendant waives this minimum period.
> (3) **Sentence Recommendation.** By local rule or by order in a case, the court may direct the probation officer not to disclose to anyone other than the court the officer's recommendation on the sentence.

FED. R. CRIM. P. 32(e). Once the attorneys receive the draft presentence report, they should review it thoroughly.

It is vitally important that the presentence report is comprehensive, complete, and accurate. If the presentence report applies the incorrect version of the United States Sentencing Guidelines, misapplies a Guidelines provision, mistakenly states the statutory provisions for incarceration, fine, or restitution, or omits some material fact or essential part of the sentence, it can result in an illegal or faulty sentence. In the end, it is the sentencing judge's responsibility to ensure that it is all correct. Yet, as advocates for their respective parties and as officers of the court, prosecutors and defense attorneys should ensure that the presentence report is completely correct. Of course, defense attorneys' primary responsibility is to their clients and thus may be ethically bound not to point out mistakes that inure to their clients' benefit.

Judges heavily rely on the information in presentence reports to determine appropriate sentences. In many cases, the only thing that judges know about the offenders they sentence is the information contained in the presentence reports. Sentencing judges may not have presided over the offender's pretrial hearings, the change of plea hearing, or the trial. Often sentencing judges have not even seen the offender before the day of sentencing. Before entering the courtroom, however, the judge will have reviewed the presentence report thoroughly and from that document will have formed an impression of the offender and may have even arrived at some impression of the sentence that would be appropriate for the offender. For these reasons, the presentence report is the single most important document judges rely upon at sentencing hearings.

Presentence reports are important for an offender's sentence even beyond the influence it has on the sentencing judge. An offender's presentence report will also follow the offender into the correctional institutions where the offender will serve the sentence. Indeed, information in the presentence report may influence the institution where the offender will serve time. Information in the presentence report may also influence where within any given institution an offender is housed. Gang affiliation disclosed in a presentence report, for example, may dictate housing the offender in one part of an institution versus another for the offender's protection. The failure to include information about an offender's gang affiliation in a presentence report may result in the offender being housed in a part of the institution with a rival gang, endangering the offender and others. At the same time, an offender may not want others to know that they are a gang member. Information in the presentence report can also influence the programs for which the offender is eligible. For example, if the presentence report fails to include information about an offender's substance abuse history or addiction, the offender may not be eligible to participate in drug treatment programs while incarcerated.

The presentence report is also important for an offender while on supervised release. The information contained in a presentence report may inform the offender's probation officer about the identity of victims for purposes of no contact orders or about the offender's prior criminal associates and the need for the offender to avoid contact with them. Probation officers may use the information in the presentence report to determine the need for the offender to receive treatment programming, substance abuse or mental health evaluations, or education. Probation officers also use the information in presentence reports to determine an offender's risk level on supervised release, which in turn impacts the intensity of supervision such as the number of visits with the probation officer, unannounced home visits, and the like.

Thus, ensuring the presentence report is complete and accurate is one of the most important aspects of sentencing advocacy. Yet, all too often attorneys neglect this task, relying on the probation officer to get it right. Some attorneys accept the information in the presentence report without verifying it or, as important, augmenting it with more information to ensure that it completely and accurately portrays the offense conduct and the offender.[7]

Few probation officers are lawyers, yet they are required in drafting presentence reports to apply the Guidelines in light of statutory provisions and judicial precedent. In short, they are required to exercise lawyer-like skills. It is my experience that probation officers perform this task with amazingly good results. Many become experts in the Guidelines and sentencing law, despite the lack of a formal legal education. Nevertheless, their interpretations of the Guidelines are not infallible. Attorneys should never assume that probation officers have correctly applied the Guidelines. Good attorneys check every paragraph of a presentence report, particularly the application of the Guidelines.

In reviewing the presentence report, attorneys should start at the beginning and not assume that anything is correct. This includes making sure the probation officer applied the correct version (year) of the Guidelines. Guidelines do change, and the court should apply the Guidelines in effect at the time of the sentencing hearing. 18 U.S.C. § 3553(a)(4)(A)(ii) (instructing courts to apply the Sentencing Guidelines issued by the United States Sentencing Commission that are "in effect on the date the defendant is sentenced."). A violation of the Ex Post Facto Clause occurs, however, when an offender is sentenced under Guidelines promulgated after his offense, and the new version prescribes a higher range.[8] In those circumstances, a sentencing court must apply the version of the Guidelines that were in effect at the time of the offender's offense. It almost goes without saying, then, that effective sentencing advocacy requires attorneys to determine if an offender's sentence would be less had the offender been sentenced under the version of the Guidelines in effect at the time of the offense when that version is different from the version of the Guidelines in effect at the time of the sentencing hearing.

Attorneys should carefully review the facts set out in the offense conduct section of the draft presentence report both for mistakes and for omissions. It is generally easier to spot mistakes than recognize omissions. It is often very difficult to realize something is missing from a presentence report. Of course, attorneys can compare the draft presentence report against their own Presentence Investigation Statements, but it is possible that the attorneys also omitted facts that, upon reflection, are important. When attorneys review the probation officer's calculation of the advisory Guidelines, it sometimes highlights the importance of omitted facts.

Attorneys should have submitted their own Guidelines calculations to the probation officer in the party's Presentence Investigation Statement during the officer's investigation period. Nevertheless, attorneys should carefully review the calculations in the draft presentence report as if for the first time, making sure that all applicable adjustments have been applied and that the probation officer did not include inappropriate adjustments. It is in conducting this review that it sometimes becomes apparent that the attorneys failed to bring to the probation officer's attention a key fact. For example, in a case in which an offender had pled guilty to being a felon in possession of a firearm, a probation officer may conclude in the draft presentence report that the offender qualifies for a reduction in the offense level for possession of the firearm solely for lawful collection or sporting purposes. Perhaps, however, the prosecutor knows that the discovery file contains a statement the offender made to an officer that he also possessed the firearm for personal protection as well, an admission that would make the reduction inapplicable. The prosecutor may have failed to bring this to the probation officer's attention in the first instance through oversight, or perhaps the officer simply missed it. Conversely, if a probation officer failed to apply this reduction, the defense attorney may want to investigate what evidence within or outside the discovery file that would support the reduction.

The parties should also carefully review the criminal history calculation section of the presentence report. This requires attorneys to review the criminal history to ensure that the dates and descriptions of the charges of conviction and any narratives of offense conduct are accurate. It also requires attorneys to ensure that the probation officers correctly scored the number of points for each conviction. Chapter 4 of the Guidelines is quite complicated, and whether convictions score points and how many points they score can be very difficult sometimes to get correct. Attorneys should once again not simply assume the probation officer correctly scored the criminal history points. Attorneys should go through Chapter 4 of the Guidelines and verify the accuracy of each criminal history score. Attorneys for both sides may ask the probation officer for courtesy copies of the underlying court documents on which the officer relied in scoring an offender's criminal history score if it would help ensure an accurate calculation.

Lastly, parties should review the offender's history and characteristic section of the presentence report. For defense attorneys, this often involves ensuring the client confirms the accuracy of the information. For prosecutors, the draft presentence report is often the first time the prosecutor learns this type of information about the offender.[9] Prosecutors should review this portion of the presentence report for any facts which, in the prosecutor's view, may have an impact on sentencing. If the presentence report states, for example, that the offender grew up living in a series of foster homes where he was physically and sexually abused, the prosecutor can reasonably expect that these facts will form the basis for a defense downward variance motion and may impact the ultimate sentence. The information in the presentence report may be accurate, but it may also not be based on anything more than what the offender told the probation officer, with nothing to corroborate the claims. The prosecutor may identify this as a subject for further investigation by law enforcement officers to verify that accuracy of the information. On the flip side, defense attorneys should be alert to the possibility that an offender may deny abuse, even when it occurred, for any number of psychological or other reasons. When defense attorneys suspect possible past abuse, despite their clients' denials, they should try to investigate it and work with their clients to overcome any reluctance to reveal past abuse.

Defense attorneys should go through the presentence report line by line with their clients. Some clients will have reading skills that enable them to read through the presentence report on their own, while others may not have such reading skills. Still other offenders may not speak English, requiring the use of an interpreter. Whatever the case, defense attorneys should carefully review the entire presentence report with their clients and ensure the accuracy of all information in the presentence report.

D. Making Formal Objections to the Draft Presentence Report

After attorneys have thoroughly reviewed the draft presentence report, they must respond to it in writing to inform the probation office of any corrections, additions, or objections the parties have to the draft report. In the federal system, Federal Rule of Criminal Procedure 32(f) sets out the requirements for the attorney to make objections to the presentence report.

> **(f) Objecting to the Report.**
>
> **(1) Time to Object.** Within 14 days after receiving the presentence report, the parties must state in writing any objections, including objections to material information, sentencing guideline ranges, and policy statements contained in or omitted from the report.
>
> **(2) Serving Objections.** An objecting party must provide a copy of its objections to the opposing party and to the probation officer.
>
> **(3) Action on Objections.** After receiving objections, the probation officer may meet with the parties to discuss the objections. The probation officer may then investigate further and revise the presentence report as appropriate.
>
> **(g) Submitting the Report.** At least 7 days before sentencing, the probation officer must submit to the court and to the parties the presentence report

> and an addendum containing any unresolved objections, the grounds for those objections, and the probation officer's comments on them.

FED. R. CRIM. P. 32(f).

Effective sentencing advocacy requires attorneys to put careful thought into whether to lodge objections and to what portions of the presentence report they should object. How attorneys articulate objections can also be very important. Just as crucial is the need for attorneys to correct any errors and provide additional information to supplement the presentence report when they find the draft presentence report contains omissions of important information.

Some courts have found that a party's failure to lodge an objection to a portion of the presentence report can constitute a waiver.[10] Other courts have found that a party does not necessarily waive a sentencing argument by failing to lodge an objection to a draft presentence report.[11] Objecting to the draft presentence report may not be sufficient if the party does not later assert that objection to the judge at the sentencing hearing.[12] In short, parties should be careful to lodge all objections they have to the draft presentence report or run the risk that a court may later find the party waived the right to challenge the sentence based on that ground.

Some objections to presentence reports may go directly to the determination of the ultimate sentence, such as objections to the Guidelines calculations. Other objections to presentence reports may be directed at facts contained in the offense conduct section that can indirectly have an impact on the calculation of the Guidelines range and the ultimate sentence. Still other objections may be focused on the offender's criminal history or characteristics.

Objections to the Guidelines calculations most directly affects the offender's ultimate sentence. These are, perhaps, the most important objections to presentence reports, and they often require a great deal of thought, analysis, and research. It is important that attorneys carefully and precisely state the basis for their objections to presentence reports and provide the calculation of the Guidelines they believe to be correct. Although objections are directed in the first instance to the probation officer, the objections will be passed along to the sentencing judge. The goal in making objections is not simply to preserve error but to persuade the probation officers and ultimately the judge to adopt the attorney's position. Attorneys should not pass up this advocacy opportunity. At the sentencing hearing, a party is generally more likely to succeed if the presentence report is drafted in their favor than if the party is fighting to have the court change the presentence report calculation. All too often, though, attorneys lodge pro forma objections to the presentence report, figuring that they will spend the time later in a sentencing memorandum to fully articulate and explain the basis for the objection. This is a mistake. The time and effort should be spent in lodging the initial objection, not later. The goal here is to persuade the probation officer to change the presentence report before it goes to the sentencing judge so that the attorney is not in the position later of trying to persuade the sentencing judge to rule contrary to the presentence report.

Thus, objections to presentence reports should be considered an important form of written advocacy and drafted with the same tone and structure an attorney would use in a sentencing memorandum. An objection to a Guidelines calculation should focus on the language of the Guidelines themselves and cite to appropriate subsections, definitions, and commentary. The objection should also cite to legal precedent, when available and appropriate. Indeed, a well-written objection to the presentence report can form the template for a sentencing memorandum.

Precision in making objections to the Guidelines is important if the attorney hopes to persuade the probation officer and judge to adopt the attorney's position. For example, there is a four-level enhancement under Guidelines Section 2K2.1(b)(6)(B) if a prohibited person (a felon, for example) possesses a firearm in connection with another felony offense. If the probation officer finds this enhancement applies, the officer will identify the felony or felonies the officer believes the offender committed while possessing the firearm. A party objecting to this Guidelines enhancement should precisely state the defect the attorney believes exists by identifying the element of the felony offense the attorney believes was not met, stating the facts that support that position, and citing statutory language or case law supporting the attorney's conclusion. A simple objection to application of the Guidelines enhancement, without a thorough and reasoned explanation, is unlikely to persuade the probation officer to change the presentence report. On the other hand, I recognize that there may be some instances when attorneys may not want to reveal the details of challenge as a litigation tactic so as not to reveal too much to opposing counsel in advance of a sentencing hearing. In these instances, attorneys need to assess the likelihood of persuading the probation officer against the costs of revealing the precise nature of the challenge in advance of the sentencing hearing and make their best judgment as to what will likely be the most successful tactic.

Attorneys should be cautious when objecting to facts in the offense conduct section of the presentence report for several reasons. First, "[a] defendant who falsely denies or frivolously contests" relevant conduct that the sentencing judge finds is true may jeopardize any reduction for acceptance of responsibility. USSG §3E1.1, cmt. (1)(A). Second, if the parties entered into a written plea agreement that contained factual stipulations, objecting to facts in a draft presentence report in a manner inconsistent with the stipulations in the plea agreement may give rise to a claim that the party has breached the plea agreement. When, however, a party believes the draft presentence report has incorrectly stated the facts, good attorneys will precisely explain the error and direct the probation officer to source information to aid the officer in making the correction.

Attorneys should likewise be thoughtful in how they object to the offender's criminal history portion of the draft presentence report. There are several types of objections that could be made in this section. Defense attorneys may object to the very fact of conviction, if they believe offenders were not convicted of a listed offense, and prosecutors may object if they believe the probation officer omitted convictions. It is important here for attorneys to be very thorough in their review and how they articulate objections. Oftentimes an offender may have been charged within several counts but not convicted of them all. It may be necessary to double-check the underlying documents to ensure the criminal history accurately reflects the counts of conviction. As part of their presentence investigation, probation officers will often have obtained underlying court documents and will share these with the attorneys upon request.

More often, objections to the criminal history portion of a draft presentence report focus on two areas: the narrative and the scoring of criminal history points. Probation officers will often include a short summary of the offense conduct leading to that conviction beneath each listed conviction in a presentence report, at least when the probation officer is able to garner that information from court documents. Charging documents are often the source for these narratives. Defense attorneys in particular should object to facts alleged in these narratives if they believe the facts are not completely accurate. The best objections are those that precisely state the facts to which the offender is objecting as opposed to a blanket objection to the narrative. A surgically narrow objection reflects a greater degree of acceptance by the offender for his past criminal conduct; a series of blanket denials to all narratives in the criminal history section runs the danger of portraying the offender as someone who, though he cannot deny the convictions, denies ever committing wrongs.

Objections to the scoring of criminal history points will be based on Guidelines provisions. Each conviction scores points based in large part on the length of the sentence imposed, including time served for revocation of supervised release, probation, and parole. Calculating this time is often not easy. Not all convictions score points for various reasons, including the age and nature of the conviction. And for some convictions, not all the points scored may be counted against an offender (i.e., only four so-called one-point convictions can count toward an offender's criminal history score). Attorneys should not only lodge an objection if they believe the score is incorrect but articulate why they believe it is incorrect and provide the probation officer with the correct calculation.

Occasionally the parties have objections to the section of a draft presentence report relating the offender's personal history and characteristics. Here, again, attorneys should use caution and be deliberate and careful in voicing objections. Defense attorneys should object to portions of the draft presentence report relating the offender's childhood, education, employment history, and other such facts to ensure that they completely and accurately reflect the offender's background. If necessary, the defense attorney should attach to or include with the objection any reports or other documents to support the attorney's objection. The sentencing judge will consider the offender's history and characteristics under the Section 3553(a) factors in arriving at the appropriate sentence, including in deciding whether a variance from the advisory Guidelines range is appropriate. Thus, it is crucial that the defense attorney objects to this portion of the presentence report if there are material mistakes or omissions.

The offender's history and characteristics portion of a presentence report can also have a significant impact on the type of sentence the offender serves. Effective sentencing advocacy includes not just a focus on the number of years in prison, but also on the quality of life during those years in prison. Thus, attorneys should object if the presentence report contains references to gang membership that are inaccurate because that may affect the offender's security classification and housing. Attorneys should object if the offender's medical or mental health history is inaccurate because that, too, could affect the facility where the offender is housed. Attorneys should also ensure that the offender's drug use history is accurate. The instinct for offenders may be to minimize their drug use history. Yet, if the presentence report fails to reflect that the offender has a history of struggling with substance abuse, the offender may be ineligible for drug treatment in prison and, in the federal system, completion of some drug treatment programs can result in a reduction in the offender's sentence. However, defense attorneys may, in rare cases, counsel their clients not to waive the confidentiality of mental health records if the defense attorneys know they contain more damaging information (such as homicidal ideations or threats) than beneficial information. This requires defense attorneys to review such records before making the decision whether to assist the probation officer in gaining access to them.

One final note on making objections to draft presentence reports: it has been my experience that probation officers are often quite approachable and willing to discuss the draft presentence report with attorneys. Before making objections to a presentence report, particularly when it comes to Guidelines provisions, it may be advisable to call the probation officer to discuss any mistakes the attorney believes the officer made. This informal conversation can only help. The probation officer may be able to provide an explanation that shows that the draft presentence report is correct, saving the attorney from lodging a meritless objection. Remember that the sentencing judge will be informed about all objections and the probation officer's response. Judges form impressions, just like everyone else, of attorneys' competence and credibility. Those impressions may impact the judge's receptiveness to attorneys' arguments. Attorneys who make a series of meritless objections to a draft presentence report may have difficulty then persuading the sentencing judge of the merits of a good objection. Conversely, a conversation with the probation officer may persuade the probation officer that the draft presentence report contains a mistake and will enhance the likelihood that the officer will change the final presentence report in a manner consistent with the attorney's objection. This informal discussion with the probation officer, then, can be a productive form of sentencing advocacy. Attorneys may also consider sending the probation officer a copy of their sentencing memoranda, especially any argument for the appropriate sentence under the Section 3553(a) factors. In some districts, probation officers make sentencing recommendations to the district court judge, and the parties' sentencing memoranda may influence the probation officer's recommendation in those instances.

Last, Rule 32(f)(3) provides that the probation officer may meet and confer with attorneys about objections. The actual practice of such meet and confer meetings differs from district to district, sometimes probation officer by probation officer, and sometimes case by case. There is also nothing in the rule that prevents the attorneys from meeting separately from the probation officer to try to work out and negotiate agreements about disputed issues. Likewise, attorneys can initiate a request of the probation officer to meet and confer with the attorneys, even if it is not the normal practice. Whether these meetings or attempts to negotiate resolution of disputed sentencing issues is practical or appropriate in a given case is something only the attorneys can determine. As a general matter, however, there is little downside to at least engaging in a conversation with opposing counsel, with or without the probation officer's involvement, to determine whether a settlement can be reached on disputed issues. At the very least, an attorney often comes away from such meetings with a better understanding of their opponent's position and would then be in a better position to litigate the issue. In the best of cases, the attorneys may reach a compromise, perhaps with the assistance of the probation officer, that resolves disputed sentencing issues to the mutual benefit of both sides. Attorneys should not lightly disregard this opportunity for sentencing advocacy.

E. Reviewing the Final Presentence Report

After the parties lodge objections to the presentence report, the probation officer will complete and file a final presentence report. The final presentence report will include any objections the parties made, along with a response by the probation officer and an indication of whether the officer changed the presentence report in light of the objection. It is important for attorneys to review the final presentence report carefully and thoroughly. Defense attorneys have an obligation to review the final presentence report with their clients.

First, an attorney should review the final presentence report to ensure that the probation officer accurately reflected the attorney's objection. The attorney should note the response and whether the officer changed the presentence report in light of the attorney's objection. If not, the attorney will have to decide whether to maintain that objection at the sentencing hearing and whether to address it in a sentencing memorandum. An attorney may be persuaded by the probation officer's explanation for why the officer did not alter the presentence report. On the other hand, the attorney may continue to disagree with the officer and find it necessary to litigate the matter at the sentencing hearing.

Second, attorneys should review the final presentence report to discover what objections the opposing party made that the probation officer accepted or rejected. The opposing attorney should anticipate that any rejected objection to the draft presentence report may be litigated at the sentencing hearing and will need to be addressed in a sentencing memorandum.

It should be noted here that there may be a tension in the timing of writing and filing of sentencing memoranda and the filing of the final presentence report. Rule 32(g) requires that a probation officer file the final presentence report at least seven days before the sentencing hearing. Nevertheless, local rules or court orders may require attorneys to file sentencing memoranda farther in advance of the sentencing hearing. When that is the case, communication with opposing counsel and the probation officer to identify the issues that require briefing is that much more important so that the attorneys can address in their sentencing memoranda all disputed issues. As I will discuss in the following chapter, a sentencing memorandum is the first opportunity attorneys have to directly persuade the sentencing judge. Attorneys should use this form of written sentencing advocacy to its full advantage, which is not possible if they are unaware of all the disputed issues.

9

Sentencing Memoranda

A sentencing memorandum is an opportunity to advocate in writing on behalf of a party. The parties may, but generally are not required to, file sentencing memoranda or sentencing briefs in advance of contested sentencing hearings. Whether required or not, attorneys should take advantage of this opportunity to advocate for their clients in writing by filing sentencing memoranda in any contested sentencing. In a sentencing memorandum, attorneys have the ability to logically address each of the contested sentencing issues, summarize any pertinent facts, and provide legal authority for their position. Effective advocacy involves taking every opportunity to argue one's position. Sentencing memoranda serve as a means of preparing a judge in advance of the sentencing hearing. Unlike with juries, attorneys have an opportunity to advocate to judges as factfinders and decision-makers before the sentencing hearing. Through written advocacy, attorneys may influence judges' perceptions of offenders and appropriate sentences before the judges ever enter the courtroom. Only when there are truly no factual or legal issues for the judge to resolve, the ultimate sentence is predetermined by agreement, or a mandatory minimum or maximum sentence controls the outcome of the sentence, should attorneys consider forgoing the opportunity to advocate for their clients in written sentencing memoranda.

Effective written advocacy is essential at sentencing hearings for several reasons. First, judges are often persuaded by written advocacy as much or more than oral advocacy. Judges are trained in legal reasoning and are guided by statutory language and precedent. They think in terms of elements, factors, burdens of proof, and the like. Speaking to judges in a written language they understand can be effective in persuading them to adopt a party's position. Attorneys often fail to appreciate how important written advocacy is, instead focusing on oral advocacy at sentencing hearings. Judges are not like jurors, however. They are much more focused on the law, elements, factors, and precedent than spellbinding oratory and emotional appeals. Since judges are accustomed to written advocacy, they may reach conclusions about the merits of an issue based on written advocacy alone. Attorneys who wait until sentencing hearings to impress judges with spellbinding oral advocacy may enter courtrooms at a distinct disadvantage and find that the oral advocacy they counted on failed to move judges off positions they reached after having read the presentence report and opposing counsels' sentencing memoranda. Although all judges strive to keep an open mind, the reality is that written advocacy can influence a judge's perception and reception of the merits of oral arguments.

Second, judges will often reach preliminary decisions about disputed sentencing issues based on the written submissions. Unlike jurors who know nothing about a case and issues until opening statements and must absorb everything during the course of a trial, sentencing judges come into the sentencing hearing already very well informed about the offender and the offense. It has been my experience that judges come into sentencing hearing well-prepared, having carefully read the presentence report and the parties' written briefs, and have often conducted their own independent research on disputed Guidelines or legal issues. Attorneys who wait to advocate at the sentencing hearing, or who place too little emphasis on writing a persuasive sentencing memorandum, may face an uphill battle. Thus, it is important that attorneys devote sufficient time and effort to write persuasive sentencing memorandum.

Writing effective sentencing memoranda is much like any effective legal writing. Sentencing memoranda should be well-organized. The tone and style of the writing should be tailored for the audience. The writing should be concise and precise, yet thorough and complete. Attorneys should provide supporting legal authority, when appropriate, while acknowledging contrary authority when it exists. Finally, good sentencing memoranda, like all good legal memoranda, clearly specify the relief the party is seeking from the judge. I will elaborate a little on each of the attributes.

A. Organization

All legal writing should be organized so as to help the reader, a judge, to follow the writer's reasoning. However, I recommend that attorneys organize sentencing memoranda in a manner consistent with the sentencing procedure the court will follow at the sentencing hearing. What I mean by that is attorneys should address issues in their sentencing memoranda in the same order that the court will address them at the sentencing hearing.

In federal sentencing hearings, judges are required under Title 18, United States Code, Section 3553(a) to first calculate the sentencing Guidelines. Only after establishing the advisory Guidelines range are judges to move on to address other factors under Section 3553(a). Thus, it follows that attorneys should address disputed Guidelines issues first in their sentencing memoranda. As noted in a prior chapter, the Guidelines are also organized in a sequential manner. The sentencing judge must first determine the base offense level under Chapter 2, then determine whether any offense characteristics in Chapter 2 should result in upward or downward adjustments to the base offense level. Only after all Chapter 2 adjustments are made does the judge move on to Chapter 3 adjustments, and only after that does the judge move on to determine an offender's criminal history score, and so on. Only after determining the Guidelines range do judges decide whether a departure from that Guidelines range is appropriate. It follows, then, that any section of a sentencing brief addressing Guidelines issues should follow the same order as the Guidelines themselves. Attorneys should strive to write sentencing memoranda in a manner that aids judges in making sentencing decisions. Attorneys who organize their briefs in a manner that aids judges are going to be more persuasive than those who do not.

Of course, the Guidelines are only the starting point in determining an offender's sentence. There are all the other factors under Section 3553(a) that a judge must consider. In addition, there are sometimes other collateral matters that require a ruling from the sentencing judge, such as restitution, forfeiture, conditions of supervised release, and the like. There are no federal rules of criminal procedure that dictate the order in which judges address these various issues. In most courts, judges will address and decide these collateral matters after resolving disputed Guidelines issues but before hearing argument from attorneys about the other Section 3553(a) factors and the ultimate disposition. In most instances, then, in makes sense for attorneys to organize their sentencing memorandum in a similar manner. It is advisable, however, for attorneys to research the order in which the particular sentencing judge addresses various issues at sentencing and organize their sentencing memoranda accordingly.

B. *Tone and Style*

In drafting sentencing briefs, attorneys should be sure to write to the audience. The audience includes, of course, the sentencing judge. The judge should be the primary member of the audience to whom attorneys focus their written advocacy. But attorneys should keep in mind that the audience may also include others. Sentencing memoranda are public documents. What the attorneys write in their sentencing memoranda may be read by offenders and victims, the public and the press. Thus, although attorneys should write sentencing memoranda with the goal of persuading the judge—the factfinder and legal arbiter—attorneys need to keep in mind the effect of what they write may have on others who may read the sentencing brief. This means that attorneys may want to change the tone or verbiage they use so as not to offend an offender or a victim or risk the press quoting something in the memorandum out of context.

With the primary goal in drafting a sentencing memorandum of persuading the judge to rule in the party's favor, attorneys should endeavor to write the sentencing memorandum in a manner that is designed to help the judge. This means that sentencing memoranda need to be concise. Judges are busy and have many hearings, including many sentencing hearings. They are reading constantly. Long and verbose sentencing memoranda are unlikely to be as persuasive as short, concise memoranda that gets directly to the point and are stripped of unnecessary verbiage.

In tension with the goal to be concise, however, is to need to be thorough and precise. It is also important that attorneys provide citations to the factual record and legal authorities upon which they are basing their arguments. Sentencing memoranda should fully address every contested issue. This includes all sentencing Guidelines issues, criminal history scoring, departures, and variances. Attorneys should also fully address any collateral consequences that are at issue, such as restitution, deportation, etc. In short, in their sentencing memoranda, attorneys should strive to provide sentencing judges with a roadmap for resolving all disputed issues at the sentencing hearing.

The more the attorney can do to aid the judge in understanding and moving through all the disputed issues, the more persuasive and effective the sentencing memorandum will be. Thus, the attorney should make sure the memorandum addresses all the issues the judge will have to decide at the sentencing hearing. Attorneys may consider using lists, charts, or other summaries to identify issues to help guide the court's understanding. An attorney should also make sure that the memorandum is precise and correct. Frequent citations to the pertinent paragraph in the presentence report or other relevant documents help the sentencing judge confirm the accuracy of the attorney's position and more clearly understand the specific issues in dispute. Attorneys should provide sentencing judges with firm grounds upon which to rule in their clients' favor such that an appellate court will affirm the district court's decision. It is incumbent upon attorneys to provide that basis for the sentencing judge instead of trusting that the sentencing judge will make the record for the attorney.

Finally, judges are properly focused on procedural error. In other words, although federal judges will ultimately decide sentences based on the totality of the factors set out in Title 18, United States Code, Section 3553(a), they must make sure before they reach the ultimate decisions that they do so in a procedurally correct manner. Significant procedural errors include failing to calculate the Guidelines correctly, failing to calculate the Guidelines range at all, or treating the Guidelines as mandatory. A judge should also not resolve a variance issue before first determining the applicable advisory Guidelines range. Similarly, in determining an offender's sentence, a judge cannot consider something in the presentence report to which the offender objected unless the judge has properly overruled the objection based on evidence. A sentencing judge may also commit a procedural error by failing to consider the factors of Title 18, United States Code, Section 3553(a), or by relying on clearly erroneous facts. For attorneys, this means they should ensure that their sentencing memoranda call upon the judge to resolve issues in a procedurally correct order and manner, and that they do not invite the sentencing judge to commit a procedural error in any way.

Judges have a vast amount of discretion in determining criminal offenders' sentences. In the federal system, this discretion is reflected in the very broad factors set out in Title 18, United States Code, Section 3553(a). In short, judges can base sentences upon the nature and circumstances of the offense, the history and characteristics of the offender, and the need to accomplish the goals of sentencing, including such things as deterrence and protection of the community. With this in mind, attorneys' sentencing memoranda should fully address all the factors a judge should consider in determining sentences. Attorneys usually will fully address the application of the Guidelines but sometimes fail to address other factors, particularly the goals of sentencing. Attorneys should use sentencing memoranda to advocate for their clients' positions about why the requested sentence would advance all the applicable goals of sentencing.

C. Legal Support

Attorneys should always provide legal support for positions they want the sentencing judge to adopt. Generally, attorneys understand this and provide ample citations to precedent or other legal authorities to support their positions. There are some practices, however, that are unproductive or problematic. The Supreme Court held the mandatory nature of the Guidelines unconstitutional in 2005, more than a decade and half ago. Yet, attorneys often still devote pages of sentencing memoranda telling judges all about that change in the law and reminding them that the Guidelines are no longer mandatory. Judges know this. Including this outdated boilerplate legal authority in sentencing memoranda is a waste of paper and the judge's limited time. Attorneys should omit it altogether.

At the same time, attorneys sometimes cite cases in sentencing memoranda for propositions that are no longer applicable as a result of the change in the law. Attorneys sometimes still cite cases about departures from the Guidelines, for example, that no longer apply because the Commission has since changed the Guidelines provisions. In a similar vein, some attorneys who practiced for years under the mandatory Guidelines scheme still seem to have failed to understand the differences between a departure from the Guidelines, which is based on departure grounds in the Guidelines themselves, and a variance from the Guidelines, which is based on the factors in Title 18, United States Code, Section 3553(a). Attorneys need to understand the difference and use those terms appropriately. They also need to understand that a judge can vary downward on the same grounds that the judge could not use to depart downward under the Guidelines.

Thorough, fact-based research is important in producing persuasive sentencing memoranda. Sentencing issues turn on facts. The best sentencing memoranda include cases where the facts are similar to the facts in the case proceeding to sentencing. Many times, I conduct my own research and find cases that are more factually relevant than what the attorneys have cited in their briefs. Although the attorneys may have cited cases correctly setting out the general legal principle, cases applying that principle to facts similar to those before me are far more persuasive and helpful.

D. Requested Relief

All good salespeople will tell you that the most important part of a sales pitch is "the close." This is when salespeople state exactly what they want the buyer to do. It is equally important for attorneys to state exactly what they want the sentencing judge to do. Attorneys should be precise in stating the relief they are requesting. With Guidelines issues, attorneys should not only clearly indicate how they believe the judge should rule on the precise issue, but also articulate how granting that request will affect the calculation of any other Guidelines provisions and the ultimate sentencing range.

When attorneys ask judges to depart or vary from the Guidelines range, they should consider whether to be precise about the relief they are requesting. In other words, defense attorneys should consider whether they should be clear not only that they want the judge to depart or vary, but also whether to precisely state how much they want the judge to depart or vary. Similarly, when prosecutors seek upward departures or variances, they should consider whether to state the extent to which they want the judge to depart or vary. Sometimes attorneys state that they will leave the degree of departure or variance within the discretion of the judge to determine.

In making the decision whether to explicitly state the extent of the requested departure or variance, attorneys should consider a number of factors. When attorneys stake out a position on the extent of a departure or variance, they set a bar that can influence the judge's ultimate decision. Anchoring bias is a common cognitive phenomenon that reflects a mental tendency for people to rely too heavily on the first piece of information they hear, especially when the information is numeric. In other words, when a person sets a starting point for a discussion, such as the price of an item in a bartered sale or the amount that a party would offer in a legal settlement, that baseline has a psychological impact on perception. That first value tends to form a mental anchor that influences what people think is reasonable. For example, if a car seller first offers to sell a car for $25,000, the consumer might think it a bargain to get the car for $22,000. Had the seller first offered to sell the car for $22,500, the consumer may not be willing to purchase it if the seller would only come down to $22,000.

In a sentencing hearing context, if a defense attorney requests a 50 percent downward variance from the advisory Guidelines range, in a judge's mind, a 30 percent reduction may not seem too great in comparison. On the other hand, were the prosecutor to acknowledge that a downward variance may be warranted but that the judge should limit the degree of variance to a 10 percent decrease from the advisory Guidelines range, then the judge may mentally conclude that a 30 percent reduction would seem too great. Judges are generally aware of cognitive biases and through mental discipline may not be as influenced by them as the general public. Experienced judges also have a body of knowledge from past cases that provides them other anchors from which to judge reasonable outcomes, unlike the consumer who may purchase a new car only once a decade. Nevertheless, judges are human and subject to the same types of cognitive biases as everyone else.

Of course, attorneys should be cautious not to stake out a ridiculous position that could negatively impact their credibility. Asking for a 90 percent downward variance based only on the fact the offender's parents divorced when the offender was young may jeopardize the defense attorney's credibility with the judge and backfire. Prosecutors who ask for a 50 percent increase in an offender's sentence because the criminal history score understates the seriousness of the offender's criminal history or likelihood of reoffending because one conviction did not score points because of its age may lose credibility with the court. Attorneys should effectively advocate for their clients and, in my view, this includes advocating for the degree of departure or variance they believe is realistically appropriate in a case.

On the other hand, staking out a precise position about a requested departure or variance can be tricky for attorneys, particularly for defense attorneys. The extent of a departure or variance may depend on how a judge rules on other issues such that it may not be possible in advance of the sentencing hearing to stake out a specific position. Offenders may also insist on their defense attorneys staking out ridiculous positions such that it may be better for client relations and the client for the defense attorneys to stake out no position. It is also possible that a judge may impose a sentence lower than the one the defense attorney requested, perhaps making the defense attorney look bad in front of the client.

Finally, attorneys should also consider whether to be precise in articulating any other relief requested. This may include requests for fines or restitution amounts, recommendations about the institution where the offender will be incarcerated, or the length or terms of supervised release. The goal is to prepare the judge thoroughly for the sentencing memorandum to know exactly what is in dispute and precisely what each party is requesting.

E. Personal or Confidential Information

In some cases, there may be some particularly personal or confidential information that is important for the judge to consider at the sentencing hearing that the attorneys do not want to include in a publicly filed sentencing memorandum. This may include reports of psychological, medical, or drug treatment history, for instance. Judges are generally reluctant to allow the wholesale sealing of pleadings because of the public's general right to know what is occurring in public courtrooms. If attorneys are unfamiliar with how the sentencing judge prefers to address such confidential information, they should inquire of the court's staff how to proceed. Some judges may permit attorneys to file the entire sentencing memorandum under seal, while other judges may prefer to have the attorney file a supplemental sentencing memorandum or attachment or include the information in a letter (with a copy to opposing counsel). When this issue arises, attorneys should again research how the particular judge before whom they will appear handles these matters and comply with that judge's preferences.

10

Preparing for Sentencing Hearings

The level and nature of attorney preparation for a sentencing hearing will differ, of course, depending on whether there are facts in dispute, witnesses who will testify, legal arguments will be required, and victims will address the court, to name just a few contingent factors. Some sentencing hearings are rather straightforward with no contested factual or Guidelines issues and no collateral matters in dispute; the only contested issue is the length of incarceration. And sometimes that is not even in dispute. These sentencing hearing obviously require little preparation. At the other end of the spectrum are the highly contested, complex hearings when nearly everything is in dispute. There are certain steps in preparing for sentencing hearings that attorneys should perform, regardless of the complexity of the hearing. In this chapter I will focus first on those basic and steps before turning to all the additional steps that may be necessary in preparing for sentencing hearings that are more complicated.

A. Basic Preparation

One of the first things attorneys should do in preparation for a sentencing hearing is to prepare a checklist. In a sentencing hearing, a judge must ensure that certain things take place. In federal court, a judge must determine the statutory penalties that apply and calculate the sentencing Guidelines range. A judge must give the parties an opportunity to be heard and to argue for upward and downward departures and variances. A judge must always afford the offender the opportunity to allocute. And a judge must advise the offender of the right to appeal.

It is the judge's duty to complete each and all of these steps, but judges can become distracted due to events in the sentencing hearing itself. A judge may have to resolve forfeiture or restitution issues, hear from victims, recalculate the Guidelines range, and the like. In the hustle and bustle of a sentencing hearing, a judge might miss one of the required steps. Good attorneys will have a checklist of these requirements prepared in advance of the sentencing hearing so that the attorney can keep track and ensure that the judge addresses each required matter. Although it is ultimately the sentencing judge's responsibility to comply with all the statutory and procedural sentencing requirements, it is in the parties' best interest to verify that the judge does so. Maintaining a checklist to make sure the judge checks all the boxes is the best method to ensure that the judge does not miss a requirement.

Attorneys should also re-review the final presentence report, particularly to determine if anything has changed since the report was completed. For example, the offender's financial or personal situation may have changed. In some instances, if an offender had pending charges when the probation officer wrote the final presentence report, those charges may have since been resolved. On the other hand, the offender could be facing new charges brought since the drafting of the presentence report. Some changes in the facts and circumstances may be of little material import to any sentencing issue, but others may significantly impact an offender's sentence. An offender who has violated conditions of release pending the sentencing hearing may have jeopardized a reduction for acceptance of responsibility. An offender who has been convicted of a charge that was only pending at the time the probation officer completed the presentence report may now have an increased criminal history score. In short, attorneys should carefully review the presentence report and alert the judge of any material changes.

Attorneys should also notify all the interested parties of the time and date of the sentencing hearing. For prosecutors, this means they should be sure to notify law enforcement officers who were involved in the investigation. A sentencing hearing is the culmination of the officers' work on a case, and they should be notified so they can be present if they wish. Prosecutors also should notify victims of the crime, if any. Sometimes this is statutorily required, while in other instances, when the victims may be indirect, it is more a matter of good practice. Defense attorneys may need to alert the offender's family of the sentencing date and time.

In preparation for sentencing hearings, defense attorneys should also solicit letters of support from family and friends. It is important that defense attorneys obtain letters of support when possible, but defense attorneys should be sure to provide them to the sentencing judge sufficiently in advance of the sentencing hearing that the judge has adequate time to read them.

Defense attorneys should also give direction to the offender's friends and family on what to include, and not include, in such letters. Although defense attorneys should not dictate the content of such letters, it is very helpful to give these interested people some direction and guidance. Most of them have never written such a letter before. Letters can be very influential when they are sincere and open a window into the offender's background and character. No one knows the offender better than the offender's family and friends. Letters that tell the offender's story without trying to make excuses or falsely portray the offender as an angel can give a sentencing judge insight into the offender that otherwise is not available from a reading of the presentence report. Defense attorneys should instruct letter writers that they should not give their opinions on the offender's innocence. After all, the judge is sentencing the offender after the offender has either admitted guilt or been found guilty. Further, letter writers will not be privy to all of the facts and may have a mistaken understanding of the events. Letters expressing claims that the offender is innocent, therefore, are not helpful and may detract from the impact of other information in a letter of support. Instead, it is far better for letters of support to provide concrete examples of the offender's kindness or other contributions to society, rather than state platitudes; I can't tell you how often I have read that an offender "would give the shirt off his back for another person." Platitudes like that contribute little to informing the sentencing judge about the offender's true character.

Defense attorneys should also prepare their clients for the sentencing hearing. This begins with describing the sentencing procedures the court will follow. A sentencing hearing will likely be the most traumatic event an offender has ever experienced. Knowing in advance the order of events at the hearing, what the judge and others will do, when the offender will have a chance to speak, and where everyone will be sitting in the courtroom will at least diminish to some degree the level of anxiety the offender is feeling the day of the sentencing hearing. Defense attorneys should fully brief their clients on what issues are in dispute and whether the government or the offender has the burden of proof or persuasion on those issues. The defense attorney should also candidly apprise the offender of the worse-case scenario, meaning the longest term of imprisonment the judge may impose under the statute, so that the offender is not surprised if the worst happens.

B. Preparation When Offenders Have Pending Charges

Sometimes offenders will have pending charges and outstanding warrants from other jurisdictions. There may be costs and benefits for an offender in getting pending charges resolved before the sentencing hearing. When offenders go to prison, especially federal prison, their eligibility to participate in some programing and employment may be seriously jeopardized if they have outstanding charges or warrants. Those outstanding matters may also affect the offender's eligibility for parole or conditions of supervised release. In the federal system, the Bureau of Prisons case workers will strive to help offenders resolve these outstanding matters if they can, but it is very difficult for case workers to do so from a prison without the assistance of a defense attorney. Some warrants may appear outstanding because of clerical mistakes and can be easily resolved. In other cases, jurisdictions may be willing to drop or resolve outstanding charges favorably when they learn that an offender is facing a long federal sentence. In some cases, a little effort by defense attorneys to get these matters resolved before the sentencing hearing could significantly benefit the offender in the long run.

Thus, if resolving the outstanding charge will not result in the accumulation of criminal history points or will not increase the offender's criminal history score under the Federal Sentencing Guidelines, it is generally advisable to get the charges resolved, if possible. This may require the defense attorney to coordinate efforts with other defense attorneys in state or federal court in other jurisdictions. It may also require obtaining the prosecutor's cooperation and even a court order if resolving the charge requires transfer of the offender to another jurisdiction temporarily in order for the offender to make an appearance in another court to be sentenced. Similarly, if the outstanding charge is included in the offense conduct comprising the federal charge, then resolving the charge will typically have no adverse impact on the offender's sentence and may even result in a slight reduction in the ultimate sentence if the offender already served some time in jail for the state offense.

For example, imagine a federal case in which a grand jury charged an offender with conspiracy to distribute drugs during a two-year period. Imagine further that during that two-year period, the offender was charged in state court with the crime of possession with intent to distribute drugs, was arrested, and spent a few days in jail before bonding out. The state charge will likely be considered part of the federal offense conduct. The state prosecutor may be willing to drop the state charge in light of the offender's federal conviction. If not, pleading guilty to that charge in state court will be unlikely to affect the offender's federal sentence because it would not score any criminal history points under the Guidelines. Either way, the offender should generally receive a reduction in his federal sentence for the time he served in custody on the state charge. This issue can become very complicated because in some instances the Bureau of Prisons may not give credit for time served depending on which government had primary jurisdiction and whether some state charges are maintained that may or may not fully overlap with the federal criminal conduct. The nuances of this complexity are beyond the scope of this book, but suffice to say that a judge can depart from the advisory Guidelines range under Section 5G1.3 to ensure an offender receives full credit for time served.

Resolving outstanding charges, however, is not always beneficial to offenders. Sometimes resolving an outstanding charge could result in an additional conviction. In the federal system, under the Guidelines, that conviction could increase the offender's criminal history points and that, in turn, could place the offender in a higher criminal history category. Under these circumstances, it would be unwise to resolve that charge before the sentencing hearing. Similarly, defense attorneys need to make sure, before resolving an outstanding charge, that a conviction on that charge will not otherwise enhance the offender's federal sentence. For example, it would be foolhardy to resolve an outstanding state drug trafficking charge if a guilty plea to that charge would count as a predicate offense for purposes of making the offender a career offender under the Federal Sentencing Guidelines. Finally, defense attorneys may need to consider the long-term consequences of a guilty plea to an outstanding charge and not just the immediate consequences. If another conviction would make an offender qualify as a career offender in the future, even if it does not have that consequence in the pending federal case, it may be inadvisable to have the offender plead guilty to the outstanding charge. Although it may affect the nature of the offender's incarceration and supervision in the case for which the offender is about to be sentenced, it may be in the offender's best interest to let the charge lie and hope that it will go away or that the government's case will get weaker with the passage of time. These are difficult judgment calls for offenders and defense attorneys to make. The point here, though, is that these are decisions and actions that should be taken in preparation for the sentencing hearing because there may not be a chance to do it later, or doing so will become much more difficult.

C. Preparation for Factually-Contested Sentencing Hearings

In some sentencing hearings, there are factual disputes that a judge must resolve. In the federal system, the existence or absence of some facts may impact an offender's Guidelines base offense level (e.g., the quantity of drugs in a drug trafficking case or the nature of the firearm in a firearms possession case) or whether certain Guideline enhancements apply (e.g., whether a drug trafficking offender possessed a firearm in connection with the drug trafficking or the number of firearms possessed in a firearms possession case or the amount of a loss in a fraud case). There may be disputes about the existence of facts that are irrelevant for purposes of the Guidelines calculation but may be relevant for purposes of the factors under Title 18, United States Code, Section 3553(a). Whatever the case may be, preparation for a sentencing hearing in which the judge will have to resolve factual disputes is materially different from preparing for other sentencing hearings.

The first task for attorneys in preparing for factually-contested sentencing hearings is to identify all the facts in dispute. Sometimes the failure to be fully prepared for factual disputes is the result of an opposing party's vague or imprecise objection to a presentence report. An attorney may have objected to a paragraph in the offense conduct section of the presentence report but failed to state what facts within that paragraph are in dispute. If an attorney is unsure what facts the opposing party is disputing, the attorney should seek a clarification from opposing counsel. If that effort proves unfruitful, the attorney should be prepared to prove every fact in the disputed paragraph.

Once attorneys identify the facts in dispute, they need to determine how they will prove the facts. This is much like preparing for any hearing or trial when facts are in dispute. Attorneys may need to obtain and mark exhibits, identify and prepare witnesses to testify, or both. It is important that attorneys begin this preparation as soon as they realize that there will be facts disputed at the sentencing hearing. In federal court in particular, some sentencing hearings can take on the appearance of minitrials. I have been in sentencing hearings that have lasted days, during which the parties called multiple witnesses. Preparing for a factually-contested sentencing hearing in some cases is every bit as important, and can take just as much work, as preparing for a trial.

In some instances, whether judges grant evidentiary hearings or limit the scope of the hearings may be influenced by whether the offender pleaded guilty or went to trial. If an offender pleaded guilty under a plea agreement, the scope of facts that the parties may dispute could be limited by the terms of the plea. If the offender was found guilty after trial, a judge may rely on the trial record and decline to accept further evidence at a sentencing hearing. For this reason, attorneys may consider asking questions at trial (such as about drug quantity) that go to sentencing factors even though the questions may not be directly relevant to issues of guilt.

1. Preparing Exhibits

When facts are in issue in a sentencing hearing, attorneys need to identify, gather, and mark any documents or tangible objects that may be necessary to offer as exhibits during the sentencing hearing. This task requires attorneys to think critically not only about what evidence exists in the government's discovery file, but what evidence could be gathered specifically for purposes of the sentencing hearing. An investigation in a criminal case need not come to an end when guilt is determined. Indeed, as noted previously, there are sometimes issues that only become known or ripe in relation to sentencing that had nothing to do with determining the offender's guilt. Attorneys should jump on the task of identifying necessary exhibits as soon as the contested sentencing issue becomes apparent. Some documents take time to obtain. If the offender's criminal history will be a contested sentencing issue, getting copies of the underlying court documents related to prior convictions can be difficult and take substantial time. Attorneys who wait to gather these documents until shortly before the sentencing hearing may find themselves without the necessary documents. Likewise, documents about an offender's history and characteristics, such as educational, medical, prison, or military service records may require the attorney to negotiate complex avenues or may take significant time to obtain. Thus, the sooner attorneys start in on identifying and gathering documents and items for use as exhibits in a sentencing hearing, the better.

When identifying and marking exhibits, attorneys need to consider two primary possible audience members: the sentencing judge and the court of appeals. Attorneys should first persuade the sentencing judge from the exhibits and testimony but also should ensure that a proper record is laid for purposes of appeal. This means, in part, considering exhibits from each perspective. What may be persuasive evidence to a sentencing judge may not translate well on the record for appellate purposes. For example, if the government seeks an upward departure or variance based on the excessive number of firearms the offender possessed, it may be more persuasive to bring all of the firearms into the courtroom during the sentencing hearing so that judge can see the vast quantity, rather than simply look at a number written on a page of the presentence report. When the appellate court later reviews the reasonableness of the judge's decision, however, the appellate judges will not have the firearms in front of them to see, so it may be best for the prosecutor to produce a photograph of the firearms in addition to bringing them into the courtroom.

Considering the potential audience members also means marking exhibits in a manner that allows the sentencing judge to easily follow the references in testimony and also makes a good record for a reviewing court. For example, each page of multiple-page documents should be numbered. Similarly, if a video recording is to be used as an exhibit, and there is a particular frame of the video that is key, creating a still-shot of that frame as a separate exhibit will allow the sentencing judge to more easily focus on the key point and will allow a reviewing court to also understand what the parties believed was important.

To present a persuasive sentencing case through exhibits, attorneys should also think outside of the box and consider what exhibits the attorneys could generate that would tell their side of the story or enhance the witness testimony. Attorneys need not feel constrained to the evidence gathered by law enforcement officers. In the course of a bank robbery investigation, for example, law enforcement officers may have taken many photographs of the bank and teller station and the like in order to gather evidence to establish the offender's guilt. But if the teller was assaulted in the course of the robbery, the officers may not have taken photographs of the teller's injuries at the hospital. At sentencing, the nature and extent of the teller's injuries may be very important, though they are facts that were not material to the offender's guilt. Likewise, if the offender confined hostages in a small room for an extended period of time, at sentencing it may be persuasive for the judge to have a sense of how small the room was to appreciate the extent to which their confinement was stressful or traumatizing, yet such details would have little relevance for purposes of establishing the offender's guilt. The prosecutor may consider sending the law enforcement officers back to the bank to take measurements and photographs, perhaps even stage people in the same small room to show the cramped conditions.

Attorneys should also consider how to convey information to the judge in persuasive ways through demonstrative exhibits. Timelines, summary charts, graphs, and similar visual aids may be extremely persuasive. They often help witnesses tell their stories. Visual aids also often allow people to see connections or draw conclusions that would be less apparent from the raw data. In short, attorneys should consider ways to present information to judges in a compelling and persuasive manner through exhibits in much the same way they would do so in a jury trial.

2. Preparing Witnesses

When attorneys must call witnesses to testify at a sentencing hearing, it is imperative that they prepare the witnesses for the testimony. Testifying can be difficult. And testifying at a sentencing hearing is different than testifying before a jury. The extent of the witness preparation necessary will depend on the identity of the witness and the nature of the subject matter about which the witness is testifying.

Preparing a civilian witness to testify requires more time and effort than preparing a law enforcement officer to testify. But attorneys owe it to witnesses and their clients to prepare every witness to testify. Testifying is a nerve-wracking experience for everyone. This is true for even the most experienced law enforcement officer who has testified many times. Attorneys often do not appreciate this because they are seldom, if ever, on the stand themselves. The less nervous witnesses are, however, the more effective they are. It is an important part of sentencing advocacy, then, for attorneys to take efforts to reduce the stress of testifying. It is helpful for attorneys to fully explain to witnesses what they will experience and the process that will occur at the sentencing hearing. Attorneys should either show witnesses a diagram of the courtroom or take them to the courtroom and show the witness where everyone else in the courtroom will be located, where the witness will stand to be sworn in, and where the witness will sit while testifying. Attorneys should explain the sequencing of questioning and about the differences between direct and cross examination. Attorneys should inform the witness that the judge may also ask the witness questions during the sentencing hearing.

Preparing a witness to testify is not the same thing as telling a witness what to say or even how to say it. Attorneys should not improperly try to influence what a witness is going to say. It is also important that attorneys refrain from trying to influence how a witness is going to testify. In other words, attorneys should not use witness preparations to provide acting lessons to witnesses. Attorneys should not tell witnesses, for example, that they should be more remorseful or passionate, or act more scared or excited, during their testimony. That is not to say that attorneys cannot instruct witnesses about inappropriate courtroom behavior, such as swearing unnecessarily. Further, attorneys may inform witnesses that it is okay for them to show their true emotions in court. Witnesses should tell only the truth as they know it, and they should testify in a manner that is natural to them. Likewise, it is appropriate to instruct witnesses to be respectful to the opposing attorney, answer questions with a "yes" or "no" when appropriate, not to argue with the opposing attorney, and provide similar instructions that will help the witness effectively testify.

It is critically important that when preparing witnesses to testify that attorneys are clear with witnesses about the absolute necessity to testify truthfully. Witnesses may, however, interpret what attorneys say during witness preparation sessions as suggesting that the witness testify in a particular manner. Thus, attorneys should be ever vigilant and self-conscious about the words they use during witness preparation to ensure that witnesses understand that attorneys only want witnesses to tell the truth and do so in their own words.

When, in relation to the timing of the sentencing hearing, attorneys prepare witnesses may depend on the nature of the testimony, the number of witnesses that need to be prepared, and other logistical considerations. Generally speaking, attorneys should try to prepare witnesses as close to the sentencing hearing as possible, yet far enough in advance of the hearing to allow the attorney to adjust the presentation of the case in light of information learned or developments that arise during the preparation. Attorneys will almost always have to revise the outlines of questions for witnesses in light of the preparation. Through a witness preparation session, attorneys may come to learn that a witness knows of some fact of which the attorney was previously unaware or did not know the witness knew. An attorney may also determine there is a need to adjust the form or order of questions as a result of going over the witness's testimony during a preparation session. Also, sometimes witness preparation results in the attorney realizing there is a need to add a witness or exhibit. Thus, witness preparation needs to take place sufficiently in advance of the sentencing hearing to allow for these potential changes. On the other hand, the farther in advance of the sentencing hearing the preparation occurs, the more likely it is that the witness will forget what the attorney told the witness during the preparation session. Further, the larger the time gap, more likely it is that something may change with the witness before the proceeding. A witness may be arrested, suffer medical issues, or be approached by others trying to influence the witness's testimony. Although it is possible the witness would bring the matter to the attorney's attention before the sentencing hearing, the witness may not. The attorney could be surprised during the sentencing hearing by a witness who has changed testimony. Or the attorney may have lost the opportunity at the sentencing hearing to exploit the witness tampering attempt or to otherwise act on the information. In the end, determining the timing of the witness preparation sessions requires attorneys to exercise judgment and engage in careful planning.

Attorneys should assume that anything they say to the witness during witness preparation will come out during the sentencing hearing. Thus, attorneys must ensure that nothing is said to witnesses that the attorneys would not want the judge to hear. Along this line, attorneys should never criticize or denigrate the judge, opposing counsel, or anyone else for that matter. This includes not suggesting to the witness that the opposing counsel will try to "pull the wool over the witness's eyes" or use tricky or deceptive questioning. Nor should the prosecutor label the offender (such as calling him an "animal"), attack the offender's character, call the offender any names, or even describe the offender's conduct in pejorative terms. Not only would it be embarrassing and potentially harmful to the prosecutor's case for this to come out at the sentencing hearing, making such statements to a witness may also improperly influence the witness's testimony.

When preparing witnesses to testify at sentencing hearings, it is essential that attorneys do not provide information to the witness that the witness did not previously know. Witnesses have finite information about certain facts relevant to a case. The attorneys, however, have access to all the facts of a case. Were the attorneys to disclose facts to a witness of which the witness was otherwise unaware, it may inadvertently and unintentionally influence the witness's testimony. Even advising a witness that other evidence exists that corroborates the witness's testimony may alter the manner of the witness's testimony. It is often best for witnesses to remain ignorant of everything to do with the case outside their own personal knowledge, at least until they have finished testifying.

Attorneys should begin and end every witness preparation session with an admonition that the witness must tell the absolute truth. Attorneys should explain that everything else they will discuss during the prep session is designed to help the attorney ask better questions to elicit the truth and prepare the witness for the process so that they are better able to convey the truth. It helps to get the witness to verbally acknowledge that they understand this and will commit to telling only the truth. Prosecutors should counsel government witnesses about how important it is for witnesses to be neutral truth tellers. Prosecutors should emphasize that witnesses should not be the least concerned with the offender's ultimate sentence or how the witness's testimony could impact that sentence. Similar advice is appropriate for defense witnesses. It may be much more difficult for some defense witnesses, such as family members, to be neutral and not skew or exaggerate or prevaricate because of the emotional attachment to the offender. Yet, defense attorneys need to explain to theses witnesses that their testimony will be of little value if the judge does not believe it. Judges have a lot of experience assessing the credibility of witnesses and will quickly discern when witnesses are coloring their testimony or shading the truth in a manner to favor one side or the other.

In advance of a witness preparation session, attorneys should provide witnesses with copies of any prior statements the witnesses have made on the subject matter about which they are anticipated to testify. It is important when providing these statements to witnesses that attorneys tell them that the purpose of doing so is to remind them about what they previously said. Attorneys should emphasize that by providing these materials to the witnesses the attorneys are not telling the witnesses that they are compelled to say the same thing at the sentencing hearing. Attorneys should explain that is it possible that the witness may have previously made a misstatement, or that law enforcement officers accidentally mis-recorded what the witness said, or that the witness may have a different recollection of events.

Before discussing the subject matter of the witness's testimony with the witness during a witness preparation session, an attorney should first inquire of the witness whether there is any change in the testimony or recollection. This inquiry will be aided, of course, when the attorney has provided the witness with an opportunity in advance to review the witness's prior statements and testimony. The attorney should also inquire more generally of the witness whether there have been any other changes in circumstances that could affect the witness's testimony, such as drug use, medications, health issues, memory issues, or contact with people about the witness's status as a witness or the witness's testimony.

During a witness preparation session, the attorney should go through the outline of questions the attorney has prepared for the witness. As a result of going through the draft questions with the witness, the witness will be better prepared for and less anxious about the witness's testimony. An attorney can go through the questions informally, in the sense of asking the questions in a casual setting (such as a conference room) or can have the witness pretend the witness is on the stand and proceed to ask questions as if the witness were in court. Of course, an attorney can do both. Sometimes it is helpful for nervous witnesses to go through the process as if the witness were on the stand to help them adjust to the process as it will actually occur in the courtroom. Either way, when going through the outline of questions, the attorney should remember not try to influence the witness's testimony. Witnesses will even ask sometimes, "Is that what I should say?" or "Is that how you want me to answer the question?" Again, the attorney should emphasize that the witness should simply tell the truth. The attorney may, however, want to rephrase the draft question to better elicit the desired testimony. Inevitably, the process of going through the questions with the witness will result in the attorney revising the draft outline of questions at least once.

During the process of witness preparation, the attorney should show the witness each exhibit about which the witness may testify. The exhibit should be marked as an exhibit and be in the same condition that it will be when offered into evidence at the sentencing hearing. The witness should review the exhibit carefully, and the attorney should ensure that the witness has personal knowledge of the exhibit and, when appropriate, lay a foundation for admission of the exhibit.[1] To alleviate witness nerves, the attorney should explain the process of presenting an exhibit to a witness and moving it into evidence. What is routine for attorneys can be a strange and quirky process to a lay person. It helps put a witness at ease, then, when an attorney explains the process: the attorney will approach the witness and hand the witness the exhibit, ask the witness a series of questions about the exhibit to lay a foundation for its admission, then will address the court and move for admission of the exhibit, at which time the opposing attorney may or may not object, and the court will then issue a ruling on admission of the exhibit. The attorney should explain to the witness that only after the court rules that the exhibit is admitted can the witness talk about what the exhibit is or what it says or contains. Again, although this is second nature to attorneys, this is an unfamiliar and perhaps strange process to a lay person.

When the witness being prepared is a government cooperator, it is imperative that the prosecutor cover the nature of the witness's cooperation at great length during the witness preparation session. The prosecutor should have the witness review any cooperation or informant agreements and any plea agreements. It is helpful for the prosecutor to inquire of the witness what they understand these agreements mean for the witness, particularly as to any potential benefit the witness has or may receive as a result of cooperating. If a witness is incorrect, it is important that the prosecutor work with counsel to correct the cooperator and make sure they fully understand the agreement. For example, if a plea agreement provides that the cooperator *may* receive a reduction in the cooperator's sentence, it would be incorrect for the cooperator to testify that the cooperator *will* receive a sentencing reduction. The agreement itself may not, and probably will not, itself be an exhibit at the sentencing hearing. But, if the cooperator gets it wrong, the attorney may use the plea agreement to refresh the cooperator's recollection or to impeach the cooperator's testimony. Also, cooperators need to fully understand, for their own benefit, what they may or may not get as a result of cooperating. Similarly, cooperators must understand the adverse consequences that could arise if they were to lie during their testimony. Because the benefits a cooperator may receive is part of a legal framework, it can sometimes be difficult for cooperators to fully understand the process and what they are and not getting from their cooperation. Prosecutors need to be prepared to go over this part of the cooperator's testimony as many times as necessary to ensure that the cooperator fully understands it and is capable of articulating that understanding when the cooperator testifies. Whenever cooperators are represented by counsel, which is almost always, the government should insist that the cooperator's attorney is present during the witness preparation session. Although most defense attorneys will insist on being present anyway, some find it a waste of their time. It is important to have the cooperator's attorney present to help work with the cooperator to correct any misunderstandings and also to ensure that the witness understands the necessity of testifying truthfully.

Witness preparation involves more than attorneys reviewing direct examination questions with witnesses. It also involves reviewing possible cross examination questions with them. Cross examination is considered "the 'greatest legal engine ever invented for the discovery of truth'"[2] because attorneys are skilled at dissecting testimony and impeaching witness. Attorneys owe it to witnesses to adequately prepare them for cross examination. Attorneys should also recognize that witnesses properly prepared for cross examination will be more effective at the sentencing hearing. Attorneys should be careful when addressing cross examination with witnesses. First, an attorney should fully explain that they are reviewing possible cross examination questions that the opposing attorney may or may not ask to prepare the witnesses for testifying. Second, the attorney should again emphasize that they are not telling the witness what to say or not say in response to the questions by opposing attorney; the witnesses must only and always just tell the truth. Third, attorneys should be cautious never to describe the opposing attorney, or the nature of cross examination questions, in a negative or derogatory manner. For example, an attorney should not describe cross examination as process by which the opposing attorney will try to "trick" the witness or describe an opposing attorney as "sneaky." To the contrary, attorneys should explain that cross examination is the opportunity for the opposing attorney to ask the witness questions and that the opposing attorney is duty bound to zealously represent their clients. Attorneys should instruct witnesses never to take questions personally or get defensive or argue with the opposing attorney. Rather, witnesses should answer the opposing attorney's questions directly and truthfully.

It is helpful to witnesses when attorneys explain how the nature of cross examination questions is different from direct examination questions. Attorneys should explain the difference between leading and non-leading questions and emphasize that there is nothing at all improper or underhanded for an attorney to ask leading questions. Attorneys can explain that when a witness has already told the whole story during direct examination, it would be a waste of time to make the opposing attorney ask nonleading questions to get to the point the attorney wants to focus on. Thus, leading questions allow an attorney to get straight to the point. Attorneys should encourage witnesses to try to answer opposing attorneys' questions with a "yes" or "no" answers when witnesses can do so, and discourage witnesses from arguing with opposing counsel. On the other hand, prosecutors should instruct witnesses to say so if they truly believe that they cannot truthfully answer questions with "yes" or "no."

In preparing witnesses for cross examination, attorneys should carefully explain the ways in which opposing counsel may attempt to impeach a witness's testimony. These include questions about the witness's potential bias, the witness's memory, any criminal history or other bad acts the witness has committed in the past, and prior inconsistent statements. With bias, it is helpful to encourage witnesses to simply be frank about any bias they may have. For example, a witness may have a racial or gender bias. A witness may even stand to benefit in some way if the offender is sentenced to a long term in prison. Whatever the potential bias issue may be, that does not mean the witness is necessarily testifying falsely. A witness can have a bias and still testify truthfully as to a fact. What will adversely affect a witness's credibility is to falsely disclaim a bias. If a witness is cross examined as to a potential bias, it is likely the opposing counsel has some evidence to back up the question. If the witness falsely denies the bias, the opposing counsel may reveal that evidence either during the cross examination or later through other evidence. With that explanation provided to the witness, attorneys can encourage the witness to be frank in revealing any potential bias the witness may have so that together the attorney and witness would have an opportunity either to dispel it, or to disclose the potential bias up front during direct examination so that it does not appear that the witness was attempting to conceal it.

It is similarly helpful to discuss with witnesses the questions the opposing attorney may ask on cross examination going to the witness' memory. It is important that witnesses understand that their memories are faulty, as is everyone's memory. Our minds trap some facts and retain them, while others are hardly noticed in the first instance and not long retained. Also, our memory of some facts may be inaccurate because in the process of perceiving the facts, they were filtered through preconceptions or biases or underwent alteration through a similar process during recall. The bottom line is that witnesses need to understand that their memories are not infallible. On the other hand, there are some facts which were so clear at the time of perception, are of a nature unlikely to be affected by inherent biases or the like, and so firmly placed in memories that witnesses can have confidence in testifying about them.

With these thoughts in mind, attorneys should advise witnesses to be firm in their testimony when they have confidence in their memories about events but refrain from asserting absolute certainty about matters when they are not so confident. Some witnesses may feel pressure to claim certainty when in truth they lack confidence in the accuracy of their own recollections. Attorneys should assure witnesses that it is acceptable to qualify answers based on their memory. Witness may say, for example, that they are "fairly certain" or "almost absolutely sure," or use similar phrases about their memory of a fact. It is also helpful to advise witnesses to dispense with unnecessary detail when testifying. The more detail included in testimony, the more likely the witness will make an error in recollection. This is particularly true the less important the detail was in the first instance.

When witnesses have prior criminal convictions that are open for use to impeach the witness, attorneys should cover this issue with them. Attorneys should explain that certain convictions are seen as reflective of a person's truthfulness. Attorneys should identify the benefits of having the attorney elicit testimony about the prior convictions during direct examination instead of waiting until cross examination. These benefits include allowing more freedom for the witness to testify in their own words, rather than having to respond to leading questions, and avoiding the appearance that the witness is attempting to hide their criminal past from the judge. Finally, attorneys should tell witnesses that it is best to be frank and open about criminal history when asked about it and not to be defensive or evasive. A witness should simply admit the prior convictions and not try to explain them away or minimize their culpability. It is helpful if the witness understands that the more defensive and evasive the witness is about criminal history, the more likely it is that the opposing attorney will focus on the criminal history and the longer the witness will be asked about it.

Finally, good attorneys will explain the technique lawyers use to impeach witnesses with prior inconsistent statements. Unless someone has been confronted by a lawyer with a prior inconsistent statement, the process can be startling and disturbing. Thus, attorneys should explain the concept first, then provide advice about responding to an attorney's attempt to impeach a witness's testimony in this manner. First, witnesses need to understand that it is very likely that they will say something in court that could be perceived to be inconsistent with prior statements. An inconsistent statement may be a result of a faulty memory, access to new information since making the prior statement, or recent refreshment of recollection. Alternatively, the apparent inconsistency may have resulted from a poorly worded question during direct examination or when the witness last spoke about the matter or a poorly worded or misworded answer either in the sentencing hearing or before. Whatever the case, in all likelihood there is an innocent explanation for what appears to be an inconsistent statement that has nothing to do with the witness's honesty. It is important to emphasize to witnesses that some of the time, the inconsistencies tend to be minor or not real inconsistencies at all. The point for attorneys to get across is that witnesses should not panic when it becomes apparent that the opposing attorneys are attempting to impeach the witness's credibility with a prior inconsistent statement.

Second, the attorney should explain how the questions will sound during the opposing attorney's impeachment attempt. The attorney should explain that the opposing attorney will likely first reference the in-court testimony that the attorney believes is inconsistent with a prior statement. Next, the attorney will usually refer to the circumstances surrounding the witness's prior statement, noting where and when it was made and often referencing facts that would show that the witness understood the importance of being accurate (such as whether the witness was under oath at the time or speaking to someone the witness knew to be a law enforcement officer). The final step of the impeachment process is the confrontation of the witness with the prior inconsistent statement. The attorney should explain to the witness that the opposing attorney will usually phrase the confrontation question is a manner that demands only a yes or no answer.[3] The attorney should encourage the witness to answer such a question with a yes or no answer, if possible, and not to equivocate or try to explain the apparent inconsistency. The attorney should also explain to the witness that the point of impeachment with a prior inconsistent statement is to show inconsistency, and not necessarily to show that one statement is more accurate than the other. Thus, the opposing attorney is not looking for an explanation and it is unlikely the attorney will give the witness an opportunity to explain an apparently inconsistent statement. Finally, the attorney should assure witnesses that if the attorney believes the opposing counsel pointed out an important inconsistency that needed an explanation, on re-direct examination the attorney will give the witness the opportunity to explain the apparent inconsistency.

Attorneys should provide witnesses with some orientation about the physical setting of their testimony. At the very least, attorneys should show witnesses a floorplan or diagram of the courtroom, pointing out where they will enter the courtroom and the location of the witness chair, the jury, and the judge. In some situations, a more extensive courtroom preparation session may be appropriate. Some witnesses, such as children or crime victims, may be especially nervous about testifying. A courtroom can be a very intimidating setting. Thus, in some cases it may be advisable to show the courtroom to the witness and, if possible, even let the witness take a seat in the witness chair. It may even be helpful to go through some questions with the witness while they are sitting in the witness chair to get them accustomed to answering questions in that setting.

By the end of the witness preparation session, it will inevitably be necessary for the attorney to revise the outline of direct examination questions. Sometimes the changes are minor, reflecting a change in the words used to ask questions in a way that allows the witness to more readily understand the question. In other cases, the witness preparation session may require major revisions to the outline of questions, the addition or removal of exhibits to be shown to the witness, or other significant alterations. Attorneys should resist the urge to make the testimony fit the outline, or to make do with an outline that does not fully elicit the testimony the witness has to offer. This urge to make do can be hard for attorneys to resist because witness preparation occurs shortly before the sentencing hearing at a time when there are a lot of other demands on the attorney's time, along with all the work attorneys have pending in other cases. Nevertheless, it is important that attorneys revise witness outlines as soon after the preparation sessions as possible to ensure that they have captured all the changes that are needed to make the witness's testimony as persuasive as possible.

Finally, but importantly, attorneys also need to explain to witnesses that in a sentencing hearing, the judge is the factfinder and what that means. It means, among other things, that answers should be directed to the judge. To be persuasive, it is important that witnesses make eye contact with the judge. It is also very important that witnesses understand that the judge may very well ask them questions. Most witnesses may not realize that in a sentencing hearing, the judge may also examine them in addition to the attorneys. Witnesses need to be prepared for this. Attorneys should explain that, as the factfinder, it is important that judges have all their questions answered and that sometimes the judge thinks of questions the attorneys did not. Attorneys should instruct witnesses not to be worried or intimidated if the judge asks questions and counsel witnesses to answer the judge's questions just like they would answer questions from attorneys.

D. *Legal Arguments*

When sentencing hearings involve legal disputes, such as disagreements about the application of the Federal Sentencing Guidelines, attorneys should prepare for argument before the court. Not all judges will entertain oral argument on legal disputes. The parties should have addressed the legal issues in their sentencing memoranda, and judges may feel that is adequate for them to rule on the legal issues. Indeed, some judges may file orders ruling on disputed legal issues before the sentencing hearing. When attorneys believe that oral argument would be valuable, they should ask for oral argument in their sentencing memoranda.

To prepare for oral argument, attorneys should re-read the presentence report, their own and their opposing party's sentencing memoranda, and any key statutory provisions or case precedent. Attorneys should also update their legal research. Sentencing law changes frequently. It is not uncommon for the courts to issue new opinions on the sentencing issues in dispute between the time the parties submitted their sentencing memoranda and the time of the sentencing hearing. Finally, attorneys should consider preparing demonstrative exhibits, annotated copies of Guidelines provisions or statutes, timelines, charts, or other visual aids that may assist the sentencing judge in understanding the legal issues. These may also be the same demonstrative exhibits prepared for an evidentiary sentencing hearing, or they may be demonstrative exhibits created for a sentencing hearing without contested evidentiary issues, based off uncontested portions of the presentence report. Attorneys may consider creating such demonstrative exhibits solely for the purpose of communicating with and persuading the sentencing judge during the argument stage of the sentencing hearing, regardless of what demonstrative exhibits were or were not used in connection with the presentation of evidence.

E. Working with Crime Victims

When crimes have resulted in victims, certain issues may arise at sentencing hearings, including the right of victims to be heard, victim restitution, and victim expectations. Prosecutors need to assess the crime victim issues and be prepared to address them at the sentencing hearing.

Crime victims have certain statutory rights, and it is the prosecutor's statutory duty to ensure that those rights are maintained. I will discuss those rights in greater detail in a later chapter on victims, but it is sufficient here to note that those rights include the right of crime victims to address the court at the time of sentencing. Certain crime victims may do this by providing the sentencing judge with written victim-impact statements, but they also have the right to orally address the court at the time of the sentencing hearing. In advance of the sentencing hearing, prosecutors need to meet with the crime victims, or have a victim coordinator do so, to ensure the victims are fully informed of their rights and to determine if they want to provide victim impact statements in writing or orally. If victims wish to address the court orally, prosecutors should ensure they are fully briefed about the layout of the courtroom, the sentencing procedures so that the crime victims understand when during the hearing they will have an opportunity to speak, and explain to them that their statements should be made to the judge and not the offender.

Some crime victims may be due restitution. Sometimes restitution is statutorily mandatory, while for some crimes it may be the result of a plea agreement. Sometimes the amount of restitution is not in dispute, but sometimes an offender will contest whether a particular victim is factually entitled to restitution at all or contest the amount of restitution the victim has claimed. Prosecutors must try to obtain restitution owed under the law. The prosecutor has the burden to prove up the basis for the victim's restitution. This means that prosecutors should work diligently to develop the evidence necessary to prove up crime victims' claims. Victims may have difficulty understanding the need for them to prove anything and may be defensive about the obligation. Prosecutors have to tread carefully here to make sure that victims understand the need to help the prosecutor help them by gathering whatever evidence is required to establish a factual basis for the court to award restitution. It should be noted that many legal issues can arise in calculating the amount of restitution, such as the extent to which expenses or legal fees can be considered as part of recoverable losses. The nuances of these legal issues are beyond the scope of this book, but attorneys should be aware of them, and prosecutors should be prepared to explain them to crime victims who may expect restitution for expenses not allowed under the law.

Preparing to prove up restitution may also involve preparing the crime victims to testify at the sentencing hearing about restitution claims. Prosecutors need to explain to victims that testifying in support of a restitution request is different from making a victim-impact statement. When testifying, the witness will be placed under oath, questioned by the prosecutor, and cross-examined by the defense attorney. And, again, the prosecutor should alert the crime victim that the judge may also ask questions. In contrast, when victims make oral victim-impact statements at sentencing hearings, they are not under oath, and they are not questioned by anyone.

Prosecutors should also prepare victims for sentencing hearings. Sentencing hearings are one of, if not the most, emotional and difficult proceedings for crime victims to endure, even if they do not have to testify or choose not to make a victim-impact statement. Crime victims are likely to have certain expectations coming into a sentencing hearing about both the procedure and the sentence that the court will impose. These expectations may not be realistic or correct. Victims' expectations may be based on popular culture or a misunderstanding of the facts or the law. Prosecutors need to manage these expectations. Although victim coordinators can help prepare victims for sentencing hearings, this is one area where prosecutors should not fully delegate this duty. Rather, prosecutors should meet personally with crime victims to prepare them for all aspects of the sentencing hearing. Prosecutors should explain the judge's sentencing discretion, describe any statutory limitations on sentencing, describe the role of sentencing Guidelines, and answer questions from the victims about the sentencing hearing.

For offenders, facing and hearing from crime victims may be one of the most difficult parts of the sentencing hearing and one of the most traumatic events in their lives. Defense attorneys need to prepare their clients for this event. Defense attorneys should explain the purpose and nature of victim-impact statements and describe the procedure for when and how they will take place during the sentencing hearing. It is important that defense attorneys to also counsel their clients to maintain their composure. Offenders should not react negatively to victim testimony or victim-impact statements, even if the offenders do not believe the persons are truly victims or believe the victims are partially responsible in some way. Judges will typically, and understandably, be sympathetic to victims. A negative reaction by an offender to a victim may adversely color the judge's view of the offender. As I will discuss in the following chapter, while the order in which judges progress through the various stages of sentencing may differ from courtroom to courtroom, the last part of every sentencing hearing is the pronouncement of the sentence. Thus, an offender who reacts inappropriately to a victim-impact statement may face consequences when the judge imposes the sentence.

11

Conducting Sentencing Hearings

The next several chapters are devoted to the sentencing hearing itself. In this chapter, I will identify the various stages of federal sentencing hearings and briefly discuss each stage. In the following chapters, I will delve into some of these stages in much greater detail. In that sense, this chapter forms an outline for several of the following chapters. Before I begin, though, it is important to recognize that the exact order in which some of the stages occur may differ significantly from courtroom to courtroom. No procedural rules prescribe an exact order in which a judge must conduct a sentencing hearing. The order I have set out below and follow in subsequent chapters is the order I have personally adopted. It is not the only order judges use and perhaps not even the best order. I use the order here for purposes of organizing the following discussion.

A. *Opening of Court and Initial Procedures*

At the start a sentencing hearing, the judge will open up court by pronouncing the name and case number of the case and identifying the attorneys and parties. The judge will identify the offense or offenses of conviction and typically describe the date and manner in which the offender was determined guilty (i.e., by means of a guilty plea or a jury verdict). It is at this stage that I describe the mandatory minimum and maximum penalties prescribe by statute for the offense of conviction. Other judges may do this at a different time during the sentencing hearing, but at some point, the judge must state the statutory penalties.

Next, I question the parties to make sure they have received and had adequate time to review the presentence report. The Federal Rules of Criminal Procedure mandate that sentencing judges ensure the defense attorney has reviewed the presentence report with the offender. Federal Rule of Criminal Procedure 32(i)(A) requires that a judge "must verify that the defendant and the defendant's attorney have read and discussed the presentence report and any addendum to the report." FED. R. CRIM. P. 32(i)(1)(A).

At this point I also have the parties identify for me or confirm the objections to the presentence report that they are maintaining at the sentencing hearing. Between the time the parties lodged objections to the draft presentence report and the sentencing hearing, much may have changed. The parties may have resolved objections, or parties may have decided not to pursue prior objections either because further research persuaded them that the objections were unwarranted or because they have decided not to maintain the objections for strategic reasons. Attorneys should alert the sentencing judge as soon as they can if they know that they will not be pursuing a previously-lodged objection, but sometimes these decisions are made at the last minute. It is important for attorneys to recognize that it is the position they take on objections to the presentence report at the time of the sentencing hearing that controls, not the position they took when they filed objections to the draft presentence report.[1]

Once I have made a record of all the outstanding objections to the presentence report, I then summarize the Guidelines calculation as determined by the probation officer and reflected in the presentence report. At this point in a sentencing hearing, I address each paragraph of the presentence report setting out the Guidelines calculation, from the base offense level, through any Chapter 2 or Chapter 3 adjustments, the criminal history points and criminal history category, and the advisory Guidelines range of imprisonment. Again, other judges may do this at a different point in the proceeding, but at some point, in the federal system, Title 18, United States Code, Section 3553(a) requires the sentencing judge to calculate the Guidelines.

B. Presentation of Evidence

Typically, when the parties wish to present evidence on any issue, whether it is on disputed Guidelines, departure motions, variance motions, Section 3553(a) factors, fine amount, or restitution, I will take that evidence next. Sometimes the resolution of the evidentiary issues will require a sentencing judge to recalculate the Guidelines. At other times, the factual disputes have no effect on the Guidelines calculation at all or do not affect the Guidelines, depending on how the judge rules. When the evidence affects the Guidelines, I will announce my ruling on the disputed factual issues. If my findings affect the Guidelines calculation, I will then recalculate the Guidelines.

C. Resolution of Guidelines Issues

Sometimes Guidelines issues are disputed, but as a matter of legal interpretation. This involves the judge applying the Guidelines to the undisputed facts in the presentence report. This will also include ruling on motions to departure from the advisory Guidelines range. Departure motions can include motions by prosecutors for reducing sentences under Guidelines Section 5K1.1 in exchange for offenders providing substantial assistance to the government in the investigation and prosecution of others. Addressing motions to depart from the advisory Guidelines range for substantial assistance requires the court to conduct this portion of the proceeding in a manner to minimize disclosure of the offender's cooperation, for his own protection. This typically requires the court to conduct this portion of the hearing in a closed setting or under seal.

D. Resolution of Fine Issues

In federal court, it has been my experience that criminal fines are seldom imposed because most offenders are indigent or restitution obligations predominate. Occasionally an offender may appear to have the ability to pay a fine and may dispute that ability or the amount of fine to be imposed. In those cases, I typically take up the fine issue next, after I have resolved Guidelines issues about the length of incarceration have been resolved.

E. Resolution of Supervised Release Issues

In some cases, offenders will object to imposition of any supervised release or, more often, object to certain conditions of supervised release the probation officer recommended in the presentence report. When the government seeks imposition of a supervised release condition that the probation officer did not recommend in the presentence report, I will typically take up these issues next, after resolving terms of imprisonment and fine issues.

F. Resolution of Collateral Consequences Issues

When cases involve disputed collateral sentencing consequences, such as restitution, forfeiture, registration as a sex offender, or the like, I will address them next in a sentencing hearing. In some cases when parties have presented evidence on these issues, I may announce my ruling on the issues after the parties have presented their evidence. If there are other factual matters in dispute on which I have heard evidence, though, I will address these collateral matters after handling all other issues.

G. Victim Impact Statements

In cases involving victims, absent some other compelling reason, I will hear from victims immediately before I hear from the attorneys about the ultimate disposition of the case and before I hear the offender's allocution. I prefer to hear victim impact statements before I hear from the attorneys in case the attorneys wish to comment on or incorporate the victim impact statements into their arguments. I also prefer to hear from victims in close proximity to when I hear from the offender in allocution. When cases involve victims, it strikes me that what they and the offender have to say is often very important in making my decision about the ultimate sentence. Again, other judges may have victims speak at other points in the hearing, including very early in the proceedings or even after the offender's allocution. Attorneys should find out in advance of the hearing the order on this matter in particular because it may impact how and when they address victim impact.

H. Resolution of Variance Motions and Final Argument on Disposition

After resolution of all evidentiary and legal issues, I provide each attorney an opportunity to argue about any variance from the advisory Guidelines range and the ultimate sentence they believe I should impose. Federal Rule of Criminal Procedure 32 requires sentencing judges to allow attorneys for each party to speak.

> **(4) Opportunity to Speak.**
> (A) By a Party. Before imposing sentence, the court must:
> (i) provide the defendant's attorney an opportunity to speak on the defendant's behalf;
> (ii) address the defendant personally in order to permit the defendant to speak or present any information to mitigate the sentence; and
> (iii) provide an attorney for the government an opportunity to speak equivalent to that of the defendant's attorney.

Fed. R. Crim. P. 32(i)(4). Even in cases when the parties have presented evidence on Section 3553(a) factors, I will not make my decision about those factors or pronounce my ruling on them until after I have heard from the attorneys and the offender.

I. Allocution

The last stage in my sentencing hearings is the offender's allocution. As noted in the preceding section, Federal Rule of Criminal Procedure 32(i)(4) requires the court to permit an offender to speak. Of course, offenders do not have to say anything, and I assure them that if they do not wish to speak that I will not hold it against them in any way. But when offenders do wish to give an allocution, I have them do it immediately before I pronounce sentence. Although Rule 32(i)(4) is written in such a way as to suggest an order (defense attorney speaks, then the offender, and finally the prosecutor), it does not dictate that order. I have the offender speak last because it seems appropriate to me that the offender, the person most impacted by my decision, has the right to have the last word about the sentence.

J. Imposition and Judgment

The final stage of the sentencing hearing is the pronouncement of the sentence. Here, I will announce whether I am imposing a sentence within the advisory Guidelines range, or whether I am varying from the advisory Guidelines range. If I vary, I will explain why. If I chose not to vary, I will explain why not. I will expressly state how I believe any applicable Section 3553(a) factors impacted my assessment of the appropriate sentence. I will then formally pronounce sentence, including the term of any period of incarceration, fine, forfeiture, restitution, and terms of supervised release. The last thing I do before adjourning the hearing is advise the offender of his right to appeal. The probation officer will provide me with a draft judgment shortly after the sentencing hearing.[2] I will review, edit, if necessary, sign the judgment, and then have it filed.

Having summarized the stages of a sentencing hearing and the order in which I take them up as a judge, I cannot overemphasize the need for attorneys to know as much as possible about the sentencing judge. Attorneys need to learn the order in which their sentencing judges address the stages of a sentencing hearing so that they can be prepared, and they can prepare their clients and victims. Attorneys should thoroughly research their sentencing judges for other information as well, such as whether their judges routinely pose questions of witnesses at sentencing hearings, whether they want copies of sentencing exhibits in advance of trial, and the like. Attorneys should also research judges to determine if the judges have previously ruled on an issue that will be in dispute at the sentencing hearing. If the judge has ruled favorably to the attorney's side, the attorney should cite that authority to the judge; if not, the attorney should be prepared to distinguish the prior case from the one now before the judge. Recall that effective advocacy means knowing one's audience.

12

Evidentiary Sentencing Hearings

It is not uncommon for attorneys to present evidence in contested federal sentencing hearings. "It is well-established that, 'when a defendant disputes material facts in his PSR, the sentencing court must either refuse to take those facts into account or hold an evidentiary hearing.'" *United States v. Cochrane*, 608 F.3d 382, 383 (8th Cir. 2010) (quoting *United States v. Morehead*, 375 F.3d 677, 679 [8th Cir. 2004]). In some cases, offenders may object to and deny all relevant criminal conduct, requiring the government to attempt to prove all the material facts relevant for sentencing. Indeed, as noted previously, some contested sentencing hearings take on the appearance of mini-trials (even not-so-mini-trials). Presenting evidence at a sentencing hearing, though, is unlike presenting evidence at a trial for multiple reasons. Unlike trials, except for privileges, the Federal Rules of Evidence do not apply. Nor does the Confrontation Clause apply at sentencing hearings. But the Due Process Clause does apply. Also, presenting evidence to judges is different from presenting evidence to jurors in several ways, not the least of which is that parties can submit exhibits to judges in advance of the hearing. Unlike jurors, judges can question witnesses and counsel, opening the possibility of a more effective communication through a conversation. In this chapter, I will discuss these differences and examine other considerations pertinent to presenting evidence at a sentencing hearing.

A. Inapplicability of the Federal Rules of Evidence

When judges serve as factfinders, as they do in sentencing hearings, it is important for attorneys to consider whether and to what extent the Federal Rules of Evidence apply to the proceedings. How attorneys advocate and what evidence attorneys present to sentencing judges turns on this determination. In sentencing hearings, the short answer is that except for privileges, the Federal Rules of Evidence do not apply. *See* Fed. R. Evid. 1101(c) (noting that privilege rules apply to all proceedings). To be effective sentencing advocates at hearings involving evidentiary disputes, it is not enough, however, to simply accept this truism. Understanding why the Federal Rules of Evidence do not apply, and why they even exist in the first instance, is critically important for appreciating how to advocate to judges in a sentencing hearing involving evidentiary disputes.

For as long as there have been jury trials, there have been rules about evidence.

Evidence rules evolved at common law precisely because they were deemed necessary to control what evidence juries were entitled to receive.[1] As Professor John Henry Wigmore, the famous expert on the rules of evidence, once explained, the rules of evidence are "based on the purpose of saving the jurors from being misled" due to jurors' "inexperience in analyzing evidence, and their unfamiliarity with the chicanery of counsel."[2]

The Federal Rules of Evidence are a product of and a partial codification of the rules of evidence at common law. The Federal Rules of Evidence reflect the historic, fundamental, and persistent underlying belief that jurors need protection from unreliable evidence. Jurors are deemed unable on their own to determine if evidence is reliable. The law also assumes jurors are easily misled by irrelevant and prejudicial evidence and incapable of disregarding such evidence even if they recognize it as such. Indeed, for this very reason, Rule 104(c) requires judges to conduct hearings on the admissibility of evidence "so that the jury cannot hear it" under certain circumstances or when "justice so requires." FED. R. EVID. 104(c).

When it is understood that the Federal Rules of Evidence were designed to protect unsophisticated jurors from unreliable evidence and the chicanery of clever counsel, it is not surprising that the Federal Rules of Evidence, except for privilege, do not apply in a great number of proceedings when judges serve as fact finders. Importantly for this book, those proceedings include sentencing hearings. *See* FED. R. EVID. 1101(d)(3) (listing sentencing hearings, among other proceedings, when the Federal Rules of Evidence do not apply, except for privileges). In theory, trained judges are experienced in analyzing evidence and familiar with the chicanery of counsel and thus do not need the protection that the Federal Rules of Evidence provide to laypersons. The rationale is that judges can exercise the mental discipline so as not to be unduly influenced by potentially prejudicial evidence and give proper weight to potentially unreliable evidence. As a result, there is no limitation on the information a sentencing judge may consider in a sentencing hearing. *See* 18 U.S.C. § 3661 (stating that "[n]o limitation shall be placed on the information concerning the background, character, and conduct of a person convicted of an offense which a court of the United States may receive and consider for the purpose of imposing an appropriate sentence.").

To understand how to effectively advocate to a judge in a sentencing hearing, though, it is still important that attorneys understand the reasons for the rules of evidence even though they do not govern the admissibility of evidence at sentencing hearings. Underlying many of the Federal Rules of Evidence is a rationale for why the drafters concluded that certain evidence was unreliable. For instance, Rule 404(a) prohibits the admission of character evidence to prove that a person acted in conformity with that character because of the belief that a person's character is a poor predictor of behavior. FED R. EVID. 404(a)(1) ("Evidence of a person's character or character trait is not admissible to prove that on a particular occasion the person acted in accordance with the character or character trait.").[3] On the other hand, Rule 406 permits the admission of habit evidence for the purpose of showing that a person acted on a particular occasion consistent with that habit because of the belief that a habit is a good predictor of behavior. FED. R. EVID. 406 ("Evidence of a person's habit or an organization's routine practice may be admitted to prove that on a particular occasion the person or organization acted in accordance with the habit or routine practice."). The difference between character and habit is not always easily discernable. But an attorney who understands the underlying rationale and the distinction is in a better position to argue about the weight a judge ought to afford such evidence, even when the rules of evidence do not apply.

In other instances, the Federal Rules of Evidence prohibit admission of evidence not because the evidence is deemed unreliable or lacks probative value but because a policy judgment was made that admission of the evidence may deter socially beneficial conduct. For example, Federal Rule of Evidence 407 bars admission of evidence of subsequent remedial measures because we, as a society, want people or companies to take remedial measures to prevent future harms.[4] Were we to allow a litigant to use evidence against a company that the company changed the design of a product to make it safer after a person was injured, it would deter companies from making safer products. For similar reasons, the Federal Rules of Evidence bar admission of settlement negotiations,[5] offers to pay medical expenses,[6] plea negotiations,[7] and liability insurance.[8] This is not because the nature of this type of evidence makes it unreliable. It is because we, as a matter of social policy, want to encourage people to settle their disputes, pay medical expenses for others without having it be taken as an admission of fault, enter into plea negotiations without fear that what is said during negotiations will be used against parties, and for companies and people to carry insurance without it being offered as proof that the party intended to act negligently. In short, to be effective sentencing advocates, attorneys need to understand the reasoning underlying each rule to effectively argue how much weight the judge should give to evidence and why.

As a threshold matter then, to be effective sentencing advocates, attorneys should understand that the Federal Rules of Evidence do not apply at a sentencing hearing. That means the rules will not bar an attorney from presenting evidence in a sentencing hearing that would otherwise be inadmissible in a trial. Likewise, it also means that invoking the rules of evidence will not prevent the other side from presenting evidence that would be inadmissible under the Federal Rules of Evidence. In short, effective sentencing advocacy requires attorneys to learn how to deal with evidence in a hearing when there are no rules.

Generally speaking, it is inadvisable for attorneys to object to the admission of evidence at a sentencing hearing by invoking a rule of evidence. Although Federal Rules of Evidence simply do not apply at a sentencing hearing, in practice attorneys nevertheless repeatedly object to evidence by invoking the rules. Sentencing judges will simply overrule such objections as a matter of course, and perhaps attorneys thus think there may be no downside to lodging objections by citing the evidence rules. If a judge happens to forget that the Federal Rules of Evidence do not apply and sustains an objection, however, there is a potential that on appeal, it could be found to be reversable error, requiring a resentencing. Voicing an objection based on the Federal Rules of Evidence in a sentencing hearing also runs the risk of leading the sentencing judge to question the attorney's general competence, perhaps decreasing the attorney's persuasiveness.

That the Federal Rules of Evidence do not apply at a sentencing hearing does not mean, however, that they are irrelevant. As I discussed above, the Federal Rules of Evidence were enacted to protect jurors from exposure to unreliable evidence. The nature of the evidence that makes it unreliable under the evidence rules may also make it unreliable at a sentencing hearing. The task for attorneys at a sentencing hearing, then, is to persuade the sentencing judge to give such unreliable or irrelevant evidence little or no weight. To do this effectively, attorneys need to identify the reason under the rules of evidence that caused the drafters of the Federal Rules of Evidence to deem the piece of evidence unreliable. Attorneys should then articulate how that same reasoning should cause the sentencing judge to hesitate to rely on the evidence. For example, if an attorney introduces hearsay into evidence at a sentencing hearing, objecting to the testimony by invoking the hearsay rules will be ineffective. But arguing to the judge that the hearsay would be inadmissible had the rules applied and that the particular hearsay testimony at issue is unreliable because it lacks indicia of reliability may be effective in persuading the judge to either disregard the evidence completely or give it little weight. In short, instead of invoking the rules of evidence in sentencing hearings, attorneys should challenge the evidence in argument by invoking the reasoning underlying the rules of evidence.

Although the rules of evidence do not apply in sentencing hearings, that does not mean that proponents of evidence should ignore the evidence rules. Judges are trained and experienced in the rules of evidence. Judges understand that the rules exist to weed out unreliable evidence. It follows then that even when an attorney does not lodge an objection to the admission of evidence based on the rules of evidence, the judge is nevertheless likely to recognize that the evidence would not be admissible in a jury trial. As a result, the judge will likely be more skeptical of such evidence and give it less weight. Knowing this, effective attorneys should still strive to present evidence at a sentencing hearing that would be admissible under the rules. And when attorneys must present evidence that would be inadmissible under the rules of evidence, they should do so in a way that would bolster the reliability of the evidence. That is, attorneys should try to corroborate such evidence or provide additional background information that would show a judge why the evidence is nevertheless reliable. In argument, attorneys should acknowledge when they or opposing counsel presented evidence that would not have complied with the rules of evidence and explain why the reasons for the various rules should or should not lead the judge to give weight to such evidence.

B. Applicability of the Confrontation Clause

The Confrontation Clause in the Sixth Amendment to the United States Constitution protects criminal offenders from the "admission of testimonial statements of a witness who did not appear at trial unless [the witness] was unavailable to testify." *Crawford v. Washington*, 541 U.S. 36, 53–54 (2004). Nevertheless, this vital right does not apply at sentencing hearings.[9] This is because after an offender's guilt has been established, it has been deemed essential that judges should not be limited in the type of information they can rely on in determining the most appropriate sentence for an offender.[10] That does not mean, however, that the rationale for the Confrontation Clause is irrelevant to sentencing hearings. The rationale for the Confrontation Clause is important for sentencing hearings because sentencing judges recognize that confrontation through cross examination makes testimony more reliable. Cross examination has been recognized as "beyond doubt the greatest legal invention ever invented for the discovery of truth." 5 Wigmore § 1367 (Chadbourne ed.1974). Thus, judges will give more weight to evidence that withstands the crucible of cross examination than they will to hearsay evidence.

C. Applicability of the Due Process Clause

The Due Process Clause applies in sentencing hearings. Under the Due Process Clause, hearsay statements may be used at sentencing only if they bear "some minimal indicium of reliability beyond mere allegation." *United States v. Robinson*, 482 F.3d 244, 246 (3d Cir. 2007) (internal quotation omitted).[11] The Due Process Clause does not, however, incorporate the right of offenders to confront or cross-examine witnesses in sentencing hearings.[12] Determining whether hearsay evidence is sufficiently reliable to support a sentencing decision depends on the facts of the particular case and is committed to the sound discretion of the sentencing judge. In reviewing the reliability of hearsay and double hearsay evidence, courts consider factors such as the consistency of the hearsay testimony, the timing and nature of the declarant's statements, and the witness's impressions of the declarant's demeanor, as well as other corroborating evidence.

It is important to point out that Federal Rule of Criminal Procedure 32 does not require courts to allow parties to confront or cross examine witnesses. This contrasts with Rule 32.1, governing supervised release revocation hearings. Rule 32.1 specifically requires courts to allow parties to cross-examine witnesses. The difference is that at a supervised release revocation hearing, judges often resolve factual issues about whether the offender violated the conditions of supervised release, and thus may be punished. This, then, is akin to a finding of guilt, requiring greater due process rights. When testimony at a revocation hearing addresses only the extent of punishment, not whether the offender violated conditions and may be revoked, the Due Process Clause does not require that offenders be able to cross-examine witnesses. Chapter 28 discusses advocacy at revocation hearings and covers this issue in more detail. The point for purposes of this chapter is that the parties do not have either a statutory or constitutional right to confront or cross examine witnesses in sentencing hearings. That said, judges generally allow parties to cross-examine witnesses at sentencing hearings. As noted above, judges are also more likely to give greater weight to testimony that stands up to cross examination.

D. *Presentation of Evidence*

To be persuasive in the presentation of evidence at a sentencing hearing, attorneys need to keep in mind that the sentencing judge is the factfinder. This means that evidence should be presented in a manner that ensures the judge can see, hear, and comprehend the evidence. Attorneys are so trained and used to presenting evidence to jurors as factfinders that they sometimes forget to reorient the presentation of evidence to the judge when the judge is the factfinder. As a practical matter, orienting the evidentiary presentation to judges means that attorneys should take several steps in preparation for and presentation of evidence in sentencing hearings. Attorneys should provide sentencing judges with copies of all exhibits, preferably in advance of the sentencing hearing. Attorneys should direct witnesses to speak to the judge in answering questions and make eye contact with the judge during testimony. If attorneys use demonstrative exhibits, attorneys need to make sure the exhibits face the judge in a way that the judge can easily see the exhibit. Attorneys should watch judges' reactions to evidence, much as they watch jurors' reactions, to assess how judges are receiving the evidence.

Because judges are factfinders, and the Federal Rules of Evidence do not apply, it opens up the possibility of presenting evidence to judges in advance of the sentencing hearings. Indeed, some local court rules or judges' orders require parties to submit copies of exhibits to the judge in advance of sentencing hearings. As a general observation, attorneys should take advantage of the opportunity to provide judges with copies of exhibits in advance of sentencing hearings, even when it is not required. This is particularly true if the evidence consists of video or audio recordings or lengthy written documents. Judges are very busy, and court time is a limited resource. If a judge can review the evidence in advance of the sentencing hearing in chambers and on the judge's own schedule, it allows the judge to be better prepared for the sentencing hearing while simultaneously reducing the expenditure of limited courtroom time.

Attorneys should consider a few matters, however, when providing judges with exhibits in advance of a sentencing hearing. Not all exhibits are self-explanatory. Judges may not know what it is they should be looking for in a video or in a lengthy document without some direction from the attorney. I can tell you from experience that it is frustrating to receive such evidence in advance of a hearing without a clue as to what I should be looking for in a long video or in hundreds of pages of medical records. Attorneys can provide such direction in their sentencing memoranda. Attorneys can also provide direction to judges in exhibit lists by not just listing the exhibit numbers and description of the exhibit, but by also providing some explanation about the exhibit (e.g., Exhibit 34: Videotape of traffic stop showing offender resisting arrest beginning at 23:45 hr). Finally, attorneys can assist the judge by highlighting or underlining pertinent parts of a documentary exhibit or even by adding marginal commentary to the exhibit to explain the significance of an entry.

Even when attorneys submit exhibits to judges in advance of sentencing hearings, attorneys should carefully consider the extent to which attorneys have witnesses discuss the exhibits in the sentencing hearing. Although some exhibits may not need further explanation, others may. A judge may be able to fully comprehend

an exhibit and appreciate its import. To be persuasive, however, it may be best to have a witness discuss the exhibit and explain in more detail its significance. The fact the judge had the exhibit in advance of trial to examine is still helpful because the judge will at least be familiar with its general outlines and may be able to better understand the testimony. Attorneys should not assume, however, that the judge focused on the portion of the exhibit that is most important in the attorneys' mind. It may also be important to have witnesses provide some explanation of an exhibit so there is a good record for purposes of appeal.

Attorneys may find, in rare instances, that it is best not to provide the judge with copies of an exhibit in advance of the sentencing hearing. It is possible that an exhibit may be confusing to a judge without an explanation that cannot be adequately provided without live testimony. Similarly, a judge may form a mistaken and prejudicial impression from viewing an exhibit in advance of a sentencing hearing without a thorough, contemporaneous explanation by a live witness. Finally, an attorney may feel that an exhibit will have more emotional impact on a sentencing judge if the judge sees it for the first time at the sentencing hearing and fear that if the judge viewed it too far in advance of trial, the impact may be lost. When attorneys are not required to submit exhibits to a sentencing judge in advance of a sentencing hearing, then these tactical considerations may persuade an attorney that it is best not to do so. These should be very rare instances, however. On balance, it is generally far better to provide the sentencing judge with copies of exhibits in advance of a sentencing hearing.

Attorneys should also cull exhibits for presentation to judges at sentencing hearings in the same way they would do so in a trial when jurors are the factfinders. Attorneys should not submit lengthy exhibits to judges without making an effort to reduce the exhibit to the relevant, pertinent part of the exhibit. For example, attorneys have submitted medical records scores of pages in length as a sentencing exhibit when the only portion of the exhibit that had any relevance to the hearing might be two pages of laboratory results. Similarly, attorneys have submitted video and audio recordings that are sometimes hours in length when the only relevant portion of the recordings may be a five-minute clip. No good attorney would submit such exhibits to jurors; attorneys would redact the exhibit to cull it down in a manner to emphasize the one relevant part of the exhibit. For some reason, when judges are the factfinders, attorneys apparently feel as if they need not do this. Conscientious judges, though, feel compelled to watch every minute of any videotape and read every page of any written exhibit submitted as evidence in a sentencing hearing. Not only does submitting extraneous and irrelevant evidence to a judge run the risk of annoying the judge and perhaps affecting the attorney's persuasiveness, it also runs the risk that the judge will miss the important part of the evidence on which the attorney wanted the judge to focus.

E. Engaging in a Conversation with the Sentencing Judge

In trials, jurors would often love to be able to ask questions of witnesses to better understand the evidence. Attorneys would love to know what jurors were thinking of evidence during a trial. In trials, the former is possible only when judges permit it under contrived circumstances; the latter is never possible except by trying to read meaning into questions when allowed or expressions when made. In trials, attorneys cannot engage in a conversation with jurors. In sentencing hearings, when judges are the factfinders, both are possible. Judges can question witnesses and attorneys. It is possible that an exchange of communication can take place, a form of conversation, which increases the likelihood of a full understanding of the attorneys' positions.

Judges act within their discretion to question witnesses at a sentencing hearing.[13] It is not uncommon, then, for judges to ask questions of witnesses during sentencing hearings. As factfinders, judges strive to fully understand the evidence. Judges may ask questions to probe deeper into areas covered by the attorneys' questions or to explore areas not addressed by the attorneys' questions. Rather than bristle at judge-questioning, attorneys should embrace and exploit such questioning. As with questions from judges during appellate arguments, questions from judges during sentencing hearings reveal what judges are thinking or at least what they may be focused on or confused about. Attorneys should pay close attention to judges' questions and witnesses' answers to them. Attorneys should then ask appropriate follow-up questions to ensure judges have a full and accurate understanding of the facts or issues that were the subject of the judges' questions.

Some judges may also welcome questions of them from attorneys about the evidence. Attorneys may want to inquire of judges whether they have questions about any exhibits submitted to the judge in advance of the sentencing hearing, for example. Similarly, if a judge's questions of a witness concern an attorney that perhaps the judge misunderstands the evidence or is mistakenly focused on a matter that appears to the attorney to be irrelevant, the attorney may want to ask the judge about it. Attorneys should always be careful not to offend the judge in these circumstances, but a respectful inquiry about the judge's concerns could be appropriate. An attorney may ask, for example, "Your honor, I want to make sure that I am providing the court with the evidence it needs to resolve this case; could you explain your concern that prompted your question to the witness so that I may be sure to address that concern with my evidence?" It is important again to know the judge and whether the judge would be receptive to such an exchange. If the judge is receptive to questions, it could open up a real conversation between the judge, the attorneys, and the witnesses that will increase the likelihood that the attorneys are effectively presenting evidence to the judge in a manner they intended and that the judge is understanding the evidence as the attorneys intended. Although the judge may disagree with the attorneys' understanding of the evidence, and will almost inevitably disagree with one of the attorneys' views of the evidence, at least a conversation will ensure that the judge fully understands both side's views of the evidence.

F. Record on Appeal

Attorneys should always have an eye on the record for purposes of appeal. This may mean that they should present evidence at a sentencing hearing that may not really be needed if all the attorney needed to worry about was persuading the sentencing judge. For a good appellate record, attorneys may need to elicit testimony that would be strictly unnecessary for the sentencing judge. For example, a sentencing judge may have had a particular law enforcement officer testify scores of times before and may be very familiar with the officer's training and experience. Nevertheless, that background familiarity is not part of a record on appeal upon which the party or appellate judges can rely. An appellate court may consider an officer's level of training and experience important in evaluating whether the sentencing court abused its discretion in crediting testimony from the witness.

Similarly, a sentencing judge may know other facts from experience, but there still needs to be an evidentiary record for purposes of appeal. For example, an experienced sentencing judge may be quite familiar with various drug quantities and be able to determine from past experience whether an offender with several ounces of methamphetamine likely possessed the controlled substances for redistribution or for personal use. Likewise, an experienced sentencing judge may well know that firearms are tools of the drug trade. Yet, if there is no testimony about these matters at the sentencing hearing, then there is no factual basis upon which an appellate court can rely to affirm a district court's findings. It is incumbent upon the attorneys to ensure that they produce evidence in the record to support factual conclusions they are relying on, even if they are otherwise confident the sentencing judge does not need the evidence to make the finding.

13

Departures for Substantial Assistance

The most frequently invoked Guidelines departure is for substantial assistance. When an offender provides substantial assistance to the government in the investigation or prosecution of another person, the government, and the government alone, can make a motion under USSG §5K1.1 for a downward departure from the advisory Guidelines range. Indeed, under Title 18, United States Code, Section 3553(e), the government may make a substantial assistance motion that would permit the court to sentence an offender even below any statutory mandatory minimum sentence. Because this is the most frequently invoked ground for departure, and because there are several unique sentencing advocacy issues surrounding such departures on this ground versus on other grounds, departures for substantial assistance deserves its own chapter. Here I will review the statutory and Guidelines provisions relating to substantial assistance, consider the implications of unsuccessful attempts to provide substantial assistance, examine the overriding security interests implicated whenever an offender cooperates against others, and discuss advocacy skills and options related to when offenders provide, or attempt to provide, substantial assistance to the government. In the next chapter I will examine other grounds for departures from the advisory Guidelines range.

A. Statutory and Guidelines Provisions

Section 5K1.1 of the Federal Sentencing Guidelines provides that "[u]pon motion of the government stating that the defendant has provided substantial assistance" in investigating or prosecuting another person, the court may depart from the sentencing Guidelines. USSG §5K1.1. There is no statutory or Guidelines requirement that substantial assistance motions be in writing. Nor are there any rules dictating the form the motion must take, unless a district court adopts local rules doing so. In practice, most substantial assistance motions are made orally, and this is in part due to security concerns that will be discussed shortly.

The authority to make a substantial assistance motion lies solely with the government. A defense attorney cannot invoke Section 5K1.1 or make a motion for a downward departure. A sentencing court likewise has no authority to grant a downward departure on the basis of substantial assistance absent a motion by the government. Section 5K1.1 grants the government the power, not an obligation, to file a departure motion when an offender has provided substantial assistance. *Wade v. United States*, 504 U.S. 181, 184 (1992). A court's authority to review a prosecutor's refusal to exercise its discretion not to move for a Section 5K1.1 departure is limited to determining whether the refusal was animated by an unconstitutional motive. An "unconstitutional motive" would exist if a prosecutor refused to file a Section 5K1.1 departure motion "because of the defendant's race or religion" or for any other reason "not rationally related to any legitimate Government end." *Wade*, 504 U.S. at 186.

The government may bargain away its substantial assistance departure discretion under the terms of a plea agreement, however, and obligate itself to move for a downward departure in exchange for the offender's substantial assistance.[1] When the government has bargained away its discretion in this manner, the only remaining inquiry is whether the aid rendered by the offender constitutes substantial assistance as that term was reasonably understood by the parties at the time that they entered into the plea agreement.[2] This may require the parties to present evidence about the offender's cooperation, if there is a factual dispute about it, and for the judge ultimately to make a judgment call about whether that assistance was "substantial."

If the government makes a downward departure motion under Section 5K1.1, the court may grant or deny the motion. In determining whether to grant a Section 5K1.1 departure motion and, if granted, the extent of the downward departure, the sentencing judge must consider certain factors. Guidelines Section 5K1.1 states:

> (a) The appropriate reduction shall be determined by the court for reasons stated that may include, but are not limited to, consideration of the following:
>
> (1) the court's evaluation of the significance and usefulness of the defendant's assistance, taking into consideration the government's evaluation of the assistance rendered;
> (2) the truthfulness, completeness, and reliability of any information or testimony provided by the defendant;
> (3) the nature and extent of the defendant's assistance;
> (4) any injury suffered, or any danger or risk of injury to the defendant or his family resulting from his assistance;
> (5) the timeliness of the defendant's assistance.

USSG §5K1.1(a).

If the government believes the extent of an offender's cooperation is sufficiently significant to warrant a sentencing reduction below any applicable mandatory minimum sentence, it may also move under Title 18, United States Code, Section 3553(e), for the court to reduce the offender's sentence below any applicable mandatory minimum sentences. Like a motion under Section 5K1.1, the discretion to file a Section 3553(e) motion lies solely with the government. An offender cannot file such a motion and, absent such a motion by the government, the court may not sentence an offender below an applicable statutory mandatory minimum sentence. In some instances, the government may make a motion under Guidelines Section 5K1.1, but not under 18 U.S.C. § 3553(e), essentially establishing a floor below which the judge cannot go in awarding a sentencing reduction for substantial assistance.

Title 18, United States Code, Section 3553(e) provides:

> **Limited authority to impose a sentence below a statutory minimum.**—Upon motion of the Government, the court shall have the authority to impose a sentence below a level established by statute as a minimum sentence so as to reflect a defendant's substantial assistance in the investigation or prosecution of another person who has committed an offense. Such sentence shall be imposed in accordance with the guidelines and policy statements issued by the Sentencing Commission pursuant to section 994 of title 28, United States Code.

18 U.S.C. § 3553(e). Importantly, when determining whether to grant the motion, and the extent of any departure, a sentencing court may only consider the offender's cooperation and no other factors under Section 3553(a). This is because a judge has no authority to sentence an offender under a statutory minimum sentence except on grounds expressly authorized by Congress. Thus, in advocating for a sentencing departure under a Section 3553(e) motion, attorneys should be careful not to create error by arguing that the judge should consider any other factors or information other than the offender's cooperation.

B. Unsuccessful Attempted Substantial Assistance

Sometimes offenders do their best to cooperate, but that cooperation does not rise to the level of substantial assistance in the government's view such that the prosecutor does not make a motion for a Section 5K1.1 or Section 3553(e) departure. When this occurs, defense attorneys have two options. First, a defense attorney may file a motion to compel the government to make a Section 5K1.1 departure motion. As noted, the government has sole discretion in determining whether to make a Section 5K1.1 departure motion. Thus, a defense attorney can base a motion to compel the government to act only upon a showing of evidence that the government either breached a plea agreement in which it promised to make a Section 5K1.1 departure motion, or the government's refusal to make the motion is premised on an improper basis under the Constitution. An offender has the burden of proof on motions to compel a Section 5K1.1 departure motion. When the motion is premised on an allegation of improper motive, the offender has the burden of making a "substantial threshold showing" of that improper motive. *Wade*, 504 U.S. at 186. Mere unsubstantiated assertions or conjecture are insufficient.

Second, if the defense attorney does not believe there are grounds to compel the government to make a substantial assistance departure motion, the defense attorney may still apprise the sentencing judge of the offender's efforts and the effects of those efforts. Indeed, prosecutors should also make judges aware of failed good-faith attempts by an offender to cooperate. Although the judge will not have the authority to depart downward from the advisory Guidelines, the sentencing judge may still consider the offender's good faith efforts to cooperate in determining the offender's ultimate sentence. A defense attorney may also file a motion asking the judge to vary downward from the advisory Guidelines range for an offender's attempt to cooperate and provide substantial assistance. This is true even if the government did not file a Section 5K1.1 departure motion and even if the prosecutor disagrees.[3]

Thus, whether the government makes a Section 5K1.1 substantial assistance departure motion, both attorneys should be prepared to address at the sentencing hearing the nature of an offender's attempted cooperation. Attorneys should be prepared to describe the nature and extent of the cooperation, opine as to whether the offender did so honestly and in good faith, and describe the impact of that cooperation on the offender and others.

C. Secrecy and Security Issues Relating to Substantial Assistance Motions

When offenders cooperate with the government in the investigation and prosecution of others, they put themselves and their loved ones at risk. The criminal world can be violent, and criminals generally abhor cooperators. Criminals have many pejorative terms for those who cooperate, such as snitch, snake, and rat. Not surprisingly, then, some offenders who have cooperated with the government in an effort to earn a Section 5K1.1 departure motion have ended up injured or killed, and sometimes their family members have suffered as well. In my district, we have had offenders killed because they cooperated with the government's investigation. In one case in our district, an offender cooperated but ultimately declined the government's Section 5K1.1 departure motion, willingly accepting a very long sentence rather than risk any possibility that he would be labeled a snitch out of concern for his own safety and that of his family.

It is essential then for all involved in the criminal justice system that an offender's cooperation be kept as secret as possible. In public courtrooms with public access to court files, keeping cooperation secret is not an easy goal to attain. Attorneys should make every effort possible, however, to maintain the confidentiality of an offender's cooperation. This includes, at a minimum, ensuring that any document reflecting cooperation is filed under seal. This means that any plea agreement or other pleading mentioning the offender's cooperation be filed under seal, and that any publicly filed document not include a word about cooperation. This is why Section 5K1.1 departure motions are often made orally so as to minimize the chance that a written motion would somehow be disclosed or fall into the wrong hands.

Maintaining the confidentiality of an offender's cooperation also requires that the portion of the sentencing hearing when an offender's cooperation or a Section 5K1.1 departure motion is discussed is conducted outside the presence of the public, and the proceedings are sealed. Some judges accomplish this by emptying the courtroom, while others may take up the matter at sidebar when white noise prevents anyone else in the courtroom from hearing the discussion. It has been my experience that attorneys are not always sufficiently disciplined about the need for keeping an offender's cooperation out of the public record. I have conducted sentencing hearings, for example, when the offender's cooperation and the government's substantial assistance motion is taken up at sidebar and under seal and then, shortly after we resume the hearing in open court, one or both of the attorneys will mention the offender's cooperation in the open on the unsealed record. Attorneys should be vigilant so as not to disclose offenders' cooperation in any way in the public record.

Still, there are many means that criminals and criminal organizations have developed to defeat efforts by the criminal justice system to protect cooperators from retaliation. For example, some criminal organizations have associates who pay for access to the federal courts public filing system and routinely search docket reports of suspected cooperators to determine if there are indications of cooperation. Although courts can and do seal pleadings dealing with cooperation from the public, criminals may view the very existence of a notation on the docket sheet that a sealed document was filed at or near the time of the sentencing hearing as a sign that the offender has cooperated. Criminals are also sufficiently savvy enough to know about mandatory minimum sentences and the Guidelines. They are often able to reconstruct an offender's likely statutory and Guidelines sentencing ranges. If an offender's judgment reflects a sentence below a mandatory minimum or below the anticipated Guidelines range, criminals may then assume the offender cooperated. With advisory Guidelines, now, this assumption has less validity because a court may vary below the advisory Guidelines range for any number of reasons. Criminals are not always so discerning.

Similarly, those wishing to harm cooperators work hard to get copies of offenders' presentence reports. When offenders arrive at federal prisons, they are often confronted by other inmates who demand that the offender get a copy of the offender's presentence report, which may include information about the offender's cooperation. If the offender does not produce the presentence report, the other inmates may assume the offender cooperated. Presentence reports are court property, filed under seal, and the parties are not allowed to disseminate copies of the presentence report to anyone else. Nevertheless, enforcers at prisons will attempt to get around this through various efforts, including having the offender or family member attempt to get a copy from the offender's defense attorney. There are also efforts sometimes made to have third parties purport to be working on behalf of offenders in an alleged innocence project effort or the like and directly solicit the court for copies of offenders' presentence reports, ostensibly to help the offenders when, in reality, they are working for a criminal organization intended to identify cooperators.

Effective sentencing advocacy may, however, compel a defense attorney to ensure that when an offender has not cooperated, there are publicly filed documents that clearly indicate the lack of cooperation. This is one reason why defense attorneys will sometimes have their clients enter guilty pleas under plea agreements that are bare bones and do not really provide their clients any benefits except to have it in writing that it was a noncooperation plea deal. This allows noncooperating offenders to go to prison and readily produce documentation to the enforcers to prove that the offender did not cooperate. In these cases, defense attorneys may want a plea agreement to be filed publicly and to explicitly state that the offender is not cooperating. This, of course, runs the risk of highlighting the fact that other offenders are cooperating when their plea agreements are filed under seal. Defense attorneys have an obligation to zealously represent the interest of each client individually and separately, though, so this may obligate a defense attorney on one case to ensure documents show a client is not cooperating even though that effort may highlight in another case that another client is cooperating.

This is a complicated and troubling issue for attorneys, the court, and the prisons. It is critically important that attorneys are fully aware of the need to protect offenders who cooperate from retaliation for doing so, and that attorneys remain vigilant to keep offenders' cooperation completely confidential at all times.

D. Advocacy and Substantial Assistance

When the government makes a motion for a downward departure for substantial assistance under Guidelines Section 5K1.1, there is a role for attorneys to advocate. The government should fully and precisely describe the nature and extent of the offender's cooperation, addressing each of the factors under Section 5K1.1. Prosecutors should explain why they are making the recommendation to depart to the extent they recommend. Defense attorneys should be prepared, however, to ensure that the government's description of the offender's cooperation is complete and accurate. Each attorney may opine as to the significance of the offender's cooperation and the extent of the downward departure. Here, as in any form of advocacy, words matter. The words attorneys use to describe an offender's cooperation—"completely truthful" v. "largely candid," "helped the government dismantle and destroy the drug organization" v. "allowed the government to make marginal inroads investigating the drug organization"—can have a significant impact on the judge's perception and assessment of significance of the cooperation and the extent of departure warranted. In the end, the goal of sentencing advocacy, including advocacy related to substantial assistance departure motions, is to persuade sentencing judges. Thus, attorneys should put very careful thought into how they articulate their positions about a substantial assistance motion.

The government is in the best position to assess the usefulness of an offender's cooperation. Judges will have little basis upon which to make such an assessment, not knowing all the facts or how the offender's cooperation fits into or advances the government's other cases, especially when it involves an ongoing investigation. Likewise, the defense attorney will not have access to all the government's information or an appreciation of how the offender's cooperation fits into the government's overall investigation strategy. Thus, in advocating for a substantial assistance motion, the government clearly has the advantage. Nevertheless, the government can jeopardize that advantage by doing a poor job articulating the grounds for the departure and the extent of the recommended departure. Defense attorneys can enhance their own position at this stage of a sentencing hearing by participating as much as possible in the offender's cooperation and by insisting that the government keep the defense attorney as informed as possible. This means, for instance, that defense attorneys should attend any debriefing or proffer the offender provides as part of the cooperation effort. It also means that the defense attorney should have the offender fully apprise the defense attorney of what the offender said if called to testify before the grand jury. Further, if the offender testifies during a hearing or trial as part of the offender's cooperation, the defense attorney should be personally present and take notes to be used later when discussing the offender's cooperation with the judge.

E. Substantial Assistance After Sentencing

Under Rule 35 of the Federal Rules of Criminal Procedure, the government may move for a reduction of an offender's sentence for substantial assistance provided after the sentencing hearing. Rule 35(b) provides:

> **Reducing a Sentence for Substantial Assistance.**
> (1) **In General.** Upon the government's motion made within one year of sentencing, the court may reduce a sentence if the defendant, after sentencing, provided substantial assistance in investigating or prosecuting another person.
> (2) **Later Motion.** Upon the government's motion made more than one year after sentencing, the court may reduce a sentence if the defendant's substantial assistance involved:
> (A) information not known to the defendant until one year or more after sentencing;
> (B) information provided by the defendant to the government within one year of sentencing, but which did not become useful to the government until more than one year after sentencing; or
> (C) information the usefulness of which could not reasonably have been anticipated by the defendant until more than one year after sentencing and which was promptly provided to the government after its usefulness was reasonably apparent to the defendant.
> (3) **Evaluating Substantial Assistance.** In evaluating whether the defendant has provided substantial assistance, the court may consider the defendant's presentence assistance.
> (4) **Below Statutory Minimum.** When acting under Rule 35(b), the court may reduce the sentence to a level below the minimum sentence established by statute.

FED. R. CRIM. P. 35(b). Like with Section 5K1.1 departure motions, Rule 35(b) motions are within the sole discretion of the government to make. Offenders cannot move courts under Rule 35(b) to reduce their sentences, nor can judges do so on their own authority. And like Section 5K1.1 departure motions, offenders may only challenge the government's failure to make Rule 35(b) motions if the failure to do so constitutes a breach of a plea agreement or if the government's refused to make the Rule 35(b) motion for an unconstitutional reason.

Sometimes it occurs that at the time of the offender's sentencing hearing, the government does not make a Section 5K1.1 departure motion for substantial assistance because the government has not yet been able to fully use the offender's cooperation to advance another case. In other instances, the government makes a Section 5K1.1 departure motion at the sentencing hearing and later makes a Rule 35(b) motion for the same offender, either because of new cooperation after the sentencing hearing or because the full fruition of the offender's prior cooperation did not occur until after his sentencing hearing.

Defense attorneys may want to consider whether it is in their clients' best interest to seek a delay in the sentencing hearing in situations when offenders have cooperated, and it appears possible that in the near future that cooperation will constitute substantial assistance. Prosecutors will likely be reluctant to share with defense attorneys the status of an ongoing investigation, but in other cases the information may be readily apparent to defense counsel. Perhaps, for instance, an offender has cooperated against a co-conspirator whose trial is scheduled only a few weeks hence when it is likely the government will call the offender as a witness. Or, perhaps, the prosecutor has advised the defense attorney that the offender will be testifying before the grand jury in a week or two. Although it is always possible, with Rule 35(b), that the government will ultimately make a motion to reduce the offender's sentence to reward the offender for cooperating, the defense attorney has more control and influence over the matter at the time of sentencing than will be possible at any later date. On the other hand, the defense attorney should weigh the consequences of delaying the sentencing hearing. If the offender is incarcerated, that means more time in a local jail or holding facility without access to the programming and treatment options that would be available to the offender in prison. If the offender is released pending the sentencing hearing, a delay in the sentencing hearing may provide the offender more opportunities to show strides in rehabilitation or, conversely, violate the terms of presentencing release. As noted, when an offender attempts to cooperate but the government does not make a Section 5K1.1 departure motion because in its view the cooperation did not amount to substantial assistance, a defense attorney may ask a court to vary downward under Section 3553(a) for the offender's attempted cooperation. Even if the government later moves for a reduction of an offender's sentence for substantial assistance under Rule 35(b), a court is barred from considering any cooperation the offender provided before the sentencing hearing. Thus, an offender's unsuccessful attempt before sentencing to provide substantial assistance cannot be considered by a sentencing judge except in the form of a motion for a downward variance, even if the government later moves for a reduction under Rule 35(b) for post-sentencing cooperation.

Finally, for defense attorneys to assess how to approach this issue, it is important to know that Rule 35(b) motions may be conducted ex parte, without the presence of the offender and without defense counsel. Federal Rule of Criminal Procedure 43(b) provides, "[a] defendant need not be present … [when t]he proceeding involves the correction or reduction of sentence under Rule 35 …." Fed. R. Crim. P. 43(b)(4). Further, an offender does not have a right to counsel during Rule 35(b) sentence reduction proceedings.[4] The reason many constitutional rights afforded to offenders at sentencing hearings are not required in Rule 35(b) proceedings is because of the Rule's discretionary nature and because an offender faces no new threat of loss of liberty in a Rule 35(b) hearing. Indeed, a Rule 35(b) motion can only serve to reduce an offender's sentence. As a practical matter, it is also often the case that by the time the government makes a Rule 35(b) motion, the defense attorney may no longer represent the offender. This is all the more reason that defense attorneys may wish to delay sentencing hearings or seek a variance for attempted cooperation rather than count on the government later filing a Rule 35(b) motion.

Although offenders have no legal right to counsel or to be present or participate in Rule 35(b) motions, judges often have both defense counsel and offenders participate in these hearings. When judges do not routinely involve offender and defense counsel in Rule 35(b) hearings, defense counsel may want to advocate for a seat at the table. Defense counsel should recognize that there are benefits and detriments to having offenders and defense attorneys participate in Rule 35(b) hearings. One benefit is that the offender and defense attorney may have information relevant to the Rule 35(b) motion that the prosecutor does not. One factor in determining the extent of any departure for substantial assistance is the extent to which the cooperation has exposed the offender and his family to harm. The offender is likely to have greater access to this information than the government. Defense counsel may also view the offender's cooperation as more significant than the government and may be able to articulate why it was more significant. On the other hand, for an offender to participate in a Rule 35(b) hearing, the offender either must be brought back to the district or participate by phone. Transportation of an offender back to the district to appear in court exposes the offender to the hardship of travel, including repeated strip searches, and the interruption and possible loss of programming and job opportunities in the institution where the offender is serving time. Such travel may alert other inmates that the offender has cooperated. Even participation by telephone can be problematic in that other inmates may learn or discern the purpose of the phone call, just like they would the purpose of the offender being transported back to the district for a hearing. When an inmate participates in a Rule 35(b) hearing by telephone from a prison, it requires staff to retrieve and move the inmate to another room where the offender can have access to a telephone. Other inmates may become aware of this movement, draw a conclusion that the inmate has cooperated, and thus expose the offender to potential harm for cooperating. Defense counsel and offenders may want to consider having offenders waive their right to personally participate in Rule 35(b) hearings for these reasons. Offenders may still benefit from working with their defense counsel to prepare for the hearings and from having the defense attorney participate in the hearing on the offender's behalf, while simultaneously avoiding the potential adverse impact of having the offender personally appear in person or telephonically in the hearing.

As a practical matter, it may be difficult in any event for a defense attorney to try to get a seat at the table in a Rule 35(b) hearing if one is not offered. As noted, most judges allow offenders to participate and appoint counsel. When judges do not do so though, and the motion is made ex parte, defense counsel may not even be aware of it in advance and thus may have no chance to ask to participate or for the offender to be present. Even if the defense attorney somehow becomes aware that the motion will be filed, the defense attorney may no longer be representing the offender; these hearings sometimes take place years after the sentencing hearing. If a defense attorney becomes aware or believes the government may file a Rule 35(b) motion, the first advocacy step may be to contact the prosecutor and express a desire for the offender and defense counsel to participate. If the prosecutor is open to the idea, then that may help the effort. The defense attorney may need to file a motion to request the court to allow the offender to participate. If the offender is indigent, the motion may need to also request the appointment of counsel. In districts where courts routinely handle Rule 35(b) motions ex parte with the government only, this all may be a hard sell. However, it may be worth it.

14

Other Departures

As noted in Chapter 4 of this book, the Guidelines contain provisions in Chapter 5 identifying grounds that do, and do not, support departures from advisory Guidelines ranges. And as also was noted, grounds for departures are also occasionally found in Chapter 2, Chapter 3, and Chapter 4 Guidelines provisions. Federal judges have historically departed downward from the Guidelines with much greater frequency than they have departed upward.[1] Of course, a large percentage of these downward departures are for substantial assistance under USSG §5K1.1. Even when those substantial assistance departures are not considered, however, judges still tend to depart downward far more often than they depart upward.

In deciding whether to seek an upward or downward departure from the Guidelines, attorneys should first search the Guidelines for departure provisions. Then they should research the case law on departures, recognizing that the Guidelines and the case law applying them have changed over time. Attorneys should also consider the interplay between departures and variances. Finally, in arguing for departures, attorneys need to marshal evidence, persuasively weave the evidence into the departure ground, and consider the extent of departure sought.

A. *Searching for Departure Grounds*

As part of a party's Presentence Investigation Statement, attorneys should carefully comb the Guidelines to identify possible departure grounds. They should do so again after receiving the draft and final presentence report. This search requires attorneys to carefully read the Guidelines provisions applicable to the case in Chapters 2, 3 and 4. In all likelihood, attorneys will not have a good feel for whether a departure for under- or over-statement of criminal history might be appropriate until they receive the draft presentence report after the probation officer has compiled the offender's comprehensive criminal history. Other grounds for departure are based on the facts of the offense or offender and are more likely to be readily determinable at the time attorneys draft their Presentence Investigation Statement.

In their Presentence Investigation Statements and in objections to draft presentence reports, attorneys should identify any departures they believe might be applicable that would be favorable to their client's position. Prosecutors should also identify any potential departures that would be favorable to the offender, even if the prosecutor fully intends to oppose any such departure. Indeed, in the Presentence Investigation Statement, the prosecutor can articulate why the court should not depart downward. Even if a party does not identify or support departure grounds that may be favorable to the other side, they should at least take note of them because they may have to litigate the issue later. Attorneys may realize that there are factual gaps and, to effectively advocate for or against a departure, further investigation is warranted. For example, application note 7 to USSG §2L1.3 provides that a downward departure may be appropriate in a case involving immigration offenses on the basis of cultural assimilation, which considers such things as the offender's age when the offender first began residing in the United States, whether and how long the offender attended school in the United States, and the offender's duration of residence in and outside the United States, among other things. None of this information that is important for determining whether this departure is appropriate may have been uncovered in the normal course of the criminal investigation. Thus, it may be necessary to conduct further investigation to determine whether there are facts that would or would not support this departure. These facts may often already be contained in the PSR, but not always.

Indeed, it is important for both sides to investigate potential grounds for departures, upward and downward, as soon as the potential for them becomes apparent. For example, when an offender is charged with being a felon in possession of a firearm, but the context in which the offender possessed the firearm was a shooting or killing, there is a potential upward departure under Guidelines section 5K2.6. Because of this departure, the sentencing hearing can turn into a minitrial, in some cases resembling a murder trial. This will require substantial investments in time and resources to investigate the case far beyond what would be necessary if the offender was being sentenced only for being a prohibited person in possession of a firearm.

B. Departure Case Law

During the two decades that the Guidelines were mandatory, departures were the only means by which judges could sentence offenders outside the Guidelines range. Thus, departures became a hotly contested area of sentencing litigation. This in turn resulted in a large body of case law on departures. Since the Guidelines have become advisory only, litigation over and legal opinions about departures has dropped off considerably. That is because attorneys now often rely on motions to vary from the advisory Guidelines range instead, for reasons explained in the next section.

Attorneys should therefore be discerning when researching and cautious before relying on Guidelines departure precedent. Most of the case law about departures is from the time of mandatory Guidelines, and opinions may be worded in a manner that may no longer be binding or persuasive. Further, the Federal Sentencing Guidelines Commission has amended many of the departure Guidelines as part of efforts to reform the federal criminal justice system. As a result, some departure grounds (such as age of the offender) that the case law once said was a prohibited ground for a departure is no longer prohibited.

With that caution in mind, attorneys seeking or resisting departures should carefully research the case law for analogous cases when courts have addressed the departure ground. Departure grounds are fact-intensive in nature. Further, even when grounds exist to support a departure, judges are not bound to do so. Judges have a degree of discretion to decide whether to depart or not to depart from the advisory Guidelines range. Thus, prior cases will rarely constitute binding precedent compelling or prohibiting a departure. On the other hand, these cases are valuable sources for making effective arguments for or against departures. Attorneys may find in them arguments they had not considered or identify facts which were key for other judges' departure decisions that may lead attorneys into further investigation into their own cases to look for similar facts.

C. Interplay Between Departures and Variances

In considering whether to seek a departure, attorneys have to consider how departures and variances relate to each other. A party may seek a departure from the advisory Guidelines range, or seek a variance under the Section 3553(a) factors from the advisory Guidelines range, or both. A tactical consideration is whether attorneys should seek one, or both, based on the same facts.

Generally speaking, attorneys should seek departures when there is a colorable basis for doing so, but argue in the alternative that the judge should vary on the same ground even if the judge finds a departure inappropriate. The propriety of a departure may turn on the precise language of the Guidelines departure provision, as interpreted by precedent. However, in varying from the advisory Guidelines range, judges are not bound by the language of any Guidelines departure provisions. Thus, judges may find they have more leeway to sentence outside the advisory Guidelines range through a variance than by way of a departure.

On the other hand, if a party succeeds in persuading a judge to depart from the Guidelines range based on a particular fact, then it is unlikely that the judge will also vary downward based on the same reason (although there is nothing in Section 3553[a] that would strictly prohibit it). Thus, if a departure would be a close call and a hard sell, it may be more effective for the attorney to ask for a variance on the same grounds instead of asking the judge to depart and risk losing the issue on appeal.

If an attorney chooses to seek both a departure and a variance on largely the same grounds, the attorney may want to consider articulating departure and variance grounds slightly differently so as to increase the chance that a judge may both depart and vary. Certainly, the grounds for a variance are generally much more comprehensive than the narrower grounds for a departure. For example, an offender may seek a downward departure because of the offender's youth under Guidelines Section 5H1.1, but a downward variance motion may include age as only one of many grounds, along with the absence of a father figure, childhood abuse, or others. Even when the grounds overlap, attorneys may want to articulate the grounds differently. For example, Guidelines Section 5H1.11 provides that "[m]ilitary service may be relevant in determining whether a departure is warranted, if the military service … is present to an unusual degree and distinguishes the case from the typical cases covered from the guidelines." In moving for a downward departure under this Section, the defense attorney may focus on the offender's military career, exposure to combat, and field decorations and medals. In moving for a downward variance, on the other hand, the attorney may focus on the sacrifice the offender made for the United States, the extent to which military discipline decreases the likelihood of reoffending, or other consequences or attributes of military service that have nothing to do with the offender's accomplishments as a soldier.

Finally, attorneys should be disciplined about their use of terminology. Departures and variances are two separate things; sentencing judges address them procedurally differently, and appellate courts review them under different standards. Despite that, too many attorneys loosely use the terms interchangeably both in written submissions and in oral argument. When judges fail to be clear whether they are departing or varying, appellate courts will often reverse the judge and remand the case for resentencing.[2]

D. Marshalling Evidence and Facts to Support or Oppose Departures

Once attorneys have identified potential departure grounds, and certainly once they determine either to seek a departure or learn that the opposing side intends to seek a departure, attorneys should turn their attention to how they intend to make a factual record for or against a departure. In many cases, all the facts necessary to support or oppose a departure may be found in the uncontested portions of the presentence report and it is a simple matter of identifying and marshalling those facts into a coherent and persuasive argument.

In other instances, supporting or opposing a departure may require further investigation and development of facts. If the offender served in the military, for example, it may require attorneys to investigate the offender's military history, which may in turn involve issuing subpoenas for records or finding witnesses able to testify about the offender's military service. There is often little time before the sentencing hearing to conduct such investigations and to gather necessary evidence. Thus, as soon as attorneys become aware of potential departure grounds, they need to determine quickly whether further investigation is needed and, if so, move quickly to gather the necessary evidence. In some cases, attorneys may find it appropriate to move for a continuance of the sentencing hearing so as to have time to get the evidence and fully develop the record.

E. Effective Advocacy For or Against Departures

Attorneys should put careful thought into how they intend to present evidence and argue in support of or against departure grounds. Some departure motions may require testimony from live witnesses. Others may rely on documentary or other exhibits. Still others may rely on the uncontested portions of the presentence report. Whatever the case, attorneys should consider how best to present the evidence in a persuasive manner.

In some cases, live testimony may be the most persuasive form of evidence. Relying on medical records in support of a downward departure for mental health history may factually support the departure, but additional testimony from a family member about how the offender's mental health problems have impaired the offender's judgment in the activities of everyday life may be more effective. A list of an offender's military commendation may factually support a departure for military service; the medals themselves or photographs of the medals, however, may be far more persuasive in making the point. Even when the factual basis for the departure is contained in the uncontested portions of the presentence report, attorneys should still think about the most persuasive way to present those facts to the judge. For example, if an upward departure is premised on the extraordinary number of firearms an offender possessed, rather than rely on a cold recitation of the number of firearms in the presentence report, a prosecutor may bring all the firearms into the courtroom, or at least offer into evidence photographs of all the firearms. Similarly, if the ground for a departure is that the offender's criminal history score understates the seriousness of the offender's criminal history or likelihood of reoffending, the prosecutor may consider ways to summarize or chart the aggravating nature of the criminal history. The prosecutor may determine how many of the offenses the offender committed while other charges were pending or while the offender was on probation or parole, or how many involved firearms or violence, or the like. The goal in advocacy is to be persuasive. To persuade another person requires communicating with logic, reason, or emotion in a manner that compels the listener to adopt the advocate's position.

In arguing for a departure, attorneys should focus more on logic and reason, the language of the Guidelines provision and the facts, than on emotional arguments. Unlike the Section 3553(a) factors, which may lend themselves more toward an emotional appeal, departures are tied to the language of the Guidelines and precedent. Thus, judges will be more focused on logic and reason in making rulings on departures than emotions; attorneys should follow suit in their arguments.

F. *The Extent of Departure*

When arguing for or against departures, attorneys should stake out a position about the extent of the departure, if any, they believe is appropriate. Again, departures are tied to the Guidelines, and thus the extent of departures should generally be tied to the structure of the Guidelines themselves. In determining whether the extent of a district court's departure was reasonable, appellate courts consider the extent to which the departure was tied to the structure of the Federal Sentencing Guidelines.[3] In contrast, variance motions are not tied to the Guidelines and thus can be more open-ended and less tied to some preexisting structure.

With this in mind, attorneys should articulate arguments about the extent or degree of departure in a manner that invokes the structure of the Guidelines. In some instances, attorneys may find the basis for the structure within the applicable Guidelines provision. For example, if a prosecutor moves for an upward departure because the offender trafficked in substantially more than 25 firearms under Section 2K2.1, cmt. n.13(c), then the prosecutor may want to seek a departure that is proportionate to the increases that applied for lower numbers of firearms. Section 2K2.1(b)(5) provides a 4-level enhancement for trafficking in firearms (whether the offender trafficked in one firearm or a hundred). A different Guidelines section that applies to prohibited persons who possess firearms, Section 2K2.1(b)(1), provides incremental increases in the offense level for various quantities of firearms involved in such an offense (2-levels for 3–7 firearms, 4-levels for 8–24 firearms, 6-levels for 25–99 firearms, etc.). Thus, if an offender charged with firearms trafficking trafficked in 75 firearms, then a prosecutor may argue that upward departure of two additional levels (beyond the four-level enhancement that applies for trafficking in "more than 25 firearms") may be appropriate because it reflects the incremental increase in offense level for someone involved with between 25 to 99 firearms. A departure motion articulated in this manner would be one tied to the structure of the Guidelines.

In other instances, attorneys may need to turn to other Guidelines provisions to determine the degree of an upward departure in order to tie the motion to the structure of the Guidelines. For example, if an offender was not prohibited from possessing firearms but was convicted of the crime of possessing a firearm on an airplane, the applicable Guidelines is Section 2K2.5. That section does not provide for any enhancement for the number of firearms possessed. Imagine, however, that the offender tried to board an airplane with a dozen firearms. Under these circumstances, a prosecutor may want to seek an upward departure for the number of firearms. To articulate the basis for the extent of the departure, the prosecutor could turn, for example, to the provision in Section 2K2.1 that provides for increasingly greater offense level enhancements based on the greater the number of firearms the offender possessed.

The most effective attorneys will provide the sentencing judge with a reasonable basis for determining the extent of a departure that has some connection to the structure and rationale of the Guidelines. Absent such guidance, a judge may be reluctant to depart at all. With a reasonable, structured basis upon which to determine the extent of a departure, it is more likely the judge will exercise discretion to depart from the advisory Guidelines range. And the more likely it is that an appellate court will affirm the judge.

Good sentencing advocates are also reasonable about the extent of departure they request. Under the case law, the greater the departure, the more searching is the appellate review of the judge's exercise of sentencing discretion. *See Gall v. United States*, 552 U.S. 38, 50 (2007) ("We find it uncontroversial that a major departure should be supported by a more significant justification than a minor one."). Appellate courts are more likely to reverse a significant departure than a slight departure. Attorneys should not get so greedy that they risk reversal on appeal. Attorneys should recall that they can ask for a more significant variance. Although appellate courts review all non-Guidelines sentences for abuse of discretion, sentencing judges have more leeway in the extent of variances than they do the extent of departures because the former need not be tied to the Guidelines structure. *See Gall*, 552 U.S. at 47–49 (stating that appellate courts "take the degree of variance into account and consider the extent of a deviation from the Guidelines," but do not employ "rigid mathematical formula that uses the percentage of a departure as the standard for determining the strength of the justifications required for a specific sentence" and appellate courts "must give due deference" to sentencing judges' determination about the extent of variance warranted by a given factor).

G. Grounds for Departures

As noted, the Guidelines contain many provisions addressing departures from the advisory Guidelines range. The Guidelines discourage departures on some grounds but not on other grounds. Here, I will briefly examine each of the departure grounds addressed in the Guidelines and discuss some advocacy tips for and against departures. To be clear, this is not an examination of the law on departure; the cases are legion in this area. Rather, the focus here is on how to be effective sentencing advocates. The point of examining departure provisions under the Federal Sentencing Guidelines is primarily intended to alert the reader to reasons the Sentencing Commission identified that may justify higher or lower sentences so that attorneys can consider those reasons in sentencing advocacy. Attorneys practicing in state courts may use the same reasoning discussed below, even when the Guidelines do not apply.

1. Offender's History and Characteristics

Several Guidelines provisions in Section 5H address factors pertaining to offenders' histories and characteristics that may, or may not, justify a departure from the advisory Guidelines range. These include departures based on an offender's age, education and vocational skills, mental and emotional condition, physical condition (including substance abuse or addictions), employment record, family ties and responsibilities, criminal livelihood, military service, charitable contributions, public service, and lack of guidance as a youth. To be sure, the Guidelines make it clear that race, sex, national origin, creed, religion, and socio-economic status are "not relevant in the determination of a sentence." USSG §5H1.10. The Guidelines also note that an offender's role in the offense and criminal history are relevant in determining a sentence but are accounted for in the Guidelines and are not a basis for a departure. USSG §§5H1.7, 5H1.8.

Section 5H1.1 addresses departures from the advisory Guidelines range based on an offender's age.

> Age (including youth) may be relevant in determining whether a departure is warranted, if considerations based on age, individually or in combination with other offender characteristics, are present to an unusual degree and distinguish the case from the typical cases covered by the guidelines. Age may be a reason to depart downward in a case in which the defendant

> is elderly and infirm and where a form of punishment such as home confinement might be equally efficient as and less costly than incarceration. Physical condition, which may be related to age, is addressed at §5H1.4 [Physical Condition, Including Drug or Alcohol Dependence or Abuse; Gambling Addiction].

USSG §5H1.1. As will be discussed in connection with variances on this ground, age can be a double-edged sword in the sense that for every argument that youth or old age may justify a departure from the advisory Guidelines range, prosecutors can often articulate why the offender's age may be an aggravating factor.

Section 5H1.2 provides that "education and vocational skills are not ordinarily relevant in determining whether a departure is warranted" but "may be relevant in determining the conditions of probation or supervised release for rehabilitative purposes, for public protection by restricting activities that allow for the utilization of a certain skill, or in determining the appropriate type of community service." USSG §5H1.2. Thus, this provision identifies potential grounds for further restricting or limiting an offender's freedom on probation or supervised release, as opposed to identifying grounds for decreasing the severity of punishment by departing downward from the advisory Guidelines range of imprisonment.

Section 5H1.3 recognizes that "[m]ental and emotional conditions may be relevant in determining whether a departure is warranted, if such conditions ... are present to an unusual degree." USSG §5H1.3. It also notes that a downward departure may be appropriate under this section "to accomplish a specific treatment purpose." *Id.* Finally, this section notes that mental or emotional conditions may be relevant in determining conditions of probation or supervised release. *Id.* To be clear, mental and emotional conditions as used in this provision are not the same thing as diminished capacity. Unlike diminished capacity, this Guidelines section is not focused on the degree to which a mental or emotional condition had any causal relationship to the crime of conviction. Rather, it is more focused on the extent to which an offender's mental or emotional impairments may exacerbate the severity of imprisonment or render the offender more vulnerable to manipulation, violence, or abuse in prison.

The Sentencing Commission amended Section 5H1.3 in 2010 to change the status of mental and emotional conditions from a specific offender characteristic that was "not ordinarily relevant" to one that "may be relevant." USSG App. C, Vol. III at 348 (Amendment 739) (codified at USSG §5H1.3 ["Policy Statement"]). The amendment also reiterates that a downward departure for mental or emotional conditions may also be used to accomplish a specific-treatment purpose. USSG App. C, Vol. III at 348 (Amendment 739) (codified at USSG §5H1.3) (cross-referencing USSG §5C1.1, comment. [n.6]).

Section 5H1.4 addresses physical condition, including drug or alcohol dependence or abuse and gambling addictions. Section 5H1.4 provides that "[p]hysical condition or appearance, including physique, may be relevant in determining whether a departure is warranted." For example, a downward departure may be warranted under this section if a male offender had an immature appearance or a slight physique because that offender may be more susceptible to abuse or manipulation in a male prison than other offenders.[4] That section also notes that an extraordinary physical impairment may be a reason to depart downward, for example when that condition makes home detention as sufficient but far less costly than imprisonment. USSG §5K5H1.4. On the other hand, Section 5H1.4 counsels against a downward departure for alcohol dependence or substance abuse. It notes that "[s]ubstance abuse is highly correlated to an increase propensity to commit crime." *Id.* Section 5H1.4 recognizes, however, that a downward departure may be appropriate to accomplish a specific treatment purpose. *Id.* Finally, Section 5H1.4 flatly rejects a gambling addiction as a valid basis for departing from the Guidelines. *Id.*

Section 5H1.5 asserts that an offender's employment record is "not ordinarily relevant in determining whether a departure is warranted" and may only be relevant in determining conditions of probation or supervised release. USSG §5H1.5.

Section 5H1.6 provides that family ties and responsibilities "are not ordinarily relevant in determining whether a departure may be warranted" and explicitly states they are "not relevant" if the offense involved a minor victim. USSG §5H1.6. That section does note, however, that "[f]amily responsibilities that are complied with may be relevant to the determination of the amount of restitution or fine." *Id.* The phrase "complied with" refers, for example, to child support responsibilities; if an offender is in arrears on child support, then it is hard to justify a reduction in restitution or a fine because of an obligation the offender otherwise ignores anyway. The application notes to Section 5H1.6 place even more restrictions on a departure under this section.

> (B) A departure under this policy statement based on the loss of caretaking or financial support of the defendant's family requires, in addition to the court's consideration of the non-exhaustive list of circumstances in subdivision (A), the presence of the following circumstances:
>
> (i) The defendant's service of a sentence within the applicable guideline range will cause a *substantial, direct, and specific loss of essential* caretaking, or essential financial support, to the defendant's family.
>
> (ii) The loss of caretaking or financial support substantially exceeds the harm ordinarily incident to incarceration for a similarly situated defendant. For example, the fact that the defendant's family might incur some degree of financial hardship or suffer to some extent from the absence of a parent through incarceration is not in itself sufficient as a basis for departure because such hardship or suffering is of a sort ordinarily incident to incarceration.
>
> (iii) The loss of caretaking or financial support is one for which *no effective remedial or ameliorative programs reasonably are available*, making the defendant's caretaking or financial support irreplaceable to the defendant's family.
>
> (iv) The departure effectively will address the loss of caretaking or financial support.

USSG §5H1.6 cmt. n.1 (emphasis added). In short, a downward departure related to family ties and responsibilities under the Guidelines is subject to a lot of limitations and conditions.

Section 5H1.9 states that "[t]he degree to which a defendant depends upon criminal activity for a livelihood is relevant in determining the appropriate sentence," citing the career offender provisions in Chapter 4 of the Guidelines. In other words, Section 5H1.9 suggests that the fact an offender has made a career out of crime is not a basis for a departure because it is already considered in the Guidelines. The government may move for an upward departure on this ground, however, when offenders are effectively career offenders in the common sense meaning of the term, even if the offenders do not technically qualify as career offenders under the Guidelines.[5] Some creative defense attorneys have even invoked Section 5H1.9 as a basis for a downward departure, arguing the fact the offender did not make his living committing crime decreased his likelihood of reoffending, thereby arguably justifying a decrease in the sentencing range.[6]

Section 5H1.11 addresses military, civic, charitable, or public service, employment-related contributions, and prior good works. In short, it provides that military service "present to an unusual degree" may be a basis for a departure, but none of the other service or employment-related contributions or good works are valid grounds for downward departures.

Finally, Section 5H1.12 asserts that "[l]ack of guidance as a youth and similar circumstances indicating a disadvantaged upbringing are not relevant grounds in determining whether a departure is warranted."

2. Offense Conduct and Consequences

Several Guidelines provisions address departures related to the nature of the offender's criminal conduct and the impact that conduct may have on others. Several of these sections provide that upward departures may be appropriate based on the nature and extent of injuries to victims. Other sections provide that upward departures may be warranted based on the nature of the criminal conduct regardless of the impact it had on victims. Still other provisions indicate that downward departures may be appropriate based either on the conduct of victims or when the crime avoided a greater harm.

It is to be expected that the Guidelines would provide for upward departures based on harm to victims. The Guidelines providing upward departures may be appropriate when the offender's conduct caused death, physical injury, or extreme psychological injury to, or abduction of, victims when that conduct is not otherwise accounted for in the calculation of that range. USSG §§5K2.1, 2.2, 2.3 & 2.4. When the conduct caused injuries, these sections indicate that the extent of the upward departure should be tied to the extent of the injuries and the number of victims. Section 5K2.5 also provides that an upward departure may be appropriate when an offender's conduct caused property damage or loss not accounted for in the Guidelines range, and that the extent of an upward departure should be tied to the extent of the harm. Likewise, Section 5K2.7 indicates that an upward departure may be appropriate when the offender's conduct causes a significant disruption of a governmental function, and the extent of the upward departure should be tied to the significance of the disruption. Similarly, Section 5K2.14 provides that an upward departure may be appropriate if the offender's conduct significantly endangered national security, public health, or public safety, even if no injury occurred. Finally, Section 5K2.8 addresses upward departures for extreme criminal conduct in relation to victims. Section 5K2.8 provides:

> If the defendant's conduct was unusually heinous, cruel, brutal, or degrading to the victim, the court may increase the sentence above the guideline range to reflect the nature of the conduct. Examples of extreme conduct include torture of a victim, gratuitous infliction of injury, or prolonging of pain or humiliation.

USSG §5K2.8.

Two Guidelines provisions authorize upward departures based on the nature of weapons used, regardless of whether the use of the weapons caused injury. Section 5K2.6 provides that an upward departure may be appropriate when offenders use weapons or dangerous instrumentalities, even if the offender did not injury anyone. Similar to the victim-based departure provisions, Section 5K2.6 counsels that the extent of the upward departure should be tied to the dangerousness of the weapon, the manner in which the offender used it, and the extent to which the weapon endangered others. It also notes that "a substantial sentence increase" may be warranted when an offender discharged a firearm. Section 5K2.17 provides that an upward departure may be warranted if the offender possessed a semiautomatic firearm capable of holding a high-capacity magazine in relation to a crime of violence or a drug trafficking offense. Similar to Section 5K2.6, the extent of departure under Section 5K2.17 should be tied to "the degree to which the nature of the weapon increased the likelihood of death or injury."

Section 5K2.9 provides that an upward departure may be warranted if the offender committed the offense to facilitate or conceal another crime. For example, an offender prosecuted for bank robbery may merit a longer sentence if the purpose was to obtain funds for a terrorist operation.

Two Guidelines provide that a downward departure may be warranted in relation to offense conduct. Section 5K2.10 provides that a downward departure may be appropriate "[i]f the victim's wrongful conduct contributed significantly to provoking the offense behavior." USSG §5K2.10. This section identifies a number of factors relating to the characteristics of the offender and victim in relation to each other, and the nature of the conduct by each, in determining the extent of any departure. Section 5K2.10 provides that this departure ordinarily should not apply to cases involving child victims or to non-violent crimes generally. Section 5K2.11 provides that a downward departure may be appropriate if the offender committed the crime to avoid a perceived greater harm. Section 5K2.11 identifies a mercy killing as an example of when a departure on this ground may be appropriate. Section 5K2.11 also notes that a downward departure may be warranted when the offender's conduct did not cause the harm or evil the law was intended to prevent, such as when a war veteran possesses an explosive device as a trophy from his service.

A court may also depart upward for dismissed or uncharged conduct connected to the offense of conviction.

> The court may depart upward to reflect the actual seriousness of the offense based on conduct (1) underlying a charge dismissed as part of a plea agreement in the case, or underlying

> a potential charge not pursued in the case as part of a plea agreement or for any other reason; and (2) that did not enter into the determination of the applicable guideline range.

USSG §5K2.21. The language of this departure provision also suggests that a departure is appropriate on this ground when the dismissed or uncharged conduct is tied to the offense of conviction.[7]

3. Offenders' Mental States

There are two Guidelines provisions addressing potential departures from the advisory Guidelines range based on the offender's mental state. Section 5K2.12 provides that a court may depart downward from the advisory Guidelines range if the offender's criminal conduct resulted from coercion or duress. Section 5K2.13 provides for a potential downward departure based on diminished capacity.

Section 5K2.12 provides:

> If the defendant committed the offense because of serious coercion, blackmail or duress, under circumstances not amounting to a complete defense, the court may depart downward. The extent of the decrease ordinarily should depend on the reasonableness of the defendant's actions, on the proportionality of the defendant's actions to the seriousness of coercion, blackmail, or duress involved, and on the extent to which the conduct would have been less harmful under the circumstances as the defendant believed them to be. Ordinarily coercion will be sufficiently serious to warrant departure only when it involves a threat of physical injury, substantial damage to property or similar injury resulting from the unlawful action of a third party or from a natural emergency. Notwithstanding this policy statement, personal financial difficulties and economic pressures upon a trade or business do not warrant a downward departure.

USSG §5K2.12 (emphasis added). The emphasized language of this provision recognizes limitations placed on its application. The language suggests that any coercion or duress must be significant and must involve a threat of physical harm or substantial financial harm.[8]

Section 5K2.13 provides:

> A downward departure may be warranted if (1) the defendant committed the offense while suffering from a significantly reduced mental capacity; and (2) the significantly reduced mental capacity contributed substantially to the commission of the offense. Similarly, if a departure is warranted under this policy statement, the extent of the departure should reflect the extent to which the reduced mental capacity contributed to the commission of the offense.
>
> However, the court may not depart below the applicable guideline range if (1) the significantly reduced mental capacity was caused by the voluntary use of drugs or other intoxicants; (2) the facts and circumstances of the defendant's offense indicate a need to protect the public because the offense involved actual violence or a serious threat of violence; (3) the defendant's criminal history indicates a need to incarcerate the defendant to protect the public; or (4) the defendant has been convicted of an offense under chapter 71, 109A, 110, or 117, of title 18, United States Code.

USSG §5K2.13 (emphasis added). As noted by the emphasized words, § 5K2.13 qualifies and places limitations on a court's authority to depart downward for diminished capacity.

4. Voluntary Disclosure of Offense

Section 5K2.16 provides that a court may depart downward from the advisory Guidelines range when an offender voluntarily discloses criminal conduct to authorities before they discovered the conduct, if it was unlikely that authorities would otherwise have discovered it. The Guidelines give, as example, an offender voluntarily disclosing his crime because he felt compelled to do so by a sense of remorse. Although this example envisions a human offender, this departure ground is also available for organizations. When corporations have internal compliance programs or auditing units, they sometimes discover crimes committed by employees acting on behalf of corporations. If the employee was acting within the scope of employment on behalf of the corporation, then the corporation itself may have criminal liability. A corporation that discloses the crime to authorities may benefit from this departure ground in that case, regardless of the consequences for the individual employee.

This ground for departure has two requirements: the offender must voluntarily disclose the crime and accept responsibility for it, and it must have been unlikely that the crime would have been discovered. Courts have concluded that the second requirement is an objective test. In other words, a court must find that it was unlikely that authorities would have uncovered the crime. That the offender subjectively believed it would not be discovered does not matter. Courts have recognized that this may be an anomaly in the wording of a departure that is presumably based on the offender's motivation to turn himself in, but have found that the plain language of the guideline provision controls.[9] If an offender would otherwise qualify for this departure and subjectively believed the crime would never have been discovered, even if, for instance, unbeknownst to him the authorities were investigating the crime, a defense attorney may want to argue for a downward variance on this ground.

5. Aberrant Behavior

Section 5K2.20 provides that, except for certain crimes (including those involving minor victims), a court may depart downward "in an exceptional case if (1) the defendant's criminal conduct meets the requirements of subsection (b); and (2) the departure is not prohibited under subsection (c)." USSG §5K2.20(a). Subsection (b) allows a court to depart downward for aberrant behavior:

> only if the defendant committed a single criminal occurrence or single criminal transaction that (1) was committed without significant planning; (2) was of limited duration; and (3) represents a marked deviation by the defendant from an otherwise law-abiding life.

USSG §5K2.20(b). Subsection (c) further prohibits a court from departing downward for aberrant behavior if certain circumstances were present:

(1) The offense involved serious bodily injury or death;
(2) The defendant discharged a firearm or otherwise used a firearm or a dangerous weapon;
(3) The "instant offense of conviction is a serious drug trafficking offense"; or
(4) The defendant has either of the following: (A) more than one criminal

> history point; or (B) "a prior federal or state felony conviction or any other significant prior criminal behavior, regardless of whether the conviction or significant prior criminal behavior is countable under Chapter Four."

USSG §5K2.20(c).

Aberrant behavior does not necessarily mean the same thing as an offender having a crime-free history. An offender with a history of committing misdemeanor theft charges may be found to have acted in an aberrant manner when he committed an environmental crime. Motions for downward departures on this ground are more persuasive when offenders can also provide some causal explanation for why the offender acted in an aberrant manner in this particular instance. If the defense attorney can plausibly explain that the offender committed the instant offense only because a unique set of facts occurred that will unlikely ever occur again, then it can give the court some confidence that a longer sentence is unnecessary to achieve the goal of specific deterrence.

Because Section 5K2.20 contains multiple limitations on its application, it may not apply in many cases when the offender's conduct otherwise appears to be aberrant. In those cases, as with other cases when the language of the Guidelines departure provisions contains restrictions, defense attorneys may consider moving for a downward variance for aberrant behavior.

6. Dismissed or Uncharged Conduct

Section 5K2.21 provides that a court may depart upward from the advisory Guidelines range:

> to reflect the actual seriousness of the offense based on conduct (1) underlying a charge dismissed as part of a plea agreement in the case, or underlying a potential charge not pursued in the case as part of a plea agreement or for any other reason; and (2) that did not enter into the determination of the applicable guideline range.

USSG §5K2.21.

Attorneys should consider the possibility of a court departing upward on this ground in negotiating plea agreements or sentencing agreements. Indeed, this departure is often a motivating factor for the parties to reach a plea deal when there is litigation risk for both parties in relation to the most serious crime of conviction. In some cases, it may be in an offender's best interest to plead guilty to an offense that carries a lower statutory maximum sentence to limit the offender's upward exposure. On the other hand, it may be in the government's best interest to negotiate a plea to a less serious crime rather than risk losing at trial on the more serious offense. The parties may even agree that the departure applies and agree to the extent of the upward departure or agree to litigate the extent of the upward departure.

Of late, I have found that the parties often reach this type of agreement somewhat frequently when offenders are convicted of distributing drugs that resulted in the death of a user. To hold the offender accountable for the death as part of a charge, the government must prove the drug to whom the offender distributed was the but-for cause of death. Most of the time, this is hard to prove, although it is typically easy for the government to prove that the drug was one of contributing factors in the victim's death. If the government proves beyond a reasonable doubt at trial that the drug was the but-for cause of death, it carries a substantial mandatory minimum sentence and increases the maximum statutory penalty. At sentencing, the government can seek an upward departure if it can prove by a preponderance of the evidence that the drug was a contributing factor in the victim's death, even if it was not successful at trial in proving the drug was the but-for cause of death. Because there is substantial litigation risk on both sides, the parties often reach agreements that allow the offenders to plead guilty to distribution without the statutory enhancement for causing death but also agree to upward departures from the advisory Guidelines range in some amount on the ground that the drug the offenders distributed contributed to some extent in the users' deaths.

7. Discharged Terms of Imprisonment

Sometimes when offenders are sentenced, they have already been convicted of relevant criminal conduct in state court and may or may not have already served a sentence for the crime. For example, an offender may have been convicted in state court of possession with the intent to deliver a controlled substance, and that conduct was part of a larger drug trafficking conspiracy for which the offender was later convicted in federal court. The drug possession would be considered part of the relevant criminal conduct for purposes of the federal sentencing, and so the Guidelines strive to ensure that offenders do not serve prison time twice for the same conduct by giving them credit for that time. For these purposes, "relevant conduct" is defined as actions "that were part of the same course of conduct or common scheme or plan as the offense of conviction." USSG §1B1.3(a)(2). If the offender has not yet served the state court sentence, the court can accomplish this by running the state sentence concurrent with the federal sentence under Guidelines Section 5G1.3.

But what if the offender has already served his state time? Under Guidelines Section 5K2.23, a court may depart downward if an offender has completed serving a sentence for conduct that would have resulted in a reduction of the sentence under Guidelines Section 5G1.3 if the offender had not completed serving that sentence at the time of the sentencing hearing. Because statutory penalties trump the advisory Guidelines, however, it should be noted that a court may not depart downward below any statutory mandatory minimum sentence, even under these circumstances.[10] It is also important to note that a court is not required to depart downward under these circumstances; a sentencing judge still retains the discretion to decline to depart downward under this section if it deems other facts do not warrant a downward departure.[11]

8. Other Grounds

This chapter has not covered all the grounds for departure in the Guidelines and has focused instead on the primary ones that are most likely to influence attorneys' sentencing advocacy strategies. It is also important for attorneys practicing in federal court to recognize that a court may depart from the advisory Guidelines on any ground based on circumstances not adequately taken into consideration in the Guidelines. USSG §5K2.0(a).[12] For purposes of this book, the important take away for attorneys is that they recognize that the Guidelines themselves provide grounds for adjusting offenders' sentences to fall outside the advisory Guidelines range to tailor a sentence that better fits the crime and the criminal. It is also important for attorneys to be aware of these grounds at all stages of a criminal case because they may need to take departure grounds into account in connection with the presentence investigation and plea negotiation and the like.

The reader should also recognize from this chapter that the departure provisions are constricted in their application by the language of the departure provisions. As we will see in the next chapter, variances are not tethered to such statutory language restrictions. As a result, it is often easier for attorneys to simply seek a variance than to seek a departure. Nevertheless, the departure provisions are important for purposes of variances. Grounds for departures in the Guidelines provide suggestions for grounds for variances. Likewise, the language in the departure provisions also provides suggestions for attorneys in how to advocate for or against variances that are premised on grounds that are similar to departure provisions. Thus, even when attorneys chose to dispense with departures and turn straight to the more flexible variance tool, they should never lose sight of the principles underlying the departure provisions and use those provisions to more effectively argue for and against variances.

15

Variances

After the Supreme Court's *Booker* decision that ended the era of mandatory Guidelines, the federal sentencing system returned to an indeterminate sentencing scheme granting judges wide discretion to impose sentences within the statutory minimum and maximum limits. In that respect, then, the federal sentencing scheme is similar to most state sentencing schemes in many ways. In the federal system, however, the Guidelines are still intended to restrict the exercise of judges' discretion by establishing the default sentence.[1] That is, absent an intentional variance from the Guidelines, judges are expected to impose within-Guidelines sentences. This reflects a belief that sentences imposed within the advisory Guidelines range avoid unwarranted sentencing disparity, one of the primary evils targeted by the Sentence Reform Act of 1984. Although district judges may not presume within-Guidelines sentences are reasonable, appellate courts reviewing those sentences do so presume in the sense that they presume the district court's exercise of its discretion was reasonable. Variances, then, reflect sentencing judges' exercise of discretion to impose individualized sentences, adjusting sentences based on the unique facts of the offense conduct or the offender's history and characteristics. It is here, with variances, that attorneys have the greatest opportunity to affect the ultimate sentence through effective advocacy skills.

After the *Booker* decision made Guidelines advisory, federal judges have varied from the Guidelines in a significant number of cases. Judges have more often varied downward to impose sentences below the advisory Guidelines range and have varied upward much less often.[2] During fiscal year 2018, judges varied downward in approximately 23 percent of cases, but varied upward in only two percent of cases.[3] As one can imagine, the frequency with which judges vary from the advisory Guidelines range differs significantly from district to district and judge to judge and also differs dramatically based on the crime of conviction. In short, judges do exercise the power to vary from the advisory Guidelines. No other component of federal sentencing provides attorneys a greater opportunity to affect sentences through effective advocacy. It is because variance motions are so important that this is easily the longest chapter in this book.

Because the Guidelines are no longer mandatory, attorneys frequently forego making motions for departures from the Guidelines because they can just as easily, or more easily, move for variances from the Guidelines. Unlike many of the Guidelines departure provisions that contain restrictions, limits, and conditions, there are no such constraints on variances. Judges have wider discretion in deciding whether to grant variances, and in determining the extent to which they vary, than they do with Guidelines departures. As a result, variances have become a very important part of almost every sentencing hearing as they are the means by which courts may custom-tailor sentences to fit the crime and the criminal. Indeed, it is a rare case when defense attorneys do not seek some sort of variance at sentencing.

To be an effective advocate in federal sentencing, attorneys need to have a thorough understanding of the statutory structure and provisions that guide judges' exercise of discretion to vary from the advisory Guidelines sentence. Naturally, then, this chapter starts a re-examination of the language of Title 18, United States Code, Section 3553(a) to analyze how that language gives rise to and structures courts' evaluation of motions to vary from the Guidelines. Next, there follows a discussion a large number of common grounds for variances from the Guidelines range. This discussion includes advocacy techniques and the nature of evidence that could be produced to support variances on each ground. The penultimate part of this chapter briefly discusses the broadest of all possible grounds for a variance: "other." Finally, the chapter ends with an examination of preserving for appeal an objection to judges granting or denying a motion to vary.

A. Variances and Section 3553(a)

The first sentence of Title 18, United States Code, Section 3553(a) provides the legal authority for judges to vary from the advisory Guidelines sentence. It states that "[t]he court shall impose a sentence that sufficient, but not greater than necessary" to achieve the goals of sentencing identified in Section 3553(a)(2). This sentence reflects a parsimony principle, that is a Congressional direction that judges be careful not to impose sentences any longer than needed to achieve the goals of sentencing. Section 3553(a) identifies factors that judges must consider in determining what sentence will achieve those goals. A court must first determine the advisory Guidelines range, but that range is only one of the factors judges are to consider. The other factors include the nature and circumstances of the offense, the goals of sentencing, the need to avoid unwarranted sentencing disparities, and the need to provide restitution to victims. Importantly, a judge may vary not only from the advisory Guidelines range of incarceration but may also vary from any other advisory Guidelines range, including the advisory Guidelines fine range and the Guidelines range for the length of supervised release. Judges may also vary from the Guidelines range when imposing sentences upon revocation of supervised release.

A court may vary for any reason that falls under any of the very broad categories in Section 3553(a). A judge may also find a variance is appropriate based on a combination of factors, even if the judge concluded that a variance from the advisory Guidelines range was not warranted based on any single factor.[4] Finally, judges may vary based on factors that are already reflected in the calculation of the offender's advisory Guidelines sentence. For example, even if an offender's advisory Guidelines range was reduced for acceptance of responsibility, a judge may vary further downward from the advisory Guidelines range if the judge believes that the degree to which the offender accepted responsibility merits a greater decrease. Conversely, even if an offender's advisory Guidelines range was increased due to reckless endangerment during flight, a judge may vary further upward from the advisory Guidelines range if the judge believes that the extent to which the offender endangered others during his flight from law enforcement merits an increase greater than that provided by the Guidelines.

Thus, in considering grounds for variances from the Guidelines range, attorneys should not overlook the Guidelines themselves. If Guidelines adjustments apply but do not adequately account for the degree to which the factor is present, it may give rise to a ground to vary from the advisory Guidelines range. Conversely, if a Guidelines adjustment does not technically apply for some reason based on the language of the Guidelines provision, but the spirit of the Guidelines provision is implicated by the facts of the case, then attorneys may consider seeking a variance on that ground.

Judges may vary from the advisory Guidelines range sua sponte; their authority to vary is not dependent upon a motion by one of the parties. Further, judges need not give advance notice to the parties before varying from the advisory Guidelines range. Due process does not require that judges provide parties with notice of their intent to vary from the Guidelines range.[5] Nor do the Federal Rules of Criminal Procedure require judges to give advance notice of variances.[6] Parties also may not claim unfair surprise or claim error based on an inability to present mitigating evidence when judges impose sentences outside the advisory Guidelines range because, after *Booker*, parties are on notice that the sentencing Guidelines range is advisory.[7]

Generally, judges are required to provide some explanation in open court for the sentence imposed. *See* 18 U.S.C. § 3553(c) (noting that the district court must "state in open court the reasons for its imposition of the particular sentence"). When judges impose sentences within the advisory Guidelines range, appellate courts do not usually require much more than an explanation from the judge that the judge has considered the Section 3553(a) factors and found that a Guidelines sentence was appropriate. More of an explanation may be necessary when an offender raises issues or presents evidence implicating specific Section 3553(a) factors that, if not specifically addressed by the sentencing judge, may leave a court of appeals without any guidance as to how or even if the sentencing judge specifically resolve that issue. Further, when sentencing judges impose sentences outside the advisory Guidelines range, appellate courts require judges to provide a more detailed explanation of how and why the judges arrived at the sentences under the Section 3553(a) factors so that the appellate courts have some ability to evaluate the reasonableness of the sentences on appellate review. If an appellate court cannot discern how the judge analyzed the Section 3553(a) factors to reach a non–Guidelines sentence, the court may remand the case for resentencing.

Attorneys who have successfully advocated for a non–Guidelines sentence should ensure that the judge has articulated a sufficient basis for that sentence so that it survives appellate review. This means that attorneys may need to ask the sentencing judge to specifically address Section 3553(a) factors at issue. Good sentencing advocates will ensure that the judge not only addresses the factors advocated by the attorney, but also the factors advocated by opposing counsel. A judge's failure to explicitly consider a Section 3553(a) factor advocated by the losing party may result in a remand.

Finally, it is important to recognize the benefits and detriments of variance motions, particularly in relation to Guidelines-based adjustments. As will be discussed further below, some of the grounds attorneys can raise to support a variance could also support adjustments or departures under existing Guidelines provisions. Those Guidelines provisions, however, may not be precisely tailored to address the unique facts in a case. Variances, however, are a flexible and robust means by which courts can adjust sentences to fit the offender and the crime, unencumbered by the language and limitations of Guidelines provisions. Thus, although calculation of the Guidelines ranges is a required first step, attorneys need not resort to the Guidelines and litigate the applicability of Guidelines provisions as they had to when the Guidelines were mandatory, but, rather, can wield the more agile variance weapon to achieve their goals. This ability to individually tailor sentences through the means of variances advances the goal of imposing sentences that truly fit the crime and the offender. But they come at a cost of disparity in sentencing. Untethered to Guidelines language, variances do not channel courts' exercise of discretion. The result is that with every variance, the danger of disparate sentencing increases. Defense attorneys have an obligation to zealously represent individual clients and thus cannot and should not have their decision-making about whether to seek a variance in any given case be influenced by a more global concern about the increase in disparity in sentences. Prosecutors, on the other hand, should consider the impact of disparity in sentencing and balance the need in any particular case to seek a variance against the interest in maintaining a system that dispenses justice equally and evenly.

B. Common Grounds for Variances

Variance grounds can be sorted into five broad categories. In some cases, the nature and circumstances of the offense may call for a sentence outside the advisory Guidelines range. In other cases, the unique history and characteristics of the offender may give rise to arguments for the judge to impose a sentence higher or lower than that suggested by the advisory Guidelines. The offender's conduct in relation to the imposition and resolution of the criminal charges may also lead a judge to find that the advisory Guidelines range should be adjusted. Judges may also vary from the advisory Guidelines because they have a policy disagreement with the Guidelines themselves, leading them to believe that the Guidelines inaccurately reflect the seriousness of the criminal conduct or an offender's criminal culpability. Finally, the broader goals of sentencing identified in Section 3553(a) may lead a judge to find that a sentence above or below the advisory Guidelines range is appropriate.

1. Nature and Circumstances of the Offense

The nature and circumstances of the offense is often a ground that gives rise to variance motions. This is because the Guidelines do not always account for all possible offense characteristics or may not provide enhancements or reductions that the extent parties believe are warranted by the facts. As we discussed, the Guidelines provide a base offense level for offenses and in almost every instance also provide for possible increases or decreases from the base offense level based on specific offense characteristics that may typically be found in connection with that type of offense. The Guideline section for bank robbery, for example, provides for enhancements from the base offense level based on specific offense characteristics such as the amount of money stolen, whether and how a firearm or other dangerous weapon was used, and whether a victim was abducted. *See* USSG §2B3.1. The Sentencing Commission did not, by any stretch, attempt to provide Guidelines adjustments, though, for every specific offense characteristic that may, or even often, exists in connection with offenses. Rather, they did so only for the most frequent and common facts that reflect on the seriousness of the offense or the offender's culpability. Every case is different in some way, and there may be facts that demonstrate that the offense conduct is more or less serious than a typical case.

Thus, it is important for attorneys to carefully consider the particular facts of an offense and determine whether there are facts present, or absent, that would suggest that the Guidelines fail to adequately reflect the seriousness of the offense or the offender's criminal culpability. Returning to our bank robbery example, assume the case involved a robbery by an offender using a fake handgun that neither qualified as a firearm or a dangerous weapon. In such a case, the offender's Guidelines range would not be enhanced for possession of a weapon. Nevertheless, there could be an argument that the nature of the offense warrants an upward variance. A fake gun may have been just as capable as a real firearm of causing fear and psychological or emotional trauma for victims, yet the Guidelines would not have taken that into account. Similarly, if the robber had used a note demanding money, but the note was particularly frightening, an upward variance may be appropriate. Imagine, for example, that the robber had followed the teller, knew the name of the teller's minor child, and threatened to torture and kill the child (by name) if the teller tripped an alarm. That type of note suggesting greater planning and carrying a greater potential for psychological harm may warrant a greater sentence than a note simply demanding the teller hand over money, particularly if the victim actually suffered a psychological injury.

Conversely, if the offense did not include facts that seem to be presumed in the Guidelines, or included facts of less severity than presumed, then perhaps they may support a motion for a downward variance. Defense attorneys should consider what facts are presumed in the Guidelines and compare those facts to the case in front of the attorney. Imagine in our bank robbery case that the facts involved an offender walking into the bank in an intoxicated state and approaching the teller in an agitated manner; the teller reads into the offender's slurred but vague words that he is robbing the bank, and the teller hands over money. The offender, who did not initially intend to rob the bank, nevertheless takes advantage of the teller's mistaken fear and walks out of the bank with the cash. Those facts may give rise to a downward variance because arguably the Guidelines provisions for bank robbery presume that the offender intended to commit the robbery from the beginning, not only after stumbling into the opportunity. As another example, in a drug trafficking case, a creative defense attorney may think of all the aggravating characteristics of the "typical" drug dealer, identify those absent in the instant case, and argue that a downward variance is appropriate on that basis. Drug dealers often possess or carry firearms, generate a large amount of proceeds, use violence, and so forth. The absence of any of these typical characteristics could provide a basis to argue that a downward variance is appropriate because the Guidelines were formulated with the typical drug dealer in mind, and the attorney's client is not the typical drug dealer.

In short, the nature and circumstances of the offense may support motions for either upward or downward variances. But it requires attorneys to carefully analyze the applicable Guidelines section, discern the typical offense the Guidelines intended to cover, and identify all the offense characteristics the Sentencing Commission identified and chose to include in the Guidelines section. Then it requires attorneys to carefully comb the facts of their cases to identify facts present or absent that distinguish their cases from the case the Sentencing Commission contemplated when drafting the Guidelines provision for the typical offense. Attorneys should then determine if the differences are significant enough to warrant a variance in either direction.

Mens Rea

An offender's state of mind when committing an offense may give rise to an argument for the court to vary upward or downward from the advisory Guidelines range. People commit crimes for any number of motives, some more base than others. Motive is not an element of most offenses,[8] but motive does tell a lot about an offender's criminal and moral culpability, the extent to which the offender poses a future danger, and whether the offender is likely to reoffend. Thus, there may be reasons to vary from the advisory Guidelines based on an offender's motive.

Effective sentencing advocacy requires attorneys to consider an offender's motive and compare it against the so-called typical motive for crimes that may be presumed under the Guidelines to determine if the actual motive would support an upward or downward variance from the advisory Guidelines range. For example, the typical motive for a bank robbery would be greed. If the motive for a bank robbery in a particular case, though, was to obtain money to fund a terrorist operation, that may justify an upward variance from the advisory Guidelines range. Conversely, if the motive for the bank robbery was to get money to pay for medicine for the offender's minor child, perhaps that may be a ground for a downward variance.[9]

In short, attorneys should evaluate an offender's motive for committing the crime. If that motive is not obvious or was not developed as part of the investigation, the attorneys may want to investigate the motive. Because motive is not an element of most crimes, law enforcement officers understandably do not always devote resources to uncover the motive. For example, when an offender is a felon and is found with a firearm, the offender's motive for possession of the firearm may not be relevant. When appropriate, attorneys may want to offer evidence at the sentencing hearing showing the offender's motive in support of a variance motion. Sometimes an offender's motive may be aggravating while on other occasions it may be mitigating. For example, if there is evidence the felon offender obtained a firearm shortly after a physical altercation with his wife in which he threatened to kill her, the motive for obtaining and possessing the firearm may be aggravating. Conversely, if the felon offender obtained a firearm shortly after his girlfriend's ex-boyfriend threatened to kill her, the motive for obtaining and possessing the firearm may be mitigating.

Role in the Offense

Section 3B of the Federal Sentencing Guidelines contains provisions for upward enhancements for offenders occupying an aggravating role in the offense (USSG §3B1.1) and for downward adjustments for offenders occupying a mitigating role in the offense (USSG §3B1.2).[10] These provisions, though, do not always permit judges to impose sentences that fully reflect offenders' roles, for several reasons. Under the Guidelines provision for aggravating role, for example, an offender may receive a 2-level, 3-level, or 4-level enhancement for role in the offense, but whether these provisions apply depends in part on the nature of the leadership role, the nature of the criminal activity, and the number of people involved. *See* USSG §3B1.1. It may be the situation though, that in a particular case, the facts do not technically support a role enhancement under the Guidelines, but in a more general and less technical sense the facts would support a role enhancement in the form of a variance. Or, perhaps, the offender had such an aggravating role because of the number of people the offender supervised or the manner in which the offender supervised them (i.e., through force or threats or torture) that a four-level enhancement for aggravating role fails to fully reflect the aggravating nature of the offender's role. Similarly, under the Guidelines provision for a mitigating role, an offender may receive a 2-level, 3-level, or 4-level reduction in the offense level depending on whether the offender occupied a minor role, a minimal role, or a role in between minor and minimal. *See* USSG §3B1.2. The unique facts of a case, however, may lead a court to conclude that an offender is not technically eligible for a role reduction under the Guidelines, but under a variance approach the court could find a reduction in the sentence appropriate. With either aggravating or mitigating role adjustments, a court may find that the unique facts of a case may call for an enhancement or reduction greater than the four-level maximum provided under either section or less than the two-level minimum allowed under either section. Or a court may find that even though a Guidelines role adjustment is warranted under the Guidelines, the adjustment does not precisely reflect the seriousness of the offender's role, and a minor adjustment in the form of a variance is appropriate. Finally, other Guidelines provisions may indicate that a role adjustment under Section 3B should not apply in particular types of offenses. For example, if an offender is convicted of being an accessory after the fact, USSG §2X4.1, application note 2 provides that a role enhancement would not normally apply. Yet, a party may believe that the unique facts of a given case suggest that a role adjustment in the form of a variance should apply even though the Guidelines might suggest otherwise.

Thus, for various reasons, although the Guidelines generally provide a basis for a court to adjust an offender's sentence based on role in the offense, a variance based on role may still be appropriate in addition to, or despite of, the Guidelines role adjustment provisions. Attorneys should recognize that in some cases, the Guidelines role adjustment provisions are too restrictive or imprecise enough to truly reflect the nature of an offender's role in the offense. When that is the case, attorneys should move for a variance from the advisory Guidelines range on that ground, even if the offender's offense level was already adjusted for role under the Guidelines.

Extreme Conduct

The facts of a case may warrant an upward variance from the advisory Guidelines range because the nature of the criminal conduct was extreme in some way not reflected in the Guidelines. Remember that the Guidelines base offense level and various offense-characteristic adjustments were determined based on a conception of the average mine-run case. Thus, using our bank robbery case again as an example, the Guidelines provide a base offense level of 20 and provide for adjustments if the offense conduct involved certain facts, such as the use of a firearm or dangerous weapon, or when a victim sustained an injury. *See* USSG §2B3.1. The unique facts of a given case may, however, persuade a court that the enhancements fail to fully capture the extreme nature of the conduct. Imagine, for example, that a bank teller not only suffered an injury, but that the robber intentionally tortured the teller in the process of inflicting the injury. Or imagine that the robber injured multiple people. Guidelines Section 2B3.1 has no provision for increasing the offense level for the wanton infliction of pain or for more than one victim. Were those facts present in a case, an upward variance from the advisory Guidelines range may be the only means by which to reflect the extreme nature of the criminal conduct.

As noted, the Guidelines contain a provision for an upward departure for extreme conduct. *See* USSG §5K2.8 (extreme conduct). Nevertheless, this Guidelines provision may not always apply or fit well to the conduct at issue. For example, Section 5K2.8 envisions a single victim; if the offender engaged in extreme conduct with multiple victims, a departure may not capture the full extent of criminal culpability.[11] The extreme conduct may also have involved victims that were not part of the offense of conviction. Imagine, for example, that an offender pled guilty to sexual exploitation of a child whom he sexually abused one time, but uncharged conduct shows that the offender sexually tortured another child who was not included in the offense conduct. That extreme conduct would not support a departure because it was not part of the charged conduct, but it could be taken into consideration by way of a variance. Finally, the extreme conduct Guidelines departure provision is directed at physical or mental abuse of a victim. It does not encompass extreme conduct of other sorts, such as causing extreme financial loss or extremely endangering national security. Thus, although prosecutors may seek upward departure for extreme conduct, they may also find it appropriate to argue for an upward variance in the alternative, or to simply ask for an upward variance instead of an upward departure.

Prosecutors should consider an upward variance for extreme conduct when the facts of a case would support it. If a prosecutor's view of the facts is that the offender's conduct was egregious and truly out of the ordinary, it may call for an upward variance. And this holds true whether the nature of the conduct involved physical or mental harm to a person, economic or other loss, or danger of injury, loss, or damage.

Victim Impact

When offenders' crimes have a significant or unusually harsh impact on victims, an upward variance from the advisory Guidelines range may be appropriate, whether the harm is physical, mental, or financial.[12] Prosecutors should consider seeking an upward variance from the advisory Guidelines range on victim-impact grounds when the victim or victims have suffered in an extraordinary manner. A variance on this ground may be justified based on the extreme nature of the injury done to one victim, or it may be justified based on an extraordinarily large number of victims, even if the injury suffered by an individual victim was not extraordinary.

Prosecutors should be careful, however, to base any upward variance motion on reliable facts. Victims are not always accurate in their victim impact statements. Victims are not usually trained in the law or always focused on fact-based analysis. And by their very nature, victim impact statements are often drafted by victims under a highly-charged emotional state. Judges, however, can only vary upward on victim impact grounds based on facts that show that the offender's conduct harmed the victim. For example, if a victim claimed the former investment broker offender defrauded her out of $100,000, but the evidence shows that only $25,000 of that was due to fraud and rest of the loss was due to a drop in stock value unrelated to the fraud, it could be error for the judge to vary on the mistaken belief that the offender's criminal conduct caused the victim to lose $100,000.

Victim impact seems quintessentially a basis for only an upward variance, but one can envision circumstances when it could serve as a basis for a downward variance as well. Imagine, for instance, a fraud case in which an offender defrauded 50 people. Under USSG §2B1.1(b)(2)(A), there would be a two-level enhancement in the offender's base offense level based on the number of victims. If, though, no single victim was defrauded of more than a small amount of money (say less than $500), and if law enforcement officers recovered the proceeds from the offender and used it to restore the victims' losses such that no victim actually lost any money in the end, then conceivably there could be an argument that a downward variance would be appropriate because the two-level enhancement overstates the seriousness of the victims' harm. The point here is only that defense attorneys should carefully examine victim-based Guidelines enhancements to determine if any of them overstate the harm to victims and consider raising victim impact, or the lack thereof, as a basis for a downward variance.

Dismissed or Uncharged Conduct

Judges may consider dismissed or uncharged criminal conduct in arriving at an appropriate sentence. There are any number of reasons why the government may dismiss or not charge criminal conduct, yet advocate for the judge to consider it for purposes of sentencing. The government may dismiss charges or agree not to charge an offender as part of a plea agreement. The government may dismiss charges or not charge an offender because the government concluded that it did not have sufficient evidence to prove the offender's guilt beyond a reasonable doubt, but it does have enough evidence to prove his guilt by a preponderance of the evidence, the standard that applies in sentencing hearings. The government may not have charged an offender with conduct because it did not know of the conduct by the time of the offender's guilty plea but learned about it before the sentencing hearing. And, finally, the government may not have charged the offender with conduct before his guilty plea because the offender committed the criminal conduct after his guilty plea and before his sentencing hearing.

If the dismissed or uncharged conduct is within the scope of the relevant criminal conduct of the crime of conviction, then it may be used to determine the offender's Guidelines offense level and sentencing range. As noted, a court may also depart upward for dismissed or uncharged conduct connected to the offense of conviction under Guidelines Section 5K2.21. However, as noted in the last chapter, the language of that Guidelines section suggests that an upward departure is appropriate on this ground only when the dismissed or uncharged conduct is tied to the offense of conviction. Hence, an upward variance based on dismissed or uncharged conduct may be more appropriate than an upward departure when the criminal conduct is not relevant conduct for purposes of determining an offender's advisory Guidelines range, and when an upward departure is not available because the conduct was not directly tied to the offense of conviction.

General Aggravating or Mitigating Factors

Although I have listed some commonly articulated grounds for upward or downward variances premised on offense conduct characteristics, attorneys are not limited to these specific grounds. Indeed, attorneys should think creatively in considering the offense conduct against the Guidelines provisions to determine if grounds exist that would be appropriate for a variance from the advisory Guidelines range. In conducting this analysis, it is important for attorneys to consider the "typical" offense contemplated by the Guidelines in arriving at the base offense level and adjustments for specific offense characteristics. A variance may be appropriate whenever the facts of a case differ significantly from what arguably were the typical facts presumed by the Sentencing Commission in setting the base offense level or the levels applied to specific offense characteristics.

2. History and Characteristics of the Offender

The second broad category of grounds for varying from the advisory Guidelines range is an offender's history and characteristics. Here the focus is on the offender and no longer on the crime the offender committed. It involves looking at the offender as a person whose past and personality influenced their criminal conduct and may influence their future conduct. The task here is to identify those facts that distinguish an offender from the "typical" offender contemplated by the Sentencing Commission in arriving at the advisory Guidelines range and then arguing why and how those facts should justify a greater or lesser sentence. In other words, the question is whether there is something about the offender's past or the offender's nature that means the offender poses a greater or lesser risk of future criminal conduct, or that the offender has greater or lesser degree of criminal or moral culpability. The case law reflects several commonly asserted variance grounds based on offenders' history and characteristics.

Aberrant Behavior

Some offenders live lives of constant criminal conduct, while other offenders find themselves in the criminal justice system because some unusual confluence of circumstances led them to commit crimes that were otherwise outside the offenders' normal pattern of behavior. When the offense conduct is truly aberrant behavior, it may justify a downward variance from the advisory Guidelines range. The justification for a variance here is twofold. First, truly aberrant behavior suggests that the offender may be less criminally or morally culpable than another person for whom such conduct is common. Second, if the offense conduct was not normal for the offender, it also suggests that the offender poses a lower risk of reoffending or presenting a danger to the community than another person for whom such conduct is routine.

As noted in the last chapter, the Guidelines contain a departure provision for aberrant behavior. There are limits, however, to the application of this departure. Guidelines Section 5K2.20 exempts certain crimes from its application (including crimes involving minor victims) and also indicates that a court cannot depart when: (1) the offender committed more than one criminal act or transaction; (2) the criminal conduct occurred over a period of time; (3) the offender did not otherwise lead a law abiding life; (4) the offense involved serious bodily injury or death; (5) the offender discharged a firearm or otherwise used a firearm or a dangerous weapon; (6) the offense of conviction is a serious drug trafficking offense; (7) the offender has more than one criminal history point; and (8) the offender has any prior federal or state felony conviction or engaged in any other significant prior criminal behavior, regardless of whether it resulted in criminal history points under the Guidelines. *See* USSG §5K2.20(b) & (c).

Given all the limitations and restrictions to the application of Guidelines Section 5K2.20, most defense attorneys will opt for seeking a downward variance on aberrant behavior grounds instead of a downward departure on that ground unless it is clear that the offender will qualify for a departure under Section 5K2.20. Even then, it would be wise for a defense attorney to seek a downward variance on the same ground in the alternative. If there is any question whether an offender qualifies under Section 5K2.20, then arguing for a variance would be better because it would involve less litigation risk, including a risk of having an appellate court reverse the sentencing judge who erroneously granted a downward departure for aberrant behavior.

Even when defense attorneys ask judges to vary instead of departing downward for aberrant behavior, however, it is advisable for both attorneys to take clues from Section 5K2.20 on what may be important to emphasize to the judge. Little or no criminal history and an otherwise law-abiding and productive life may suggest that the criminal conduct in a particular case was aberrant behavior for an offender. Similarly, a single criminal act or a short period of conduct constituting the criminal offense is far more likely to appear as aberrant behavior than would multiple criminal acts or conduct spanning a long period of time. It is also important whenever possible, however, to provide evidence showing the judge that some unusual event or circumstance occurred that led to the criminal conduct. If an offender can show that some event, particularly an emotional or traumatic event, led inexorably to the offender's criminal conduct, then it helps show that the criminal conduct had a cause that led to aberrant behavior. Without a triggering event, it is harder for a judge to know whether the criminal conduct was unusual for the offender, even for an offender with no criminal history. It may have just been the case that the offender has no criminal history because the offender has not been caught before. Thus, a showing that the offender lost a job or a spouse or suffered some other type of financial or personal loss may be important in supporting a variance for aberrant behavior. The existence of some unusual event supports an argument that, but for that unusual event, the offender would not have committed the act and thus is less morally culpable. The existence of a usual triggering event also allows the defense attorney to assure the court that a lengthy sentence is unnecessary for purposes of specific deterrence and to persuade the court that this offender is unlikely to commit this offense again in the future.

Defense attorneys should recognize, too, that a variance for aberrant behavior is available even if the offender would be ineligible for a downward departure because of one of the limitations in the Guidelines. To be sure, it may be a tougher sell, but variances for aberrant behavior have no such limitations. A defense attorney may have to be creative in explaining why an offender with some criminal history is entitled to a downward variance for aberrant behavior. Perhaps the type of offense may give rise to an argument. For example, if the offender's criminal history consists of numerous driving offenses (driving while intoxicated, or without a license, or while a license was suspended), but the offense of conviction is a firearm offense, then the focus might by on why the offender's possession of a firearm was aberrant behavior for this offender, even though another driving offense would not have been.

In resisting variance motions based on aberrant behavior, prosecutors may consider focusing on the grounds, if they exist, that would prevent a court from granting a downward departure for aberrant behavior under USSG §5K2.20. Prosecutors can direct the court's attention to Section 5K2.20 and emphasize the logic behind the limitations for departures for aberrant behavior when one of the disqualifying facts are present. And conversely to defense attorneys, prosecutors may want to emphasize a lack of triggering event that could explain why the offender committed the offense. Absent some unusual event causally linked to the crime, a prosecutor can argue that there is no way to be sure the conduct was aberrant, and that the offender may very well commit the same offense in the future.

Age

Age is a tricky basis upon which to seek a downward variance. First, both youth and old age could give rise to an argument for a variance for reasons I will discuss. But if age is always a basis for a variance, that would suggest that the Guidelines were meant to apply only to the middle-aged, a proposition for which there is no support. Second, age is a double-edged sword. Or perhaps calling age a boomerang may be a more apt metaphor. For every argument a clever defense attorney can make for why age should constitute a mitigating factor, an equally clever prosecutor can make an argument for why the offender's age should constitute an aggravating factor. Thus, attorneys should be cautious in arguing for an age-based variance.

As noted in the preceding chapter, the Guidelines address age as a potential ground for departing from the advisory Guidelines range. Section USSG §5H1.1 suggests that both youth and old age may be grounds for a departure from the Guidelines. As with other departure grounds, attorneys may seek a downward departure based on age or, in the alternative, seek a downward variance based on the same ground. Unlike the aberrant behavior departure guideline, Section 5H1.1 does not contain a lot of limitations or exceptions to its application, and so there may be little difference between whether the argument is couched in terms of a departure or a variance.

There are several reasons why youth may justify a downward variance. One of the primary reasons is based on science. It is well accepted now that peoples' cognitive abilities are not fully developed until they are in their early to mid-twenties.[13] Thus, an offender in his teens who commits a rash criminal act, like a robbery, may not be as equipped mentally to assess the wrongfulness of the act as a fully grown adult and hence is arguably less criminally culpable than an older offender whose brain has fully developed. A young offender, particularly one still in his teens, may also be more vulnerable in a prison full of older adults. Lastly, a young offender may also have had little history with the criminal justice system such that, arguably, even a short prison sentence will be adequate to deter the offender, whereas a longer sentence may be necessary to deter an older offender who has been through the criminal justice system before.

Prosecutors may argue, though, that youth is not mitigating and, in some cases, can be an aggravating factor. If the crime took planning or occurred over a period of time or involved multiple acts, then the argument that the offender's undeveloped brain had anything to do with the offender's criminal conduct has less purchase. If the youthful offender has a history of involvement with the criminal justice system, the argument that a short sentence will deter the offender may be as unpersuasive as it would be with an older offender. Prosecutors may also emphasize that the offender's youth suggests that he poses a greater danger and a period of confinement is necessary to protect the community. If, in fact, the offender's brain is so undeveloped that he lacks judgment, then that means he poses more of a danger than an older offender who can use better judgment. Similarly, an offender committing a serious offense at a young age arguably may suggest that a short sentence will likely mean he will offend again. The recidivism rate is greater for younger offenders than it is for older ones.[14]

Older age may be a mitigating factor warranting a downward variance for several reasons. The primary reason is based on statistics that show that the rate of recidivism steadily and significantly declines as offenders age, especially beyond the age of 50.[15] A lengthy sentence for an older offender may also be, in effect, a life sentence and thus becomes a level of punishment that is qualitatively different from a term of years when an offender still has a hope of one day being free. And just like a youthful offender may be more vulnerable in prison than older offenders, elderly offenders may also be unusually vulnerable in prison. Even if the elderly offender does not, at the time of sentencing, have health issues that themselves may warrant a variance, the fact is that as the offender ages, such physical and mental health impairments are likely to occur, making the offender more vulnerable.

A prosecutor opposing a downward variance based on old age has several counterarguments. The fact that the older offender is before the court may suggest that this particular offender is defying the statistics and is an outlier such that the court can have no confidence that the offender's age alone decreases the likelihood of reoffending, whatever the general statistics may be. Prosecutors may also be able to argue that the offender is old enough to know better; the offender had decades to understand the difference between right and wrong, and the fact that the offender is committing crime at an advanced age means the offender is incorrigible. Finally, prosecutors can point out that if an elderly offender develops serious physical or mental impairments while incarcerated that would make the offender vulnerable, there is a program within the Bureau of Prisons, with recourse to district courts, for humanitarian or compassionate release.

Charitable Service—Good Works

Very few people are all good or all bad. Some offenders may have a history of performing charitable services or making charitable contributions. These instances occur more often in white collar cases when offenders are financially secure enough that they have time and funds to donate to others. Other offenders' life histories may exhibit examples of good deeds or laudable conduct. This may involve caring for an elderly neighbor or infirm parents, returning lost property, or conducting voluntary charitable services. These various examples of positive behavior may arguably counterbalance the criminal conduct that is the focus of the offender's sentencing hearing. The Guidelines reject this idea, however, stating, "[c]ivic, charitable, or public service; employment-related contributions; and similar prior good works are not ordinarily relevant in determining whether a departure is warranted." USSG §5H1.11. Nevertheless, although this may not be a ground for a downward departure under the Guidelines, a defense attorney can still argue this as a basis for a downward variance under the Section 3553(a) factors.

In support of motions for downward variances on the broad ground of good works, attorneys should pay attention to the timeline, causes, and motivation. Citing good works performed years before the criminal conduct may be less compelling than citing good works that occurred simultaneous with or after the criminal conduct. The former arguably suggests that the offender might once have been a good person but has turned bad, while the latter lends itself to an argument that the offender is generally a good person and made a mistake when engaging in the criminal conduct. The cause for the so-called good works is important to plumb as well. Community service performed as a result of a court-order is not a good reflection of the offender's true character. Citing charitable works performed for some ulterior motive may also backfire on an offender. On the other hand, good work performed voluntarily, especially in the form of time and labor, may reflect very positively on the offender.

Defense attorneys should be particularly cautious in arguing financial charitable contributions as a basis for a downward variance in white-collar cases when the offender gained substantial proceeds from the fraudulent conduct. It is easy to be charitable with other people's money. Indeed, distributing crime proceeds in so-called acts of charity smacks of egotism and could be argued to reflect an effort by the offender to further exploit his victims by gaining acclaim for charitable acts with the victims' money. Moreover, white collar offenders often have more opportunities and time to perform charitable work in their communities than poorer offenders. Although there may be a distinction in the extent to which charitable acts may reflect on character between poor and wealthy offenders, any act of charity is still mitigating to some degree.

In proving offenders' good works and charitable contributions, defense attorneys should elicit the assistance of their clients and their clients' family members. Documentation showing hours worked, photographs of the offender performing charitable services such as filling sandbags, or testimonials from those who benefited from the offenders' good work is far more compelling than defense attorneys' dry recitation or offenders' self-serving assertions. Offenders may need to call in chits for their good works by soliciting this type of compelling evidence.

Community Ties

The concept of community ties as a basis for a variance from the advisory Guidelines range relates to the sentencing goal of specific deterrence. The premise for this variance ground is that an offender connected to the community has a support system that lends stability to the offender's life. Unstable, unconnected people are more likely to lack support when they encounter social stressors, which increases the likelihood they will respond by reoffending. In contrast, those with a social network in the community have others to lean on in times of stress. Offenders may also be less likely to reoffend when they value the opinions of others in their community and do not want to disappoint them. This factor may be particularly important when the offender's past trouble with the law can be causally linked to a period when the offender lacked such ties, such as by disaffecting his family by using drugs or engaging in criminal conduct. This factor may also be important to establish when offenders are not United States citizens to counter a potential presumption that the offender lacks such ties. Again, the defense attorney's presentation and argument on this factor should be focused on showing that the offender has assimilated into the culture of the United States, including adopting its respect for the law, to suggest that the offender will be unlikely to reoffend.

To be persuasive here, as in so many other areas, providing the judge with evidence or testimonials in the form of live testimony or letters is more persuasive than simply relying on cold facts or data within the presentence report. A defense attorney may be able point out in the presentence report the timing of the offender's criminal conduct in relation to when the offender lacked close family ties and argue that the judge should draw a causal connection. It is far more compelling, however, to back this up with information from the family that explains events that caused the offender to lose the family connection and how the offender's trouble with the law followed. The defense attorney will want to show that the offender is now reconnected to his family and that the court can thus expect the offender to abide by the law as he has done in the past when connected to his family.

To be sure, defense counsel should be somewhat cautious here because there is a very good argument that a defendant's ability to pack the courtroom with supporters or bury the court with letters of support is not mitigating. The government might argue that someone with all of this support was advantaged and has less of an excuse for engaging in criminal behavior than another disadvantaged offender who has no family support and few friends or allies in life. The offender with all the support likely still committed the crime despite the support, so their presence in the offender's life arguably does nothing for decreasing the likelihood of reoffending or else they would have prevented the criminal conduct in the first instance. With this in mind, defense attorneys may want to emphasize that the total lack of a support system, the absence of anyone supporting the offender in the courtroom at the sentencing hearing, is itself perhaps mitigating. Of course, this is a very touchy area because a lack of a support system, as noted, may suggest a likelihood of reoffending. Thus, emphasizing a lack of support may be persuasively mitigating only when there is a sad or sympathetic explanation for why that support system does not exist that outweighs the downside of lacking such a support system.

Diminished Capacity

Offenders who suffer from a diminished mental capacity are presumably less criminally culpable than others who have the ability to fully weigh the costs and benefits, the risks and harms of engaging in criminal conduct. Diminished mental capacity is distinct from mental or emotional impairments as a ground for a downward variance. Diminished mental capacity means that the offender was suffering from some type of mental impairment at the time of the offense that can be causally linked to the commission of the offense. The cause of the diminished mental capacity can be temporary, such as through intoxication, or it can be the result of a chronic mental health issue. Such long-term mental or emotional impairments may be an additional ground for a downward variance, or it may serve as a basis for a downward variance even if it cannot be shown that it contributed to the offender's criminal conduct.

Intoxication aside, it is often difficult for defense counsel to marshal evidence to support a diminished capacity variance. Clients may not have funds to pay for or be willing to submit to examination by psychological experts, and courts may be reluctant to pay for such experts for indigent clients without strong support that such an expert is needed. Defense counsel should consider issuing subpoenas to any entity that could have evidence to support a diminished capacity argument. These include not only health care providers, but also employer and jails where the offender has been housed; jails are often very good at documenting mental illnesses. As noted in an earlier chapter, defense counsel may find doing this type of investigation more protective of their client than having the client provide the probation office with a medical waiver because the records may contain incriminating or damaging information.

As noted in the last chapter, the Guidelines contain a provision addressing diminished mental capacity as a ground for departing from the Guidelines range. That provision, though, contains qualifying language and some limitations that do not govern a motion for a downward variance on the same ground. As with other variance arguments, a defense attorney may argue for a downward departure or, alternatively a downward variance, for diminished mental capacity or may simply argue for a downward variance. In some instances, the limitations in Section 5K2.13 may bar an argument for a downward departure, and the defense attorney can only argue for a variance.

Even when the offender is seeking a downward variance for diminished mental capacity, the attorneys should be prepared to address the factors that the Sentencing Commission identified in the departure provision. For instance, the prosecutor may want to invoke the language from the departure provision, emphasizing that the offender did not have a significant diminished mental capacity or that it did not substantially contribute to the commission of the offense. And even though the limitations in the second paragraph of Section 5K2.13 do not apply to a variance, prosecutors may wish to point out to the judge that the offender would not qualify for a departure on this ground and argue why the limitations under Section 5K2.13 make sense and have equal resonance in the case of a variance. A defendant may, for example, argue that a downward variance is appropriate because a limited mental capacity made it difficult for him to fully understand his role in the offense or comprehend the full scope of the criminal conduct or its consequences.

Drug or Alcohol Dependence and Other Addictions

The fact that an offender has a substance abuse or addiction problem can provide a basis for a downward variance from the advisory Guidelines range. Defense attorneys may argue that the offender's addiction is a disease over which the offender has little control and against which the offender has heroically struggled for years. A defense attorney may argue that the offense of conviction was directly linked to the offender's addiction (e.g., robbing a bank to obtain funds to buy drugs for personal use), or that the offender's criminal history score is the result of the offender's addiction (e.g., numerous drug possession or petty theft charges).[16]

Drug and alcohol addiction or dependence, however, is also a double-edged sword. As noted in the last chapter, the Guidelines counsel against a downward departure on this ground. The Guidelines reason that "[s]ubstance abuse is highly correlated to an increased propensity to commit crime." USSG §5H1.4. Thus, although addiction to alcohol or drugs may be a disease that could mitigate offender's mental culpability, that same disease makes addicted offenders more likely to reoffend and pose a greater danger to society. In short, a drug addict can be seen as a dangerously out-of-control person who is a plague on society. In resisting downward variances on this ground, prosecutors may want to focus on this danger, particularly if the offender has committed violent crimes to support his addiction or has contributed to others' addictions by distributing drugs himself.

The reasoning behind variances for alcohol or drug addictions may be applied to other addictions. Some people have gambling addictions,[17] while others may have addictions to pornography.[18] Some people are diagnosed with kleptomania, an uncontrollable desire to steal from others, or pyromania, an uncontrollable desire to start fires. The point is that defense attorneys may want to consider whether a downward variance is appropriate when an offender's criminal conduct or criminal history may be a product of a mental disease or defect that reflects addictive or otherwise uncontrollable behavior. The argument would be similar to that for drug addiction variances; the offender's criminal culpability is reduced because the offender is not driven by greed or some rational decision-making but, rather, by an irrational addiction over which the offender has little or no control. Thus, an offender convicted of arson because he suffers from a diagnosed case of pyromania may arguably be less criminally culpable than an offender convicted of arson because he wanted to collect insurance proceeds. The government's resistance would likely be similar to that for drug addiction; the fact the offender cannot control his behavior makes him a greater danger to the community, warranting a longer sentence and not a shorter one. Again, the government may argue the reasoning underlying Section 5H1.4, which states that "[a]ddiction to gambling is not a reason for a downward departure," discourages or makes no mention of departures for other addictions. USSG §5H1.4.

Employment Record

Offenders with good employment records may argue for a downward variance, although the government may argue that an upward variance is appropriate for offenders with poor work records.[19] The reasoning behind employment as a basis for an upward or downward variance is tied to recidivism and the punishment goal of deterrence. An offender with a good work history arguably has stability and shows social responsibility that would make it seem less likely the offender will commit other crimes in the future and for whom there is less need for deterrence. Conversely, an offender with a poor work history lacks stability, is less socially responsible, and has a greater need to be deterred from engaging in a life of crime instead of a life of employment. This factor may be particularly appropriate in cases involving property or violent crimes when the offender's motivation was financial.

As noted in the last chapter, the Guidelines indicate that "[e]mployment record is not ordinarily relevant in determining whether a departure is warranted." USSG §5H1.5. In part, this may be a reflection that many factors influence a person's employment history that may be completely unrelated to an offender's likelihood of reoffending. A poor employment history may also be a product of socio-economic or social factors outside the offender's control. Attorneys seeking a variance based on an offender's employment history should try to show why the court should find a link between the employment history and the need for deterrence, or why a lack of stable employment history does not necessarily suggest the offender is likely to reoffend, especially if the offender has access to resources he previously lacked.

Family Ties, Impact, and Responsibilities

In appropriate cases, defense attorneys may seek a downward variance from the advisory Guidelines range based on family ties and responsibilities. There are two aspects to a variance on this ground. The first is that family ties may suggest a lower chance of recidivism. The other focus is on the collateral damage that a lengthy sentence will cause to the offender's innocent family.

Studies show that supportive family connections predict reduced recidivism, while breaking up families leads to increased recidivism.[20] Thus, a defense attorney may argue that an offender with close family ties is less likely to reoffend, reducing the need for the court to impose a severe sentence to advance the goal of specific deterrence. Conversely, sentencing the offender to a period of incarceration may actually increase recidivism if it results in a breakup of the offender's family.

Defense attorneys may also consider seeking a downward variance based on the harm a lengthy sentence may cause to the offender's innocent family. This harm may be emotional resulting from physical separation, especially between the offender and children. There may also be financial harm, especially when the offender was historically the family's primary provider. This financial harm may result from incarceration, during which time an offender cannot work and earn a living, but it also may result from imposition of restitution or a fine. Thus, defense attorneys may seek a downward variance not only from the advisory Guidelines range of imprisonment, but also from the advisory Guidelines fine range.

As noted in the preceding chapter, the Guidelines generally discourage or completely bar downward departures from the advisory Guidelines range of imprisonment based on family ties and responsibilities and contemplates departures on this ground only as to the amount of restitution or fine. USSG §5H1.6. Defense attorneys will rarely seek a downward departure on this ground, then. Prosecutors should consider citing this Guidelines provision, on the other hand, in resisting a downward variance. Section 5H1.6 reflects a congressional disapproval of lessening an offender's punishment because of family ties and responsibilities, recognizing that hardship on an offender's family is an expected and anticipated consequence of criminal punishment. Indeed, prosecutors may wish to emphasize that the offender is the one responsible for placing his family in any hardship and to reduce the offender's sentence on such a ground is tantamount to excusing an offender's disregard for his own family when choosing to engage in criminal conduct.

Defense attorneys should be cautious about how they articulate motions for downward variances on family responsibility or impact grounds. Although it is invariably true that a term of incarceration can adversely impact family members, especially children, it is also invariably true that no one is more responsible than the offender for causing this harm to the offender's family. The offender, the prosecutor's argument may go, should have thought about this harm before choosing to commit the crime. A prosecutor may argue that to reduce the offender's sentence on this ground is to excuse the callousness of his behavior to his own family. Finally, defense counsel who suggests that a judge may harm the family, especially children, by imposing a harsh sentence risks offending the judge. The sentencing of offenders is the most emotionally difficult responsibility judges have and to lay at the feet of a judge the guilt of harming the offender's family because the offender chose to commit a crime would likely offend most judges.

Lack of Youthful Guidance or Disadvantaged Youth

A sad fact of the criminal justice system is that many offenders are the product of disadvantaged childhoods. Many offenders grew up in disadvantaged households or were transient residents of numerous foster homes. Some grew up in poverty and others in crime-ridden neighborhoods. Some offenders were physically, sexually, or emotionally abused as children. Some children grow up to model the criminal lives of adults around them, learning to commit crimes like their parents or older siblings, cousins, uncles, and neighbors. In some ways, then, it is not surprising that much adult criminal conduct can be traced back to and arguably resulted from a lack of youthful guidance or a disadvantaged youth. This may give rise to an argument for a downward variance from the advisory Guidelines range of imprisonment.

For troubled youth to be an effective ground for a variance, however, defense attorneys should articulate how a lower sentence would advance the goals of sentencing. In other words, the criminal justice system is not a program for compensating people for their unfortunate backgrounds. The criminal justice system does not award get-out-of-jail-free cards to people simply because they had unfortunate childhoods, no matter how sympathetic a person may be. One of the goals of sentencing, however, is retribution. One aspect of sentencing is to punish a person proportionate to the harm they caused society. Arguably, when society as a whole fails a child, leading him inexorably into a life of crime, it mitigates the appropriateness of seeking retribution against such an offender. A defense attorney may also argue, in some cases, that an offender will be less likely to reoffend, and thus in less need of deterrence, now that the offender has been caught up in the criminal justice system. In other words, one could perhaps argue in some cases that the very fact the offender was caught and prosecuted has been a benefit to the offender, interrupting the life trajectory and opening up possibilities of assistance in rehabilitation through services available while on supervised release or probation.

To be sure, the Guidelines discourage departures from the advisory range on such grounds. As noted in the last chapter, Section 5H1.12 provides, "[l]ack of guidance as a youth and similar circumstances indicating a disadvantaged upbringing are not relevant grounds in determining whether a departure is warranted." USSG §5H1.12. The Tenth Circuit Court of Appeals has stated that lack of guidance as a youth under Section 5H1.12 is a "forbidden" factor that can never be a basis for departure.[21] As with other grounds for which the Guidelines discourage or bar departures, prosecutors may invoke the reasoning of those Guidelines in resisting a downward variance. The government may argue that however sad an offender's childhood may have been, it does not mean the punishment for his crime should be decreased. Prosecutors may also wish to focus on whether there is a causal link between the disadvantaged childhood and the crime of conviction. Arguably, for example, a childhood of poverty may not explain an adulthood of violence. Comparing offenders against their siblings may also provide some insight to the court. If an offender has siblings who presumably grew up in the same disadvantaged situation, but those siblings did not become criminals, it undercuts the persuasiveness of the offender's argument that the disadvantaged childhood is somehow causally linked to the criminal conduct.

Consistent with a prior discussion of family support as a basis for a downward variance, a prosecutor may consider whether the fact an offender had a privileged background is aggravating. An offender who grew up in the lap of luxury and had every opportunity to lead a productive and lawful life, but who chooses to commit crimes instead, is perhaps more morally culpable and deserving of a harsher sentence than an offender who grew up disadvantaged and without such support.

Mental and Emotional Condition

An offender's mental or emotional health may support a downward variance for several reasons. An offender's mental or emotional impairment may mitigate the offender's criminal culpability.[22] A mental or emotional condition may also merit a downward variance because it decreases the likelihood the offender will reoffend.[23] A mental or emotional condition may similarly be relevant in arriving at an appropriate sentence if that condition could affect the severity of a period of incarceration. Lastly, offenders with intellectual disabilities or emotional health issues may be particularly vulnerable in prison to manipulation or harm.[24] A term of imprisonment for such an offender may be more severe than the same term of imprisonment for someone not suffering from such a condition.

Mental health conditions may be tied to diminished capacity but are not necessarily the same thing. Sometimes a mental or emotional health condition may have no direct connection to the offense conduct, and in other occasions, there may be a connection but not in a way that would support a diminished mental capacity claim. For example, an offender may suffer from a mental disease or defect, or have an intellectual disability, and yet those conditions may not have interfered with the offender's ability to know right from wrong or exercise judgment. Or, for example, an offender may have suffered from some event that caused the offender extreme emotional distress (a cheating spouse, for instance) that influenced the offender's criminal conduct but could not justify a diminished mental capacity claim.

Defense attorneys should try to make it clear through evidence and argument if they are claiming a causal link between an offender's mental and emotional health condition, and thus arguing the offender is less criminally culpable. Alternatively, a defense attorney could argue that a downward variance is warranted regardless of any such causal link. If they are making the former argument, it will be important for defense attorneys to establish that the mental or emotional condition existed at or before the time of the criminal conduct, and then prove through expert testimony or otherwise how the condition may have interfered with the offender's judgment, even if it did not rise to the level of diminished mental capacity defense. For example, an offender with an intellectual disability and emotional problems may have a stunted or non-existent social life and unhealthy interpersonal relationships, and thus may be more likely to turn to internet pornography, including child pornography. Although this would not support a diminished mental capacity claim, it may ameliorate the degree of criminal culpability.

On the other hand, if the import of the mental or emotional condition is that a term of imprisonment will be more severe for the offender than it would be for other offenders or make the offender more vulnerable in prison, defense attorneys need to be prepared to show how that is the case. Again, this may be proved through expert testimony or by data from public sources. Keeping in mind that the Federal Rules of Evidence do not apply at a sentencing hearing, a defense attorney can turn to publications and studies and present those findings in evidence without having to rely on live testimony or experts. The point is that effective sentencing advocacy is more than asking a judge to infer or assume vulnerability; it requires the proponent to persuasively show how a term of incarceration would adversely impact the offender. Defense attorneys may also want to emphasize the language in Section 3553(a) instructing judges to structure sentences that provide offenders "with needed educational or vocational training, medical care, or other correctional treatment in the most effective manner." 18 U.S.C. § 3553(a)(2)(D).

On occasion, offenders with untreated mental health issues receive treatment for the first time in their lives as part of the conditions of pretrial release or even possibly while incarcerated pending trial or sentencing. When this occurs, it may also give rise to an argument for a downward variance. A defense attorney may argue, for example, that the offender poses a decreased likelihood of reoffending now that the offender is being treated for an underlying mental health issue that could have been or was a contributing factor to the criminal behavior.

In resisting a motion for a downward variance on this ground, prosecutors may wish to focus on a lack of connection between the condition and the criminal conduct, or between the condition and impact of incarceration on the victim. Prosecutors may need to conduct their own research and produce evidence to show that the Bureau of Prisons is capable of caring well for an offender with mental or emotional conditions like those at issue in a case. Finally, a mental condition may also serve as a basis for an upward variance, or at least a basis to resist a downward variance, when that mental condition suggests the offender continues to pose a danger to society.[25]

Military Service

Offenders who have served their country in the military may be deserving of a downward variance from the advisory Guidelines range. The Supreme Court has noted, "Our Nation has a long tradition of according leniency to veterans in recognition of their service, especially for those who fought on the front lines[.]" *Porter v. McCollum*, 558 US 30, 43 (2009).[26] That does not mean, of course, that courts are required to vary downward simply because the offender once served in the military.[27] As noted in the previous chapter, the Guidelines Section 5H1.11 provides that a court may depart downward for military service, but with limits. It states, "Military service may be relevant in determining whether a departure is warranted, if the military service, individually or in combination with other offender characteristics is present to an unusual degree and distinguishes the case from the typical cases covered by the guidelines." USSG §5H1.11. In contrast, a court may vary downward for military service without a showing that the military service was of an unusual degree that distinguishes the case in some way.

As a matter of sentencing advocacy, defense attorneys seeking a downward variance for military service need to find some way to persuade a judge that an offender's past military service justifies a lower sentence. Defense attorneys can simply assert that prior military service of any kind calls for leniency as a way of compensating the offender for past service. This type of quid pro quo argument may be more compelling if the offender's service was of particular merit, especially if the offender fought in combat. Past heroic military service may be more deserving of mercy. This may be enough for some judges. The difficulty with that broad approach, however, is that it is not tied in any way to the goals of sentencing that judges must keep in mind at all times in fashioning the appropriate sentence. Prosecutors may also, and with some justification, respond to such a broad argument by arguing that military service does not give a veteran a license to commit crime or a get-out-of-jail-free card.

A more persuasive argument for a variance is one that ties the offender's military service to one of the goals of sentencing. In some cases, military service may have taken a mental or emotional toll on the offender that perhaps had some causal connection to his criminal conduct. In that event, military service decreases the offender's criminal culpability and the severity of the offense (unlike another offender who committed the crime out of base greed alone, for instance). When there is a connection between the military service and the offense conduct in this way, it may also address the goal of deterrence in that providing the offender with needed treatment may do more to prevent future offenses than imprisoning the offender. In other cases, the offender's military service may have caused physical, mental, or emotional damage that makes the offender more susceptible to abuse in prison or calls for a sentence fashioned in a manner to address the offender's need for treatment. This may be particularly important if the offender was a prisoner of war and imprisonment may trigger or exacerbate the offender's mental health problems. Of course, as with other variances tied to mental health issues, it may open up an opportunity for prosecutors to argue that the offender poses a greater danger to the community, whatever the source of the mental health issues, which militates in favor of a more severe sentence.

Non-Violent Offender

Defense attorneys may argue for a downward variance based on the absence of aggravating factors, such as the absence of violence in the offense conduct. The same can be said about the absence of the use of firearms, or employment of children, or other aggravating factors. Generally speaking, the absence of aggravating factors is not a compelling mitigating factor in favor of a downward variance. This becomes a more compelling argument depending on the nature of the offense and the propensity of other offenders committing similar crimes to engage in aggravating conduct.

For instance, firearms and violence are tools of the drug trade. Some drug organizations are particularly violent. If an offender convicted of conspiring to distribute drugs as a member of a violent, gun-toting organization did not, however, personally engage in any violence or carry a firearm when all around him did, then in contrast to others, the absence of the aggravating factors may be more mitigating.[28] In contrast, the fact that an offender convicted of filing false tax returns did not engage in violence or carry a firearm is hardly mitigating at all.

Physical Condition

An offender with significant physical impairments or illnesses may warrant a downward variance because serving a period of incarceration may be particularly hard on such an offender, the physical condition renders the offender no longer a danger to the community, the offender is less likely to reoffend, or because the cost of incarcerating such an offender may outweigh the benefits, or both. As noted in the prior chapter, Section 5H1.4 of the Guidelines provides that a court may depart downward from the Guidelines range for similar reasons. As with any of the Guidelines departure provisions, attorneys may rely on the language and reasoning of those provisions in arguing for downward departures.[29]

In advocating for a variance on this ground, it is important that a defense attorney provides the sentencing judge with medical evidence or records fully describing the medical condition, but perhaps more importantly, provides the court with evidence about the practical effect the medical condition has on the offender's daily activities. This latter evidence may be in the form of expert testimony, or it may be from family or friends who can inform the court about the offender's ability to care for himself. In considering the merits of a downward variance on this ground, the court will be attempting to assess the degree to which the offender's physical condition will impact life in a prison or life on the street.

Both defense attorneys and prosecutors can contact the Federal Bureau of Prisons to inquire about the prison's ability to care for offenders based on the precise physical condition at issue. In some cases, it may be appropriate to ask the Bureau of Prisons to provide a letter or other document addressing the issue or to subpoena someone from the Bureau to testify by telephone or in person. Generally speaking, however, there is not much in the way of physically-impaired inmates that the Bureau of Prisons cannot handle. The Bureau has several facilities well equipped to take care of prisoners with even the most serious of medical issues, including a facility in Rochester, Minnesota, that has connections to and is partially staffed by medical staff from the Mayo Clinic. Thus, it is a rare case indeed when a variance motion will succeed based solely on an assertion that the Bureau cannot provide adequate medical care for an offender. A variance motion focused more on whether the physical condition makes the offender vulnerable in prison, or would make the offender less of a danger on the street, would be more likely to have purchase with a court.

Post-Offense Rehabilitation

The time period between when an attorney appears on behalf of the offender and the time of the offender's sentencing can be a vital window of opportunity when a defense attorney may be able to impact the sentence. Whether an offender is in or out of custody pending sentencing, motivated offenders can take steps to show true rehabilitation between the time of arrest and sentencing.[30] It frankly surprises me how few offenders take advantage of this opportunity. At the very least, offenders on release pending sentencing should scrupulously comply with all the terms and conditions of release.[31] Offenders could do more than the bare minimum expected of them, however, showing steps toward rehabilitation by pursuing drug treatment or mental health treatment or counseling, or by securing employment, for example. Offenders who have not yet earned a high school diploma or a General Education Development (GED) degree should use this time to earn one.[32] When the criminal conduct caused harm to victims, offenders could make some effort toward paying restitution, even if the amount is nominal, or could apologize through appropriate channels for the harm caused. Fully cooperating with the government in the investigation arguably shows an offender's intent to distance himself from former associates and past criminal conduct, even if it does not constitute cooperation in the sense of providing information against others.

Of course, the hard task for a court is to assess the degree to which these post-offense actions reflect true rehabilitation or whether they reflect an offender's attempt to game the system by going through the motions of showing rehabilitation. There is no easy way to make this assessment. The greater the effort, the more dramatic the change from the offender's past conduct, the more the effort cost or hurt the offender in terms of time and money, the more likely it is, perhaps, to reflect true change. Defense attorneys may consider supplementing the cold record about the offender's rehabilitation efforts with the testimony of those who can attest that they have seen a true change.

Conversely, prosecutors may wish to examine the offender's conduct to look for signs that the offender is just going through the motions. Prosecutors may learn that the offender's attendance at drug treatment session, or his attitude while attending, was poor if the prosecutors looked into the matter. Prosecutors may also want to look at the offender's past history in this regard to see whether it is common for him to seek treatment while sentencing is pending, only to drop it immediately after sentencing. Likewise, it may be instructive to examine what the offender has done toward rehabilitation compared against what the offender could have done. Paying, or failing to pay, $100 toward restitution during the same period the offender spent $300 on cable television may speak volumes about the sincerity of the offender's rehabilitation. Similarly, attending a half-dozen drug treatment sessions while missing a dozen may also be insightful into an offender's true efforts to rehabilitate.

With rehabilitation as a basis for a downward variance, judges will often focus primarily on the specific deterrence goal of sentencing. An offender who has truly been rehabilitated is less likely to reoffend. If deterred from committing crimes in the future, then the offender will pose less of a danger to society. A longer sentence may not be necessary then to deter a truly rehabilitated offender. Thus, evidence and argument focused on the effect the offender's efforts at rehabilitation have on the likelihood of reoffending will likely have the greatest impact with judges.

Remorse or Lack of Remorse

When offenders show remorse or regret, not at getting caught and their own plight, but remorse and regret over the wrongs they have committed, it suggests that they will be less likely to reoffend or pose a danger to society. Unrepentant offenders, on the other hand, are more likely to reoffend and are less likely to feel empathy for victims, making them a greater danger to society. Thus, a shorter sentence may be necessary to achieve the goals of sentencing for remorseful offenders, while a longer sentence may be necessary for those who lack remorse for their crimes.

For offenders, remorse can sometimes be a tricky business. It is human nature to feel sorry for ourselves. Any offenders facing sentencing sanctions will naturally feel regret about the consequences of their actions that will be visited upon them and their family. Offenders may also, however, truly regret the harm they caused victims and feel remorse for the crimes they committed. Thus, expressions of remorse, or conduct reflective of remorse, is subject to conflicting interpretations. It may reflect remorse over the personal consequences for the offender and the offender's family, or it may reflect remorse over the harm the offender caused others. The former may not be worthy of a lesser sentence, whereas the latter may. Indeed, offenders who show no remorse for the harm they have caused others and who feel only regret for the adverse impact their convictions will have on themselves and their loved ones may be deserving of a harsher sentence.

Remorse is also tricky for offenders in the sense of how one shows extraordinary remorse worthy of a downward variance. Simply pleading guilty and admitting the criminal conduct does not warrant a variance from the advisory Guidelines range; the Guidelines provide for reductions in the offense level already for acceptance of responsibility. Indeed, a court may find an offender's lack of remorse justifies an upward variance even when the offender has pleaded guilty and accepted responsibility.[33] To be worthy of a downward variance for remorse, it should be something more. Remorse, though, is a state of mind and, as such, is provable largely through an offender's own self-serving statements.

An offender's written or oral statements reflecting sincere remorse is a minimum necessary showing to support a motion for a downward variance on this ground. Occasionally, this may be sufficient. I have heard, and believed, statements from several offenders that reflected a true, sincere, and deeply felt remorse for the harm they caused by their criminal conduct that gave me some confidence that the offenders were very unlikely to reoffend. Conversely, statements by offenders peppered with comments blaming others or circumstances or fate for leading the offenders to commit crimes, or statements full of self-pity or implications that the judge will hurt the offenders' family members by imposing a harsh sentence, are likely to hobble or destroy any hope of a downward variance.

No matter how articulate or sincere such statements of remorse may be, defense attorneys may want to search for other ways to show their clients' true remorse.

Contemporary letters expressing remorse written to family members or others, letters that are clear on their face were not written in anticipation of the sentencing hearing, may be very compelling. Likewise, any efforts to compensate victims, especially when restitution is not mandatory, may go a long way in showing remorse.

It is also tricky for prosecutors to succeed in seeking an upward variance from the advisory Guidelines range for lack of remorse. When offenders plead guilty, that alone suggests a degree of remorse that seems inconsistent with an upward variance for lack of remorse. On the other hand, prosecutors should be cautious about implying that an offender's decision to exercise the constitutional right to go to trial and require the government to prove its case to a jury beyond a reasonable doubt means that the offender lacks remorse. Exercising constitutional rights is not an indication of lack of remorse.

Evidence of a lack of remorse can arise from the offense conduct itself. Cold-blooded conduct in the commission of the offense, for example, may reveal a lack of remorse.[34] Offenders may also display a lack of remorse by conduct committed between the date of the crime and the sentencing hearing. Comments made on recorded jail calls or in letters may reflect an offender's lack of remorse. Certainly, the attitude an offender exhibits in hearings or statements made during allocution may show the offender lacks remorse.[35]

Criminal History

The Guidelines provide that a court may depart upward or downward from the advisory Guidelines when "reliable information indicates that the defendant's criminal history category substantially" over- or under-represents "the seriousness of the defendant's criminal history or the likelihood that the defendant will commit other crimes." USSG §4A1.3(a) & (b). A court may also vary upward or downward from the advisory Guidelines range under Title 18, United States Code, Section 3553(a). A departure requires the criminal history category "substantially" mischaracterizes the offender's true criminal history in some way. In contrast, a court may vary when an offender's criminal history is incongruent with the criminal history category even if the incongruency is not "substantial." Otherwise, there is little difference between a departure and a variance on this ground. Indeed, in assessing the reasonableness of a variance on this ground, appellate courts look to the law on departures.[36] Nevertheless, a court may vary even though it chose not to depart on the same ground because the standards justifying departures under the advisory Guidelines are narrower than the factors enumerated in Section 3553(a).[37]

When seeking a variance based on an over- or under-statement of criminal history, it may require attorneys to look behind the listing and summary of convictions in the presentence report and research the facts of the criminal conduct that resulted in the convictions. Arguably, not all convictions resulting in the same number of criminal history points are the same. For example, an OWI conviction when an offender's blood/alcohol level as .001 over the legal limit is perhaps less significant than if it were .3 over the legal limit. Conversely, an OWI conviction arising from an event when the offender drove the wrong way on an interstate causing a multi-car pileup may reflect that the offender is more of a danger to society than in other mine-run OWI cases. The timing of prior convictions may also give rise to an argument. The Guidelines assess criminal history points for any prior sentence exceeding one year and one month imposed within 15 years of the offender's offense conduct. USSG §4A1.2(e)(1). If the sentence was imposed 14 years, 11 months, and 29 days before the offense conduct, an argument could be made that it overstates the seriousness of the offense because passage of a single day would have resulted in no criminal history points for this conviction. Conversely, if the conviction occurred 15 years and one day before the offense, an argument could be made that the artificial cut-off resulted in an understated criminal history score. The point here is that attorneys should carefully examine offenders' criminal histories in presentence reports, not only to ensure that they were properly scored, but also to consider whether there are things about the criminal history that would warrant a variance from the advisory Guidelines.

3. Offender Conduct in Relation to Charge and Resolution

How offenders act in relation to criminal charges and in resolving the criminal charges may also give rise to grounds for courts to vary from the advisory Guidelines range. This may include an offender waiving indictment and agreeing to plead guilty before even being formally charged. Offenders may also take certain actions to show extraordinary accepted responsibility for the criminal conduct. How offenders comport themselves on pretrial or presentencing release may give rise to motions to vary both upward and downward from the advisory Guidelines range. When an offender attempts to cooperate, it may serve as a basis for a downward variance even if the cooperation was not sufficiently substantial to persuade the government to file a departure motion under USSG §5K1.1. Arguably, when offenders waive the right to appeal a sentence, it may reflect a degree of acceptance worthy of a downward variance. Finally, a downward variance may also be appropriate if an offender served time on state charges already for the same conduct.

Waiver of Indictment

Sometimes, particularly in white collar cases, the government may approach an offender before bringing criminal charges, inform the offender of the impending charges, and then attempt to negotiate a pre-indictment plea agreement. Because the Constitution requires the federal government to indict offenders on felony charges, a pre-indictment plea agreement would require the offender to waive the right to make the government present evidence to a grand jury and seek an indictment, and the offender would have to agree to be charged by way of a criminal information. The benefit to the government is that this saves limited grand jury resources. Time before grand juries is limited; when offenders waive indictment, it allows the government to more efficiently use the grand jury time to charge other offenders.

When an offender accepts the opportunity to work out a pre-indictment plea deal, it may support a basis for a downward variance. Although the government is motivated out of an effort to save resources, however, that fact is not a compelling reason for a downward variance. Rather, defense attorneys should emphasize that the importance of the offender's decision to waive the right of indictment is that it reflects an extraordinary level of acceptance of responsibility and remorse. That, in turn, arguably shows the offender is less likely to reoffend. In that sense, then, waiving indictment is seldom a stand-alone ground for a downward variance and is often cited instead as conduct showing acceptance of responsibility.

Acceptance of Responsibility

Waiving indictment is not the only way for offenders to show extraordinary acceptance of responsibility worthy of a downward variance. Indeed, the government does not offer many offenders the option of waiving indictment and pleading guilty to criminal information. Offenders may show extraordinary acceptance of responsibility, though, by promptly confessing to law enforcement officers when first confronted, for example, or by consenting to searches of their property upon request. These events almost invariably occur before defense attorneys are involved, such that defense attorneys cannot usually directly influence the offender's conduct at this stage. Nevertheless, defense attorneys can point out this behavior at the time of sentencing, when it occurs, as evidence of extraordinary acceptance of responsibility. Offenders may also promptly plead guilty after being charged, cooperate fully with the government's investigation, and not dispute Guidelines calculations. If the offense involved losses to victims, making restitution payments before being ordered to do so may show extraordinary acceptance of responsibility. Letters of apology to crime victims may similarly show extraordinary acceptance of responsibility. Cooperating with the government to forfeit property likewise arguably shows acceptance of responsibility. All these types of acts can demonstrate an extraordinary level of acceptance of responsibility.

In some cases, an offender is facing multiple charges in more than one jurisdiction, or may be facing a civil or regulatory action at the same time arising out of the same conduct that led to the criminal charge. For example, a company prosecuted for an environmental crime may also be facing civil or regulatory action by the Environmental Protection Agency. An offender in that position may work out a global plea or agreement in which it resolves all criminal, civil, and administrative actions against it in a manner showing that it is fully accepting responsibility for its actions in all spheres.

As with other variance grounds, attorneys should look to the Guidelines for guidance in this and other areas. The application notes to USSG §3E1.1 identify a number of things that offenders can do to show acceptance of responsibility. These include (a) truthfully admitting the criminal conduct; (b) voluntarily terminating or withdrawing from the criminal conduct; (c) voluntarily paying restitution before adjudication of guilt; (d) voluntarily surrendering to authorities promptly after commission of the offense; (e) voluntarily assisting authorities in recovering the fruits and instrumentalities of the crime; (f) voluntarily resigning from the office or position held during the commission of the offense; (g) engaging in post-offense rehabilitation efforts; and (h) manifesting acceptance early. USSG §3E1.1 (cmt. n.1). Arguably, offenders who can check off several of these examples of acceptance may deserve a further reduction in the sentence for super acceptance. Conversely, the Guidelines indicate that an offender who frivolously objects to relevant criminal conduct may not be showing acceptance of responsibility. *Id.* And certainly, an offender who engages in conduct that is obstructive (USSG §3E1.1 [cmt. n.4]) or lies to a probation or pretrial officer (USSG §3C1.1 [cmt. n.5(E)]) may exhibit a lack of acceptance of responsibility. Attorneys should keep these Guidelines provisions in mind in assessing variance arguments, even if the conduct is not present to such a degree as to affect the Guidelines calculations themselves.

In short, there can be degrees of acceptance of responsibility. Defense attorneys should explore every opportunity for offenders to show acceptance of responsibility, and prosecutors should be alert to conduct that detracts from a conclusion that offenders have fully accepted responsibility for their conduct. As with other grounds, it is often best for defense attorneys to articulate how extraordinary acceptance relates to the goals of sentencing; it arguably shows the offender is less likely to reoffend and thus is not in need of a severe sentence for purposes of deterrence. And prosecutors should point out the need for a more severe sentence when offenders have not truly accepted full responsibility for their criminal conduct because it suggests they need more punishment to deter them from committing offenses in the future.

Conduct on Pretrial Release

How offenders comport themselves on pretrial or presentencing release can hurt them or help them. That conduct can thus support grounds for upward or downward variances from the advisory Guidelines range. Offenders who violate the trust courts place in them when the courts allow the offenders to be free on pretrial release may be deserving of a sentence above the advisory Guidelines range. Such conduct reflects a degree of incorrigibility and lack of respect for the law that suggests a more severe sentence is necessary for purposes of deterrence. If the violation involved other criminal conduct, particularly conduct involving violence or weapons, an upward variance may also be warranted to protect the community.[38]

A court may vary upward for violations of pretrial release even when the court does not impose an enhancement for obstruction of justice under USSG §3C1.1 or declines to take away an offender's acceptance of responsibility reduction under USSG §3E1.1 for the same conduct. Conversely, a court may vary upward even when the conduct on pretrial release resulted in an obstruction enhancement or loss of an acceptance of responsibility reduction.[39] Indeed, when the conduct is sufficiently egregious, a court can vary upward even when the conduct has resulted in an enhancement for committing an offense while on release under USSG §3C1.3.[40]

Conduct on pretrial release less often justifies a downward variance unless it also reflects extraordinary acceptance of responsibility. In other words, offenders who engage in conduct showing extraordinary acceptance of responsibility of the type discussed above while on pretrial release may have a good argument for a downward variance. Offenders who only refrain from violating pretrial release conditions do not. Offenders are expected to comply with conditions of pretrial release, and simply having no violations on pretrial release is hardly grounds for a downward variance.

That said, there may be factors that show extraordinary conduct on pretrial release that may warrant a downward variance. For example, an offender with a severe heroin addiction who manages to beat the addiction while on pretrial release may have shown such a strength of character that a court can have some faith that the offender can show the same self-discipline not to offend again in the future. Or, for example, an offender who had a poor work or other achievement record but who, while on pretrial release, obtained steady employment, earned an educational degree, or otherwise showed a real transformation while on pretrial release may have an argument that a downward variance would be warranted. In short, it will likely take more than simply not violating conditions of pretrial release for an offender to get a downward variance from most judges.

When offenders do violate terms of pretrial release, defense attorneys should investigate the cause for the violations. Again, it is far easier for offenders with ample support systems and family structure to comply while the disadvantaged offenders with no support system may struggle. There may also have been unusual events in the offender's life, such as the death of a loved one or some other crisis, that the defense attorney could emphasize, not to excuse the violation, but to place the violation in context and argue why it mitigates the seriousness of the violation or the likelihood the offender will reoffend.

Attempted Cooperation

For offenders to receive a reduction under USSG §5K1.1 for cooperating, the government must make the motion and will do so only if that cooperation constituted substantial assistance. Sometimes offenders attempt to cooperate and do everything in their power to provide substantial assistance, but for reasons outside their control, the cooperation never reaches that level. Perhaps the cause is that the government does not use the assistance provided because of a lack of resources, the government shifted its focus on other targets, or some other reason. Or, perhaps, the assistance was not substantial for reasons out of everyone's control, such as a target fleeing the country or dying.

When offenders have done all that is within their power to provide substantial assistance but fail to earn motions from the government, they may argue that they are entitled to some reduction in their sentence for their efforts through a downward variance. This may be especially true when their cooperation assisted the government in some manner but just did not quite rise to the level of being "substantial." When offenders seek variances on this ground, defense attorneys should be cautious about how they handle the motion for several reasons. The assistance the offender provided is almost assuredly still confidential and may relate to an ongoing investigation, so defense attorneys should not disclose it in any publicly filed sentencing memorandum or by making statements about it in open court. Disclosure of an offender's attempt to cooperate may also be as dangerous to the safety of the offender and the offender's family as it would be if the assistance was substantial. Thus, defense attorneys should work with prosecutors to ensure that they can raise the motion in a way that will not jeopardize either the government's or the offender's interests.

In moving for a downward variance on the ground of attempted cooperation, it is often best that defense attorneys not take the tone that the government has somehow acted improperly or in bad faith. Defense attorneys seldom possess the information that prosecutors do about ongoing criminal investigations and prosecutorial decisions, and prosecutors may not be able to disclose that information even in the face of accusations of bad faith. Nor is it necessarily effective for defense attorneys to argue that the offender is entitled to a reduction as a reward for making an effort to cooperate, as if the offender has earned a get-out-of-jail free card. On the other hand, if a defense attorney has a good faith belief that the government has breached a plea agreement by not making a motion when one is appropriate, the defense attorney may move to enforcement the plea agreement at the time of sentencing. Because knowledge that an offender has cooperated or even attempted to cooperate may place the offender in danger while incarcerated, litigation over this issue should be addressed in camera or in a sealed record.

An approach that may meet with more success is for defense attorneys to focus on the offender's intent and how the offender's efforts reflect on the offender's criminal culpability and the likelihood of reoffending. In other words, a defense attorney may emphasize that an offender's good faith efforts to cooperate reflect a desire to break with his criminal associates, accept responsibility for his past wrongs, and change the trajectory of his life. A defense attorney can emphasize that effort to cooperate shows that the offender does not need a severe sentence to be deterred from future criminal conduct. A focus on the offender's efforts and character is more likely to succeed with a judge, and not provoke a strong resistance from the government, than a tone that the offender has been cheated out of a substantial assistance departure motion. Again, the most effective sentencing advocacy is to tie arguments directly to the goals of sentencing upon which judges invariably focus.

Waiver of Appeal

Offenders sometimes agree to waive their right to appeal their sentences. Arguably, this reflects a high degree of acceptance of responsibility. An offender willing to waive the right to appeal the sentence is an offender who is willing to fully accept what is coming to him without complaint, a defense attorney may argue. This may be true to a degree. On the other hand, when offenders waive their appeal rights, it is almost always the result of a plea negotiation involving the government making a charging or sentencing concession in exchange for the offender agreeing not to appeal the sentence. When an appeal waiver is the result of a quid pro quo with the government, then the waiver is much less a reflection of acceptance of responsibility than it reflects a bargained for exchange. Thus, defense attorneys may consider asserting an appeal waiver as warranting a downward variance, but prosecutors should be quick to point out when offenders already received some sentencing concession in exchange for that waiver. Similarly, in some districts, prosecutors insist on an appeal waiver in exchange for any plea agreement and not in exchange for a charging or sentencing concession. In such a case, this too may give rise to an argument for a downward variance by suggesting that the government condition unfairly deprived the offender of a right he would otherwise have.

4. Time Served but Not Credited in Sentence

In some instances, a downward variance may be appropriate for the judge to adjust a period of incarceration to reflect credit for time the offender served in custody for conduct that was part of the crime of conviction. Sentencing courts have no authority to instruct the Bureau of Prisons how to calculate offenders' time-served credit. Title 18, United States Code, Section 3585(b) provides that an offender "shall be given credit toward the service of a term of imprisonment for any time he has spent in official detention prior to the date the sentence commences." Section 3585(b) also provides that this time served credit must not have been "credited against another sentence." 18 U.S.C. § 3585(b). The United States Supreme Court has held that a district court may not award credit at sentencing, because "Congress has indicated that computation of the credit must occur after the defendant begins his sentence." *United States v. Wilson*, 503 U.S. 329, 333 (1992).

When sentencing judges believe that offenders deserve credit for time served, and yet have concerns that the Bureau of Prisons may not give offenders the credit, the judges may depart downward under Section 5G of the Guidelines or vary downward to achieve that result.[41] In appropriate cases then, when there may be a question about whether an offender will receive credit for time served in state custody on state charges for conduct that also comprises the basis for the federal charge, defense counsel may find a motion for a downward variance proper. As mentioned previously, this area of the law is full of pitfalls and can be very complicated. I will not attempt to parse through all the legal issues here, but attorneys should be aware that credit for time served is complicated and deserves significant attention from them.

5. Judges' Policy Disagreements with the Guidelines

In *Kimbrough v. United States*, 552 U.S. 85 (2007), the Supreme Court held that "district courts are entitled to reject and vary categorically from the crack-cocaine Guidelines based on a policy disagreement with those Guidelines." *Spears v. United States*, 555 U.S. 261, 266 (2009) (clarifying *Kimbrough*). At the time of *Kimbrough*, the applicable guideline provision treated one gram of crack cocaine as equivalent to 100 grams of powder cocaine. In *Kimbrough*, the Supreme Court upheld the district court's decision to vary downward because of its policy disagreement with the crack-versus-powder-cocaine sentencing disparity in USSG §2D1.1. *Kimbrough*, 552 U.S. at 91. As the Court explained, the Commission generally developed the Guidelines "using an empirical approach based on data about past sentencing practices." *Id.* at 96. Crucially, however, the Commission "did not use this empirical approach in developing the Guidelines sentences for drug-trafficking offenses." *Id.* Instead, at Congress's direction, the Commission formulated Guideline 2D1.1(c) based on the "weight-driven scheme" in the Anti-Drug Abuse Act of 1986 (1986 Act), Pub. L. No. 99–570, 100 Stat. 3207 (1986). *Id.* Thus, the Supreme Court recognized that Guideline 2D1.1(c) did "not exemplify the Commission's exercise of its characteristic institutional role" to "base its determinations on empirical data and national experience." *Id.* at 109 (internal quotation marks omitted). The Supreme Court concluded, then, that the Commission's deviation from its characteristic institutional role in creating Guideline 2D1.1(c) afforded district courts greater leeway to vary from that guideline. *See id.* at 109–110.

Kimbrough thus gave leave to sentencing courts to vary from the Guidelines when judges have a policy disagreement with particular Guidelines provisions.[42] As a result, courts have varied based on a number of such policy disagreements. This discretion "applies to all aspects of the Guidelines" and is not limited to crack cocaine or other drug Guidelines provisions.[43] Nevertheless, most policy disagreement-based variances do relate to Guidelines provisions for drug offenses (such as methamphetamine and heroin) which, like the crack cocaine provision, were not based on an empirical approach but, instead, were based on statutory provisions.[44] The *Kimbrough* holding has been extended, however, to cover policy disagreement with Guidelines other than drug Guidelines. Thus, courts have varied downward based on policy disagreements with disparity in the treatment of immigration cases based on the existence of fast-track programs in some but not all districts,[45] the child pornography Guidelines provisions,[46] and career offender Guidelines provisions.[47] To be clear, although most judges vary downward, particularly with policy disagreements, judges may vary from the advisory Guidelines range in either direction—upward or downward—based on a policy disagreement with the Guidelines.[48]

Sentencing judges are not compelled, however, to have a policy disagreement with the Guidelines, even when the Sentencing Commission did not base the Guidelines provision on empirical data.[49] So long as a judge recognizes that the judge has the authority to vary downward based on a policy disagreement and chooses not to do so, there is no error. For each court opinion in which a court has varied downward based on a policy disagreement with various Guidelines provisions, there are about as many opinions in which courts have declined to do so for reasons articulated in those decisions. Thus, both prosecutors and defense attorneys have grounds for arguing that judges should, or should not, vary from the Guidelines for policy reasons, and it is left the sound discretion of sentencing judges to decide what to do.

C. *Variances for Other Reasons*

The list of variance grounds discussed above is not exhaustive of the basis for courts to vary from the advisory Guidelines ranges. Rather, the goal here was to discuss grounds commonly raised and to explore how attorneys may best advocate for and against variances based on these grounds. Because sentencing judges may consider literally anything in arriving at a sentence, the range of grounds for which attorneys may argue for variances is limited only by their imaginations. It remains important for purposes of persuasion, however, that attorneys anchor their variance arguments to one or more of the goals of sentencing. Judges are charged with focusing on those goals and variance arguments that explain how and why a variance would advance one of those goals will have more purchase than arguments that seek only to appeal judges' emotions or sympathy.

D. Preserving Grounds to Appeal on Variance Motions

Appellate courts review district courts' sentencing decisions for an abuse of discretion, inquiring whether the sentence is reasonable in view of the factors listed in 18 U.S.C. § 3553(a). *See Gall v. United States*, 552 U.S. 38 (2007): "Our explanation of reasonableness review in the *Booker* opinion made it pellucidly clear that the familiar abuse-of-discretion standard of review now applies to appellate review of sentencing decisions." Reasonableness has both a procedural and a substantive component. In general, a sentence that reflects a proper Guidelines calculation and application of the Section 3553(a) factors is procedurally reasonable. A sentence is deemed substantively reasonable if it reflects the seriousness of the crime and the Section 3553(a) factors as applied to the case. A sentence which falls within a properly-calculated Guidelines range is presumed to be substantively reasonable on appeal.

Judges should explain the basis for any variance sufficiently to allow for meaningful appellate review. It is incumbent upon attorneys who have persuaded the judge to vary then to ensure that the judge adequately explains the basis for the variance. Attorneys may need to ask the court to elaborate on its reasoning if necessary. Conversely, to make a good record for purposes of appeal, a party should ask for clarification if it believes the court has failed to adequately address or state the grounds for rejecting a variance motion. For those opposing variances, it is equally important to note opposition to variances to preserve the issue for appeal. It is generally sufficient to preserve the issue for appeal when a party to object to the downward variance sentence as unreasonable.[50]

16

Fines

Criminal fines are a form of punishment that courts may impose in addition to, or in lieu of, other punishments, such as periods of incarceration. Indeed, criminal fines have long been a common form of punishment, second only to incarceration. Nevertheless, in the federal system, judges seldom impose fines. This is primarily because many offenders are indigent by the time they reach sentencing, or if they have funds, using them for restitution to make victims whole takes priority. On the other hand, the imposition of fines is the primary form of punishment for organization offenders. Whether the offender is a person or an organization, criminal fines constitute an important form of punishment and require attorneys' attention.

Effective sentencing advocacy as to the imposition of fines requires attorneys to consider several factors. In the federal system, attorneys should consider both the applicable statutory and Guidelines fine provisions. Attorneys need also to consider Constitutional provisions relating to fines. Ultimately, attorneys should then consider the burden of proof and determine how to weigh and argue factors the judge will consider in determining whether to impose a fine. Lastly, attorneys should consider the implications of arguing for imposition of a fine in lieu of a term of incarceration.

A. Statutory Fine Provisions

In the American criminal justice system, fines are statutory in origin; that is, statutes prescribe minimum and maximum fines for crimes just like they do the minimum and maximum periods of incarceration. Generally speaking, the more serious the offense, the greater the maximum fine. In the federal system, criminal statutes defining the elements of a crime often also contain punishment provisions that establish minimum and maximum periods of incarceration and fines. Some of these statutes tie the amount of fine to the amount of money involved in the criminal conduct or the nature or degree of harm caused by the conduct.[1] Many federal criminal statutes, however, simply state the court may impose a fine "consistent with this statute." That language refers to Title 18, United States Code, Section 3571, which establishes the maximum fines for individuals and organizations based on the classification of the offense as a felony, a misdemeanor resulting in death, a Class A, B, or

C misdemeanor, or infraction. 18 U.S.C. § 3571(b) & (c). Also, Section 3572(d), sometimes known as the Alternative Fines Act, provides for an alternative fine based on gain or loss from the crime. It states:

> If any person derives pecuniary gain from the offense, or if the offense results in pecuniary loss to a person other than the defendant, the defendant may be fined not more than the greater of twice the gross gain or twice the gross loss, unless imposition of a fine under this subsection would unduly complicate or prolong the sentencing process.

18 U.S.C. § 3571(d).

In determining whether to impose a fine, sentencing judges must consider all the factors at Title 18, United States Code, Section 3553(a). The judge must also consider other statutory factors, including: "(1) the defendant's income, earning capacity, and financial resources; (2) the burden that the fine will impose upon the defendant, any person who is financially dependent on the defendant, or any other person (including a government) that would be responsible for the welfare of any person financially dependent on the defendant, relative to the burden that alternative punishments would impose; (3) any pecuniary loss inflicted upon others as a result of the offense; (4) whether restitution is ordered or made and the amount of such restitution; (5) the need to deprive the defendant of illegally obtained gains from the offense; (6) the expected costs to the government of any imprisonment, supervised release, or probation; and (7) whether the defendant can pass on to consumers or other persons the expense of the fine." 18 U.S.C. § 3572(a). When offenders also owe restitution as a result of the crime, judges are to impose a fine "only to the extent that such fine or penalty will not impair the ability of the defendant to make restitution." 18 U.S.C. § 3572(b).

B. Guidelines Fine Provisions

The Federal Sentencing Guidelines provide that the sentencing judge "shall impose a fine in all cases, except when the defendant establishes that he is unable to pay and is not likely to become able to pay any fine." USSG §5E1.2. The burden is on the offender to show an inability to pay a fine.[2] The Guidelines provide a chart of minimum and maximum fine ranges tied to the offender's offense level, unless another Chapter 2 section provides for a different range. USSG §5E1.2(b) & (c). The Guidelines permit imposition of two fines: one based on the offense and one based on the costs of incarceration and supervised release.[3] USSG §§5E1.2(c)(1)(A) & (i).

In determining the amount of the fine to be imposed, a sentencing judge must consider the factors in USSG §5E1.2. These factors are similar to the statutory factors at 18 U.S.C. § 3572(a), but they are not identical. They are: (1) the need for the sentence to reflect the seriousness of the offense, promote respect for the law, provide just punishment, and afford adequate deterrence; (2) the offender's ability to pay the fine in light of his earning capacity and financial resources; (3) the burden that the fine places on the offender and his dependents; (4) any restitution that the offender has made or will be required to make; (5) the collateral consequences of the conviction; (6) whether the offender has previously been fined for a similar offense; (7) the expected costs to the government of any term of probation, imprisonment, or supervised release; and (8) any other pertinent equitable considerations. USSG §5E1.2(d).

C. Constitutional Constraints on Fines

The Eighth Amendment to the United States Constitution provides, "Excessive bail shall not be required, nor excessive fines imposed, nor cruel and unusual punishments inflicted." U.S. Const., Amdt. 8. At the time the Constitution was adopted, "the word 'fine' was understood to mean a payment to a sovereign as punishment for some offense." *Browning-Ferris Industries of Vt., Inc. v. Kelco Disposal, Inc.*, 492 U.S. 257, 265 (1989). The Excessive Fines Clause thus "limits the government's power to extract payments, whether in cash or in kind, 'as punishment for some offense.'" *Austin v. United States*, 509 U.S. 602, 609–610 (1993) (emphasis deleted). Federal courts have seldom interpreted or applied the Excessive Fines Clause outside the realm of forfeiture actions. As I will discuss in more detail in the next chapter, criminal and civil forfeiture actions are considered a form of punishment and their constitutionality judged in the context of the Excessive Fines Clause.

It is conceivable that a fine near or at the top of the statutory fine range could constitute an unconstitutionally excessive fine if imposed on an indigent offender. When courts have considered whether forfeiture actions constitute excessive fines, however, there is a presumption that they are not excessive if the value of the forfeited property is less than the statutory maximum fine. That would suggest that any fine within the statutory range would not be excessive under the Eighth Amendment. As a practical matter, this question will unlikely ever be answered because judges routinely decline to impose fines when it is clear that offenders do not have the financial ability to pay fines. Thus, although defense attorneys should always consider possible constitutional challenges to imposition of fines, they should recognize that this is unlikely to be a successful basis on which to persuade a sentencing judge to decline imposing a fine, so long as the amount of the fine is within the statutory range.

It should be noted here that the right to be free from excessive fines under the Eighth Amendment is one of the few remaining rights within the Bill of Rights that the Supreme Court has not incorporated against the states.[4] That does not mean, of course, that the excessive fines clause does not apply to the states. It may. But it does mean that there is no Supreme Court precedent for it at this time.

Some statutes, particularly public welfare statutes such as environmental crimes, provide for enhanced fines based on facts, such as how many days a waste stream was introduced into the environment. Fines, as a form of punishment, are subject to the holding in *Apprendi v. New Jersey*, 530 U.S. 466 (2000). That is, if the finding of a fact can increase the statutory maximum fine to which an offender is exposed, then that fact must be alleged in the indictment and proven to a jury beyond a reasonable doubt.[5]

D. Advocating For or Against Imposition of Fines

When attorneys advocate for or against imposition of fines as a form of criminal punishment, they should first take stock of all the statutory and Guidelines factors that judges must consider when deciding whether to impose, and the amount of, criminal fines. Attorneys' evidence and arguments should address those factors if they want to be persuasive.

Offenders may resist imposition of a fine, or a significant fine, for multiple reasons. Primary among them is an assertion that the offender lacks the financial ability to pay a fine. Unlike most other matters at sentencing, the burden of proof for whether an offender has the financial ability to pay a fines lays with the offender.[6] Offenders who refuse to provide financial information to the probation officer in connection with the preparation of the presentence report are generally found to have failed to show an inability to pay a fine unless they produce that information at the sentencing hearing.[7] It is important for both sides to recognize as well that the focus is not just on the offender's current financial status. Even if an offender cannot presently pay a fine, a court may still impose a fine if the offender has a future ability to pay a fine.

Offenders may also resist imposition of criminal fines because it would place a financial burden on others. This may be particularly true when the offender will also face a period of incarceration. Although an offender may have sufficient funds to pay a fine at the time of sentencing, if the offender is the sole or primary breadwinner for the family and will be incarcerated for a period of time, those funds may be necessary for the family's support.

It is possible that the uncontested portions of the presentence report provide an adequate factual basis for the court to determine whether the offender lacks the ability to pay a fine or that imposition of the fine will impose a financial burden on others. Effective sentencing advocacy, however, may require the attorneys to supplement the information in the presentence report with other evidence of the offender's financial status. Effective sentencing advocacy by defense counsel may necessitate that the offender produces a financial affidavit or financial records and documentation. It may also require live testimony from the offender or others. It is important to recognize that an offender's unsworn allocution is not evidence that the court can rely on in deciding a fine or any other factually-disputed matter.[8] Nor are statements by defense counsel evidence upon which the court may rely. If the goal is to persuade the factfinder not to impose a fine, then defense attorneys need to think in terms of providing the judge with evidence upon which the judge can rely to rule in the offender's favor. On the other side of the aisle, the government need not simply rely on the presentence report or the offender's financial affidavit. If a prosecutor believes that an offender may have the ability to pay a criminal fine, the prosecutor should have officers investigate the offender's finances and, if necessary, subpoena witnesses to testify or produce financial records at the sentencing hearing.

Attorneys for both sides should consider the impact any fine would have on the offender's ability to pay restitution to victims. Money from an offender in the form of fine payments goes into the government's coffers, but money from an offender in restitution goes to make victims whole. Although a court may require both payment of restitution and a fine, generally any funds from the offender will be applied first to the payment of the offender's restitution obligation and only after that is paid in full will funds be applied toward fulfilling the offender's fine obligation. In advocating for or against a fine when there also exists a restitution obligation, attorneys should consider the effect of all aspects of punishment as a whole. A long period of incarceration and a large restitution obligation would generally militate against imposition of a fine or imposition of a large fine, whereas a short period of incarceration and a small restitution obligation may suggest a significant fine may be appropriate.

Attorneys should also consider the implications of seeking imposition of a fine in lieu of a period of incarceration. There is strong debate about the propriety of imposing fines instead of incarceration when the motive for or the harm arising from the crime was financial. Some argue that fining a criminal who was motivated by greed is a greater deterrence to that offender and others similarly situated than a period of incarceration. Others argue that this smacks of buying one's way out of prison. Many low-income offenders are financially unable to pay fines, while high income offenders often are able to pay some fine. Thus, courts and attorneys should maintain perspective about fines as a form of punishment in relation to terms of incarceration.

In a similar vein, both prosecutors and defense attorneys should be cautious in how they articulate their arguments when discussing the length of incarceration and imposition of a fine. It is true that while an offender is in prison, the offender cannot earn a good salary that could be used to pay a fine. But if a sentence of incarceration is appropriate, then the effect it might have on the offender's ability to pay a fine that is also appropriate should not impact the judge's decision. It is generally best, however, for attorneys to argue the merits of the length of incarceration and the amount of a fine separately and on their own merits.

17

Forfeiture

Forfeiture is a form of financial punishment that sentencing court mays impose, in addition to terms of incarceration and fines.[1] Criminal forfeiture is an in personam proceeding against an offender personally and is part of the punishment.[2] Federal statutes authorize the government to seek forfeiture of property, real and personal, that constitutes proceeds of criminal activity or that was used to facilitate or commit the criminal conduct. The goals of criminal forfeiture are to "punish wrongdoing, deter future illegality, ... lessen the economic power of criminal enterprises ... recompense victims of a crime, improve conditions in crime-damaged communities, and support law enforcement activities like police training." *Kaley v. United States*, 571 U.S. 320, 323 (2014) (internal quotation marks and citations omitted). Courts do not order forfeiture in every case, and sometimes the government seeks civil forfeiture of assets outside the scope of the criminal prosecution.

The case law is legion on the parameters of what the government can and cannot forfeit and what evidence is required for the government to prevail. This is not a book on the substantive law of forfeiture. Yet, because forfeiture is a component of some sentences, it is proper to broadly examine the law of forfeiture so as to discuss sentencing advocacy as it relates to forfeiture. The focus of the discussion here about forfeiture, then, is on forfeiture as a form of punishment and how a party's position on forfeiture may impact effective advocacy on other forms of punishment.

There are several factors to consider when thinking of effective sentencing advocacy in relation to forfeiture. First, there are Constitutional implications. Second, attorneys should consider the statutory authority for the court to impose forfeiture orders. Third, there are rules establishing procedures required to provide offenders with due process in connection with criminal forfeiture. Fourth, in formulating an effective sentencing advocacy strategy, attorneys should consider the interrelation between forfeiture and restitution. Similarly, and lastly, attorneys should consider how the offender's position about forfeiture, that is the offender's willingness or unwillingness to forfeit property to the government, may reflect on an offender's acceptance of responsibility and remorse and, thus, how it may impact the offender's sentence of incarceration. Were an offender to challenge facts related to the forfeiture, it may suggest a lack of acceptance of responsibility, while a purely legal challenge to a forfeiture action may not.

A. Constitutional Implications of Forfeiture

The Eighth Amendment to the United States Constitution provides, "Excessive bail shall not be required, nor excessive fines imposed, nor cruel and unusual punishments inflicted." U.S. CONST. AMEND. VIII. Criminal forfeiture is a fine within the meaning of the Eighth Amendment's excessive fines clause.[3] Courts must undertake "a fact-intensive analysis under the Eighth Amendment Excessive Fines Clause to ensure that the forfeiture is not an excessive penalty, and courts may forfeit less than what the statute requires if necessary to preserve the forfeiture by tailoring it to fit within the broad boundaries of constitutional proportionality." *United States v. Bieri*, 68 F.3d 232, 236 (8th Cir. 1995) (internal quotation marks and citation omitted). The "principle of proportionality" embodied in the Excessive Fines Clause requires that "[t]he amount of the forfeiture must bear some relationship to the gravity of the offense that it is designed to punish." *United States v. Bajakajian*, 524 U.S. 321, 334 (1998). Nevertheless, the Constitution does not require strict proportionality, meaning that the amount of forfeiture need not be precisely equal to the crime. Rather, the forfeiture of property violates the Constitution's excessive fines clause only if it is "grossly disproportionate to the gravity of the defendant's offense." *Id.*, at 336–37.

The United States Supreme Court has declined to establish a strict test for determining proportionality, but lower courts have provided some guidance. Generally, an offender must make a prima facie case that the value of the property being forfeited is grossly disproportionate to the seriousness of the crime. A monetary forfeiture order is constrained by the Excessive Fines Clause only when it is imposed as punishment for some offense.[4] Forfeiture does not per se violate the Eighth Amendment simply because the amount to be forfeited exceeds the maximum fine under the sentencing Guidelines.[5]

There are no Guidelines provisions pertaining to forfeiture. Nevertheless, the Guidelines provisions for fines may be informative of the constitutionality of a forfeiture order. In considering whether a forfeiture order constitutes a violation of the Excessive Fines Clause, courts look to the Guidelines fine range. If the value of the property forfeited falls within that range, it will generally be found not to be excessive. If value of the forfeited property exceeds the Guidelines fine range, then it may be excessive. That fact alone, however, is not enough to find forfeiture constitutes an excessive fine.

Finally, criminal forfeiture is a matter alleged in an indictment and, unless the offender agrees as part of a plea or sentencing agreement, must be decided by a jury. The rule announced in *Apprendi v. New Jersey*, 530 U.S. 466 (2000), however, does not apply to forfeiture orders because forfeiture statutes do not establish any statutory maximum and are not a determinate scheme.[6] Thus, the jury need not determine the exact property to be forfeited; it need only find that proceeds of or property used to facilitate the crime is to be forfeited. It is then up to the sentencing court to determine the precise property that will be forfeited. On the other hand, if a criminal case goes to jury trial, then either party may request that the jury make a finding as to the specific property to be forfeited. FED. R. CRIM. P. 32.2(b)(5)(A). The burden of proof for forfeiture, whether decided by judge or jury, is by a preponderance of the evidence.[7] In other words, the government must prove, by a preponderance of the evidence, a factual nexus between the crime of conviction and the property subject to forfeiture.

B. Statutory Provisions

As with all other components of criminal sentences, an understanding of forfeiture begins with an examination of the statutory provisions. As this is not a book on substantive law of forfeiture, the review here is cursory and only for the purpose of providing context for a discussion of sentencing advocacy related to these components. It is important to understand that criminal forfeiture is of rather recent origin and is wholly statutory-based. Congress enacted the first criminal forfeiture statutes in the 1970s when Congress passed the Racketeer Influenced and Corrupt Organization Act[8] and the Continuing Criminal Enterprise statues[9] providing for criminal asset forfeiture. In 1986, though, Congress passed the Comprehensive Forfeiture Act (CFA)[10] to provide for criminal forfeiture for a whole host of criminal offenses identified in the Act. In 1986, Congress also amended the forfeiture statute dealing with drug offenses to give courts the authority to order the forfeiture of an offender's substitute assets when the forfeitable property is unavailable for a post-conviction forfeiture.[11]

Each of the criminal forfeiture statutes define the scope of the government's forfeiture authority. They also contain directly, or by reference to other forfeiture statutes procedures, requirements and conditions for the government's seizure or control of assets subject to forfeiture. To the extent that the government pursues criminal forfeiture, then, it is important that both prosecutors and defense attorneys become familiar with the statutory authority for forfeiture, and the procedures connected with sentencing for the government to pursue forfeiture of assets as part of an offender's punishment. In addition to the procedures prescribed in the forfeiture statutes themselves, the Federal Rules of Criminal Procedure also addresses criminal forfeiture proceedings.

C. Rules on Criminal Forfeiture

Rule 32.2 of the Federal Rules of Criminal Procedure governs criminal forfeiture as part of a criminal sentence. Rule 32.2 reflects the basic requirements of due process: notice and an opportunity to be heard. Under Rule 32.2(a), a court cannot enter a judgment of forfeiture unless the indictment or information gave notice of the government's intent to seek forfeiture. Nevertheless, the pleading need not identify the property with any specificity. It is sufficient for the government to give notice of its intent to forfeit property constituting proceeds of criminal activity or property used to facilitate the commission of crimes. If the charging document does not specifically identify the property to be forfeited, though, then the government must provide further notice through other means to specifically identify the property it seeks to forfeit.

Rule 32.2(b) provides that "[a]s soon as practical" after a guilty verdict or guilty plea on a forfeiture count, "the court must determine what property is subject to forfeiture under the applicable statute." FED. R. CRIM. P. 32.2(b)(1)(A). The sentencing judge must "determine whether the government has established the requisite nexus between the property and the offense" or the amount of money to be forfeited if the government seeks a money judgment in lieu of specific property. *Id.* Unless the offender stipulates to the facts establishing the basis for forfeiture of the property, the court must hold an evidentiary hearing, separate from the sentencing hearing. FED. R. CRIM. P. 32.2(b)(1)(B). This is because once the court determines the property to be forfeited, it must enter a preliminary order of forfeiture specifically identifying the property. FED. R. CRIM. P. 32.2(b)(2). The judge must enter the preliminary order of forfeiture "sufficiently in advance of sentencing to allow the parties to suggest revisions or modifications before the order becomes final" as part of the judgment. FED. R. CRIM. P. 32.2(b)(2)(B). For forfeiture to become final, it must be orally pronounced by the judge at sentencing[12] and included in the judgment.

It is important for defense counsel to ensure that offenders understand the legal effect of a forfeiture order. A court's criminal forfeiture judgment affects only the offender's interest in the property being forfeited. The judgment does not affect the rights of other third parties who may have innocent ownership interests in the property to be forfeited. For example, the offender's innocent spouse may have a half-interest in the residence that the offender used as part of a drug operation. The forfeiture of the offender's interest in the house may not affect the spouse's interest. Rule 32.2 provides for collateral proceedings for the determination of third-party's interests in forfeited property. Those collateral proceedings are not part of the offender's criminal case or sentencing. For obvious reasons, offenders may be very worried about how the forfeiture of property may affect their loved ones, so defense attorneys may need to explain all this to offenders to help them through the sentencing proceedings.

D. Relationship Between Forfeiture, Restitution, and Fines

"Criminal forfeiture is ... separate from restitution, which serves an entirely different purpose." *United States v. Newman*, 659 F.3d 1235, 1241 (9th Cir. 2011). The amount an offender owes for one does not depend on the amount owed for the other. Nevertheless, as noted above, one of the purposes of criminal forfeiture is to seize property so as to liquidate it to restore victims' losses.[13] It follows then that the forfeiture statutes authorize the government to transfer forfeited property to victims as restitution.[14] The government is not, however, required to do so.

Conversely, a district court generally has no authority to offset an offender's restitution obligation by the value of forfeited property the government seized.[15] In other words, through forfeiture the government is entitled to take property from an offender as part of punishment, and through restitution the government is entitled to take property from an offender to compensate victims of the offender's crime. The government may choose not to use forfeited property to compensate crime victims, and if it chooses not to, the offender cannot compel the government to do so, nor may the court reduce the amount of restitution the offender owes.

The value of property seized is sometimes identical or close to the amount of restitution owed to crime victims. When the basis for the criminal forfeiture is that the property constitutes proceeds of the crime, and when the proceeds come at the expense of crime victims, the amount of restitution owed (the crime victims' losses) may be the same as the value of the forfeited property (the crime proceeds). Thus, offenders may be required to pay restitution and forfeit the same amounts.

When the government makes the nexus between the crime and property to be forfeited, then a court must order forfeiture of the property regardless of the financial impact on the offender. Likewise, when restitution is mandatory, and the government has proved the recipient is a victim of the offender's crime and the amount of restitution owed, then the court must order payment of restitution regardless of an offender's ability to pay. Fines, however, are subject to an offender's financial ability to pay. Thus, as a practical matter, criminal forfeiture and restitution orders have a direct impact on criminal fines. Depending on an offender's financial resources, the value of property forfeited, and the amount of restitution owed, an offender may not have the ability to pay a criminal fine.

E. Sentencing Advocacy About Forfeiture

Effective sentencing advocacy as it relates to forfeiture requires consideration of several matters. Initially, attorneys should recognize that they need to consider criminal forfeiture along with all the other forms of punishment at every stage of a prosecution, just as they should consider the length of incarceration. This means that prosecutors should consider criminal forfeiture as part of charging decisions, and both prosecutors and defense attorneys should consider forfeiture in plea negotiations. This may be particularly true when offenders may also be subject to an order of restitution at sentencing. Although the court cannot compel the government or third parties to apply the value of forfeited assets to paying restitution obligations, the government may agree to do so as part of a negotiated plea agreement.

Both attorneys also need to understand and ensure compliance with all the procedures surrounding criminal forfeiture. This includes proper notice in the charging document. The attorneys must obtain a jury or court finding as to the particular property to be forfeited. Attorneys need to ensure entry of an accurate preliminary order of forfeiture. Finally, attorneys should also ensure inclusion of the correct forfeiture language and description of property in both the court's oral and written judgments at the time of sentencing.

When the sentencing judge, instead of a jury, makes the finding about the particular property to be forfeited, the judge may make the requisite nexus finding either by way of an offender's admission or stipulation to facts or through an evidentiary hearing. Offenders must decide whether to agree to or fight forfeiture of property. It may be in an offender's best interest to stipulate to forfeiture as part of a negotiated plea agreement or to show acceptance of responsibility. On the other hand, if there is a colorable basis to challenge the factual nexus between the crime and the property the government seeks to forfeit, an offender may wish to challenge the government's forfeiture action.

When the parties intend for an offender to stipulate to forfeiture, it is vitally important that the attorneys ensure that there is a factual basis in the record showing the requisite nexus between the crime and the property to be forfeited. It is not enough that an offender simply agrees to forfeit the property.[16] An offender has to agree to facts that would establish the nexus authorizing forfeiture. These facts may be contained in a plea agreement, in the uncontested portions of a presentence report, in a sentencing agreement, or in a written stipulation of fact signed by the offender.

When an offender contests the factual basis for forfeiture, the sentencing judge must hold an evidentiary hearing, and that hearing must take place before the sentencing hearing. When this occurs, the attorneys should use all the advocacy skills in the preparation and presentation of witnesses and evidence in the forfeiture hearing that they would bring to bear in a contested evidentiary sentencing hearing. Effective sentencing advocacy requires attorneys to fully prepare witnesses and exhibits for forfeiture hearings, and also prepare charts, summaries, and other demonstrative exhibits for presentation to the court. Attorneys also need to use all the skills in oral judicial advocacy that would apply at a sentencing hearing with equal force at a forfeiture hearing.

18

Restitution

"[R]estitution is part of a sentence," *United States v. Perillo*, 897 F.3d 878, 883 (7th Cir. 2018). Yet, a sentence of restitution is not criminal punishment.[1] There is a lot of substantive law on the books addressing restitution. Several federal statutes authorize courts to order restitution within the court's discretion and under certain circumstances. Other statutes mandate orders of restitution regardless of an offender's ability to pay. Again, this book will not delve deeply into the substantive law on restitution. Rather, the focus here will be on effective advocacy about restitution as a part of a criminal sentence. This necessitates some review, though, of the substantive law on restitution.

There are several factors for attorneys to consider when thinking of effective sentencing advocacy in relation to restitution. First, there are constitutional implications. Second, attorneys should consider the statutory authority for the court to impose restitution orders. Third, there are Guidelines applications addressing restitution that attorneys should consider. Lastly, attorneys should consider how the offender's position about restitution, that is the offender's willingness and efforts to pay restitution, may reflect on an offender's acceptance of responsibility and remorse and, thus, how it may impact the offender's sentence of incarceration.

A. Constitutionality of Restitution Orders

Under the current federal restitution framework, when judges order restitution, they do so upon a guilty verdict or entry of a guilty plea.[2] The court need not base its restitution order on facts from the trial or guilty plea. Rather, the court determines the factual basis for restitution on its own under a preponderance of the evidence standard. Because a sentence of restitution is not criminal punishment, "there is no constitutional requirement that the facts needed for [a] district court's fashioning of a restitution order be found by a jury or found beyond a reasonable doubt." *United States v. Reifler*, 446 F.3d 65, 116 (2d Cir. 2006). Further, a district court is only required to ascertain by a preponderance of the evidence "a reasonable approximation of losses supported by a sound methodology" before imposing restitution.[3] Because restitution is not punishment, restitution does not violate the Excessive Fines Clause or Cruel and Unusual Punishments Clause of the Eight Amendment because it is already inherently proportional to the harm caused and is inherently linked to an offender's culpability.[4]

B. Statutory Provisions

As with forfeiture, criminal restitution is a product of statutory creation. And like the statutory basis for forfeiture, the statutory basis for restitution is of relatively recent origin.[5] An understanding of restitution and how attorneys should advocate at sentencing about restitution begins with an examination of the statutory provisions. As this is not a book on substantive law of restitution, the review here is cursory and only for the purpose of providing context for a discussion of sentencing advocacy related to this component of sentencing.

There are several federal statutes addressing restitution. Some statutes give sentencing courts discretion to impose restitution while other statutes require courts to impose restitution regardless of an offender's ability to pay. In 1982, Congress passed the Victim Witness Protection Act (VWPA),[6] which is the primary statute used to impose restitution in criminal cases. Restitution under the VWPA is discretionary. In the decade following passage of the VWPA, Congress enacted several mandatory restitution statutes. In 1992 and then in 1993, respectively, Congress enacted two narrow statutes that include mandatory restitution provisions in certain limited circumstances, including the Child Support Recovery Act (CSRA),[7] and the Violence Against Women Act.[8] Then in 1996, Congress passed the Mandatory Victims Restitution Act (MVRA),[9] which made restitution mandatory for most federal crimes, including fraud, when a victim suffers a loss. Whether the restitution statute is discretionary or mandatory, when courts do order restitution, they must order full restitution for the victims' loss, regardless of the offenders' ability to pay. Court may, however, order offenders to make payments under a payment schedule if they are unable to make a lump sum payment at the time of sentencing. Under the MVRA, a court may alternatively order community restitution when there is no identifiable victim.

Procedurally, the imposition of restitution as part of a criminal judgment begins with the probation office investigating victims' losses and including that information in the presentence report.[10] As with other factual conclusions in the presentence report, the parties may object to facts about restitution obligations, including whether the person is even a "victim" of the crime of conviction. The judge must resolve the factual dispute in an evidentiary sentencing hearing. The government bears the burden of proving by a preponderance of evidence that the person seeking restitution fits within the definition of victim in the applicable statute and must also prove that the victim suffered the loss claimed in the amount alleged. Generally speaking, a "victim" is a "person directly and proximately harmed as a result of the commission of" a crime. 18 U.S.C. § 3663A(a)(2). A court may hold a restitution evidentiary hearing to address the restitution dispute before the sentencing hearing, as part of the sentencing hearing, or even hold a separate restitution evidentiary hearing after the sentencing hearing if sufficient evidence is not available by the time of the sentencing hearing.[11]

C. Guidelines Provisions

It is important that attorneys understand that "loss amount" as that term is used to determine an offender's Guidelines offense level may not be identical to the "loss amount" established for purposes of restitution. Most financial crimes fall under Guidelines Section 2B1.1. Under this Guidelines provision, loss amount is often the driving force in determining the offender's offense level. Under the Guidelines, the government must prove by a preponderance of the evidence the actual or intended loss amount attributable to an offender's conduct. The Guidelines, unlike the restitution statutes, do not require losses to be ascribed to specific victims. Further, the Guidelines loss amount can include all relevant criminal conduct as defined under USSG §1B1.1.

In contrast, under restitution statutes, victims can be compensated only for actual loss, not intended loss. In other words, when calculating loss amount for purposes of establishing a Guidelines range, courts may look at the amount of loss the offender intended to cause, even if that loss did not occur or the victim has been repaid. Restitution, on the other hand, addresses real, actual loss to victims, regardless of what losses might have occurred or what losses the offender may have intended to cause. Losses must also be attributable to specific, identifiable victims. Importantly, absent an agreement by the parties, restitution can also be based only on conduct that constitutes the crime of conviction, not on relevant criminal conduct as that term is used under the Guidelines.[12] Thus, the loss amount under the Guidelines is more flexible and expansive in scope than loss amount under the restitution statutes.

It is possible, though, for the Guidelines loss amount to be the same as the restitution loss amount. For purposes of restitution, prosecutors must establish both factual and legal causation in essentially the same way they must establish causation of actual loss under the Guidelines—by proving but-for and proximate causation.[13] It follows then, that when the government is relying on actual loss amounts for purposes of determining the Guidelines offense level, in most cases the Guidelines loss amount figure will be the same as the restitution loss amount figure.

Section 5E1.1 of the Guidelines directs judges to order restitution when all other conditions of the applicable restitution statute are met. USSG §5E1.1(a)(1). Under the Federal Sentencing Guidelines, "If a defendant is ordered to make restitution and to pay a fine, the court shall order that any money paid by the defendant shall first be applied to satisfy the order of restitution." USSG §5E1.1(c). Section 5E1.1(d) also authorizes courts to impose "community restitution" in certain drug trafficking offense cases when there are no identifiable victims, "taking into consideration the amount of public harm caused by the offense and other relevant factors." USSG §5E1.1(d). The amount of community restitution cannot "exceed the fine imposed under §5E1.2." *Id.* This has been interpreted as meaning that if the court does not impose a fine, it cannot impose community restitution. "As a consequence of those [limiting qualifications], community restitution is infrequently imposed, even though the implementing Guideline provides that the court 'shall' impose it." Catharine M. Goodwin, Jay E. Grenig, & Nathan A. Fishbach, FEDERAL CRIMINAL RESTITUTION at § 4:20 (West 2009).

D. Sentencing Advocacy About Restitution

Effective sentencing advocacy requires attorneys to consider the implications of the decisions they make at every stage of a criminal case on restitution as part of offenders' sentences. This includes how charging decisions, plea and sentencing negotiations, and forfeiture actions may affect restitution. These decisions can also influence other Guidelines applications and strength of possible non-Guidelines sentencing options.

In charging and plea decisions, prosecutors should consider the effect on availability of restitution. As noted, restitution is available to victims only for the crime of conviction; restitution cannot be based on relevant criminal conduct. In other words, if the offender is not charged and convicted of an offense based on conduct that caused a victim's loss, the court cannot order restitution to the victim even if the conduct leading to the loss was clearly part of the broader offense conduct. Thus, to achieve the goals of the restitution statutes, prosecutors should consider the implication of charging decisions and hesitate to dismiss charges as part of plea negotiations if the effect would be to prevent the government from seeking restitution for victims.

In negotiating plea agreements, attorneys should also understand that offenders can agree to pay restitution even when the restitution statutes would not otherwise require it. Likewise, offenders can agree to pay restitution for relevant conduct victims even though they would not be required to do so under the restitution statutes. Offenders may be willing to pay restitution, even though they may not have to do so by statute, because prosecutors may be willing to make other charging or sentencing concessions to secure restitution for relevant crime victims. For example, a prosecutor may be more willing to dismiss a charge for a crime that involved victim loss if the offender would be willing as part of a plea agreement nevertheless to pay restitution to that victim. Offenders may also consider paying restitution beyond that required by the restitution statutes as a means of showing extraordinary acceptance of responsibility worthy of a downward variance from the advisory Guidelines range.

Offenders must also consider whether to litigate restitution issues. There may be legitimate factual issues about whether a person is a victim of a crime. There may be significant factual and legal causation issues involving disputes about intervening causes, proximate causation, and but-for causation. Some of those same issues may be directly related to establishing loss amount as well for purposes of determining the Guidelines offense level. Although offenders have a right and should contest disputed facts, they should be ever mindful of the Guidelines provisions for acceptance of responsibility and not frivolously contest relevant offense conduct. Offenders have more freedom to contest non-offense conduct, however, and that may pertain to some restitution issues. On the other hand, the sentencing judge may be less sympathetic to downward variance motions based on acceptance of responsibility theories when the judge believes the offender is attempting to shirk financial responsibility for victim losses tied to the offender's criminal conduct, even if the offender is able to prevail on technical restitution issues.

Finally, defense attorneys may also want to consider the benefits when offenders make pre-sentencing restitution payments. When it appears clear that an offender will owe restitution, the amount of restitution is fairly discernable, and the offender has the financial capacity to do so, the offender should make restitution payments before the sentencing hearing. Making restitution payments, even in nominal amounts if that is all an offender can afford, can go a long way in persuading a judge that the offender feels true remorse for the crime and fully accepts responsibility to the harm the offender's conduct caused others. It may even be sufficient itself to establish acceptance of responsibility, even if the offender would otherwise not be eligible.[14]

Conversely, prosecutors may consider opposing downward variances or even reductions for acceptance of responsibility when an offender has failed to make any effort whatsoever to make restitution payments before a sentencing hearing, when the offender clearly has the financial means to do so and the victims' losses are not fairly debatable. A failure to make voluntary restitution payments is a good argument against an extraordinary acceptance of responsibility departure or variance motion, even if other grounds may exist.[15] Likewise, an offender's failure to make voluntary restitution or otherwise preserve available assets to be able to make restitution can serve as a basis for denying an offender a Guidelines offense level reduction for acceptance of responsibility.[16]

19

Supervised Release

Federal courts impose terms of supervised release for most offenders sentenced to terms of imprisonment. Supervised release is a term of supervision that follows a term of incarceration in the federal system. The length of the terms of supervised release depends on the classification of the offense and other statutory provisions and can vary from one year to life on supervised release. While offenders are on supervised release, they must abide by certain mandatory and discretionary terms and conditions the court imposes at the time of sentencing. When a court imposes a term of supervised release as part of a sentence, the court must impose certain mandatory conditions. Other statutory conditions are discretionary, and courts are to impose these discretionary conditions only to the extent that they are reasonably related to the Section 3553(a) factors and only when any resulting deprivation of liberty is reasonably necessary to achieve the goals of sentencing. A sentencing judge can also impose conditions of its own invention, termed "special conditions," so long as they are again reasonably related to the Section 3553(a) factors and impair the offender's liberty no more than is necessary to achieve the goals of sentencing. Sentencing courts have broad discretion to fashion special conditions of supervised release.

"Congress designed supervised release as the successor to parole in the federal criminal system, because it believed that the parole system provided inadequate supervision." *United States v. Armstrong*, 187 F.3d 392, 394 (4th Cir. 1999). Congress designed supervised release to be "a form of postconfinement monitoring overseen by the sentencing court." *Johnson v. United States*, 529 U.S. 694, 696–97 (2000). "[T]he supervised release term constitutes part of the original sentence, and the congressional intent is for defendants to serve their full release term." *United States v. Buchanan*, 638 F.3d 448, 455 (4th Cir. 2011). As the Supreme Court has explained, "Congress intended supervised release to assist individuals in their transition to community life. Supervised release fulfills rehabilitative ends," providing "individuals with postconfinement assistance" through court supervision. *United States v. Johnson*, 529 U.S. 53, 59 (2000). Another purpose of imposing a term of supervised release is to protect the public.

Supervised release may involve significant impairment of offenders' liberty interests. Violations of the conditions of supervised release may also result in a revocation of supervised release and the reincarceration of offenders. Thus, it is important that attorneys provide proper attention to the imposition of supervised release, both in number of years and in conditions. In considering sentencing advocacy pertaining to supervised release, attorneys should first examine the applicable statutory and Guidelines provisions. Then they should consider what the case law says about the findings judges must make when imposing conditions of supervised release and the legal basis for challenging those conditions. After discussing these considerations, I will turn to discuss sentencing advocacy in connection with supervised release.

A. Statutory Provisions

Title 18, United States Code, Section 3583 addresses supervised release and provides that a court "may include as a part of the sentence a requirement that the defendant be placed on a term of supervised release after imprisonment" and must place an offender on supervised release if required by the offense of conviction or if the offender was "convicted for the first time of a domestic violence crime." 18 U.S.C. § 3583(a). The maximum length of a supervised release term varies according to the severity of the initial offense. 18 U.S.C. §§ 3583(b). The term commences on the day the offender "is released from imprisonment and runs concurrently with any Federal, State, or local term of probation or supervised release or parole for another offense to which the person is subject or becomes subject during the term of supervised release," but it is tolled during any period in which the offender "is imprisoned in connection with a conviction for a Federal, State, or local crime unless the imprisonment is for a period of less than 30 consecutive days." 18 U.S.C. § 3624(e).

In considering whether to impose supervised release at all, and if so, what conditions the court should impose, courts are to consider some of the factors set forth in Title 18, United States Code, Section 3553(a). Courts must consider the factors set out in Title 18, United States Code, Section 3553(a)(1), (1)(2)(B), (a)(2)(C), (a)(2)(D), (a)(4), (a)(5), (a)(6) and (a)(7). *See* 18 U.S.C. § 3583(c). In imposing a term of supervised release, courts are not to consider the factor identified in 18 U.S.C. § 3553(a)(2)(A), that is, the need "to reflect the seriousness of the offense, to promote respect for the law, and to provide just punishment for the offense." *See* 18 U.S.C. § 3583(c), (d), & (e) (each listing the factors from Section 3553[a] that are to be considered and each omitting Section 3553[a][2][A]).

While on supervised release, offenders must abide by certain specific conditions. 18 U.S.C. § 3583(d). These include a prohibition against committing any federal state or local crimes, paying restitution if owed, not unlawfully possessing or using controlled substances, and providing DNA samples. *Id.* In addition, the court may impose special conditions of supervised release, provided such a condition: (1) is reasonably related to the factors set forth in section 3553(a)(1), (a)(2)(B), (a)(2)(C), and (a)(2)(D); (2) involves no greater deprivation of liberty than is reasonably necessary for the purposes set forth in section 3553(a)(2)(B) (deterrence), (a)(2)(C) (protection of the public), and (a)(2)(D) (correctional treatment); and (3) is consistent with any pertinent policy statements issued by the Sentencing Commission under 28 U.S.C. § 994(a). 18 U.S.C. § 3583(d). Section 3583(d) thus requires that conditions of supervised release to be connected to the offense and necessary for either the offender's rehabilitation or protection of the public.[1]

B. Guidelines Provisions

Section 5D of the Guidelines addresses supervised release. Section 5D1.1 instructs that courts must impose a term of supervised release (1) when required by statute or (2) when imposing a sentence of more than one year. USSG §5D1.1(a). In any other case, courts may, but are not required, to impose a term of supervised release. USSG §5D1.1(b). The Guidelines suggest, however, that courts not impose a term of supervised release when it is not required by statute and the offender "is a deportable alien who likely will be deported after imprisonment." USSG §5D1.1(c). The reasoning is that a deported alien offender will not be subject to the court's control unless the alien offender returns to the United States and because the alien offender should be adequately deterred by the prospect of new prosecution for illegally returning to the United States. USSG §5D1.1 (cmt. n.5). The application notes to Section 5D1.1 list several factors that courts should consider in determining whether to impose a term of supervised release. USSG §5D1.1 (cmt. n.3). These include: (1) the statutory factors at Title 18, United States Code, Section 3583(c); (2) the offender's criminal and substance abuse history; and (3) whether the offender was convicted of, or the case involved, domestic violence or stalking.

Section 5D1.2 sets out the advisory length of supervised release courts should impose. The length of supervised release is correlated to the seriousness of the offense, as reflected in the offense classification, with longer terms of supervised release recommended for more serious offenses. USSG §5D1.2. As with all other Guidelines, statutory provisions trump Guidelines provisions of supervised release. Thus, if a statute provides a mandatory minimum term of supervised release for an offense, then that becomes the advisory Guidelines range regardless of how it would otherwise be calculated under Section 5D1.2. If offenders qualify under the safety-valve provisions in the drug offense Guidelines such that they are not subject to a mandatory minimum sentence, then they are likewise not subject to any mandatory minimum term of supervised release under the statute or Guidelines.

C. Court Findings When Imposing Conditions of Supervised Release

Courts deem supervised release conditions affecting offenders' significant liberty interests as qualitatively different from those that do not. Generally, judges should explain on the record the reasons for imposing special conditions of supervised release.[2] Courts need only provide a generalized statement of reasoning for imposing most conditions of supervised release.[3] When judges impose conditions that restrict offenders' liberty interests, however, judges need to make an individualized determination that the facts of the case and the offender's history and characteristics justify imposition of such a condition. When a condition affects an offender's liberty interests, granting a probation officer the discretion to decide whether such conditions will be imposed is tantamount to improperly delegating to the probation officer the authority to decide the nature or extent of the offender's punishment. Thus, the sentencing judge must make that decision and not leave it in the discretion of a probation officer to decide whether to impose the condition. Ultimately, the sentencing judge should not impose conditions of supervised release that constitute a greater deprivation of liberty than reasonably necessary to accomplish the goals of sentencing. Conditions that affect offenders' liberty interests include requiring offenders to participate in residential treatment or any other type of civil commitment.[4] They also include any condition that may involve physical contact with or physical restriction of an offender,[5] limit offenders' contact with their children,[6] require an offender to take medication,[7] or require offenders to undergo mental health treatment.[8]

The point here is not to identify every possible condition that can affect offenders' liberty interests. Rather, it is to provide the reader a sense of the type of conditions that do. Attorneys should be alert to whether a condition might affect an offender's liberty interests and do research for controlling case law to find if a court has so determined. It will be important at the sentencing hearing that the judge makes sufficient findings about any such condition, or the case may be remanded for resentencing. Indeed, in recent years, courts of appeal have increasingly reversed and remanded cases for resentencing when courts have imposed conditions of supervised release without making a sufficient finding or when courts have imposed conditions that were unjustified by the facts or under the factors at Title 18, United States Code, Section 3553(a).

D. Sentencing Advocacy Relating to Supervised Release

It is important for both defense attorneys and prosecutors to devote sufficient attention to supervised release. Defense attorneys should carefully consider any special conditions of supervised release proposed in the draft presentence report. Defense attorneys should object to any condition that is either not supported by the facts or imposes too great a deprivation of the offender's liberty interests to be justified. Indeed, defense attorneys may consider whether to object to imposition of any term of supervised release when it is not mandated by statute if a term of supervised release would not advance the goals of sentencing. Failure of a defense attorney to object to a term or condition of supervised release may constitute a waiver of any right to appeal the imposition of a term or conditions of supervised release.[9]

Defense attorneys should be concerned not just with the degree to which a condition of supervision impairs a liberty interest or a burden, but also with the potential implications for the offender's success on supervised release. Although some conditions may seem to offenders to be an inconvenience or burden, those conditions may be important for the offenders' successful rehabilitation. It may ultimately be in an offender's best interest to be subject to such conditions. Although defense attorneys have a duty to zealously advocate for their clients, they should also counsel their clients and advise them about what is in their clients' best interests. Some conditions, such as evaluations and treatment for anger management or drug abuse, could greatly assist some offenders to address some root causes of their criminal conduct and avoid becoming involved in the criminal justice system again. In short, defense attorneys should hesitate to object to conditions that could help offenders succeed just because offenders do not like the conditions. Of course, if the offender insists, then the defense attorney should follow their client's wishes.

At the same time, defense attorneys should consider the consequences if their clients fail to comply with conditions. Violations of conditions of supervised release can lead to prison time. Thus, defense attorneys may want to object to conditions of supervised release that an offender is likely to violate because of the offender's history and characteristics or may violate unintentionally because the nature of the condition is too vague or broad. The wording of conditions of supervised release are typically stock language drafted at the national level or local level by probation officers. Sometimes the wording is imprecise or too broad. Defense attorneys may consider, as a form of effective sentencing advocacy, objecting to the language of a condition of supervised release as opposed to the entire condition. A judge may be more willing to modify the language to satisfy a defense attorney's concerns than a judge may be to eliminate the condition altogether. When defense attorneys challenge the language of a condition of supervised release, it is most effective for them to propose the language they would like to see in its place. An objection without a proposed solution is often ineffective. To the extent the defense attorney can find support in the case law for the proposed language, all the better.

When an offender objects to supervised release or a condition of supervised release, the burden is on the government to show they are justified. The government bears the burden of showing that a particular condition of supervised release is appropriate and involves no greater deprivation of liberty than is reasonably necessary to serve the goals of supervised release.[10] The presentence report itself may contain sufficient uncontested facts to provide a factual basis for imposing a condition of supervision. For example, a condition barring an offender from consuming alcohol while on supervised release may be justified when the offender has some history of abusing alcohol and other controlled substances. That history may be reflected in the presentence report. When offenders contest pertinent facts in a presentence report, or when the presentence report fails to contain sufficient facts to fully justify a condition of supervised release, then the prosecutor may need to present additional evidence in the form of testimony or exhibits.

Because one of the purposes of supervised release is to protect the public, the government should ensure that the court imposes appropriate conditions of supervised release that will achieve that purpose. When defense counsel has an objection to the language of a condition of supervised release, prosecutors may consider working with defense counsel and the probation office to see if the language could be amended in a way that achieves the purpose of the condition while easing the offender's concerns. Prosecutors may also consider working with probation officers to get a better understanding of how conditions to which an offender objects may be implemented in practice so as to assuage, when possible, the offender's concerns about the degree to which the condition may impair the offender's liberty interests.

For example, a condition that requires an offender to undergo a mental health evaluation and take any medication recommended by a licensed physician may appear to contemplate a form of forced medication. That is, if the doctor prescribes it and the offender does not take it, the offender may be found to violate supervised release and be sent back to prison. If in practice, however, the traditional doctor/patient relationship governs the prescription of medications such that the patient retains the option of declining to take medication prescribed, then the offender's liberty interest is not as impaired. Without talking to the probation officer to see how the officer implements this condition in practice, the prosecutor may not be aware of how to effectively advocate for the condition.

Finally, both attorneys should listen carefully to the reasons the judge articulates for imposing any special condition of supervised release to which the offender objects. As stated above, when a condition impairs an offender's liberty interests, the judge should be precise in articulating the factual basis for imposing the condition and should explain why the judge believes the condition furthered the applicable goals of sentencing. If the judge's explanation is imprecise or insufficient, counsel may need to ask for greater clarification from the judge so as to firm up the record for purposes of appeal.

20

Collateral Sentencing Consequences

Adverse collateral consequences from sentencing include potentially undesirable outcomes apart from the imposition of a term of incarceration and a fine, or even forfeiture and restitution. Collateral consequences are sometimes considered "silent" punishments because the sentencing judge does not announce or impose them at sentencing, though they follow directly from conviction and sometimes from the sentence imposed. There is a broad range of collateral consequences, many of which are outside the sentencing judge's influence.[1] Here, I will primarily focus on the collateral consequences that judges can influence and, by extension, those that attorneys can influence through effective sentencing advocacy. I will also examine, however, some of the other common collateral consequences that flow naturally from criminal convictions even though the attorneys and sentencing judges have no real ability to control them. This is because attorneys may want to argue that those adverse consequences should influence sentences judges impose.

A. The Nature of Adverse Collateral Sentencing Consequences

Like a stone thrown into a lake, a criminal conviction can have a ripple effect that radiates far beyond the immediate term of incarceration, restitution, forfeiture, or fine. This is particularly true of felony convictions. Few of these collateral consequences are indirectly within a judge's control at a sentencing hearing. There are many more collateral consequences over which the sentencing court has no control. These consequences arise from other federal, state, and local laws, and administrative and civil rules and regulations. It is important that attorneys, particularly defense attorneys, have some awareness of the most significant possible adverse collateral consequences so that offenders can make informed decisions about pleading guilty and reaching plea or sentencing agreements. It may also be important for attorneys to address whether and how the sentencing judge should consider adverse collateral consequences when sentencing an offender to a term of incarceration or payment of a fine.

1. Collateral Consequences Courts Can Influence

Judges have, at best, a limited ability to rule on or make recommendations that affect collateral sentencing consequences. There are really only two collateral sentencing consequences over which judges can even exercise limited authority: bills of costs and placement in correctional facilities.

The government can pursue collection of the costs of prosecution from offenders as part of the sentence for commission of a certain offenses. Statutes for criminal tax offenses, for example, include language allowing the government to seek the costs of prosecution as part of the offender's punishment.[2] District courts also have the authority to assess costs against criminal offenders for a violation of any non-capital offense under Title 28 United States Code, Section 1918(b).[3] Judges are not required, however, to order payment of costs of prosecution and can refuse to do so when, for example, the offender is financially unable to pay such costs.

Costs of prosecution are those costs that a federal court may tax in a civil action. These costs are enumerated in Title 28, United States Code, Section 1920 and include the following as recoverable costs: (1) fees of the clerk and marshal; (2) fees of the court reporter for all or any part of the stenographic transcript necessarily obtained for use in the case; (3) fees and disbursements for printing and witnesses; (4) fees for exemplification and copies of papers necessarily obtained for use in the case; (5) docket fees under section 1923; and (6) compensation of court-appointed experts, compensation of interpreters, and salaries, fees, expenses, and costs of special interpretation services under section 1828. Costs of prosecution do not include attorneys' fees or other expenses not specifically listed in Section 1920.[4]

Although it may seem that costs of prosecution limited to the permissible categories under Section 1920 would be a negligible concern for offenders, these costs can be substantial. In one case, the costs exceeded $55,000.00.[5] Many of the white-collar criminal statutes permit recovery of costs of prosecution and white-collar cases can entail years of investigation, scores of witnesses, and the government expenditure of tens of thousands of dollars that may be subject to payment as costs of prosecution. Thus, in certain cases, both prosecutors and defense attorneys should give this component of sentencing serious attention. Prosecutors owe it to taxpayers to collect the costs of prosecution when permitted.[6] Defense attorneys should resist the imposition of improper or inadequately supported costs of prosecution.

As for placement at correctional facilities, in the federal system the Bureau of Prisons decides where a convicted offender will be incarcerated. Sentencing judges cannot dictate the placement of an offender within the Bureau of Prisons. Certain decisions judges make at sentencing, however, can influence the type of facility where an offender may be housed. Judges can also make non-binding recommendations that the Bureau of Prisons place offenders at particular facilities.

When an offender enters the Bureau of Prisons system, the Bureau conducts an analysis of the offender to arrive at a security and classification rating for the inmate. An inmate's classification is based on a large number of factors, including the nature of the offense of conviction and whether the offense conduct involved firearms or violence, among other things. The classification and designation of inmates is a matter within Bureau of Prison's sole discretion.[7] Offenders cannot invoke the Administrative Procedures Act to seek judicial intervention in the decision because prison designations are, by statute, exempted from the Act. *See* 18 U.S.C. § 3625. An offender has no legal right to a particular classification or program and no protected liberty interest in placement in a particular facility.[8]

The Federal Bureau of Prisons relies heavily on the information in offenders' presentence reports to determine offenders' security risks and programming needs.[9] This is one reason why it is very important that the presentence report is as accurate as possible. Rule 32 does not provide a means for the court to correct presentence report after sentencing.[10] Instead, Rule 32 allows the court to resolve any objections to the presentence report at the time of sentencing and "append a copy of the court's determinations [on objections] to any copy of the presentence report made available to the Bureau of Prisons." FED. R. CRIM. P. 32(i)(3)(C). Thus, once the sentencing hearing is complete, the opportunity to alter the presentence report is over, and the Bureau of Prisons will rely on it to determine the offender's housing.

Sentencing judges can recommend that offenders be placed in particular Bureau of Prisons facilities. Such recommendations are just that: suggestions that are not binding upon the Bureau of Prisons. Having spoken with many Bureau of Prisons officials, however, I understand that they strive to comply with judges' recommendations whenever possible. Defense attorneys may want to hesitate before requesting judges to recommend specific facilities, however, because it may not be in an offender's best interest. In designating inmates to a facility, the Bureau of Prisons considers all an offender's programing needs, such as for substance abuse treatment, medical requirements, and educational needs. The Bureau of Prisons' effort to comply with a judicial recommendation to a place an offender in a particular facility may result in an offender being placed in a facility that does not have all the programming opportunities the offender needs.

2. Collateral Consequences Courts Cannot Influence

Criminal convictions can have many collateral consequences for offenders and their families that are completely outside a court's ability to influence or control. Offenders convicted of felony offenses lose the right to vote, to hold public office, to sit on a jury, and to possess firearms and ammunition. A conviction may also impact possible future sentences if the offender is later convicted of additional offenses. Many recidivist statutes—those designed to increase punishment for repeat offenders, such as Armed Career Criminals—and recidivist Guidelines provisions may be triggered by past convictions. The nature of the offense of conviction can also significantly influence a non-citizen's immigration rights and opportunities. Certain types of convictions, such as for violent felonies, may make an alien ineligible to ever become a United States citizen. Offenders convicted of sex offenses may be required to register as sex offenders, perhaps for the rest of their lives. Offenders who had worked in professional positions may lose their licenses or have restrictions placed on their licenses, affecting their ability to work in their chosen profession. Those offenders who worked in industries doing business with the United States may be barred from doing so in the future. A conviction may also impact whether the offender's property may be subject to civil forfeiture. Depending on the facts of the case and the offender's characteristics, the number and nature of possible collateral consequences may be immeasurable.

Many of these collateral consequences may seem punitive in nature. When the government is the entity imposing a sanction as a collateral consequence of a criminal conviction, such as with debarment or civil forfeiture, it may appear to be a form of double punishment in violation of the Double Jeopardy Clause. Nevertheless, courts have consistently held that such collateral consequences of a conviction are not a form of punishment for purposes of the Double Jeopardy Clause.[11]

I have not attempted here to list all the possible collateral consequences that may arise from a criminal conviction or sentence. Rather, the point here is to identify a few of the more significant and frequent collateral consequences to illustrate the nature of collateral consequences. Every case and offender are unique, so attorneys should carefully consider what collateral consequences may flow from a conviction and determine how those collateral consequences bear, if they do, on the sentence the court should impose.

B. Consideration of Collateral Consequences Before Sentencing

Defense attorneys should alert offenders of certain collateral consequences of convictions and sentences and should alert them to all collateral consequences of which defense attorneys are aware. It is important that an offender be apprised of as many collateral consequences that may flow from a conviction as may be reasonably anticipated so that they can make fully informed decisions about whether to plead guilty or go to trial. Indeed, the Supreme Court has held that defense counsel must inform offenders of adverse collateral immigration consequences. In *Padilla v. Kentucky*, 559 U.S. 356, 388 (2010), the United States Supreme Court held that the failure of defense counsel to advise his client "that a conviction may have immigration consequences" violates the offender's Sixth Amendment right to the effective assistance of counsel under *Strickland v. Washington*, 466 U.S. 668 (1984). In so doing, the Court recognized that it had "never applied a distinction between direct and collateral consequences to define the scope of constitutionally 'reasonable professional assistance' required under *Strickland*." *Id.* at 365 (quoting *Strickland*, 466 U.S. at 689). Nevertheless, it ruled that "[d]eportation as a consequence of a criminal conviction is, because of its close connection to the criminal process, uniquely difficult to classify as either a direct or a collateral consequence." *Id.* at 365–66. Although federal courts have not yet expanded the holding of *Padilla* to other collateral consequences,[12] the language of the Court's opinion suggests a broader application, and various legal scholars certainly have urged expanding its application.[13]

Aside from ensuring that offenders are aware of adverse collateral consequences, the parties may consider whether they can reach an agreement on collateral consequences to the extent any of them are within the government's control. Working with agency counsel, for example, the government and the offender may be able to reach a negotiated global agreement that the offender not be debarred from conducting business with the United States government in exchange for an agreement that the offender pay a larger fine.

C. Consideration of Collateral Consequences at Sentencing

Even when parties and courts cannot directly control or influence the collateral consequences of a conviction and sentence, that does not mean that those consequences are irrelevant for purposes of effective sentencing advocacy. In sentencing offenders, courts may be able to consider the collateral consequences of conviction in fashioning an appropriate sentence. Defense attorneys may move courts to vary from the advisory Guidelines range of imprisonment or fine, or to impose no supervised release or more lenient conditions of supervised release, because offenders will suffer other collateral consequences from sentencing that are punitive in nature.[14] For example, a defense attorney may argue that the court should not impose a fine or impose a reduced fine for an offender who faces debarment or loss of a professional license as a collateral consequence of conviction because it will affect the offender's financial ability to pay a fine. The Federal Sentencing Guidelines note that courts may consider collateral consequences in determining imposition of a fine. Section 5E1.2(d)(5), which covers individuals, states that "any collateral consequences of conviction, including civil obligations arising from the defendant's conduct" should be considered in determining a fine within the Guidelines range. Section 8C2.8, applicable to organizations, includes similar guidance. These Guidelines provisions support the proposition that judges may properly consider collateral consequences, such as debarment, that affect an offender's financial position in imposing a fine within the Guidelines range.

On the other hand, prosecutors may consider arguing against such reductions in fines or other variances from the Guidelines if it would arguably treat an offender of means more favorably that someone else similarly situated. A number of courts of appeal have reversed variances when judges have done so based on collateral consequences for this reason.[15] Prosecutors may also emphasize at sentencing that many collateral consequences are distinct from sentencing sanctions because they are focused on future conduct and potential harm while criminal sentences are imposed as punishment for past wrongs. For example, a term of imprisonment and a fine may be imposed as punishment for a doctor who engaged in Medicare fraud. Those sanctions are imposed as punishment for that past wrong—the fraud the doctor committed. The loss of the offender's medical license and debarment, in contrast, are consequences that may flow from conviction, but are directed at preventing the doctor from committing similar crimes in the future. They are not imposed as punishment for past wrongs but, rather, to prevent the offender from committing future wrongs.

21

Argument by Counsel

The key moment for attorneys in sentencing hearings is when they attempt to persuade the judge to adopt their positions through oral argument. This moment is the culmination and climax of the attorneys' sentencing advocacy efforts. Up to this point, attorneys have endeavored through every stage of the case to place their clients in the best possible position for sentencing. The attorneys have carefully tended to the preparation of the presentence report, drafted persuasive sentencing memoranda, and perhaps even presented evidence to the judge. Now the whole case comes down to persuading one person—the judge—of the merit of their clients' positions. The outcome of an attorney's entire sentencing advocacy efforts up to this point comes down to the moment when the attorney stands up, faces the judge, and uses oratory skills to convince the judge to rule in their clients' favor.

As I pointed out in Chapter 2, persuading a judge is not like persuading a jury and is even different in some ways from persuading a group of judges sitting on an appellate panel. As I pointed out in Chapter 2, in sentencing hearings, a sentencing judge sits as a jury of one. A lone judge resolves any factual disputes, sustains or overrules objections to the presentence report, weighs the merits of the attorneys' arguments, is influenced (or not) by victim impact statements and the offender's allocution, and pronounces sentence. Persuading this lone judicial officer is ultimately the key to the outcome of the entire proceeding.

It is surprising, then, that there is so little written about skillfully advocating to judges in sentencing hearings, and often so little thought is devoted by attorneys to this task.[1] I encourage the reader to re-read Chapter 2 so as to recall the fundamentals of effective judicial advocacy. I will not repeat those points in this chapter. Rather, here I will focus on this one moment in time during a sentencing hearing when the attorneys present the equivalent of a closing argument to the judge. Effective sentencing arguments require thorough preparation, resulting in an organized outline to structure the attorneys' oral presentation. The content of effective sentencing arguments focuses on the goals of sentencing, marshalling the unique facts of the offense and offender in a manner that persuasively explains how the advocated-for sentence advances those goals. The style of an effective sentencing argument is one that carefully employs the right mixture of logos, ethos, and pathos based on the nature of the offense and offender.

A. Preparing a Sentencing Argument

The first essential step in the process of presenting an effective sentencing argument is thorough preparation. Indeed, in my mind, this is the basis for all effective advocacy. In relation to a sentencing argument, what this means is that attorneys should draft an outline of their sentencing argument well in advance of the sentencing hearing. I confess that as a practicing attorney, I seldom did this myself except in the most complex and high profile of cases. As a judge, I seldom see attorneys speaking from any notes during argument. Rather, all too often I observe attorneys doing as I did: speak extemporaneously, with little organization or structure. The result is often a disjointed, rambling series of observations and comments with a weak opening and often a weaker closing. In contrast, I can immediately tell when attorneys come prepared with an outline for their sentencing argument, not only because I can see the pieces of paper they reference during their remarks, but because the argument is demonstratively better and more persuasive.

Sentencing arguments are similar to closing arguments in trials, or should be to be effective. Sentencing arguments are most like closing arguments in bench trials because the sentencing judge has been the factfinder and decision-maker and the focus of all advocacy efforts throughout the sentencing hearing. As with a bench trial, the sentencing judge has the benefit of written materials prepared in advance of the sentencing hearing that have already shaped and influenced the judge's perception of the matter. The sentencing judge has already absorbed the presentence report, the parties' sentencing memoranda, and any written exhibits before the attorneys stand to present their sentencing arguments. Thus, in preparing an outline of a sentencing argument, an attorney should take this into account. Attorneys should not read from their sentencing memoranda or repeat the substance of their written advocacy. Attorneys can assume that judges have read their sentencing memoranda.[2] Oral advocacy is an opportunity to highlight and emphasize portions of written advocacy, to shine a light on important points previously made in writing.

The most effective sentencing arguments are the ones that are well organized. Attorneys should have a structure to their arguments that address the key issues the judge must decide, just as closing arguments in a bench trial should be structured to address the key issues. In a bench trial, the key issues are the elements of the offense or the claim. In sentencing hearings, the key issues are the goals of sentencing. In federal court, those goals of sentencing are incorporated in the factors in Title 18, United States Code, Section 3553(a). Not all of those factors will be of equal importance in each sentencing hearing. Some will be much more important than others, just as in a bench trial some elements of an offense or claim will be more in dispute or important than others.

Preparing a sentencing argument is different in some ways, though, from preparing a closing argument in the bench trial. In a bench trial, the parties present evidence, then make closing arguments, and the judge then renders a single verdict (often later, in writing). In a sentencing hearing, on the other hand, the judge renders a series of verdicts throughout the sentencing hearing. The judge may, for example, make rulings on disputed Guidelines issues that fundamentally change the case.

An attorney may come into a sentencing hearing in a drug trafficking case with a presentence report indicating that an offender's statutory sentencing range of five to 40 years, with an advisory Guidelines range of 97 to 121 months. But during the hearing, the judge made rulings finding the offender to be safety-valve eligible and thus no longer subject to a mandatory minimum sentence, found a lower drug quantity than determined in the presentence report, and as a result of those and other Guidelines rulings, arrived at a new advisory Guidelines sentencing range of 51 to 63 months.

What this means for preparation for sentencing arguments is that attorneys need to prepare flexible outlines or contingent arguments. Attorneys will have little time during a sentencing hearing to adjust their sentencing argument to rulings the judge makes during the sentencing hearing. Thus, attorneys need to prepare those adjustments in advance of sentencing hearings. Attorneys should prepare outlines for sentencing arguments that include contingent arguments based on different outcomes based on rulings the judge may make during the sentencing hearing on disputed issues. Using the above example, had the sentencing judge ruled in the government's favor on the disputed Guidelines issue, the prosecutor may have concluded that a sentence at the bottom of the advisory Guidelines range of 97 months was sufficient to achieve the goals of sentencing. When, however, the judge ruled against the government on the disputed Guidelines issue, the prosecutor may believe that a sentence at the top of the new advisory Guidelines range of 63 months is necessary to achieve the goals of sentencing. The sentencing argument under the first scenario should look significantly different from the sentencing argument under the second scenario. Under the first scenario, the prosecutor will have little need to persuade the judge because presumably the defense attorney will likewise argue for a sentence at the bottom of the advisory Guidelines range. In the second scenario, the defense attorney will presumably be arguing for a bottom of the Guidelines range sentence of 51 months. Thus, the attorneys' arguments in the second scenario will be seeking to persuade the judge to reach contrary outcomes. For these reasons, it is important that attorneys prepare sentencing argument outlines in a way that contemplate different outcomes based on different rulings the judge may make during the course of the sentencing hearing based on disputed issues.

Finally, it is important that attorneys prepare their final remarks. All too often attorneys end their sentencing arguments weakly, having finished speaking extemporaneously and, realizing that they do not have much more to say, conclude without having given much thought to their final words. The closing remarks often sound something like, "So, judge, for the reasons I have stated, we would ask you to consider sentencing the offender to ...." Instead, the attorney's final words should be well thought out in advance, should emphasize the key points the attorney has made, and argue why those points should lead the judge to impose the desired sentence.

B. Content of Sentencing Arguments

Like closing arguments in trials, sentencing arguments should have a strong beginning, a strong ending, and a coherent, organized middle. The goal of sentencing advocacy is persuading the judge to impose the sentence the attorney believes is in the client's best interest. For offenders, that is the lowest sentence possible; for the government, it is the most appropriate sentence that achieves the goals of sentencing. As with jurors, primacy and recency effects make it likely that the judge will remember best the first and last things the attorneys say. The body of the argument should be tied to goals of sentencing.

To be persuasive, attorneys should start their arguments strong by asserting concisely the sentence the attorney believes is appropriate and why. It is often effective for attorneys to state the proposition and tell the judge the points the attorneys will make in argument. For example, a prosecutor may start by telling the judge that a sentence at the top of the advisory Guidelines range is appropriate to advance the goal of protecting the public because the offender poses a danger to the community. The prosecutor may then say that the prosecutor will focus on three factors in showing the judge why this sentence is necessary to achieve that goal: the violent nature of the offender's offense conduct, the offender's criminal history that includes multiple crimes of violence and firearms violations, and the offender's lack of remorse or even true acceptance of responsibility for the criminal conduct. An opening like this is structured, persuasive, and will help the judge follow and place into context the content of the body of the prosecutor's sentencing argument.

As with closing arguments in trials, use of a theme may be persuasive. A theme for a sentencing hearing may focus on a goal of sentencing, for example. For the government, a theme in a sentencing hearing may be the need to protect the public and the focus is on the danger the offender poses to the community. For the defense, a theme in a sentencing hearing may be on the need for rehabilitation, and the focus is on the offender's history of mental illness and addiction problems. The content of an attorney's entire argument should be consistent and built around this theme. And the close of the attorney's sentencing argument should return to this theme.

The body of sentencing arguments should focus on the goals of sentencing and the factors judges must consider when arriving at a sentence. When determining a sentence, judges are engaging in a form of fact-finding when they apply the Section 3553(a) factors. Those factors identify broad categories and goals judges must consider to determine an offender's sentence. It is up to the judge, however, to comb the presentence report and other facts in the case, fit those facts into the various factors, and then determine the weight the judge will give to each factor. For example, Section 3553(a)(2)(B) requires judges to consider the need for the sentence imposed to afford adequate deterrence to criminal conduct. The sentencing judge must decide what facts relate to this consideration. A judge may find the fact an offender has received lenient sentences in the past is relevant in that it suggests a need for a longer sentence to deter the offender. The judge may also conclude that an offender's sincere remorse is relevant as showing that a short sentence may be sufficient to deter the offender. The judge must then decide how much weight to afford these two conflicting considerations to reach a conclusion about how severe of a sentence is necessary to provide adequate deterrence. Lastly, sentencing judges must evaluate an offender's allocution, when and if presented, to discern whether it reflects acceptance of responsibility and remorse, or disdain and disrespect, and then figure out how much weight to give it in arriving at the appropriate sentence.

Appellate courts recognize that a sentencing judge is in a unique position to consider and weigh all the facts, factors, and faces. The institutional setting of a sentencing judge provides advantages unavailable to reviewing appellate judges.[3] Appellate courts recognize that sentencing judges are in a better position than appellate judges to apply and weigh the Section 3553(a) factors.[4] Appellate courts recognize that sentencing judges occupy unique positions to weigh an offender's acceptance of responsibility.[5] It is because sentencing judges are in superior positions that appellate judges afford sentencing judges considerable deference when imposing sentences.

Thus, attorneys need also to appreciate the unique position sentencing judges are in. In arguing to sentencing judges, attorneys should recognize that the sentencing judge has considerable discretion to make all these judgment calls. It is the role of advocate to assist the decision-maker by identifying the material facts and considerations and explain how the judge may and should apply them to the Section 3553(a) factors. It is the advocate's role to assist the sentencing judge in feeling comfortable that the advocated-for sentence is one that promotes all the goals of sentencing.

The body of an attorney's sentencing argument should help the judge by doing the work for the judge. Attorneys should comb the presentence report and the evidence in a sentencing hearing to identify the facts that apply to the various sentencing factors. Attorneys should marshal those facts together in a coherent and organized fashion and show the judge how they apply to the sentencing factors the judge must consider in determining the sentence. Just as in closing arguments in trials, it is an attorney's role to interpret the evidence and draw conclusions from the facts. In sentencing arguments, attorneys should tell judges what the attorneys believe the facts mean and how the attorneys believe the facts should cause the judge to reach a particular conclusion.

Sentencing arguments should end strong. Attorneys should return to their theme, their central point, the essence of what they believe the sentencing hearing is all about. What an attorney says at the end of the argument is the attorney's last words before the judge pronounces sentence. It needs, then, to be concise, firm, and persuasive. The attorney's last words should summarize the key points the attorney has made in the body of the sentencing argument and conclude by emphasizing how those points show that the requested sentence is the one that best achieves all of the goals of sentencing.

C. *Style of Sentencing Arguments*

When attorneys decide what and how they are going to argue to the judge at sentencing, they should consider adopting a style for their sentencing arguments considering the perspective of the sentencing judge. Effective legal advocates either intentionally or intuitively incorporate all three elements of classical rhetoric—pathos, ethos, and logos—to some degree when striving to persuade a decision-maker. Effective sentencing advocates recognize that they need to adjust the focus and emphasis on these elements of rhetoric in sentencing hearings. Making an effective argument to a sentencing judge calls for a different emphasis on these components than does making an effective argument to appellate courts, which may be different still from effective argument to jurors. Although Aristotle was correct when discussing the elements of rhetoric that juries constitute "an audience of untrained thinkers,"[6] that is not true of sentencing judges.

Generally speaking, lawyers should emphasize logos and ethos when arguing to sentencing judges. Judges will be focused on the goals of sentencing; federal judges will be focused on those goals as articulated in the factors in Section 3553(a). Thus, the most persuasive sentencing arguments are usually ones that emphasize the logic of the attorney's reasoning by emphasizing how the facts of the case fit within and advance sentencing goals. A sentencing argument primarily focused on an emotional appeal is unlikely to be successful.

That does not mean, however, that emotional arguments do not have a place in some sentencing hearings. An emotional appeal has far more application in a sentencing hearing than in any other district court setting. Empathy, sympathy, and mercy have a role in a judge's exercise of the broad discretion to impose the appropriate sentence. Thus, in appropriate cases where the facts evoke these emotions, attorneys may want to emphasize them as an appropriate basis upon which judges may make their sentencing decisions. For example, in a case where the severe harm the offender caused to victims came through in emotional victim impact statements, a prosecutor may want to focus on that emotional evidence when emphasizing the need for the sentence to reflect the seriousness of the crime. Conversely, in a case where the offender is the product of a broken and abusive home, mental illness, and drug addiction, it may be persuasive for a defense attorney to evoke sympathy when asking the judge to show leniency.

Effective sentencing advocates also recognize that different parts of sentencing hearings call for changing the emphasis on the rhetorical components. When arguing how the length of a term of incarceration may advance the goal of deterrence, for example, a logic argument may be more effective than an emotional appeal. On the other hand, when arguing the need for a sentence to provide just punishment, an appeal to emotion may have more purchase.

Finally, when deciding what to argue to a judge in a sentencing hearing, attorneys should pause to consider the uniquely difficult position sentencing judges occupy in determining the fate of other human beings. Sentencing is, by far, the most difficult task district court judges must perform.[7] Before becoming a district court judge myself, I thought I understood this, and I did at an intellectual level. After all, as a prosecutor, I had advocated to sentencing judges for decades to impose sentences ranging from probation to death. Intellectually, I fully understood the ramifications of my requests and felt the emotional impact of the judges' decisions, at least to a degree. Until one is actually called upon to impose a sentence upon another human being, however, one cannot fully appreciate how lonely and awesome and crushing that responsibility can be.

Although it is difficult, effective sentencing advocates should endeavor to appreciate the sentencing judge's position. The tone attorneys take in arguing to judges should reflect an appreciation that the judge is not taking lightly the awesome responsibility for sentencing the offender. Attorneys should refrain from ever placing on sentencing judges more responsibility than is their due by making arguments such as suggesting it will be the judge who separates children from the offender, or that it will be the judge's fault if an offender commits an offense because the judge gave the offender probation. These types of arguments are highly likely to offend the sentencing judge and be counterproductive.

To be sure, that is not to say that defense attorneys should refrain from emphasizing the adverse consequences their clients will suffer as a result of the sentence. It is completely appropriate for a defense attorney to argue, for example, that a prison sentence may result in the offender's loss of employment if probation is a realistic potential sentence. Rather, what I caution against here is the tone of arguments in which defense attorneys place the blame on the sentencing judge for ruining the offender's life or that of the offender's family. Pointing out the consequences of a sentence is different from blaming the sentencing judge for causing those consequences.

22

Victims

When crimes involve victims, attorneys need to consider a number of victim-related issues that may arise and significantly alter a typical sentencing hearing and impact the ultimate sentence the court imposes. Victims have certain rights at sentencing hearings, and it is the job of prosecutors to enforce those rights. Prosecutors should also assist victims in presenting victim impact statements and produce evidence in support of restitution claims. Both prosecutors and defense attorneys need to carefully consider the court's ability to rely on victim impact statements and what the attorneys can do to effectively advocate for their clients in relation to those statements.

A. *Victim Rights at Sentencing Hearings*

Crime victims have certain legal rights in criminal cases that prosecutors have a statutory duty to enforce. This is particularly true in federal court. Beginning in the 1980s, Congress enacted a number of laws addressing victims' rights. Some of those statutes created rights for victims when courts sentence offenders.

In the Crime Control Act of 1990, Congress mandated that government officials, including prosecutors, make "best efforts" to ensure that victims' rights are enforced. This requires prosecutors to confer with victims, protect their privacy, notify them of court proceedings, and provide reasonable protection from the accused. Prosecutors are also required to provide victims with a waiting area out of sight and hearing of the offender and defense witnesses and inform victims of the filing of charges, any plea agreement, the trial verdict, the sentence, and any order releasing the offender from custody. 34 U.S.C. § 20141.

The Antiterrorism and Effective Death Penalty Act of 1996 contained provisions for closed circuit televised court proceedings for victims of crime when there is insufficient room in the courtroom for all the victims. 34 U.S.C. § 20142. This includes sentencing hearings. The Act also provided for mandatory restitution for certain crime victims (including victims of fraud or violent crime) notwithstanding an offender's financial inability to pay restitution. 18 U.S.C. § 3663A.

In 1997, Congress enacted the Victims' Rights Clarification Act. Among other things, that act mandated that, notwithstanding any other law or rule, crime victims have a right to be present in the courtroom during a trial even if they may become witnesses or may become a witness at the time of sentencing. 18 U.S.C. § 3510. This law was motivated in part by the capital trial of Timothy McVey when his bombing of a federal building killed and injured so many people that it was physically impossible to have all victims and their family members present in the courtroom.

The Crimes Victims' Rights Act of 2004 enumerates specific rights of crime victims in federal criminal cases, codified at 18 U.S.C. § 3771(a). These include "[t]he right to reasonable, accurate, and timely notice of any public court proceeding … involving the crime or of any release or escape of the accused," and "[t]he right to be reasonably heard at any public proceeding in the district court involving release, plea, sentencing, or any parole proceeding." 18 U.S.C. §§ 3771(a)(2) and (a)(4).

There are other federal statutes addressing victims' rights under other special circumstances as well. States have also enacted similar victims' rights acts. The bottom line is that prosecutors should become familiar with these statutes to become fully aware of victims' right to enforce those rights in sentencing hearings. As noted above, many of these rights have to do with notice of and an opportunity to be present during judicial proceedings, including sentencing hearings. It is ultimately the prosecutor's responsibility to make sure that victims are notified of sentencing hearings and enforce their right to be present and observe the sentencing hearing and speak to the judge.

Federal Rule of Criminal Procedure 32 provides that the presentence report must identify any victims of the crime and describe the financial, physical, and psychological impact the offense had on the victim and the victim's family. Prosecutors should also ensure that the crime victim, or the victim's family members, have an opportunity to address the court before imposition of sentence and to submit crime victim impact statements if the victims wish.

Defense attorneys should also be familiar with victims' rights and how victims may exercise those rights, even though defense attorneys clearly have no obligation to enforce those rights. Defense attorneys should ensure that their clients are fully aware that victims have certain rights and explain to offenders how the victims can and will exercise those rights. Defense attorneys should also explain to offenders how victim impact statements may influence the judge's decisions.

B. Presentation of Victim Impact Statements

At the sentencing hearing, prosecutors should ensure that the judge hears from any victims who wish to make a victim impact statement. When the time comes to do so, prosecutors should help the victim by directing them to the location where they are to sit or stand when presenting their statements. There are no rules about where in the courtroom or how victims are to present statements to the court. Some judges have victims speak from a lectern; others have victims speak from counsel tables or witness boxes. In any event, prosecutors should find this out in advance of the sentencing hearing so that they can help the victims.

In some instances, victims may be so overcome with emotion that they cannot follow through with making a statement. If a victim has written the statement and intended to read from the written text, a prosecutor could offer to read it for the victim, with leave of the court. The impact that a crime had on victims is a very important factor in determining the appropriate sentence. Thus, prosecutors should do what they can to make sure that the court hears the statement in some way.

For some offenders, listening to victim impact statements can be gut-wrenching, so defense attorneys need to prepare offenders for victim impact statements. While the victims are making statements, defense attorneys should monitor their clients to make sure that the offender is not reacting in a way that could adversely affect the sentence. There is not necessarily a correct way to respond to a victim impact statement other than, hopefully, the offender's demeanor reflects empathy and remorse. The demeanor should be sincere, or the judge may see through the façade of feigned remorse. At the very least, defense counsel should work with offenders so that they do not act dismissive or reflect a hateful or angry demeanor. A neutral demeanor is preferable to one that suggests the offender is openly hostile to the victims.

Victim impact statements vary significantly in eloquence and emotional impact. As important, they are not invariably against an offender's sentencing interests. Some victims may plead that the court impose the longest sentence and harshest conditions possible. Other victims, however, profess forgiveness. Some victims may, indeed, plead with the court to impose a light sentence. Attorneys often will not know in advance of the sentencing hearing just what a victim is going to say, and they need to be prepared for any eventuality.

C. Court's Ability to Rely on Unsworn Victim Impact Statements

Victims can present victim impact statements to the court in writing or orally in open court. In neither case are the statements under oath. When victim impact statements are made in open court, the victims are not subject to cross examination. Courts may rely on statements made by victims even when they are not made under oath, unless the court relies on statements that are materially false or unreliable.[1]

D. Advocacy in Reference to Victims

At the time of sentencing, attorneys have an opportunity to speak. Sometimes the court has attorneys present arguments about the sentence that they believe the judge should impose before hearing from victims and sometimes after the victims have spoken. If attorneys are required to speak before the court hears from victims, the attorneys may want to reference what the attorneys anticipate the victims will say. If the victims have already spoken, then the attorneys may wish to comment on their statements.

The most persuasive attorney comments upon victim impact statements are those that are tied to the factors in Section 3553(a). A victim impact statement that reflects that the offender's crime caused the victim significant financial, physical, or emotional harm may suggest that the goal of imposing a sentence that reflects the seriousness of the offense is a compelling reason for a longer sentence. A victim impact statement in which the victim expresses a fear that the offender will harm the victim, or some other victim, in the future implicates the sentencing goal of protecting the public. On the other hand, a victim who expresses forgiveness and speaks sympathetically of the offender may suggest a defense argument focusing on rehabilitation would be appropriate. In any event, attorneys should give careful thought about how to weave victim impact statements into their overall argument about the sentence that the judge should impose.

23

Allocution

Offenders have a right to speak to the sentencing judge before the judge imposes the sentence. The right to allocution is "firmly entrenched in our criminal jurisprudence" because it provides an opportunity for an offender to personally plead for leniency with the sentencing judge. *United States v. Machado*, 886 F.3d 1070, 1087 (11th Cir. 2018). It also "reaffirms human dignity in the face of severe punishment."[1] Allocution is deemed such a vital part of sentencing that a sentencing judge's failure to afford an offender the opportunity to allocute is generally considered plain error, requiring reversal and remand for resentencing. As a matter of sentencing advocacy, however, offenders and defense attorneys must struggle with the question of whether to allocute and what to say in allocution. There is also the question of what role defense attorneys should play in guiding offenders about allocution and crafting allocution statements. I will discuss those and other aspects of allocution in this chapter.

A. *Right and Role of Allocution*

Offenders have a constitutional right to personally address the judge at sentencing.[2] This right was further codified in Federal Rule of Criminal Procedure 32. That rule provides that "[b]efore imposing sentence, the court must … address the defendant personally in order to permit the defendant to speak or present any information to mitigate the sentence." Fed. R. Crim. P. 32(i)(4)(A)(ii). Of course, offenders are not required to speak, but judges must give them the opportunity to do so.[3] A judge's failure to personally address an offender and afford the offender an opportunity to speak almost always constitutes reversible error.[4] In some rare and factually unusual circumstances, courts have found a judge's failure to address an offender and offer an opportunity to speak does not constitute plain error, but these circumstances are so unusual that attorneys should presume that it will constitute plain error. Finally, judges must directly address the offender. A judge making inquiry of a defense attorney about whether the offender wishes to speak does not comply with the rule or the Constitution.[5]

B. Impact of Allocution

Although the law recognizes allocution as an essential and important part of a sentencing hearing, it is a fair question whether, in practice, allocution is effective. Whether an allocution is effective may turn on a number of factors. A sincere statement accepting responsibility, showing remorse, and apologizing, particularly to victims, may be effective in persuading a judge to show compassion. On the other hand, a statement full of self-pity or, worse, one blaming others, may be particularly ineffective and could even result in the judge finding a lack of remorse or acceptance of responsibility.[6] Such an allocution statement could result in a longer sentence.[7] In a study of the impact allocution statements had on the sentences federal judges imposed, a little more than a quarter of the judges generally found offenders' allocution to be "extremely" or "very" important in determining the offenders' sentences, while about three quarters of them found allocution to be "somewhat important," "not very important," or "not important at all."[8] The actual effectiveness of an allocution in determining the sentence imposed will often depend, of course, on how "good" the allocution is, and that often turns on how well the offender exhibits true remorse for the criminal conduct.

In some instances, offenders may have trouble feeling true remorse if they believe the sentence far exceeds the harm caused by the offender's criminal conduct. This may especially be true when the crime of conviction carries a significant mandatory minimum sentence. In such cases, an offender's allocution may focus less on remorse and more on deterrence, expressing how the punishment will effectively deter the offender from ever committing the offense again.

In answering the question of whether allocutions are "effective," though, it is important to consider what other purposes allocutions serve beyond persuading the sentencing judge to show mercy by decreasing the sentence. Allocution also provides offenders with an opportunity to directly participate in the offenders' own sentencing hearings. This, in turn, may help offenders feel heard and more willing to accept the punishment imposed. Additionally, the right of an offender to participate may help legitimize the fairness of the sentencing hearing in the eyes of the offender's family and friends, and the public at large. Allocution may, on occasion, also help victims heal when the offender expresses true remorse. Finally, the right of allocution is important to ensure that offenders can air publicly allegations of wrongdoing by the government. Although an allocution that accuses the government of entrapment or fabricating charges may not be the most effective in persuading the judge to impose a more lenient sentence, in a free democracy, it is essential that offenders always have the right to speak out publicly against the government.

C. The Decision to Allocute

An offender must ultimately decide if they wish to make a statement in allocution. Whether to do so may depend on an offender's general perception of the effectiveness of allocution. This, as noted, may depend on exactly what the offender intends to say. There are other factors, though, for offenders and their attorneys to consider as well.

Like the decision to testify at a trial, the decision to speak at a sentencing hearing may depend in part on the offender's ability to speak effectively. By this I do not mean that only well-educated, articulate offenders should allocute. Indeed, some of the most sincere and effective allocutions come from the mouths of the most unsophisticated offenders.[9] Rather, what I mean here is that an offender may have a very short temper or is so emotionally charged about the crime such that it raises a real risk that a well-intended allocution would degenerate into a disastrous one.

Offenders must also consider the legal consequences of anything they say in allocution on the case at hand or in other pending or potential cases. What an offender says may very well be used against the offender in the very sentencing hearing in which the offender allocuted. Few judges warn offenders of this consequence.[10] Defense attorneys, on the other hand, should always warn offenders that what they say in a sentencing hearing could be used against them in that hearing and in other proceedings. Likewise, the use of an offender's allocution statements in subsequent proceedings does not violate that offender's due process rights if the making of such statements was an effective waiver of his Fifth Amendment rights. It is difficult for offenders to allocute after trial because if they succeed in having the conviction overturned on appeal, any incriminating statements made in allocution could be used against them in a future trial.

Offenders may also have to consider whether a judge may interpret a failure to make a statement in allocution as an indication that the offender has failed to accept responsibility. Although this is a legitimate concern,[11] in practice it has been my observation that judges respect an offender's right to remain silent and do not consider an offender's silence in any way. And, as mentioned, the Constitution prohibits judges from doing so.

Judges do generally value hearing from offenders in allocution. As one judge put it, for most offenders, allocution is the judge's "only window into their minds and souls."[12] Generally speaking then, defense attorneys should hesitate to discourage offenders from making statements in allocution. It may be important for the judge and offender to have at least some level of human interaction, even if the offender's allocution is no more than to give an apology. In some cases, it may appropriate to have the offender provide an allocution in the form of a written letter to the judge, filed as an exhibit for the sentencing hearing, if the offender is reluctant to allocute or the defense attorney is otherwise concerned about the offender allocuting. Although a letter may not be quite as effective as hearing the offender speak in open court to the sentencing judge, it is not a far second. I have received such written allocutions before, and I have found some of them moving when it is clear the offender is writing from the heart.

D. Defense Attorneys' Role

Defense attorneys have a responsibility to prepare their clients for allocution.[13] Defense attorneys should explain the purpose of allocution, along with all the costs and benefits that may flow from making a statement in allocution.[14] A defense attorney may work with an offender to craft the offender's statement, helping the offender edit out statements that may harm the offender before the court or in another pending or potential action. Defense attorneys may also encourage offenders to write out their allocution statement so that the defense attorney can help the offender craft the allocution statement, but also so that at the sentencing hearing the offender will have something in writing to work from. The defense attorney may also encourage the offender to practice giving the statement to the defense attorney or others. Defense attorneys should be cautious, however, not to exert too much influence over the content of an allocution statement. The words in allocution need to be from the offender, however inartful they may be, so that the sincerity of the offender's statement will ring true. A sentencing judge is likely to detect an allocution statement written by a defense attorney.

When an offender is unable to communicate effectively or is too nervous or emotional at the sentencing hearing to carry through with making an allocution statement, then the defense attorney may offer to read the statement to the judge on behalf of the offender. This is another reason for encouraging offenders to write their allocution statements down in advance of sentencing hearings. When attorneys read offenders' allocution statements, they should strive to invest them with an appropriate tone and, to the extent discernable, the tone the offenders intended. Reading an allocution without any emotion or modulation in voice is less effective than reading an allocution with feeling. Of course, there is a line of theatrical performance which defense attorneys should not cross.

Defense attorneys should also warn offenders that some judges ask questions or engage in a conversation with offenders when they make statements in allocution. Not all judges do this, and once again it is important for attorneys to know the judge who will be sentencing the offender. But even judges who do not have a history of asking offenders questions during or about their allocution may do so in a particular case. Offenders should be counseled to understand that judges are attempting to learn and understand the offender and are often looking for signs of true remorse. Offenders should be counseled to greet judges' questions as an opportunity to provide sincere and heartfelt responses and to avoid being defensive or blaming others.

Defense counsel may wish to advise their clients about things that may not be wise to say during an allocution. Generally speaking, offenders should not use the opportunity to just apologize to their families, especially when there were crime victims involved in the offense conduct. It speaks ill of an offender who has harmed a victim who then apologizes during the allocution to the offender's family but never mentions the victim. It is not wise for offenders to speak directly to their family members in the courtroom because it sometimes triggers a response from the family members that the defense attorney cannot predict or control and that may be against the offender's best interest. It is also generally ill-advised for offenders to use the opportunity to argue with the judge about why they are not a bad person. As has been noted, judges recognize that the vast majority of offenders are not bad people, and the judges are sentencing the offenders for the offenders' conduct and not character. It could insult an occasional judge if the offender's comments seem to accuse the judge of being unfair by basing the judge's sentence on the offender's character. And defense counsel should caution offenders from saying anything that may incriminate them for conduct that is not the subject of the sentencing hearing or when the offender has contested guilt through trial or motions and needs to preserver the assertion of innocence to potentially succeed on appeal.

Lastly, if an offender stands up to make a statement in allocution, the defense attorney should stand with the offender as a sign of support for the offender and to mark the importance of the statement.

E. Attorney Comments About Allocution

Depending upon how the sentencing judge structures the order of various parts of the sentencing hearing, attorneys may or may not have an opportunity to comment upon offenders' statements in allocution. Often, the offender's allocution is the last stage in the sentencing hearing before pronouncement of sentence. When, however, attorneys have an opportunity to speak or argue about the final disposition after an offender's allocution, the attorneys should consider whether to comment on the allocution. In this regard, there is a question both of whether an attorney legally can comment and then a question of whether an attorney should comment on an offender's allocution.

Whether attorneys may comment about what an offender says, or fails to say, in an allocution has seldom arisen in the case law aside from capital cases. In some death penalty trials, judges allow offenders to make allocution statements to the juries during the penalty phase of the trials. These allocutions, like any other allocution, do not expose the offender to cross examination. Generally speaking, courts have held that when offenders make statements in allocution, the government may comment on the allocution without violating an offender's Fifth Amendment rights.[15] Death penalty cases show that prosecutors may legally comment upon an offender's allocution in noncapital cases as well.

Nevertheless, it is far safer for prosecutors to limit any comments to what the offender said and how the offender said it than to comment on what the offender did not say. It is fair for a prosecutor to point out, for example, that in the offender's allocution, the offender blamed others or that the offender's words betrayed a callous attitude toward victims. It may be entirely appropriate for a prosecutor to point out that the offender only apologized to his family and not the victims or the victims' family, for instance, or to comment on the lack of any statements in allocution showing remorse. Nevertheless, to suggest that the judge should base a sentence, even partially, on an inference about what an offender did not say when given an opportunity to speak strays far enough away from the uncontested facts of a case to invite a finding of error on appeal and treads perilously close to commenting on an offender's right to remain silent.

The question then becomes whether either attorney should comment on an offender's allocution. Generally speaking, I believe comment by attorneys on an allocution to be unnecessary and ineffective. The sentencing judge can see and hear the offender as well as the parties and will draw the conclusions from the allocution that the judge thinks appropriate without help from the attorneys. That said, if there is something the attorneys know outside the record that reflects upon the allocution, they may want to try to put it on the record.

24

Imposition of Sentence and Judgment

An attorney's responsibilities at sentencing do not end when the judge reaches the point of pronouncing sentence. Attorneys should pay close attention to the court's pronouncement of the sentence in light of their client's best interests. What the judge says, or fails to say, in pronouncing the sentence can be extremely important. Attorneys should attentively listen to the judge's pronouncement of the sentence for many reasons. Judges sometimes make mistakes and may state some aspect of the sentence incorrectly. Judges may also fail to explain adequately the basis for their rulings or sentences or state something inconsistent with the judges' intended sentences. Attorneys should also ensure that judges have addressed each issue that required attention and fully complied with all the constitutional and statutory requirements of sentencing. Even after the attorneys leave the courtroom, their sentencing advocacy work is still not done. Attorneys should attentively review the written judgment to ensure that it is correct and consistent with the oral pronouncement of sentence because if there is an error, parties have only a limited window to get the error corrected.

A. Attorneys' Responsibilities to Parties at Pronouncement

A judge's pronouncement of sentence is the most significant moment in any sentencing hearing. This is, of course, true for the offender whose fate hangs in the balance. The pronouncement of sentence can also be traumatic for the offender's family and loved ones; the offender's fate is theirs as well. A judge's pronouncement of sentence can also greatly impact crime victims yearning for a sense of closure. It is even a potentially difficult time for law enforcement officers who have invested time and effort into the case. The attorneys, whose work and efforts have been focused on this outcome, feel the impact of the pronouncement of sentence. And, quite frankly, it can be, and often is, a difficult moment for the judge. There is nothing pleasant for judges in sentencing offenders.

Effective sentencing advocates have already prepared their client and associates (such as family members, victims, and agents) for this moment to the extent possible. Good attorneys have explained to them when in the sentencing hearing the judge will pronounce the sentence and what it will sound like. The attorneys have encouraged the offender, family members, victims, and others to show restraint in their reaction. Effective sentencing advocates would have explained to these people the appeal process that will follow should they dislike the sentence the judge imposed. To be sure, some of them will likely dislike the judge's sentence.

At the moment the judge pronounces sentence, there is little more that prosecutors can do about reactions to the sentence but to ensure that any co-counsel and agent sitting at counsel table remain calm and professional regardless of the sentence imposed. For defense attorneys, their job is far more difficult because it is their clients who are being sentenced. Because a judge can still change a sentence, for better or for worse, during the pronouncement itself, it is wise for offenders to remain calm and not react with a violent or angry outburst. Such a reaction may cause some judges to consider changing their minds to impose longer sentences. Defense attorneys should endeavor to lend their moral support and presence to provide some comfort to the offender. In courtrooms where judges require offenders to stand when the court pronounces sentence, defense counsel should stand with their clients, side-by-side, while the judge pronounces sentence.

Finally, defense counsel should ask if the offender has any questions about the sentence imposed before the judge leaves the bench so that any ambiguity can be resolved before the opportunity to change the oral pronouncement has passed. For example, if the judge recommends the offender be incarcerated at a facility in close proximity to the offenders' family, an offender who has family members located in several states may wonder how that recommendation would work out under the circumstances. It may be appropriate at that time to clarify for the judge which family members are the ones the offender wants to be near or to have the judge recommend a particular state or region.

B. Listening to Pronouncement of Sentence

Attorneys should ensure that the judge does not misspeak and impose a sentence inconsistent with any sentencing rulings the judge has made during the hearing. This is essential because it is the sentence pronounced by the judge orally at the sentencing hearing that is the actual sentence imposed, regardless of what is in the written judgment. Federal Rule of Criminal Procedure 35(c) states: "As used in this rule, 'sentencing' means the oral announcement of the sentence." In other words, if the written judgment differs from the oral announcement, the oral announcement controls. This is because an offender has a constitutional right to be present at sentencing.[1] If the oral pronouncement is ambiguous, an appellate court may consider the entire record, including the written judgment, to resolve the ambiguity.[2] Thus, attorneys should listen carefully to ensure that the judge pronounces the correct term of years, fine amount, and term and conditions of supervised release. When attorneys believe that a judge may have misspoken, they should speak up and draw the judge's attention to the mistake to ensure that it is corrected.

Attorneys should also pay careful attention to a judge's stated comments to make sure the judge did not rely on a mistake of fact, a contested fact not proven, or reach an erroneous legal conclusion. That is not always easy. A judge's erroneous characterization of evidence may not be the same as an erroneous finding of fact.[3] Likewise, attorneys need to pay careful attention to make sure that judges do not rely on contested facts in arriving at a sentence unless the judge has resolved the factual dispute one way or the other. If a judge relies on a fact in a presentence report to which an offender has objected, then it may result in the sentence being reversed if the government has not offered evidence to prove the disputed matter.[4] Again, attorneys should point out such a mistake to the judge. From the offender's point of view, the absence of the contested fact from the court's analysis may cause the judge to re-evaluate the sentence to be imposed. From the prosecutor's point of view, it is important to make sure that the judge has not relied in error on a contested fact when the judge would have imposed the same sentence without that fact in consideration. Both attorneys should bring to the court's attention any time the judge appears to rely on a contested fact that was not proven by the party bearing the burden of proof.

Attorneys should also listen carefully to how judges articulate any deviation from the advisory Guidelines range. Just like many attorneys, some judges are not always careful in clarifying whether they are departing from the Guidelines or whether they are varying from the Guidelines. The distinction can be important. As discussed, Guideline departure provisions often contain limitations or conditions to their applications, whereas variances do not. Courts of appeals also afford sentencing judges more discretion when varying from the Guidelines than when they depart from them. If there is any doubt whatsoever whether a judge is departing or varying from the advisory Guidelines range, attorneys should ask the judge to clarify. If necessary, attorneys should not hesitate to point out that the judge may not have been careful in the label the judge attached to the decision.

Although it is ultimately the sentencing judge's responsibility to comply with all sentencing procedures and constitutional requirements when imposing a sentence, attorneys have a responsibility to monitor this and ensure that the judge fulfills this responsibility. In federal court, judges may commit procedural error by failing to consider sentencing factors or applying them in the wrong order. Similarly, an appellate court may reverse and remand for resentencing a case when a judge forgets to give an offender the opportunity to exercise the right of allocution or fails to advise the offender of the right to appeal after pronouncing the sentence. It is in both side's best interest to ensure the judge complies with all the constitutional and statutory requirements. To help make sure this happens, attorneys should go to sentencing hearings with a checklist and make sure that the judge covers everything and does so in the correct order.

When a judge has resolved contested Guidelines issues, attorneys should listen attentively to hear whether the judge indicated an intent to impose the same sentence under the Section 3553(a) factors, regardless of whether the judge erred in resolving the disputed Guidelines issues. In other words, judges sometimes state that they would have imposed the same sentence after considering all Section 3553(a) factors even if they incorrectly applied the Guidelines. When judges do not make it clear, attorneys may consider inquiring of the judge whether they would have imposed the same sentence regardless of any errors in relation to the Guidelines calculations. This can make a significant difference on appeal. If a judge has erred in the resolution of disputed Guidelines provisions but announces that the judge would impose the same sentence even if the judge made a Guidelines error, then an appellate court will likely find any such Guidelines-related error to be harmless and will affirm the sentence. If an appellate court finds the judge made a Guidelines error, but it is not clear from the record whether the judge would have imposed the same sentence, then the appellate court must remand the case for resentencing. This is particularly true if the judge sentenced the offender at the bottom of the advisory Guidelines range because it suggests, absent an affirmative statement from the judge to the contrary, that the judge would have imposed a lower sentence but for the Guidelines error (assuming, of course, that the Guidelines error would have resulted in a lower advisory Guidelines range). Similarly, an appellate court may assume the judge would have imposed a higher sentence if the Guidelines error would have resulted in a higher advisory Guidelines range if the sentence imposed was at the top of the range the judge mistakenly found. This could also be important if the judge made any procedural errors. If a judge announces that the judge would have imposed the same sentence under the Section 3553(a) factors regardless of any procedural or Guidelines errors, then an appellate court may review the judge's sentence for harmless error.

If the offender was charged in multiple counts but pled guilty to one or more counts under a plea agreement that called for the dismissal of other counts, then at the sentencing hearing, the judge must pronounce the disposition of those other counts. The judge should call upon the prosecutor to inquire whether the prosecutor is moving to dismiss those counts, and if the prosecutor so moves, the court should grant the motion and pronounce those counts dismissed. Both the prosecutor and defense counsel need to monitor the hearing carefully to make sure the court does not overlook this step.

Attorneys should also be familiar with the law in their circuits about technicalities in pronouncing sentence. Again, this is not a book on substantive sentencing law. Nevertheless, it is worth noting, to make this point, that circuit courts of appeal differ, for example, on whether it constitutes plain error if a judge fails to orally pronounce the sentence imposed on each count or whether it is sufficient if the written judgment does so.[5] Attorneys should be aware of any circuit-specific nuances like this so as to avoid error.

C. Comparing the Orally Announced Sentence Against the Written Sentence

Because the oral pronouncement of sentence controls in any conflict with the written judgment,[6] it is important that attorneys studiously review the written judgment immediately after it is filed to ensure that it accurately reflects the judge's oral pronouncement of sentence. The oral pronouncement and the written judgment should be consistent. Even if the oral pronouncement was correct and controls over a mistaken written judgment, the written judgment follows the offender through the correctional system. Errors in the written judgment could affect the offender's classification and other liberty interests. Showing that the written judgment was wrong and convincing officials that the oral pronouncement controls may be difficult, at best. It is far better to make sure the written judgment is corrected immediately. If there is a mistake, an attorney may be able to get it corrected by filing a motion under Rule 35 or Rule 36, the topic of the next chapter.

25

Challenging Judgment Before Appeal

After a judge pronounces sentence in the courtroom, there is little the parties can do to alter that sentence short of an appeal. District courts are generally bound by the sentences they orally pronounce.[1] In short, a federal judge generally cannot modify a term of imprisonment once it has been imposed. A judge generally cannot amend a sentence simply because the judge had a change of heart or mind.[2] Rather, once a judge pronounces a sentence, there are only three circumstances in which the judge may change the sentence. The first two circumstances arise when judges have made an error in imposing the sentence. The last is when Congress later changes the Guidelines in a manner that would have benefited the offender.

In very narrow and limited circumstances, parties may have an opportunity to request that a court alter the judgment after the sentencing hearing but before the deadline for parties to file an appeal. Parties may file a motion to correct a sentence during this short time period when the judge has made some error while imposing the sentence. The rationale for granting judges this authority is to avoid the waste of judicial resources that would ensue if an appeal and remand were always required to correct an erroneous sentence. Two Federal Rules of Criminal Procedure dictate when judges may alter a criminal judgment.

Rule 35(a) provides a short window after sentencing for the court to correct errors in the sentence. Rule 35(a) states:

> **Correcting Clear Error.** Within 14 days after sentencing, the court may correct a sentence that resulted from arithmetical, technical, or other clear error.

Fed. R. Crim. P. 35(a). Thus, for example, if an attorney realizes after the hearing that the judge forgot to provide the offender the opportunity to provide an allocution, then the attorney could file a motion under Rule 35(a) to have the judge reconvene the sentencing hearing to permit the offender to allocute.[3] Under Federal Rule of Criminal Procedure 35(a), a court loses any power it may have had to correct an "arithmetical, technical, or other clear error" in the sentence fourteen days after pronouncing sentence.

Rule 36 grants district courts slightly broader authority to correct errors at a later time. Rule 36 states:

> **Clerical Error.** After giving any notice it considers appropriate, the court may at any time correct a clerical error in a judgment, order, or other part of the record, or correct an error in the record arising from oversight or omission.

FED. R. CRIM. P. 36. This rule, though, authorizes courts to correct only clerical errors, which exist when the court intended one thing but through a clerical mistake or oversight did another.[4] Rule 36 may not be used to make a substantive alteration to a sentence.[5]

Finally, a judge may alter a judgment if Congress later amends the Guidelines in a manner that would have resulted in a lower sentence. Title 18, United States Code, Section 3582(c)(2) grants judges the discretion to modify a sentence when an offender has been sentenced to a prison term based upon a sentencing range that thereafter is lowered when the Sentencing Commission amends the Guidelines. In deciding whether to reduce a sentence under Section 3582(c)(2), the district court must first determine whether the offender is eligible for a sentence modification.[6] Section 3582(c)(2) authorizes a judge to reduce an offender's sentence only if two criteria are met. First, the offender must have been sentenced "based on a sentencing range that has subsequently been lowered by the Sentencing Commission." 18 U.S.C. § 3582(c)(2). Second, Section 3582(c)(2) requires that any reduction must be "consistent with applicable policy statements issued by the Sentencing Commission." *Id.*

In short, there is little attorneys can do to change a sentence once the judge has imposed it. For purposes of a book on sentencing advocacy, this has two implications. First, it emphasizes the importance of effective sentencing advocacy. It shows how important it is that attorneys are thoroughly prepared, that they fully and effectively litigate issues, and that they use all their persuasive skills to influence the sentencing judge before the judge imposes sentence. Second, it highlights the need for attorneys to pay close attention to the imposition of sentence and be alert to any errors the judge may make when imposing sentence. Otherwise, it is only when a judge makes a clear mistake, or when Congress changes the sentencing law, that the sentencing judge can change a sentence once it is imposed. After that, the only avenue of relief available is appeal.

26

Sentencing Advocacy and the Audience

This is a book on effective sentencing advocacy with the overriding focus on how attorneys can effectively persuade sentencing judges to impose sentences that are in the best interests of their clients. The focus of these advocacy efforts, the primary audience to whom attorneys are directing all their persuasive powers, are sentencing judges. The reality, however, is that there are other audience members in the courtroom who hear and may be affected by what attorneys say in sentencing hearings. In addition to the sentencing judge, other people may read attorneys' sentencing briefs, and there are always other people hearing the attorneys' statements and arguments in the courtroom. What attorneys say in writing and orally in relation to a sentencing hearing can impact how these other audience members view the fairness of the proceeding, the degree of emotional trauma they may feel, their opinions of the attorneys, and even how they may act in the future themselves.

In short, when attorneys speak in relation to a criminal sentencing, they are potentially speaking to many people. The message they want to convey to the judge may be different from the message they want others to receive. Any book on sentencing advocacy should acknowledge that other audience members will, and perhaps should, influence attorneys' sentencing advocacy. Thus, it is appropriate to examine how and why attorneys may want to tailor their advocacy to be responsive to these other members of the sentencing audience.

A. Other Audience Members

It is first appropriate to identify the other audience members, besides the judge, who will hear the attorneys' words before addressing how attorneys may want to tailor their sentencing advocacy in recognition of these people. Besides the judge, the focus of the attorneys' advocacy efforts, there are others that attorneys may wish to influence through their written and oral advocacy. First among these is the offender. The judge will directly address the offender at some point, but in their remarks, attorneys may want to directly address the offender. Regardless, the attorneys should consider the effect their words may have on the offender.

As a practical matter, offenders sometimes insist that their attorneys make arguments that are borderline frivolous or irrelevant for purposes of sentencing. For offenders to feel their attorneys are advocating fully for them and that they are being treated fairly, defense attorneys sometimes make these arguments even knowing they will be ineffective. Defense attorneys may do with a kind of "wink and nod," such as by introducing the argument by saying "Mr. Offender wants you to know, your honor, that...." It has been my experience that judges understand what defense attorneys are doing in these instances and do not let it influence their decision-making.

Related to the offender are the offender's family members, loved ones, and friends. The offender's sentence will often have a significant impact of these people. They are often the collateral damage of an offender's crime. It has also been my observation from reading letters of support from family members that they do not know the true facts of the case but, rather, have relied on an inaccurate version the offender gave them. The offender's family may also be paying for the offender's representation or may have been working closely with defense counsel throughout the case to assist in the offender's defense. Or the offender's family may be partially to blame for the offender's life of crime. The offenders' parents may have neglected or abused the offender, for example, or engaged in criminal conduct themselves and thus served as poor role models for the offender.

There are other people, beyond the offender and the offender's family, to consider as well. Crime victims could be affected by both attorneys' comments. The attorneys' characterization of crime victims or descriptions of the victims' experiences or injuries may dramatically affect the emotional impact of the sentencing proceedings on crime victims. For prosecutors, the law enforcement officers who worked on the investigation will be listening carefully to what the prosecutor says and may even read the prosecutor's sentencing memorandum. How law enforcement officers act in the future, how they investigate or pursue other cases, may turn on what the prosecutor says and the words the prosecutor chooses.

Courtrooms are open to the public, which means that members of the press may be present. In the audience there may also be courthouse staff members, student groups observing proceedings, and private citizens simply interested in court proceedings. Attorneys should recognize that in the audience may also be those seeking information for nefarious reasons. People may attend to find out if the offender cooperated with law enforcement officers or to gather information about the nature and extent of a government's investigation into criminal activity.

The audience of attorneys' sentencing advocacy may also extend beyond what attorneys say orally. In addition to the sentencing judge, others may read the attorneys' written submissions, such as the attorneys' sentencing memoranda. These may include members of the press. It may include attorneys for other offenders whose cases may be related to the offender being sentenced or may have cases with legal issues similar to those being addressed in the sentencing hearing. It may be defense attorneys representing offenders against whom the offender cooperated. It may also include appellate judges who might read the pleadings when handling the case on appeal.

There is also a wider audience, beyond those who immediately hear the attorneys in the courtroom or read the attorneys' pleadings. If members of the press report on the sentencing hearing, then anyone who consumes the news reports are members of the extended audience. Those people who attended the sentencing hearing may also repeat to other people what they heard or thought they heard. To the extent that word gets out about what was said during a sentencing hearing, prosecutors may want to consider the effect their words might have on other targets of criminal investigations or others similarly situated as the offender who may also be tempted to commit similar crimes. Prosecutors also need to be concerned not to disclose information in a sentencing hearing that, if word gets out about it, may adversely impact a pending investigation. Defense attorneys may need to consider how what they say in a sentencing hearing may be interpreted by potential future clients. Lastly, both attorneys may want to consider how other members of the bar and the bench may react to what the attorneys say or do during sentencing hearings. Attorneys' reputations are key to their future success. That said, defense attorneys' primary responsibility is to their clients; their relationship with their clients may have to take precedence sometimes over their reputations with the court. Judges who have an understanding of and appreciation for this relationship will understand. There may be nothing to be done by those who do not.

B. *Tailoring Advocacy to Account for Other Audience Members*

The sentencing judge, the ultimate decision-maker, should remain the primary focus of attorneys' communication at sentencing. Nevertheless, while maintaining the essence of their arguments so as to persuade the judge, attorneys may want to alter the tone or adjust the verbiage so as not to offend others, or in a manner designed to influence the actions of others. Sometimes this is a very difficult task. Attorneys should be cautious not to sacrifice the persuasiveness their arguments will have on judges in an effort to appease another member of the audience. In the end, it is up to the attorneys to weigh the degree to which they tailor their arguments for other audience members. Here are some factors, however, for attorneys to consider in making that difficult judgment call.

Offenders and their family members deserve to be treated with dignity and respect. Yet, defense attorneys may think it effective in persuading the judge to be brutally candid with the judge about an offender. For example, in arguing for a lighter sentence, a defense attorney may want to emphasize that the offender has a severe learning disability or is naive and easily manipulated by others. Or, for example, the defense attorney may want to be frank with the judge about the disadvantaged childhood the offender had as a result of neglectful or abusive parents. If the defense attorney shies away from blunt descriptions of the offender's handicaps, or tempers their comments about the offender's parents out of a sensitivity not to offend the offender or the offender's family members, it may blunt the persuasive impact of the attorney's argument.

If a defense attorney speaks before victims make their statements, the defense attorney may need to consider the effect the attorney's words may have on the victims. Victim statements can be very powerful. If a defense attorney phrases an argument in a manner that offends a crime victim or reflects a lack of empathy for a victim, it may influence the victim's conduct in a manner adverse to the offender. A victim may have been reluctant to speak until provoked by a defense attorney's comments, or the attorney's comments may embolden a victim who was otherwise reluctant to speak to make a victim impact statement or prompt another victim to make statements more adverse to the offender's interest. Defense attorneys should consider their comments from the victims' perspectives then, when appropriate, tailor the comments in such a way to still make the point the attorney wanted to make but in a manner so as not to offend victims.

Defense attorneys may also consider addressing law enforcement officers or their work. If a defense attorney commends law enforcement officers or the way officers handled the investigation, it will signal the offender and the offender's family that the allocution should take a different tone than if the defense attorney attacks law enforcement officers or criticized their work. As a practical matter, defense attorneys need a good reputation among law enforcement because sometimes the defense attorneys' clients are cooperating with law enforcement officers, and it is in those clients' best interests that there exist a professional and positive relationship between them. Good defense attorneys develop working relationships with prosecutors and law enforcement officers such that they can, when appropriate and justified, attack law enforcement officers' conduct without jeopardizing this relationship. On the other hand, sometimes a defense attorney has a client who will insist on attacking law enforcement officers during the offender's allocution if the defense attorney has not. In those instances, it is in the offender's best interest for the defense attorney to air the criticism so as to spare the possible adverse consequences if the sentencing judge finds the offender's allocution attacking law enforcement officers off-putting.

Prosecutors may consider tailoring their comments to achieve goals other than persuading the sentencing judge. Like defense attorneys, prosecutors may consider the impact their statements may have on the offender and the offender's family. At the same time, prosecutors have to consider what victims will think of their comments. Prosecutors want to be seen as advocating on behalf of crime victims and to a degree should do so. This may suggest that strong words condemning the offender would promote that goal. Similarly, law enforcement officers who have worked hard on the case and may have themselves been in harm's way during the course of the investigation may also be expecting a degree of invective in the prosecutor's comments. In the end, however, prosecutors have a responsibility to see that justice is done, and that includes treating everyone in the process with respect. Prosecutors should not lose sight of their duties and goals in an effort to curry favor with crime victims or law enforcement officers. Prosecutors should feel free to vilify offenders' acts when appropriate but should refrain from vilifying offenders personally. If a prosecutor makes a personal attack on an offender, it may actually backfire if the judge believes the personal attack was inappropriate.

Prosecutors may also consider the impact their words may have on other targets of the criminal investigation or other criminal associates. A prosecutor may need to be cautious in making arguments so as not to inadvertently disclose the direction an ongoing investigation is taking if doing so may jeopardize that investigation. On the other hand, if other targets of an investigation are already aware they are targets, then a prosecutor may want to consider the impact the prosecutor's argument may have on them. A strident, take-no-prisoner tone in argument may trigger another target into deciding to fight charges, or it may trigger in them an urgency to work out a plea deal with the government.

Similarly, prosecutors may need to consider tailoring their comments at sentencing to send a message to others who may be tempted, like the offender, to commit similar crimes. Here, a prosecutor may intentionally take a strident tone with the hope that word gets out to others to deter them from engaging in similar criminal conduct. This may be most effective in white collar cases when the offender was part of a profession or industry that is closely watching and reporting on the criminal case.

Finally, both attorneys may want to consider how the press will report their words. In high profile cases, the press may cover the sentencing hearing closely and may have read the parties' sentencing memoranda. Both defense attorneys and prosecutors should be cautious about what they say, keeping in mind that what they say in a particular sentencing hearing may come back to haunt them in future cases. Prosecutors may also need to choose their words carefully to reflect a Department of Justice priority, such as a focus on suppressing violent crimes or firearms offenses, and thereby further the Department of Justice's general deterrence goals.

The point of this chapter, in short, is to encourage attorneys to broaden their perspective and to think carefully about how their arguments and words may impact others besides the sentencing judge.

27

Sentencing Organizations

It is settled law that corporations and other legal organizations may be held criminally responsible for the criminal acts of their employees or agents acting within the scope of their authority.[1] The sentencing of organizations is fundamentally different from the sentencing of people, including the sentencing of employees and agents of such organizations.[2] The most glaring and obvious difference is that an artificial entity, like a corporation, cannot be incarcerated. That reduces the sentencing options for organizations and, in turn, places a greater emphasis on the remaining means of punishment. Financial punishment predominates as the most logical means of punishing organizations. Financial punishment can take the form of fines, restitution, and forfeiture. Courts may also place organizations on probation as well, however, and through terms and conditions of probation, control to some degree how the organization operates while on probation. These conditions may have a significant financial impact on the organization as well.

Sentencing an organization, a legal artificial person, is different from sentencing a natural person in many other ways, too. Thus, effective sentencing advocacy when the offender is an organization requires consideration of different issues than present themselves when the offender is a human being. This chapter first examines statutory and Guidelines provisions addressing criminal punishment for organizations. Next, I will address seriatim the different forms of punishing an organization, fines, forfeiture, restitution, and probation. Finally, I will discuss sentencing advocacy when an organization sits in the offender's chair.

A. *Statutory Provisions*

The minimum and maximum fines that courts may impose on organizations are set by statute just as they are for human offenders. As one might predict, the fine range is higher for organizations than for individuals in part because of an organization's likely ability to pay a greater fine and because incarceration is not an option. Under Title 18, United States Code, Section 3571, the fine for an individual convicted of a felony offense faces a maximum fine of $250,000; for an organization the maximum fine is double that: $500,000. The alternative fines provision under Title 18 United States Code, Section 3571(d), the section providing that the maximum fine can be twice the gross gain or twice the gross loss to a victim, also applies to organizations. Here, the gross gain to the entire organization is considered, which may be significantly greater than the gross gain to any individual offender. Thus, the potential fine for the organization could be incrementally larger.

Title 18, United States Code, Section 3572(a) identifies factors courts must consider when determining the amount of any criminal fine. Two of the factors in Section 3572(a) pertain in particular to the fining of organizations. The factor at Section 3572(a)(7) is "whether the defendant can pass on to consumers or other persons the expense of the fine." Although individual offenders may, on occasion, be able to pass the costs of fines onto others, organizations are more likely to be able to do so. And the factor at Section 3572(a)(8) states: "if the defendant is an organization," in determining the amount of the fine to impose, judges should consider "the size of the organization and any measure taken by the organization to discipline any officer, director, employee, or agent of the organization responsible for the offense and to prevent a recurrence of such an offense."

Under Title 18, United States Code, Section 3561(a) a court may also sentence an organization to a term of probation. A probationary term for an organization is designed to promote six objectives: (1) "just punishment"; (2) deterrence; (3) incapacitation; (4) rehabilitation; (5) restitution to crime victims; and (6) determinacy.[3] In other words, the same goals of sentencing for individuals reflected in Section 3553(a), and an elimination of parole such that the sentence imposed is the sentence served. In determining whether the imposition of a term of probation is appropriate in a particular case involving an organizational offender, judges also consider Guidelines provisions in Chapter 8 about the sentencing of organizations, the topic of the next section.

B. Guidelines Provisions

Chapter 8 of the Federal Sentencing Guidelines enumerates criteria to assist federal judges when sentencing organizations. Section 8A provides instructions on the application of the other provisions of Chapter 8. Importantly, the application notes to Section 8A provide definitions applicable to the remaining sections. Section 8B addresses restitution, remedial orders, community service, and compliance programs. Section 8C addresses fines and provides a fine table. Section 8D contains provisions related to requirements and conditions of probation for organizations. Finally, Section 8E addresses special assessments, forfeitures, and costs. I will examine each of these sections to highlight aspects most important for purposes of sentencing advocacy.

Under Chapter 8B, the court can order an organization to pay restitution to crime victims in much the same manner that it can order an individual to pay restitution. Section 8B1.2, however, also allows courts to impose remedial orders on organizations, meaning that a court can order an organization to remediate a past harm or act to arrest the harm that has occurred and prevent future harm from the criminal conduct. For example, if a company committed an environmental crime, a court may order the company to remediate the environmental harm by paying for the clean-up of the spill or discharge and to take remedial action to prevent further spills or discharge. The court can even require an organization to create and finance a trust fund for purposes of paying for remediation of expected future harm from the criminal conduct. Section 8B1.3 authorizes a court to impose community service "reasonably designed to repair the harm" as a condition of probation. Finally, Section 8B2.1 sets out the criteria for an effective compliance and ethics program designed to prevent and uncover criminal conduct by and within organizations.

Section 8C addresses fines for organizations. The Guidelines adopted a complicated scheme for determining an organizational fine range. It begins with establishing a base fine amount and then multiplying that base amount by a "culpability score" to set a minimum and maximum fine range. Section 8C2.4 sets the base advisory Guidelines fine for organizations.

Fines for Organization Table

Offense Level	*Amount*	*Offense Level*	*Amount*
6 or less	$8,500	23	$3,000,000
7	$15,000	24	$3,500,000
8	$15,000	25	$5,000,000
9	$25,000	26	$6,500,000
10	$35,000	27	$8,500,000
11	$50,000	28	$10,000,000
12	$70,000	29	$15,000,000
13	$100,000	30	$20,000,000
14	$150,000	31	$25,000,000
15	$200,000	32	$30,000,000
16	$300,000	33	$40,000,000
17	$450,000	34	$50,000,000
18	$600,000	35	$65,000,000
19	$850,000	36	$80,000,000
20	$1,000,000	37	$100,000,000
21	$1,500,000	38 or more	$150,000,000
22	$2,000,000		

The base fine is the greater of either the fine provided in the chart in Section 8C2.4 corresponding to the total offense level, the pecuniary gain, or the pecuniary loss from the offense. Section 8C.2.5 then identifies factors for determining a culpability score. Points are assessed to an organization based on factors such as the size of the organization, the extent to which high-level employees were involved in the criminal conduct, whether the organization exhibited a culture of tolerance or a history of criminal activity, and whether the crime involved a violation of a court order or the organization obstructed justice. Points may be subtracted from the culpability score based on whether the organization had a compliance program, self-reported the crime, cooperated in the investigation, or showed acceptance of responsibility. Sections 8C2.6 and 8C2.7 provide a chart and instructions on applying the culpability number against the base fine amount to arrive at a fine range.

Corporate Culpability Chart

Culpability Score	*Minimum Multiplier*	*Maximum Multiplier*
10 or more	2.00	4.00
9	1.80	3.60
8	1.60	3.20
7	1.40	2.80
6	1.20	2.40
5	1.00	2.00
4	0.80	1.60
3	0.60	1.20
2	0.40	0.80
1	0.20	0.40
0 or less	0.05	0.20

Finally, Section 8C2.8 identifies about a dozen factors courts should consider in determining the amount of fine to impose within the advisory fine range.

Section 8C does not stop there. Section 8C2.9 notes that whatever fine the court determines is appropriate, the court should add to that amount "any gain to the organization from the offense that has not and will not be paid as restitution or by way of other remedial measure." USSG §8C2.9. Section 8C also contains additional provisions essentially noting that the statutory maximum and minimum fine amounts control over the Guidelines fine amounts (USSG §8C3.1), addressing whether the court should order the fine due immediately (USSG §8C3.2), reducing the fine based on the ability to pay (USSG §8C3.3), and reducing the fine if members of a closely held organization are also fined as individual criminal offenders for the same offense conduct (USSG §8C3.4).

Section 8C.4 of the Guidelines addresses grounds for upward and downward departures from the advisory Guidelines fine amounts. As with individual offenders, there is a provision for the government to make a motion for a downward departure from the advisory Guidelines fine range in exchange for the organization providing substantial assistance to the government in the investigation and prosecution of another. USSG §8C4.1. Grounds for upward departures from the advisory Guidelines fine range include criminal conduct that created a risk of death or bodily injury (USSG §8C4.2), a threat to national security (USSG §8C4.3), a threat to the environment (USSG §8C4.4), or a threat to the integrity or continued existence of a market (USSG §8C4.5). An upward departure may also be appropriate if an organization bribed, attempted to bribe, or conspired to bribe a public official in connection with the criminal conduct. USSG §8C4.6. The Guidelines also provide that if an organization's culpability score was reduced because it had a compliance program in place only because of a prior court order, then an upward departure is appropriate to erase the effects of that reduction. USSG §8C4.10. Similarly, if the organization was required by court order to have a compliance program in place but did not, then an upward departure may be appropriate. *Id.* Finally, the Guidelines provide that a court may upward depart from the advisory Guidelines fine range if the organization's culpability score is greater than 10. USSG §8C4.11. On the other hand, a downward departure may be warranted if the organization had a compliance program in place and no high-level employee was involved in or condoned the criminal conduct (USSG §8C4.11), when the organization is a public entity (USSG §8C4.7), when members or beneficiaries, other than shareholders, of the organization are themselves direct victims of the offense (USSG §8C4.8), or when the organization has paid or agreed to pay remedial costs that greatly exceed the organization's gain from the criminal conduct (USSG §8C4.9).

Section 8D addresses imposition of probation on an organization. Section 8D1.1(a) of the Guidelines, in particular, provides that a court "shall order a term of probation" when, among other things, "such sentence is necessary to ensure that changes are made within the organization to reduce the likelihood of future criminal conduct," USSG §8D1.1(a)(6), or when "necessary to accomplish one or more of the purposes of sentencing set forth in 18 U.S.C. § 3553(a)(2)," USSG §8D1.1(a)(8). Commentary to the Policy Statement concerning community service for organizations states that "[a]n organization can perform community service only by employing its resources or paying its employees or others to do so." USSG §8B1.3.

For purposes of this book, the importance of reviewing these Guidelines provisions is not so much in learning the incredibly complex substantive Guidelines law of these provisions as it is for the reader to recognize the type of conduct that the drafters of the Guidelines found important. As with individuals, federal judges must first calculate the advisory Guidelines range as part of the analysis under Section 3553(a). But the Guidelines calculation is only one of the factors a judge must consider. For state court practitioners, the same factors and considerations underlying the Guidelines provisions may provide fodder for the attorneys in formulating arguments for the sentencing of organizations in state court, even when the Federal Sentencing Guidelines do not apply. In short, whether in state or federal court, attorneys can, and should, advocate for sentences based on considerations and reasoning underlying the Guidelines even when they may not apply in a given case.

C. Fining an Organization

The imposition of a criminal fine is the principal means by which courts can punish an organization. When incarceration is not an option because a fictional entity cannot be placed in a real prison, inflicting financial punishment is the only other significant option. Regardless, a fine is a punishment that often fits the crime well for organizations. The underlying premise is that organizations are primarily motivated to commit crimes for financial gain. Unlike human offenders who may be motivated by emotions or prejudice, ideology or beliefs, a fictional entity typically exists for the purpose of generating income. It is fitting then that the form of punishment—a financial fine—fit the motive for the crime—financial gain.

Fining an organization reasonably advances the several goals of sentencing. Making an organization pay a fine meets the goal of retribution because it punishes financially the offender financially motivated to commit the crime. Similarly, a sizable fine, that is a fine in an amount greater than the profit the organization realized from the criminal conduct, advances the goal of deterrence by showing to the organization, and to other organizations, that crime does not pay. Finally, imposing a very harsh fine may also advance the goal of incapacitation by financially hobbling, if not destroying, an organization so as to prevent it from committing future crimes. For these reasons, fining organizations is often preferable to other forms of punishment, such as placing organizations on probation.[4]

This premise, however, may be faulty in some instances. Organizations can include non-profit organizations, such as churches and charities. Organizations can also include municipalities and state governments. They may also be publicly traded corporations where a fine would adversely impact innocent shareholders. They can also include organizations created for largely or wholly illegal purposes, such as criminal motorcycle gangs, for which generating income is of secondary importance to generating a means of control over gang members. And the underlying reason for any organization to commit a crime may also reflect the baser human motives of the owners, officers, and directors who run the organization. The officers or employees of an organization may be motivated to commit a criminal offense to advance some type of social or political agenda. Some members of criminal organizations, on the other hand, may commit crimes to maintain discipline or control territory or to retaliate against those they perceive to have wronged the organization.

Thus, an organization's motive for criminal conduct may not always be financial. This is important for purposes of sentencing advocacy when determining whether a fine is the most appropriate means of punishing the organization. In advocating for or against a fine with an organizational offender, attorneys should consider the degree to which the motive for the crime was financial. A fine tied to the amount of funds unlawfully obtained may be the most appropriate punishment for an organization that committed the crime for financial again. To advance the goals of sentencing, the fine should be sufficiently severe not only to erase any financial gain, but to deter the organization, and other organizations, from ever being tempted to commit the crime in the future. On the other hand, if the motive for the crime was driven by the baser motives of owners, officers, employees, or members, then a fine may not address that motive as well as other forms of punishment could. If the organization's conduct was part of a pattern or was itself very reprehensible, then a crippling fine designed to incapacitate the organization may be called for.

Generally speaking, funds offenders pay in the form of fines are deposited in the government's general accounts. When courts fine organizations, the desire to direct the fine to be paid to some other entity, rather than to have it simply enter the federal government's coffers, may be great. A prosecutor may be tempted in a fraud case, for instance, to ask the court to require the offender organization to pay a fine to a charity that may benefit the general class of individuals whom the organization victimized. Similarly, a defense attorney may propose that the organization will pay the fine to a charity as a way of suggesting that the organization is remorseful or to reduce or mitigate the amount of restitution the court may order. Nevertheless, federal appeals courts have universally held that it is impermissible for a sentencing court to direct an offender, including an organization, to make a charitable contribution in lieu of a fine, reasoning that to do so would essentially allow a judge to divert money that would have been paid to the Treasury to a private organization without statutory authorization.

D. Forfeiture of Organization Assets

As with individual offenders, courts may forfeit an organization's assets as part of the sentence. The law and purpose of forfeiture for organizations are the same as those for individuals: to deprive the offender of assets that constitute the proceeds of the unlawful conduct and to seize the assets used to commit the offense. Forfeiture advances the sentencing goals of retribution and deterrence. In certain instances, the government may also seek forfeiture of assets so as to incapacitate the organization. For example, the government has sought to forfeit company names and the trademarks of organizations so as to deprive the organizations from operating under the same names or from using trademarks that allowed the organizations to succeed.[5] Attorneys should be alert, however, to the possibility that forfeiture of some tradenames and trademarks could run afoul of the First Amendment.[6] When forfeiture of an asset, like a trademark, may incapacitate the offender organization, attorneys should consider whether that degree of punishment complies with the Eighth Amendment's excessive fines clause. In some cases, forfeiture that leads to dissolution of an organization may not be excessive punishment, especially if the organization was criminal in nature. On the other hand, forfeiture of assets that incapacitate an organization may be so disproportionate to the crime that it violates the excessive fines clause.

Forfeiture can become a more complex issue with organizational offenders than with human offenders. An organization offender might distinguish some property as not subject to forfeiture by showing that it did not own the property at the time of the offense. The court will determine the extent of the organization's property interest, however, at an ancillary hearing and will not typically resolve this issue at a sentencing hearing. FED. R. CRIM. P. 32.2(c). Likewise, an organization offender may argue that the amount of funds generated by the unlawful conduct should be decreased by the value of the "lawful goods or services that [were] sold or provided in an illegal manner ... [and not] property of any kind obtained directly or indirectly, as the result of the commission of the offense giving rise to forfeiture ...." 18 U.S.C. § 981(a)(2)(B).

E. Restitution and Organizations

Like individual offenders, a court may require organization offenders to pay restitution as part of a criminal sentence. The law on restitution is the same for organizations as it is for individuals. With organizations, however, certain issues arise more often than with individual offenders. Often the amount of restitution owed by an organization is significant simply because the scope of harm that an organization can cause is often far greater than what any individual may cause. As a result, restitution payments may be so significant that they directly impact an organization's financial capacity to pay a fine. As with individual offenders, though, payment of restitution should take precedence over payment of a fine and must do so when restitution is mandatory.

Second, because of the geographic and temporal scope of the crime and the size of any single victim's loss, the logistical cost of determining loss and restitution for individual victims may be so great as to be impracticable. The Victim-Witness Protection Act explicitly provides that a court may decline to order restitution "[t]o the extent that the court determines the complication and prolongation of the sentencing process resulting from the fashioning of an order of restitution ... outweighs the need to provide restitution to any victims." 18 U.S.C. § 3663(a)(1)(B)(ii). The Federal Sentencing Guidelines similarly provide that a court need not enter a restitution order if it finds, "from facts on the record, that (A) the number of identifiable victims is so large as to make restitution impracticable; or (B) determining complex issues of fact related to the cause or amount of the victim's losses would complicate or prolong the sentencing process to a degree that the need to provide restitution to any victim is outweighed by the burden on the sentencing process." USSG §8B1.1(b)(2).[7] Restitution may also be inappropriate when the corporation has already made remediation payments so as to make the victim whole. Thus, attorneys should consider whether these factors would make imposition of restitution impracticable.[8]

It is not uncommon for the number of victims to be "too large to be practicable" in complex cases involving securities or environmental offenses. The nature of these complex cases might make identifying victims or assessing injuries especially difficult.[9] In environmental cases, for example, restitution is often comprised of cleanup costs. The Environmental Protection Agency (EPA), however, sometimes has no way of verifying the costs incurred or who covered the expenses, and defendants might "pre-comply" beyond what the EPA wants them to do—in effect recovering more "credit" than they deserve.[10]

F. Organizations and Probation

Courts may place organizations on probation, just as they may place individual offenders on probation. In contrast, supervised release, which is imposed only upon completion of a term of incarceration, is not an option for organizations. Nevertheless, a term of probation may serve the same goals of supervised release for an organization.

A sentencing judge may impose conditions of probation that are designed to advance the goals of sentencing. A term of probation may require the organization to pay for past harms, such as an order requiring remediation efforts, thus advancing the goal of retribution. A judge may also impose a condition designed to deter the organization from committing future crimes, such as subjecting its books to examination by auditors during the term of probation. A judge may advance the goal of rehabilitating the organization by imposing terms of probation, such as by requiring the organization to adopt an internal compliance program designed to deter and detect criminal conduct by employees. In advocating for or against the length and terms of a probationary sentence for an organization, attorneys should consider how the conditions and length of probation would advance the goals of sentencing the organization.

In the federal system, there is statutory authorization for a sentencing court to require as a condition of probation that an offender, including an organization, "work in community service as directed by the court." 18 U.S.C. § 3563(b)(12). Thus, one term of probation for an organization could include a requirement that the organization's employees contribute a number of hours to community service. Ideally the community service is tied to the harm the organization caused. A fraud that victimized the elderly may call for community service directed at that population demographic. An environmental crime may call for community service in the form of restoring or cleaning up the environment.

Attorneys need to be cautious when negotiating or arguing for conditions of probation that constitute an indirect monetary sanction on an organization. It is impermissible for a court to direct an organization to make a charitable contribution to a community service organization in lieu of a fine. Such a term of probation would essentially allow a judge to divert money that would have been paid to the Treasury to a private organization without statutory authorization.[11] Similarly, although courts can order offenders to participate in community service as a condition of probation, that does not mean that a court can order an offender, including an organization, to make a financial donation or contribution to the community as a condition of probation. The idea behind community service is that offenders personally give back to the community through time and effort—sweat equity, if you will—as a means of atonement and rehabilitation. Requiring an organization to make a financial contribution as a form of community service does not further the purpose of community service. Instead, it essentially constitutes a fine under a different label.[12] In short, payments imposed as a condition of probation, including community service payments, cannot be imposed if they enhance the monetary penalties beyond the maximum fine allowed by law. Courts may, however, still impose community service as a condition of probation for organizations when the community service requires the performance of tasks by officers and employees of the organization.

G. Advocating Organizational Sentences

Sentencing organizations poses conceptual difficulties not present when sentencing individuals. Although the law recognizes an organization as a fictional, legal "person," it is not a person with a metaphysical existence. Rather, it is an entity that is comprised of people who have a property interest in the organization, be it through stock, employment, or other means. As a result, in some sense, when a judge imposes a sentence on an organization, the judge is imposing punishment on the property owners and employees comprising the organization. A fine on a corporation effectively fines its stockholders as well. The stockholders may absorb the impact of the fine by loss of equity or dividends. Or they may pass along to others, such as consumers, some or all the costs of a fine by increasing the costs of the goods or services sold, or the organization's employees by reduced compensation or reduction in force. A fine, forfeiture, or restitution order imposed on an organization may directly impact employee compensation immediately and in the future. That may, in turn, indirectly impact the family members of those employees. Thus, any financial penalty a court imposes on an organization has a ripple effect far beyond the artificial entity and may impact real people in sometimes inestimable ways.

When advocating for or against a particular sentence for an organization, attorneys should consider the impact the sentence will have on the real people comprising the organization. Prosecutors should consider whether an organization's financial penalty may result in an unduly harsh impact on innocent owners and employees of the organization. Defense attorneys may consider developing and presenting evidence to show a sentencing judge how a financial penalty may directly or indirectly impact innocent owners and employees and their families. To be persuasive, this may require something more than asking the judge to make a logical conclusion that a financial penalty will necessarily have a ripple effect. A defense attorney may wish to show through a forensic accountant's testimony or with exhibits, charts, or other means how a financial penalty will impact the organization and how that impact will in turn affect innocent owners and employees.

Both attorneys may also need to consider the societal impact of a financial penalty on an organization. A severe financial penalty that may impair the organization's survival as a going concern may adversely impact the community or communities where the organization is located. If an organization may go out of business because of the size of the financial penalty, it may not only impact the owners and employees of the organization; it may also directly impact others in the community. When a company shutters its doors, it may adversely impact other suppliers and customers, local restaurants and hotels, and other shops and businesses. It may erase a source of tax revenue for a local government that could in turn impact that government's ability to fund programs and infrastructure within the community. In short, attorneys should think outside the box and beyond the immediate parties in the case and consider the wider implications of a financial penalty on an organization. That is not to say that in some cases a severe financial penalty may not be warranted, despite the wider adverse impacts that may follow in its wake. It does mean, however, that attorneys should be aware of the impact and incorporate those implications in its advocacy to the sentencing court.

Finally, it is difficult for organizations to express remorse, a human emotion. We have explored the importance of an allocution and the need for offenders to show remorse. The face of an organizational offender will be an officer or director of the organization duly designated by the organization to plead and speak on behalf of the organization in court, including in allocution for the organization. These executives or managers, however, are unlikely to strike a sympathetic image on behalf of the organization. Defense counsel may need to work with the organization's representative to develop an allocution that speaks on behalf of all the people comprising the organization and not just the board of directors or chief executive officers of the organization. This may require that the representative meet with the owners and employees of the organization, fully inform them of the events and consequences, and elicit responses from them to pass on to the judge in a manner to show that the lowest-level employee understands the significance of and has regret for the criminal conduct and a dedication to reform as an organization.

28

Advocacy in Supervised Release Revocation Hearings

The topic of sentencing advocacy in the federal court system includes advocacy in supervised release revocation hearings. As noted in a prior chapter, federal judges impose a term of supervised release almost every time they impose a term of incarceration. A term of supervised release following prison is part of an offender's sentence. When an offender violates a term or condition of supervised release, a court may modify or revoke the offender's supervised release and impose additional conditions of supervision or send the offender back to prison. Courts determine whether the offender violated supervised release and, if so, what punishment to impose in revocation hearings. In that sense, revocation hearings are hybrid hearings in the sense that they are both hearings to determine guilt—that is, whether the offender in fact violated terms or conditions of supervised release—and sentencing hearings when a court finds that the offender did violate supervised release conditions.

To be effective advocates at revocation hearings, attorneys need to consider and address several issues. Attorneys should determine what laws and rules govern these hybrid procedures and then decide how to effectively advocate for their clients within the confines of these rules and laws. This chapter addresses both the law of supervised release and effective advocacy in revocation hearings.

A. Statutory Provisions

Title 18, United States Code, Section 3583 addresses supervised release. 18 U.S.C. § 3583. This section provides that a sentencing judge may impose a term of supervised release initially as a component of a sentence. *Id.* § 3583(a). In addition, once imposed, a judge may terminate, extend, or revoke an offender's supervised release. *Id.* § 3583(e)(1), (2), and (3). If a judge revokes supervised release and imposes a term of imprisonment, then the court may reimpose another term of supervised release to follow the new term of imprisonment. *Id.* § 3583(h). This statute also establishes maximum terms of imprisonment that courts can impose when revoking terms of supervised release. A "defendant whose term is revoked ... may not be required to serve on any such revocation more than 5 years in prison if the offense that resulted in the term of supervised release is a class A felony, more than 3 years in prison if such offense is a class B felony, more than 2 years in prison if such offense is a class C or D felony, or more than one year in any other case." *Id.* § 3553(e).

Revocation of supervised release takes two forms: discretionary under Title 18, United States Code, Section 3583(e), and mandatory under Title 18, United States Code, Section 3583(g). Section 3583(e) establishes a three-step process for discretionary revocation: (1) a finding by the judge that the offender violated a condition of supervised release; (2) a decision by the judge whether to revoke the offender's term of supervised release; and (3) following revocation, the imposition of a penalty. *See* 18 U.S.C. § 3583(e)(3) ("The court may, after considering [certain] factors set forth in § 3553[a] ... revoke a term of supervised release, and require the defendant to serve in prison all or part of the term of supervised release authorized by statute for the offense that resulted in such term of supervised release."). The burden of proof in revocation hearings is the same as at sentencing hearings—the preponderance of the evidence. *See id.* stating that courts may revoke or modify supervised release "if the court ... finds by a preponderance of the evidence that the defendant violated a condition of supervised release."

Title 18, United States Code, Section 3583(g) addresses mandatory revocation. Section 3583(g) provides:

> **Mandatory revocation for possession of controlled substance or firearm or for refusal to comply with drug testing.**—If the defendant—
> (1) possesses a controlled substance in violation of the condition set forth in subsection (d);
> (2) possesses a firearm, as such term is defined in section 921 of this title, in violation of Federal law, or otherwise violates a condition of supervised release prohibiting the defendant from possessing a firearm;
> (3) refuses to comply with drug testing imposed as a condition of supervised release; or
> (4) as a part of drug testing, tests positive for illegal controlled substances more than 3 times over the course of 1 year;
> the court shall revoke the term of supervised release and require the defendant to serve a term of imprisonment not to exceed the maximum term of imprisonment authorized under subsection (e)(3).

18 U.S.C. § 3583(g). The process set out in this subsection is similar to that of Section 3583(e) but eliminates the second step applied under Section 3583(e). Thus, this subsection entails only two steps: (1) a finding by the court that one of the four circumstances in Section 3583(g)(1)–(4) occurred; and (2) if so, revocation is automatic, and the court must impose a "term of imprisonment" as a penalty. Despite the word "mandatory," a sentencing judge does have the authority to exempt an offender from mandatory revocation when the reason for the revocation is that the offender tested positive for the use of illegal drugs. In those cases, Title 18, United States Code, Section 3583(d) provides that, "when considering any action against a defendant who fails a drug test," the court can consider "whether the availability of appropriate

substance abuse treatment programs, or an individual's current or past participation in such programs, warrants an exception" from the mandatory revocation and imprisonment directed by Section 3583(g).[1]

I should note that the United States Supreme Court recently found another supervised release provision unconstitutional. Under Title 18, United States Code, Section 3583(k), "If a judge finds by a preponderance of the evidence that a defendant on supervised release"—who is also required to register as a sex offender—"committed one of several enumerated offenses … the judge *must* impose an additional prison term of at least five years and up to life without regard to the length of the prison term authorized for the defendant's initial crime of conviction." *United States v. Haymond*, 139 S. Ct. 2369, 2374 (2019) (plurality opinion) (emphasis in original). The Supreme Court held that the statute's application of an additional five-year prison term violated the defendant's rights under the Fifth and Sixth Amendments. Justice Gorsuch, writing the plurality opinion joined by Justice Ginsburg, Justice Sotomayor, and Justice Kagan, concluded the statute was unconstitutional under *Apprendi v. New Jersey* and its progeny. The point here, though, is that the Supreme Court's holding in *Haymond* has not called into question the constitutionality of the mandatory provisions of Section 3583(g).[2]

B. Governing Rules

Federal Rule of Criminal Procedure 32.1 addresses revocation of supervised release, including preliminary proceedings related to revocation of supervise release. Subsection (b)(2) in particular governs revocation hearings. It provides:

> (2) **Revocation Hearing.** Unless waived by the person, the court must hold the revocation hearing within a reasonable time in the district having jurisdiction. The person is entitled to:
> (A) written notice of the alleged violation;
> (B) disclosure of the evidence against the person;
> (C) an opportunity to appear, present evidence, and question any adverse witness unless the court determines that the interest of justice does not require the witness to appear;
> (D) notice of the person's right to retain counsel or to request that counsel be appointed if the person cannot obtain counsel; and
> (E) an opportunity to make a statement and present any information in mitigation.

FED. R. CRIM. P. 32.1(b)(2).

The written notice of violations comes in the form of a Petition to Revoke Supervised Release, drafted and filed by the United States Probation Office. These petitions will include a summary of the alleged violation and will typically attach copies of any documentary evidence (such as urine drug testing laboratory reports). Upon the filing of the petition, which may be filed under seal, the judge will either issue a warrant or summons to compel the offender's presence at a revocation hearing.

If an offender is arrested on the warrant, there will follow an initial appearance and a detention hearing, if requested, when the government seeks detention of the offender pending the revocation hearing (a very likely occurrence whenever warrants are issued). Upon issuance of a summons, the court will ensure the offender is represented by private counsel or will appoint counsel to represent the offender. If the offender is arrested, the court will address representation at the time of initial appearance.

Courts will typically attempt to appoint the same attorney who represented the offender at the original sentencing hearing to represent the offender in a revocation hearing, when possible. Sometimes decades have passed since the original sentencing hearing, however, and the original defense attorney has changed jobs, moved, retired, or died. In other cases, the original attorney may decline the appointment. Some Federal Public Defenders' offices are so overwhelmed that they decline to represent offenders in supervised release revocation hearings because they need to give priority to other offenders. Being appointed to represent an offender for the first time in connection with a supervised release revocation hearing can present significant challenges to defense counsel. In those situations, defense attorneys typically have a very short window of time to develop rapport with their clients, learn about their clients' past and the alleged violations, and develop a defense strategy.

There is a place for sentencing advocacy at this early stage of revocation proceedings, just as there is a place for sentencing advocacy at the early stages of a criminal prosecution. Defense attorneys should carefully consider the implications of seeking release of an offender pending a revocation hearing similar to considering the implications of seeking release when offenders are arrested on charges in the first instance. Offenders will inevitably prefer to be released, but there is always a danger that if released, they will violate the conditions of release, which in turn could adversely affect them when the judge considers the appropriate sentence. This is particularly true of an offender arrested for violating the terms of supervised release. Such an offender has already likely showed an inability or unwillingness to abide by conditions of release, making it that much more likely that the offender will reoffend pending the revocation hearing. Thus, defense attorneys should have candid conversations with offenders about seeking release pending revocation hearings. More often than not, it is in the offender's best interest to remain in custody pending the revocation hearing. The defense attorney's goal then will be to advocate for scheduling the revocation hearing as soon as possible. Courts often schedule revocation hearings within ten to fourteen days of an offender's initial appearance or return of a summons. Thus, detention of an offender pending a revocation hearing is much shorter than detention of an offender pending trial.

When a summons is issued for an offender to appear at a revocation hearing, it is again important for attorneys to consider steps they can take toward effective sentencing advocacy. Defense attorneys should contact their clients as soon as possible after issuance of the summons. It is very important that the defense attorney warn the offender about the adverse consequences that would follow a failure to appear at the revocation hearing. The issuance of a summons is generally a good sign that the probation office and judge do not necessarily consider the offender a danger to the community or a flight risk. That, in turn, likely means there is a possibility that the judge may modify, instead of revoke, the offender's supervised release. Failure to appear at the revocation hearing in response to a summons, however, would likely end any chance the offender might have for a favorable outcome at the revocation hearing. Likewise, the defense attorney should have a candid conversation with the offender about the need to strictly abide by all the conditions of supervision pending the revocation hearing. Again, further violations of conditions between the issuance of the summons and the hearing may very well jeopardize any chance the offender has of a favorable disposition at the hearing.

Whether the offender is arrested or summoned to a revocation hearing, one of the first questions the offender and defense attorney will face, of course, is whether the offender will contest or dispute the allegations that the offender has violated some or all the conditions of supervision as alleged in the petition to revoke supervision. That the offender may have previously denied the violations when confronted by the probation officer does not mean that the offender cannot and should not reverse direction and admit the violation later when, in fact, the offender is guilty of violating the condition. The decision whether to admit or contest the violations will necessarily be fact specific and turn on the nature of the allegations and the weight of the evidence.

It is important that defense attorneys investigate the alleged violations. This may start with talking to the offender to find out what happened and what the offender's position is about the violations. If the offender denies the violations, the defense attorney should elicit the offender's help in trying to discover evidence to rebut the alleged violation. The offender may have names of potential witnesses or other evidence that could be helpful. If the violation involves a violation of state law, the defense attorney will want to contact the state defense attorney assigned to the state case. Even if the offender is acquitted of the conduct in state court or the state prosecutor drops the charges, it may still serve as a basis for revocation of federal supervised release. The state defense attorney may be of great assistance in defending the allegation in such cases. Conversely, if the state charges forming the basis for a revocation in federal court remain pending at the time of the revocation hearing, the offender may not be in a position to admit to the conduct because it will incriminate him in state court. Here, the defense attorney could either resist that ground for revocation or plead the Fifth, neither admitting nor denying the conduct.

At the revocation hearing, the parties may present evidence on the alleged violations when they are contested. Prosecutors assume the role of representing the probation office and prosecuting the violation allegations. The government bears the burden of proof by a preponderance of the evidence.

A word of caution is appropriate here. Defense attorneys should hesitate to rely on information or documents submitted by their clients who are contesting violations of supervised release. Once as a prosecutor, and now once as a presiding judge, I have witnessed situations when offenders have provided the defense attorneys with a letter or photograph or other document that purports to prove them innocent of the violation when it turned out the evidence was fabricated. Not only were the offenders revoked, on one of the occasions the government prosecuted the offender on a new obstruction of justice offense. It has been my observation that offenders for some reason seem to be more willing to fabricate evidence and commit perjury in a revocation hearing when they would never do so in a criminal trial. I fear, too, that because of the press for time in a revocation hearing, defense attorneys feel more need to rely on their clients and trust what their clients are providing them. My advice is that defense attorneys should independently verify the accuracy of anything their client provides them under these circumstances. In both instances I mentioned, it would have been relatively easy for the defense attorney to have discovered the falsity with a simple phone call.

C. Inapplicability of the Federal Rules of Evidence

The short story here is that the Federal Rules of Evidence do not apply in revocation hearings. *See* FED. R. EVID. 1101(d)(3). Thus, hearsay is admissible in revocation hearings. Nevertheless, the Due Process Clause does apply and, as will be discussed next, it incorporates a requirement that evidence in revocation hearings be reliable. Thus, although hearsay is admissible, the government must generally produce witnesses with knowledge of the facts unless there is good cause for not doing so.

D. Applicability of Due Process and Confrontation Clauses

Although supervised release revocation hearings involve a determination of whether an offender violated the terms and conditions of supervised release, they are not criminal trials. Thus, offenders' rights in revocation hearings are more limited rights than they would be in criminal trials.[3] This means, in part, that the Sixth Amendment's Confrontation Clause does not strictly apply to revocation hearings.[4] A right to confront witnesses is encompassed within the Due Process Clause, however, which does apply to revocation hearings. This Due Process Clause right of confrontation is considered a "qualified" right because it can be overcome if a balancing test weighing the offender's and government's interests shows good cause to not allow the confrontation.[5]

This balancing test is codified in Federal Rule of Criminal Procedure 32.1, which grants offenders the right to question adverse witnesses in revocation hearings "unless the judge determines that the interest of justice does not require the witness to appear." FED. R. CRIM. P. 32.1(b)(2)(C).[6] When an offender asserts Rule 32.1(b)(2)(C)'s cross-examination right, a court must apply a balancing test before admitting the hearsay evidence, weighing an offender's right to confront the declarant against the government's asserted grounds for not producing the witness.[7] Most courts require judges to explicitly balance the offender's constitutional interest in confrontation and cross-examination against the government's stated reasons for denying them, and may reverse and remand the case for rehearing if this is not done on the record.[8]

Courts generally analyze whether the government has asserted good cause for not producing the witness for confrontation.[9] In determining if good cause exists, judges consider the reliability of the evidence, the availability of the witness, and the availability of corroborating evidence or witnesses. A witness may be "unavailable" if the witness invokes the Fifth Amendment privilege.[10] The witness may also be unavailable if the government has tried but has been unable to find or subpoena the witness, or the witness is outside the government's national subpoena power. When live testimony would be difficult or burdensome to obtain, confrontation need not be face-to-face. Video conferencing could allow a distant witness to testify and face cross-examination with minimal inconvenience and expense. When such inexpensive means of communication are available, attorneys should assume that judges will find that due process requires the witnesses to appear by that means.

E. Application of 18 U.S.C. § 3553(a) Factors in Revocation Hearings

In arriving at the appropriate sentence when revoking supervised release, sentencing judges turn to Title 18, United States Code, Section 3553(a), just like they do when sentencing an offender upon conviction. Some courts have held that judges must consider the Section 3553(a) factors in cases of mandatory revocation under 18 U.S.C. § 3583(g), even though that section does not explicitly reference Section 3553(a), while other courts have held that judges need not consider Section 3553(a) factors in instances of mandatory revocation.[11]

Not all the Section 3553(a) factors apply, however, in a revocation proceeding. Section 3583(e), the statute governing supervised release, specifically directs courts to consider factors enumerated in "section 3553(a)(1), (a)(2)(B), (a)(2)(C), (a)(2)(D), (a)(4), (a)(5), (a)(6), and (a)(7)" when imposing a sentence upon revocation of supervised release. Absent from these enumerated Section 3553(a) factors is Section 3553(a)(2)(A), which requires district courts to consider the need for the imposed sentence "to reflect the seriousness of the offense, to promote respect for the law, and to provide just punishment for the offense." Nevertheless, some courts have held that it is not error for a sentencing judge still to consider the Section 3553(a)(2)(A) factors in imposing a sentence after revocation of supervised release when those are not the primary factors the court relied on, and the court relied on the other factors as well.[12]

It should be noted that a judge may vary from the advisory Guidelines revocation range of imprisonment, just as a judge may vary from the advisory Guidelines range of imprisonment at a sentencing hearing. A district court has broad discretion when imposing a sentence upon revocation of supervised release. Nevertheless, under 18 U.S.C. § 3553(c)(2), judges must state in open court the specific reasons for imposing a sentence outside the Guideline range in a revocation proceeding, just as they do in sentencing hearings. 18 U.S.C. § 3553(c)(2).[13]

F. The Federal Sentencing Guidelines in Revocation Hearings

One of the factors listed under Title 18, United States Code, Section 3553(a) is the sentencing range established under the Federal Sentencing Guidelines. 18 U.S.C. § 3553(a)(4). This applies in revocation hearings as well as in sentencing hearings. Chapter 7 of the Federal Sentencing Guidelines Manual addresses sentencing upon revocation of supervised release. The Sentencing Commission chose to promulgate policy statements, as opposed to guidelines, for use in hearings on violations of supervised release or probation. USSG, pt. A(1). Now that the Guidelines are advisory and no longer mandatory, though, there is little practical difference between a guideline and a policy statement. In both instances they reflect the Sentencing Commission's recommendation about the sentence to be imposed that the sentencing judge must consider but is not bound to accept.

As a philosophical matter, Chapter 7 of the Guidelines directs judges to think about sentences for violations of a supervised release differently than they think about sentences for violations of criminal statutes. Chapter 7 instructs that, in fashioning a revocation sentence, "the court should sanction primarily the defendant's breach of trust, while taking into account, to a limited degree, the seriousness of the underlying violation and the criminal history of the violator." USSG ch. 7, pt. A(3)(b).[14] "[T]he nature of the conduct leading to the revocation [is] considered in measuring the extent of the breach of trust." USSG §7(A)(3)(b).

Chapter 7 of the Guidelines provides for three grades of probation and supervised release violations. A Grade A violation is the commission of: (A) a federal state or local felony offense that constitutes (i) a crime of violence as defined in USSG §4B1.2(a), (ii) a controlled substance offense as defined in USSG §4.1.2(b), or (iii) involves possession of firearm or destructive device, or (B) any other federal, state, or local offense punishable by a term of imprisonment exceeding twenty years. USSG §7B1.1(a)(1). A Grade B violation is "conduct constituting any other federal, state, or local offense punishable by a term of imprisonment exceeding one year. USSG §7B1.1(a)(2). Lastly, a Grade C violation is conduct that either: (A) constitutes a violation of federal, state, or local law for an offense punishable by a term of imprisonment of less than one year, or; (B) any other violation of a condition of supervision. If an offender's conduct violates more than one offense, 'the grade of violation is determined by the violation having the most serious grade.'" USSG §7B1.1(b).

In another policy statement, the Guidelines establish ranges of sentences for supervised release violations that are based on violation grade and criminal history category. *See* USSG §7B1.4(a). Similar to the sentencing table in Chapter 5, there is a similarly structured sentencing table in Chapter 7 where the grade of violation appears on the vertical axis and the offender's criminal history category (as it was determined at the time of the offender's original sentencing) appears on the horizontal axis.

Revocation Table
(in months of imprisonment)

	Criminal History Category					
	I	*II*	*III*	*IV*	*V*	*VI*
Grade of Violation	*I*	*II*				
Grade C	3–9	4–10	5–11	6–12	7–13	8–14
Grade B	4–10	6–12	8–14	12–18	18–24	21–27
Grade A(1)	12–18	15–21	18–24	24–30	30–37	33–41
Grade A(2)*	24–30	27–33	30–37	37–46	46–57	51–63

* *Grade A(2) applies when the defendant was on probation or supervised release as a result of a sentence for a Class A felony.*

USSG §7B1.4(a). The advisory Guidelines sentencing range for a supervised release violation is established at the intersection of these two axes. For example, if an offender had a criminal history category of VI at the time of the offender's original sentencing hearing, and the offender commits a Grade A violation while on supervised release, the applicable advisory Guidelines range of imprisonment upon revocation of supervised release is 33 to 41 months.

Finally, as with Guidelines sentences for commissions of offenses, Guidelines sentences for violations of supervised release are subject to statutory constraints. Although a district court ultimately has broad discretion to revoke supervised release and impose a term of imprisonment, judges may only impose sentences up to the statutory maximum. For purposes of revocation, the statutory maximums are not those for the commission of the underlying offense, but, rather, the statutory maximums previously mentioned in Title 18, United States Code, Section 3553(e): five years if the underlying offense was a class A felony; three years if the underlying offense was a class B felony; two years if the underlying offense was a class C or D felony; and one year in any other case. Thus, even though the advisory Guidelines range of imprisonment for a supervised release violation may exceed the statutory range, the sentencing judge may impose a sentence only up to the statutory maximum sentence. Statutory provisions always trump Guidelines provisions.

Judges need not always revoke an offender's supervised release, even when they find the offender violated the terms and conditions of supervise release. A district court may instead modify the conditions of supervised release by adding new terms and conditions or by changing existing terms or conditions. Judges may even modify conditions of supervised release when the offender has not violated supervised release; judges may modify supervised release conditions based solely on the evidence that was available at the time of sentencing.[15]

G. *Right of Allocution in Revocation Hearings*

Because courts may revoke offenders' supervised release and send offenders back to prison, it follows that the same reasons for granting offenders a right of allocution at sentencing hearings applies equally to revocation hearings. And, indeed, courts must afford offenders the right of allocution in revocation hearings.[16] This right of allocution is codified in Rule 32.1, which dictates that an offender is entitled to "an opportunity to make a statement and present any information in mitigation." FED. R. CRIM. P. 32.1(b)(2)(E).

Effective defense sentencing advocacy includes, then, working with an offender to prepare an allocution for a revocation hearing in much the same way defense attorneys would prepare offenders for allocution in advance of a sentencing hearing. In a sense, it may be even more important for an offender to provide a compelling allocution at a revocation hearing because the offender has betrayed the court's trust and the court is focused in significant part on the offender's rehabilitation. The worst allocutions I have heard have occurred during revocation hearings when offenders blamed their probation officers for not doing enough for them, complained about conditions of supervision being too troublesome, or minimized the significance of their violations. ("It's not like I did drugs, judge; I only smoked marijuana.")

In revocation hearings, most judges are more focused on the rehabilitative goals of sentencing than they are the other goals of sentencing.[17] Probation officers are primarily concerned with helping offenders on supervised release re-integrate into society. Everyone wants to see offenders succeed on supervised release. Thus, allocution at a revocation hearing acknowledging that the offender has struggled and failed to comply with conditions of supervision, accepting full responsibility for those failures, and reflecting a sincere desire and commitment to succeed may go much further in influencing a sentencing judge than the same allocution at the original sentencing.

H. Advocacy at Revocation Hearings

The facts that give rise to a revocation hearing and the conditions that offenders allegedly violated vary significantly. Some violations are relatively minor in nature, such as violations of curfew or failing to report to probation officers in a timely manner. Most violations revolve around the failure to comply with drug testing and the abuse of alcohol and controlled substances. Still other cases involve very serious violations, including the commission of new crimes. The consequences for the offender will differ based on the number and seriousness of the violations. Some violations may result in either a modification of conditions of supervision or some relatively minor punishment such as community service, weekends in jail, or a month or two of incarceration. Other violations, however, can be very serious, including many years in prison.

Effective advocacy at a revocation hearing will depend, then, on the nature and seriousness of the conduct giving rise to the hearing. Minor violations with less severe consequences will require less preparation, while more serious violations with more severe consequences will dictate and justify a greater effort by attorneys. All revocation hearings, however, require zealous advocacy by attorneys on both sides.

Unlike sentencing hearings, the probation office will not prepare a new presentence report for a revocation hearing. Rather, the parties and the court will rely on the offender's presentence report prepared at the time of the original sentencing. It is imperative that attorneys review that presentence report carefully and consider whether and how matters may have changed since the time that presentence report was prepared. Sometimes decades have passed between the date the original presentence report was drafted and the date of the revocation hearing, and in other cases only months have passed. There may be very important changes that took place in the interim that attorneys should investigate and bring to the court's attention to be effective advocates. For example, the presentence report may reflect that at the time of the offender's sentencing, there were serious felony charges pending against the offender in another jurisdiction. It would be important to know at the revocation hearing what happened with those charges. A conviction may support an argument at the revocation hearing that the offender's criminal history is more serious than reflected in the presentence report, supporting an argument for a more severe sentence when revoking the offender's supervised release. Or, perhaps, the presentence report reflected that the offender had never received drug abuse treatment at the time of original sentencing. If, in the meantime, the offender has received such treatment, it may provide insight into the offender's addiction issues relevant to determining the appropriate disposition at the revocation hearing. The point is that unless the attorneys carefully review the presentence report, look into these matters, and bring them to the judge's attention, then the judge may be deprived of very important information.

For prosecutors, there is a significant difference in their relationship with probation officers than their relationship with law enforcement officers. At sentencing hearings, probation officers are neutral, and their role is to assist the court by providing accurate information in the presentence report. At revocation hearings, probation officers have a different role because they are the ones supervising the offenders and charged with ensuring the offenders comply with the terms of supervised release. At revocation hearings, prosecutors represent the probation office in a sense by advocating on the probation officer's behalf. Nevertheless, prosecutors and probation officers are not on the same team in the same sense as are prosecutors and law enforcement officers. Probation officers are employees of the courts, whereas law enforcement officers, like prosecutors, are employees of the executive branch of government. Probation officers also do not have an obligation, nor often the authority, to assist in any further investigation into the violations of supervised release. Probation officers may have conducted some investigation that led to the filing of a petition to revoke supervised release, but that does not mean that they have conducted all the investigation necessary to prove the violations if the offender contests them.

On a related note, defense attorneys should inspect the case's posture to determine if the probation officer asked for the same type of appearance as the prosecutor and judge. For example, the probation officer may have sought a summons, but the prosecutor asked for a warrant, and the judge approved a warrant. Or the probation officer and prosecution may have requested a warrant, but the judge found a summons sufficient. If the probation officer sought a summons, but a warrant was issued, the defense attorney should contact the probation officer to discuss why the probation office thought a summons would have been appropriate. These reasons may provide a basis for argument or, in the right case, a defense attorney may want to call the probation officer as a witness. Defense attorneys should not simply assume that probation officers are pro-law enforcement. Many probation officers enter the career because they believe strongly in rehabilitation, and their mindset may be more aligned with the defense than with the prosecution in some instances.

Thus, prosecutors may need to enlist the assistance of law enforcement officers to help investigate and prove the violations. Typically, prosecutors will turn to the law enforcement agency that was involved in the underlying case. That agency has an ongoing interest in ensuring that the offender is properly punished for the offense, and supervised release punishment is part of the sentence for the underlying offense. When the alleged violations of supervised release involve new criminal conduct, prosecutors may also turn to the law enforcement agency involved in the investigation of that new offense to assist in the prosecution of the supervised release violations. Sometimes prosecutors cannot elicit the assistance of any law enforcement officers to help investigate and prepare for supervised release revocation hearings. When that happens, prosecutors may have to do some of the work of law enforcement officers. There were many times when I served as a federal prosecutor that I made phone calls to obtain documents and find witnesses in order to prove up violations of supervised release conditions because I had no law enforcement officer helping me.

When the violation of supervised release involves an allegation of new criminal conduct, both parties should contemplate the benefits and detriments of moving forward with the revocation proceedings while the other charges are pending against the costs and benefits of awaiting resolution of the pending criminal charges before addressing the ramifications the alleged offense has on the offender's supervised release. Some judges will routinely continue revocation proceedings until after the criminal charges are resolved. This has some practical benefits. If the offender pleads guilty or is found guilty of the offense, then it negates the need to have an evidentiary hearing on the revocation violation. On the other hand, if the offender is acquitted of the charge, the prosecutor and probation officer may conclude that it is appropriate to dismiss the petition to revoke supervised release. An acquittal of the criminal charge, of course, does not necessarily bar the government from continuing to pursue the revocation petition because the burden of proof is different. Even if the government could not prove the offense beyond a reasonable doubt in the criminal case does not mean that the government could not prove the offense by a preponderance of the evidence in the revocation proceeding.

In other instances, the revocation hearing may proceed even if the criminal case has not been resolved. This may occur because the federal judge insists on moving forward with the revocation proceeding without waiting for resolution of the criminal charge. It may also occur because the government believes the offender poses a danger to the public or a flight risk. If the criminal case may take some time to resolve, and especially if the offender has bonded out or could bond out of custody on the criminal charge in the meantime, then the prosecutor may choose to proceed with the revocation petition without waiting for resolution of the criminal charges.

Defense attorneys and their clients should also consider the sentencing ramifications of proceeding with the criminal case or the revocation proceedings first. If the offender is convicted and sentenced to a term of incarceration on the criminal offense, then at the revocation hearing, the defense attorney could argue that the sentencing judge should impose a light sentence or concurrent sentence for the revocation. Conversely, if a court revokes an offender's supervised release and sends the offender back to prison, then it could affect his criminal history calculation and the length of sentence the offender faces if convicted of the criminal charge. A defense attorney should also consider Fifth Amendment issues; an offender's statements in a revocation hearing may be used against the offender in the pending criminal case. In short, part of effective sentencing advocacy requires the attorneys on both sides to consider these consequences in determining whether to advocate for the revocation hearing to proceed before or after resolution of pending criminal charges.

When a revocation hearing involves a violation that also constitutes new criminal conduct, the attorneys should recall that the focus at revocation is to punish the offender for the breach of trust and not so much for the criminal offense.

> While the nature of the conduct leading to the revocation would be considered in measuring the extent of the breach of trust, imposition of an appropriate punishment for any new criminal conduct would not be the primary goal of a revocation sentence. Instead, the sentence imposed upon revocation would be intended to sanction the violator for failing to abide by the conditions of the court-ordered supervision, leaving the punishment for any new criminal conduct to the court responsible for imposing the sentence for that offense.

USSG Chapter 7, pt. A(3)(a). Thus, in advocating for the appropriate disposition, attorneys should focus on how the criminal offense reflects on the breach of the court's trust of the offender on supervision, not on the factors that would normally guide a judge's sentencing decision for the commission of the offense itself.

When revocation hearings are factually contested, attorneys need to prepare for them in much the same way as they prepare for evidentiary sentencing hearings. The parties may need to obtain and mark exhibits, and they may need to prepare and call witnesses to testify. Some revocation hearings can, like some sentencing hearings, take on the appearance of minitrials. In preparing for these contested evidentiary revocation hearings, attorneys should engage in the same practices of preparing exhibits for the sentencing judge and providing the judge with copies of the exhibits in advance of the hearing. Attorneys should also prepare witnesses for testifying in a hearing when the judge will be the factfinder, and the judge may ask questions of the witnesses.

There remains a role for plea negotiations in revocation hearings as well, although it has been my experience that this seldom occurs. There is nothing to prevent the parties from meeting and negotiating agreements both as to the violations themselves and also to the proper disposition of the case. These agreements could be written, or they may be more informal agreements that are placed on the record orally at the revocation hearing. Effective sentencing advocacy involves efforts to reach compromises to reduce the risk of litigation for both sides. It may also be helpful in negotiations to involve the supervising probation officer in an effort to find a resolution that holds the greatest promise of helping the offender succeed on supervision.

Finally, attorneys may also file memoranda with the court in the same manner they would file sentencing memoranda. In practice, again, it has been my experience that attorneys rarely file such revocation hearing memoranda. This is understandable as a practical matter because in most cases, the facts and issues are simple enough that legal memoranda are not warranted and because there is typically a fairly short time between the offender's initial appearance or receipt of a summons and the supervised release revocation hearing. That is not always the case, however; sometimes complex factual and legal issues arise in connection with revocation hearings. Attorneys should always consider whether it would aid and persuade the judge to file a memorandum in support of the client's position at a revocation hearing.

Revocation hearings that result in imposition of a new term of imprisonment resemble sentencing hearings in some ways, but in other ways there is a different tone to the proceedings. Instead of punishing an offender for a crime, the court is punishing the offender largely for the contempt or abuse of trust the offender has shown by violating the terms of release. The goal here is more to help the offender acclimate back into society and live by its rules than it is to punish the offender for transgressions. In some instances, too, an offender may seek greater punishment at a revocation hearing in exchange for not having a further term of supervision imposed. Most offenders hate being "on paper," and some would rather do more time in prison than less time if it means they can get off paper, particularly if they have historically struggled with complying with supervision.

29

Advocacy in Probation Revocation Hearings

Judges sometimes impose terms of probation instead of terms of incarceration. Probation is a significant punishment itself. Importantly, when courts sentence offenders to probation, the judges impose terms and conditions of probation that are very similar, if not identical, to terms and conditions imposed for supervised release. And like supervised release, judges may revoke terms of probation and send a probationer to prison. Thus, part of effective sentencing advocacy includes having familiarity with the law and rules governing probation and revocation of probation. It also requires attorneys to consider advocacy tactics and skills that could be brought to bear in hearings on probation violations.

A. *The Law and Rules Governing Probation and Revocation of Probation*

Title 18, United States Code, Section 3561 is the primary statute that addresses probation in federal court. It identifies offenses for which probation is an option and the statutory maximum period of probation that a court may impose.

(a) In general.—A defendant who has been found guilty of an offense may be sentenced to a term of probation unless—

(1) the offense is a Class A or Class B felony and the defendant is an individual;

(2) the offense is an offense for which probation has been expressly precluded; or

(3) the defendant is sentenced at the same time to a term of imprisonment for the same or a different offense that is not a petty offense.

(b) Domestic violence offenders.—A defendant who has been convicted for the first time of a domestic violence crime shall be sentenced to a term of probation if not sentenced to a term of imprisonment. The term "domestic violence crime" means a crime of violence for which the defendant may be prosecuted in a court of the United States in which the victim or intended victim is the spouse, former spouse, intimate partner, former intimate partner, child, or former child of the defendant, or any other relative of the defendant.

(c) **Authorized terms.**—The authorized terms of probation are—
   (1) for a felony, not less than one nor more than five years;
   (2) for a misdemeanor, not more than five years; and
   (3) for an infraction, not more than one year.

18 U.S.C. § 3561. To be sure, there are other statutory provisions that may trump those in Section 3561. For example, Title 21, United States Code, Section 841 contains language under certain sections explicitly stating that "[n]otwithstanding any other provision of law, the court shall not place on probation." 21 United States Code, Section 841(b)(1)(A). Other statutes provide minimum terms of probation.

District courts have broad discretion to impose and apply conditions of probation. Valid conditions are ones designed to promote the offender's rehabilitation and ensure the protection of the public, without being unnecessarily harsh or excessive. When imposing probation, the sentencing judge may subject the offender to certain terms and conditions similar to those imposed for supervised release.

Chapter 7 of the United States Sentencing Guidelines governs sentences to be imposed for revocation of probationary sentences. Just as with supervised release, violations of probation are placed into one of three grades of violation. USSG §7B1.1. Likewise, Guidelines Section 7B1.3 advises the court as to which violations require revocation based on the grade of the violation. Finally, the same sentencing table found at Guidelines Section 7B1.4 is used for arriving at the appropriate advisory range of imprisonment for violations of probation and is used for violations of supervised release.

B. Advocacy in Probation Revocation Hearings

The same issues and considerations that apply to effective advocacy in supervised release revocation hearings also apply to probation revocation hearings. Here, as there, the court's focus should be on the breach of trust the offender showed by violating the probation conditions. Although the sentencing judge can certainly consider the nature and seriousness of the underlying offense, revocation of probation is not primarily intended as punishment for the underlying offense. And, as with supervised release revocation hearings, the attorneys and the judge should address the applicable factors under Title 18, United States Code, Section 3553(a).

C. Early Termination of Probation

Under 18 U.S.C. § 3564(c), a court may "terminate a term of probation previously ordered and discharge the defendant ... at any time after the expiration of one year of probation in the case of a felony, if it is satisfied that such action is warranted by the conduct of the defendant and the interest of justice." 18 U.S.C. § 3564(c). To guide its discretion under the statute, judges are required to consider the "factors set forth in [18 U.S.C. § 3553(a)] to the extent that they are applicable." *Id.* Early termination of probation may be warranted when circumstances have changed, such as when the offender has accomplished significant steps toward rehabilitation such that the original term of probation is now too harsh or inappropriately tailored to serve the general punishment goals of section 3553(a). That an offender has fully complied with the terms of probation is not, however, generally a sufficient justification for reducing the original probationary sentence.

Conclusion

Final Observations About Sentencing Advocacy

Sentencing is the culmination and ultimate goal of a criminal case. It is the swan song, the crescendo, the apex of efforts exerted from the beginning of a criminal case and throughout the prosecution and defense of that case. Criminal sentences, when structured to promote the goals of sentencing, cause lasting changes in offenders and society as a whole. Criminal sentences also have intended and unintended ripple effects that radiate out far beyond the offender standing before the judge at the sentencing hearing. Thus, sentencing advocacy deserves to be at the forefront of every prosecutor's and every defense attorney's mind and not be the product of afterthought and improvisation.

This book has sought to emphasize the importance of sentencing advocacy and the need for a renewed emphasis on effective sentencing advocacy. Attorneys must devote the attention and effort to sentencing advocacy that it demands and that offenders and society deserve. Deficiencies in this may be in part a result, at least in the federal system, of decades of mandatory sentencing Guidelines when the best sentencing advocacy could have little impact. Thus, sentencing advocacy skills once possessed atrophied and were not taught to new practitioners. It may also be a lack of resources and available continuing legal education programs focused on sentencing issues. In part, though, poor sentencing advocacy is also a product of popular culture that has placed an emphasis on the battle of increasingly rare criminal trials to determine offenders' guilt. All too often neglected have been the sentencing ramifications for those found guilty and for the more than 90 percent of offenders who plead guilty.

The overriding theme of this book has been the need for attorneys to reexamine, develop, and refine their sentencing advocacy skills. The primary emphasis of effective sentencing advocacy is to focus on the goals of sentencing. All evidence and argument should be tied to showing how a particular sentence will best advance the goals of sentencing. Judges focus on those goals when imposing sentences, and thus attorneys should likewise do so.

Of course, effective sentencing advocacy requires a familiarity with the law and procedures that form the basis and structure for sentencing offenders. To be effective sentencing advocates, attorneys should understand the contours of the sentencing laws, rules, and procedures so as to recognize and exploit the opportunities to use them to advance sentencing arguments. In this book I have primarily addressed federal law and procedures, but only so far as necessary to provide a context within which to examine and discuss sentencing advocacy skills. Attorneys practicing in state court can use the lessons learned here and apply them to the similar applicable state laws and procedures that structure sentencing in state courts.

Another principal emphasis in this book has been to treat sentencing advocacy as something more than what attorneys say or how attorneys address judges in sentencing hearings. Effective sentencing advocacy requires attorneys to focus on sentencing throughout the life of a criminal case. Decisions made during investigations, when drafting charging documents, and while negotiating pleas may have such a significant impact on sentencing options that courtroom advocacy skills are rendered relatively unimportant, or conversely those efforts may open up wide opportunities for persuasion to influence the outcome of the sentence.

Hopefully, the reader comes away from this volume with a new appreciation for the need for and opportunities that can arise from effective sentencing advocacy. Attorneys who strive to become better sentencing advocates will need to change their mindsets about the importance of sentencing advocacy. They should understand and be willing to devote the time and effort necessary to understand all the nuances of the sentencing law and procedures that form the structure for sentencing in their courts of practice. Attorneys wanting to become the most effective sentencing advocates will consciously approach their criminal cases with sentencing at the forefront of their planning and strategy. I can only hope that this book may assist those attorneys become effective sentencing advocates so that judges like me will be in the best position to impose sentences that are sufficient, but not greater than necessary, to achieve and advance all the goals of sentencing.

Chapter Notes

Chapter 1

1. Carter v. Illinois, 329 U.S. 173, 178 (1946).

2. USSG § 6A1.3(a); *see also* United States v. Marshall, 411 F.3d 891, 894 (8th Cir. 2005) ("A court may consider any evidence in its sentencing determination that has sufficient indicia of reliability to support its probable accuracy."); United States v. Simmons, 164 F.3d 76, 79 (2d Cir. 1998) ("Generally, sentencing judges are not restricted to information that would be admissible at trial. Any information may be considered, so long as it has sufficient indicia of reliability to support its probable accuracy." (Citation and internal quotation marks omitted.)

3. *See, e.g.*, Cait Clarke & James Neuhard, *"From Day One": Who's in Control as Problem Solving and Client-Centered Sentencing Take Center Stage*, 29 N.Y.U. Rev. L. & Soc. Change 11, 12 (2004) ("Sentencing is too often considered an afterthought rather than seen as a critical stage in a criminal case."); Sharon Patrick & Jill Miller, *Sentencing Advocates Enhance Reasoned Court Decisions*, 24 Crim. Just. 30, 30 (2009) ("Sentencing is the most neglected part of the criminal case, often ignored both by defense attorneys and by prosecutors until it is too late—after the guilty verdict has been returned or the plea agreement negotiated.").

4. *See* Miriam S. Gohara, *In Defense of the Injured: How Trauma-informed Criminal Defense can Reform Sentencing*, 45 Am. J. Crim. L. 1, 33 (2018) (hypothesizing that one reason criminal defense attorneys have fallen short in presenting mitigating evidence in non-capital cases is because their advocacy skills have atrophied as they "lay dormant during decades of the Guidelines and determinate sentencing era in which courts adhered to directives to exclude evidence of adversity from sentencing considerations."); *see also* D. Brock Hornby, *Speaking in Sentences*, 14 Green Bag 2d 147, 150–51 (2011) (observing that prosecutors appear to have difficulty accepting judicial sentencing discretion after 20 years of mandatory guidelines).

5. Clarke & Neuhard, *supra* note 2, at 12–13 ("Indeed, the initial prosecutor is often entirely absent from a sentencing hearing, and stand-ins regularly appear for the defense trial lawyer; clients are virtually indistinguishable from one another as they shuffle past judges.").

6. *See* Jeffrey Abramson, *Death-is-Different Jurisprudence and the Role of the Capital Jury*, 2 Ohio St. J. Crim. L. 117, 117n.1 (2004) (summarizing Supreme Court's "death-is-different" doctrine).

7. Miriam S. Gohara, *Grace Notes: A Case for Making Mitigation the Heart of Noncapital Sentencing*, 41 Am. J. Crim. L. 41, 78 (2013) (noting that capital offenders are almost always sentenced by juries rather than judges, and noncapital offenders are almost always sentenced by judges and not juries).

Chapter 2

1. My colleague, the Honorable Leonard T. Strand, Chief United States District Court Judge of the Northern District of Iowa, and I coined the term "judicial advocacy" in a law review article we wrote after finding that there was no common term in the literature to refer to the art of advocating to a district judge. *See* C.J. Williams & Leonard T. Strand, *Judicial Advocacy: How to Advocate to a Judge*, 43 Am. J. Trial Advoc. 281 (2020).

2. *See* John Munkman, *The Technique of Advocacy*, foreword (Butterworth's 2001) ("Advocacy is the art of persuasion; it is also a craft."); Murphy v. Shaw, A-0906-13T1, 2014 WL 7370131, at *8 (N.J. Super. Dec. 30, 2014) ("Advocacy is the art of persuasion."); People v. Mischley, 417 N.W.2d 537, 539 (Mich. App. 1987) ("The art of advocacy is the art of persuasion.").

3. *See* John N. Sharifi, *Approaching the Bench: Trial Techniques for Defense Counsel in Criminal Bench Trials*, 28 Am. J. Trial Advoc. 687, 687 (2005) (observing that "training in trial advocacy almost universally focuses only on the jury trial. Rarely, if ever, are trial advocacy techniques taught in the context of bench trials."). A glance at texts on trial advocacy reveal the same focus on jury trials. The National Institute for trial advocacy text, Steven Lubert & J.C. Lore, Modern Trial Advocacy (5th ed. 2015), only references bench trials in passing in three places, and Professor Thomas A. Mauet's Trial Techniques (10th ed. 2017),

addresses the topic only in a 19-page chapter in a 619-page book.

4. *See* Eric E. Bergsten, *Experiential Education Through the Vis Moot*, 34 J. L. & Com. 1, 4–5 (2015) (explaining how law school moot court programs most typically involves teaching appellate advocacy). *See also generally* John T. Gaubatz, *Moot Court in the Modern Law School*, 31 J. Legal Educ. 87, 89–90 (1981) (describing law school moot court programs).

5. *See, e.g.*, Robert F. Forston, *Sense and Non-Sense: Jury Trial Communication*, 1975 B.Y.U. L. Rev. 601, 609–10, 619–20, 631–33 (1975); Joel D. Lieberman & Bruce D. Sales, *What Social Science Teaches Us About the Jury Instruction Process*, 3 Psychol. Pub. Pol'y & L. 589, 626–27 (1997); John P. Cronan, *Is Any of This Making Sense? Reflecting on Guilty Pleas to Aid Criminal Juror Comprehension*, 39 Am. Crim. L. Rev. 1187, 1211, 1214 (2002) (emphasizing increase in comprehension and retention when oral delivery is supplemented by written materials, and opining that is unrealistic to expect jurors, unfamiliar with law, to comprehend and remember what they hear only orally).

6. *See* Alan D. Hornstein, *Appellate Advocacy in a Nutshell*, 245–46 (1998) (explaining why reading from brief is ineffective advocacy); William J. Rehnquist, *Oral Advocacy: A Disappearing Art*, 35 Mercer L. Rev. 1015, 1024 (1984) ("The Supreme Court gets more advocates than it should who regard oral argument as a 'brief with gestures.'").

7. *See* Michael Frost, *Ethos, Pathos & Legal Audience*, 99 Dick. L. Rev. 85 (1994) ("Roman rhetoricians and lawyers like Cicero and Quintilian, relying on Aristotle's rhetorical analyses, divided persuasive discourse, and legal arguments in particular, into three categories: logical argument (*logos*), emotional argument (*pathos*), and ethical appeal or credibility (*ethos*).") (footnote omitted).

8. *See generally* Jennifer Kruse Hanrahan, 2003 B.Y.U. Educ. & L.J. 299 (2003) (arguing that good attorneys use classical rhetorical devices to make effective arguments).

9. Carl Sandburg, *The People, Yes*, 181 (1937) ("'If the law is against you, talk about the evidence,' said a battered barrister. 'If the evidence is against you, talk about the law, and, since you ask me, if the law and the evidence are both against you, then pound on the table and yell like hell.'"). Interestingly, this saying has some variations. *See* David M. Wilson, *Working Toward a Common Goal: Are You One of Us?*, 48 No. 3 DRI For Def. 14, 14 (2006) ("Lore has it that Abraham Lincoln, while lecturing a group of young lawyers, advised that 'If the facts are against you, argue the law. If the law is against you, argue the facts. If the facts and the law are against you, attack your opponent.'") (no authority cited).

10. *See* Mary Beth Beazley, *Writing for a Mind at Work: Appellate Advocacy and the Science of Digital Reading*, 54 Duq. L. Rev. 415, 419 (2016) ("Appellate judges, of course, must 'solve the problem' of the appeal by reviewing those attorney arguments as they appear in written briefs, and by reading the relevant case law and the 'cold record.'")

11. *See* Samuel V. Schoonmaker IV, Kenneth J. Bartschi, *Effective Family Law Appeals*, 28 Fam. Advoc. 6, 6 (2006) (noting that "although trial court judges have a great deal of latitude to do what they believe is fair and equitable, appellate judges review cases based on a cold record and employ formal standards of review, such as the abuse of discretion standard. Arguments that might succeed in the trial court may be doomed to failure in the appellate court.").

12. Lawrence M. Friedman, *American Law in the 20th Century*, 266 (2002) ("It is thanks almost entirely to the jury that we have a huge, lumbering body of doctrine and practice called the law of evidence."). As Professor Wigmore, the famous expert on the rules of evidence, once explained, the rules of evidence are "based on the purpose of saving the jurors from being misled" due to jurors' "inexperience in analyzing evidence, and their unfamiliarity with the chicanery of counsel." John Henry Wigmore, *A Treatise on the Anglo-American System of Evidence in Trials at Common Law*, 125 (2d ed. 1923). *See also* Lawrence M. Friedman, *A History of American Law*, 135 (1973) (noting that American law distrusts jurors and as a consequence "[t]he jury only hears part of the story; that part which the law of evidence allows.").

13. Fed. R. Evid. 104(c).

14. *See* Null v. Wainwright, 508 F.2d 340, 344 (5th Cir. 1975) ("Strict evidentiary rules of admissibility are generally relaxed in bench trials...").

15. Fed. R. Evid. 104(a).

16. *See* Chris Guthrie, et al., *Blinking on the Bench: How judges Decide Cases*, 93 Cornell L. Rev. 1 (2007); Chris Guthrie, et al., *Can Judges Ignore Inadmissible Information? The Difficulty of Deliberately Disregarding*, 153 U. Pa. L. Rev. 1251 (2005); Chris Guthrie, et al., *Inside the Judicial Mind*, 86 Cornell L. Rev. 777 (2001).

17. *See* William L. Reynolds &; William M. Richman, *Justice and More Judges*, 15 J.L. & Pol. 559, 563 (1999) (arguing that "a collegiality of judges who know one another well enough to think alike and through that group think to achieve a coherent and stable body of law."); Chrisje Brants, *Wrongful Convictions and Inquisitorial Process: The Case of the Netherlands*, 80 U. Cin. L. Rev. 1069, 1111–12 (2012) ("One of the more troubling aspects of a career judiciary, however, is that experience can degenerate into routine, so that panels of judges feel no need to explain to each other what the strength or weakness of the case are as all will understand them, and that in general a process of group-think governs deliberations.").

18. *See* Irving L. Janis, *Groupthink*, 7, 270–71 (2d ed. 1983) (discussing group think among jurors); Jill M. Cochran, *Courting Death: 30 Years Since Furman, Is the Death Penalty Any Less Discriminatory? Looking at the Problem of Jury Discretion in Capital Sentencing*, 38 Val. U. L. Rev. 1399, 1447 (2004) (discussing negative effects of group

thing among jurors, particularly in death penalty cases).

19. *See* Joe S. Cecil et al., *Citizen Comprehension of Difficult Issues: Lessons From Civil Jury Trials*, 40 Am. U. L. Rev. 727, 749–50 (1991) (discussing benefits of group decision-making by jurors).

20. In some instances, judges may talk out decisions with law clerks. A law clerk may have been present during the hearing or trial and may have seen the same evidence the judge saw. Even then, though, the group dynamic is significantly different not only because of the fewer number of people involved, but also because of the disparate power relationship between a judge and a law clerk.

21. *See* Code of Conduct for United States Judges ("Code") (2019), Cannon 3(A)(2) (stating that judges "should maintain order and decorum in all judicial proceedings.") & Cannon 3(A)(3) ("A judge should be patient, dignified, respectful, and courteous to litigants, jurors, witnesses, lawyers, and others with whom the judge deals in an official capacity. A judge should require similar conduct by those subject to the judge's control, including lawyers to the extent consistent with their role in the adversary process."); Fed. R. Evid. 611 ("The court should exercise reasonable control over the mode and order of examining witnesses and presenting evidence so as to: (1) make those procedures effective for determining the truth; (2) avoid wasting time; and (3) protect witnesses from harassment or undue embarrassment.").

22. The need for speed is compelled in federal criminal cases by the Speedy Trial Act. 18 U.S.C. § 3161. In federal civil cases, Rule 1 of the Federal Rules of Civil Procedure urge rapid resolution of cases by requiring judges to "construe[ ], administer[ ], and employ[ ]" them in a manner "to secure the just, speedy, and inexpensive determination of every action and proceeding." Fed. R. Civ. P. 1. *See also* Code, *supra* note 27, Canon 3(A)(5) ("A judge should dispose promptly of the business of the court."). The commentary to Cannon 3(A)(5) elaborates on this duty and reflects the tension between judges' need to give parties their days in court and the limited number of days in a year.

> In disposing of matters promptly, efficiently, and fairly, a judge must demonstrate due regard for the rights of the parties to be heard and to have issues resolved without unnecessary cost or delay. A judge should monitor and supervise cases to reduce or eliminate dilatory practices, avoidable delays, and unnecessary costs. Prompt disposition of the court's business requires a judge to devote adequate time to judicial duties, to be punctual in attending court and expeditious in determining matters under submission, and to take reasonable measures to ensure that court personnel, litigants, and their lawyers cooperate with the judge to that end.

Id., Cannon 3(A)(5), comment.

23. *See* Mu'Min v. Virginia, 500 U.S. 415, 431 (1991) (explaining that jury voir dire enables courts to select impartial juries and assists attorneys in exercising peremptory strikes). Good trial attorneys also use that information to tailor the presentation of their evidence and argument to the particular audience of jury ultimately selected.

24. *See generally* Rachael A. Ream, *Limited Voir Dire*, 23 Crim. Just. 22 (2009) (discussing role of written questionnaires in jury selection).

25. *See generally* Thaddeus Hoffmeister, *Investigating Jurors in the Digital Age: One Click at a Time*, 60 U. Kan. L. Rev. 611, 615–16 (2012) (discussing use of internet to research prospective jurors).

26. *See generally* Katherine Allen, *The Jury: Modern Day Investigation and Consultation*, 34 Rev. Litig. 529 (2015) (discussing use of jury consultants in researching prospective jurors and assisting in jury selection).

27. There is some debate in academic circles about whether judges should, or even really do, separate their decision-making from their emotions. *See* Bruce A. Green & Rebecca Roiphea, *Judicial Activism in Trial Courts*, 74 N.Y.U. Ann. Surv. Am. L. 365, 379–84 (2018) (discussing extent to which judges are able to make unemotional decisions).

28. Paul Holland, *Sharing Stories: Narrative Lawyering in Bench Trials*, 16 Clinical L. Rev. 195, 268 (2009) (noting that bench trials are different from jury trial because as "[m]embers of the same profession, judges and lawyers share a vocabulary, a code of ethics, certain formative experiences (such as law school and the bar exam) and a responsibility for justice.").

29. *See* Hon. David J. Newblatt, *How to Convince the Judge on Motion Day in Family Court*, 85 Mich. B. J. 16, 17 (2006) ("Judges are trained and experienced. Judges will not be persuaded by gratuitous personal attacks. Hyperbole lost its effect long ago. We can tell baloney from substance and can tell whether you know the law and the facts. Talk to the judge at the judge's level."); Larkins, 23 No. 2 Litig. 16, 17 ("Although a judge, like a jury, wants to understand where justice lies in the case, a judge will rarely have a favorable reaction to an emotional or inflammatory appeal. In fact, the judge's usual reaction to such 'jury argument' is to be professionally offended.").

30. *See* Brian Wice, *Oral Argument in Criminal Cases: 10 Tips for Winning the Moot Court Round*, 69 Tex. B. J. 224, 225 (2006) ("Remember that your forum is an appellate court, not a trial court, and that your audience is composed not of jurors but of appellate judges. Some of the most talented criminal trial lawyers are far from stellar when they take on the mantle of appellate warrior. Why? Because they are unable or unwilling to recognize that the same table-pounding argument and incendiary prose that may carry the day in the trial court will be laughed at by the appellate judges whom they hold hostage for 20 minutes. It is logic, not emotion, that is the foundation of a compelling oral argument.").

31. *See* Larkins, *supra* note 35 at 70 ("Every

appearance before a judge inevitably affects every case the lawyer or his firm has or will have before that judge."); J. Thomas Greene, *Oral Argument in the District Court*, 26 No. 3 LITIG. 3, 59 (2000) ("Remember, you may lose the particular motion, but the outcome of any case seldom turns on a single decision. Continued civility coupled with meticulous preparation inevitably will carry the day (and the judge)—if not in this case, then in the next.").

32. *See* MODEL RULES OF PROF'L CONDUCT r. 3.3 (AM. BAR ASS'N 2020) ("A lawyer shall not knowingly: (1) make a false statement of fact or law to a tribunal...").

33. Some judges do permit jurors to ask questions of witnesses, at least after the questions are screened by the judge. Our former colleague, Judge Mark W. Bennett, a true judicial innovator, was among those who engaged in the practice and advocated for it. *See generally* Hon. Justice Thomas D. Waterman, Hon. Judge Mark W. Bennett, & David C. Waterman, *A Fresh Look as Jurors Questioning Witnesses: A review of Eighth Circuit and Iowa Appellate Precedents and an Empirical Analysis of Federal and State Trial Judges and Trial Lawyers*, 64 DRAKE L. REV. 485 (2016).

34. *See* HORNSTEIN, *supra* note 12 at 242 ("Finally, and perhaps most important, questions initiated by the advocate to the court are simply inappropriate.").

35. To be sure, there may be other limitations on what evidence a judge may consider independent of the Federal Rules of Evidence. Local rules, the Federal Rules of Civil and Criminal Procedure, and the United States Constitution may place limitations on the evidence a judge may consider even when the Federal Rules of Evidence do not. For example, in sentencing hearings criminal offenders retain due process rights under the Fifth Amendment, which encompasses to some extent the right to confrontation under the Sixth Amendment to the United States Constitution. *See* Morrissey v. Brewer, 408 U.S. 471, 488–89 (1972) ("[T]he minimum requirements of due process ... include ... the right to confront and cross-examine adverse witnesses (unless the hearing officer specifically finds good cause for not allowing confrontation)."). Thus, although the Federal Rules of Evidence would not bar the government from presenting hearsay testimony at a sentencing hearing, the Fifth Amendment may. More on this in a later chapter.

36. *See* Sara Klco & Francisco Armada, *Tips for Young Lawyers*, 37 No. 3 TRIAL ADVOC. Q. 13, 13 (2018) (urging young lawyers arguing cases before district judges to "Know your audience. Consider your judge's background and experience handling the issue you are asking him or her to address and tailor your pleadings and arguments based on that background and experience.").

37. *Cf.* James D. Dimitri, *Stepping Up to The Podium with Confidence: A Primer For Law Students On Preparing and Delivering An Appellate Oral Argument*, 38 STETSON L. REV. 75, 95 (2008) ("Hence, you should not treat questions from the bench as an intrusion upon your argument. Rather, you should welcome questions from the bench and strive to answer them to the court's satisfaction.") (footnotes omitted).

38. *Cf.* Andrew M. Low, *Questions from The Bench*, 27-DEC. COLO. LAW. 21 (1998) ("Responding to an appellate judge's question should be your number one priority in the oral argument. Never, never, never tell an appellate judge you will get to that point in a minute.").

Chapter 3

1. *See* Arthur W. Campbell, *The Law of Sentencing*, § 1:2 (2009). *See also* W. Lafave & A. Scott, *Substantive Criminal Law*, § 1.5, at 36–43 (2d ed. 2003) (identifying goals of criminal punishment).

2. States have adopted similar legislation reflecting these same goals. *See* Lisa Hay, *Sentencing: Thinking Like a Judge, Arguing as an Advocate*, 38 CHAMPION 20, 20 (2014).

3. 18 U.S.C. § 3551 *et seq.*

4. *See* Jelani Jefferson Exum, *Why March to a Uniform Beat? Adding Honesty and Proportionality to the Tune of Federal Sentencing*, 15 TEX. J. ON C.L. & C.R. 141, 166 (2010) (arguing that goal of imposing sentence that reflects seriousness of offense "hits directly at the heart of proportionality.").

5. *See* Ewing v. California, 538 U.S. 11, 31 (2003) (Scalia, J., concurring) ("Proportionality—the notion that the punishment should fit the crime—is inherently a concept tied to the penological goal of retribution.").

6. *See* William W. Berry III, "Mitigation in Federal Sentencing in the United States," in *Mitigation and Aggravation at Sentencing*, 247, 253–54 (Julian V. Roberts ed., 2011).

7. *See* Hon. Roger K. Warren, *A Tale of Two Surveys: Judicial and Public Perspective on State Sentencing Reform*, 21 Fed. Sent. R. 276, 280–81 (2009) (noting results of public surveys reflecting high priority people place on having punishment fit crime in assessing fairness of criminal justice system).

8. United States v. Lawrence, 254 F. Supp. 3d 441, 447 (E.D.N.Y. 2017).

9. *Id.* at 442.

Chapter 4

1. See the United States Sentencing Guidelines table reproduced in Section D of this chapter.

2. One exception to this is criminal contempt of court, in violation of Title 18, United States Code, Section 401(3). Congress provided no statutory maximum sentence for this offense, presumably because the broad scope of conduct that could constitute criminal contempt can range from refusing to testify to murder of a witness. *See* Frank v. United States, 395 U.S. 147, 149 (1969) (failure to establish maximum sentence for contempt

may reflect Congress's "recognition of the scope of criminal contempt"). For the same reason, there is no sentencing Guidelines provisions for criminal contempt. *See* U.S.S.G. §2J1.1 comment n.1 (stating that Sentencing Commission decided against promulgating criminal contempt guideline "[b]ecause misconduct constituting contempt varies significantly.").

3. *See* Johnson v. United States, 529 U.S. 694, 700 (2000) ("[P]ostrevocation sanctions [are] part of the penalty for the initial offense..."). Sentences for violations of supervised release conditions are also meant to sanction the abuse of the court's trust inherent in those violations. *See* United States v. Woodrup, 86 F.3d 359, 361 (4th Cir. 1996) (explaining that sentence imposed upon revocation punishes the defendant for failing to abide by the conditions of the court-ordered supervision and is separate from the sentence imposed for the new criminal conduct that led to the revocation).

4. "Commentary in the [Sentencing] Guidelines Manual that interprets or explains a guideline is authoritative unless it violates the Constitution or a federal statute, or is inconsistent with, or a plainly erroneous reading of, that guideline." Stinson v. United States, 508 U.S. 36, 38 (1993).

5. Not every criminal offense is listed because there are almost countless offenses buried within the United States Code, some in very obscure statutes. The Guidelines direct that if a statute is not listed in Appendix A, the court is to apply the most analogous section. *See* USSG §2X5.1 ("If the offense is a felony for which no guideline expressly has been promulgated, apply the most analogous offense guideline.").

6. Departures occur under and within the Guidelines framework. As will be discussed in greater detail later, a judge may also "vary" from the Guidelines under the Court's greater sentencing discretion conferred by Title 18, United States Code, Section 3553(a). The same grounds that may give rise to a departure may also be asserted as a ground for a variance. When raised as a variance, the Guidelines language may be informative to the sentencing judge but not binding.

7. *See, e.g.*, United States v. Stuart, 384 F.3d 1243(11th Cir. 2004) (per curiam) (noting that party seeking departure bears burden of proof by preponderance of evidence).

8. *See, e.g.*, United States v. Overstreet, 713 F.3d 627, 633–38 (11th Cir. 2013); United States v. Klups, 514 F.3d 532, 537 (6th Cir. 2008).

9. *See, e.g.*, United States v. Florence, 333 F.3d 1290, 1294 (11th Cir. 2003); United States v. Simpson, 741 F.3d 539, 558 (5th Cir. 2014). Still other courts of appeal are apparently on the fence. *See* United States v. Olsen, 519 F.3d 1096, 1105 (10th Cir. 2008) ("[O]ur circuit has never adopted the clear and convincing standard in so-called disproportionate impact cases," but "we have reserved the question of whether, in some extraordinary or dramatic case, due process might require a higher standard of proof").

Chapter 5

1. *See also* United States v. Knights, 534 U.S. 112, 119 (2001) ("Inherent in the very nature of probation is that probationers do not enjoy the absolute liberty to which every citizen is entitled") (quoting Griffin v. Wisconsin, 483 U.S. 868, 874 (1987)) (internal quotation marks omitted).

2. Section 3013 allows district courts to remit a special assessment "upon the petition of the Government showing that reasonable efforts to collect a fine or assessment are not likely to be effective." 18 U.S.C. § 3573.

3. *See* United States v. Munoz-Flores, 495 U.S. 385, 400 (1990) ("Read in its entirety, the passage clearly evidences Congress' intent that § 3013 provide funds primarily to support the Crime Victims Fund.").

4. This additional $5,000 special assessment can add up quickly. I once sentenced an offender who pleaded guilty to seven counts of conviction for which this special assessment applied. Unfortunately, the attorneys were not aware until I raised the issue at the change of plea hearing that the offender was potentially going to be responsible for a total of $35,700 in special assessments.

5. *See* Austin v. United States, 509 U.S. 602 (1993).

6. *See, e.g.*, United States v. Beecroft, 825 F.3d 991, 1001 (9th Cir. 2016) (finding gross proportionality where defendant "was ordered to forfeit a sum more than 100 times greater than the maximum fine allowable and more than 5,000 times greater than the lower-end of the Guidelines range"); United States v. Myers, 21 F.3d 826, 831 (8th Cir. 1994) (finding no gross proportionality where defendant's land was forfeited because "it was extensively involved in facilitating the marijuana-growing operation [intertwined with his money laundering conviction] by providing not only the location but an ideal concealment of the operation").

Chapter 6

1. *See* Margareth Etienne, *The Declining Utility of the Right to Counsel in Federal Criminal Courts: An Empirical Study on Diminished Role of Defense Attorney Advocacy Under the Sentencing Guidelines*, 92 Calif. L. Rev. 425, 434–35 (2004) (noting that "[m]any lawyers are surprised to find that their advocacy decisions during these earlier stages of a case could impact their client's Guidelines sentence later on if their pretrial strategies are considered indicators of the defendant's cooperativeness or remorse.").

2. *See* Etienne, *supra* note 65 at 434 (noting that offender's negative post-offense conduct occurs during time when defense counsel can influence offender's conduct).

3. *See* Scott B. Tulman, *Competent and Zealous Representation at Sentencing: Core Ethical Obligations in Criminal Defense Cases*, 2015 WL

7299814, at *8 (2015) (arguing that defense attorneys should actively work with their clients with post-offense rehabilitation efforts).

Chapter 8

1. *See* United States v. Harper, 946 F.2d 1373, 1375 (8th Cir. 1991) (explaining that presentence reports "are, in general, quite helpful, and they should normally be made as a routine matter.").

2. *See* United States v. Hazelrigg, 430 F.2d 580, 583 (8th Cir. 1970) ("The language of Rule 32 mandates a presentence report 'unless the court otherwise directs,' which appellate courts construe to be discretionary in effect.").

3. *See also* United States v. Long, 656 F.2d 1162, 1165 (5th Cir. 1981) (vacating sentence and remanding with orders to draft presentence report before resentencing, finding that judge lacked sufficient information).

4. *See* Anthony G. Amsterdam, *Trial Manual 5 For the Defense of Criminal Cases*, 286–87 (Vol. I 1988) (asserting that defense attorneys should provide information to probation officer preparing presentence investigation report).

5. My sources for this information came from responses to an email. As part of my research for this book, I asked the Chief Probation Officer for the Northern District of Iowa, John Zielke, about attorneys' practices in providing probation officers with information to aid them in their presentence investigations. Chief Zielke and his staff in turn solicited input from the other probation officers in federal districts across the United States through an email exchange. The feedback I received has been invaluable in helping me understand the national practice in this area and to appreciate the degree to which is this is often an unexploited opportunity for sentencing advocacy.

6. Incidentally, defense attorneys may consider as part of plea negotiations requesting prosecutors to provide a preview of the government's Presentence Investigation Statement. Sharing this document with the offender may help the offender have a better sense of the government's position and be able to weigh the costs and benefits of pleading guilty versus going to trial. It may also help the parties negotiate positions regarding sentencing issues.

7. *See* Patrick & Miller, *supra* note 2 at 30 (noting that "defense attorneys and prosecutors often rely on information and recommendations in the presentence report without verification or augmentation."); Clarke & Neuhard, *supra* note 2 at 27 ("The pre-sentence report forms the core of the judge's sentence and prosecutors and defense attorneys do little more than argue for minor changes around the edges.").

8. *See* Peugh v. United States, 569 U.S. 530, 533 (2013).

9. If the government sought detention of the offender at the initial appearance, the probation office would have drafted a bond report, sometimes called a Pretrial Services Report, that would include at least some limited information about the offender's background. Pretrial service officers must generate bond reports very quickly, however, and often do not have the time to delve deeply into an offender's background.

10. *See, e.g.*, United States v. Holloway, 826 F.3d 1237, 1251 (10th Cir. 2016) (requiring parties to object with specificity to presentence report); United States v. Visman, 919 F.2d 1390, 1394 (9th Cir. 1990) (noting that "[o]ther circuits have held that a defendant waives a challenge to a presentence report by failing to object in the district court" and finding that the offender "forfeited his opportunity to contest the probation officers" guideline calculation by failing to file a timely objection); United States v. Garcia, 580 F.3d 528, 542 (7th Cir. 2009) (holding that failure to object to presentence report can waive drug-quantity argument when offender "had access to the PSR, knew of his right to object, considered objecting to portions of the presentence report other than the one he now challenges, and stated on the record that he did not have any further objections when asked by the district court.").

11. *See, e.g.*, United States v. Jaimes-Jaimes, 406 F.3d 845, 848 (7th Cir. 2005) (holding that offenders do not necessarily waive sentencing arguments by accepting presentence reports without objection); United States v. Jenkins, 772 F.3d 1092, 1095–96 (7th Cir. 2014) (holding that party does not waive sentencing argument by contesting some aspects of draft presentence report and not others).

12. *See* United States v. Jones, 899 F.2d 1097, 1102–03 (11th Cir. 1990) (holding that party waives objection when, regardless of objections included in presentence report addendum, he does not articulate his arguments when afforded opportunity by district court) (overruled in part on other grounds, United States v. Morrill, 984 F.2d 1136 (11th Cir. 1993) (en banc)).

Chapter 10

1. As I will discuss in more detail in a later chapter, although the Federal Rules of Evidence do not apply in sentencing hearings, evidence that otherwise complies with the rules is generally more persuasive to a judge than evidence that would not be admissible under the evidence rules.

2. California v. Green, 399 U.S. 149, 158 (1970) (quoting 5 J. Wigmore, Evidence § 1367, p. 29 (3d ed. 1940)).

3. The most effective impeachment with a prior inconsistent statement occurs when the attorney provides the witness with a transcript of the witness's prior statement or testimony, reads it verbatim, and then simply asks the witness if the attorney read it correctly. The witness will have little choice but to say "yes."

Chapter 11

1. *See, e.g.*, United States v. Bowers, 743 F.3d 1182, 1184 (8th Cir. 2014) ("[I]f a defendant makes written objections to the factual allegations in a PSR, but tells the court during the sentencing hearing that the facts in the PSR are accurate, then the written objections are withdrawn, and the defendant waives any objection to the facts set forth in the PSR.") (internal citation and quotation omitted).

2. In some districts, the Clerk of Court prepares the judgment while in other districts, like mine, the probation officer does so.

Chapter 12

1. Lawrence M. Friedman, *American Law in the 20th Century*, 266 (2002) ("It is thanks almost entirely to the jury that we have a huge, lumbering body of doctrine and practice called the law of evidence.").

2. John Henry Wigmore, *A Treatise on the Anglo-American System of Evidence in Trials at Common Law*, 125 (2d ed. 1923). *See also* Lawrence M. Friedman, *A History of American Law*, 135 (1973) (noting that American law distrusts jurors and as consequence "[t]he jury only hears part of the story; that part which the law of evidence allows.").

3. Rule 404(a) prohibits admission of character evidence to prove a person acted in conformity with that character because the rule drafters believed a person's character is a poor predictor of behavior. *See* FED. R. EVID. 404(a)(1); C.J. Williams & Dasha Ternavska, *A Series of Unfortunate Events: The Admissibility of "Other Fires" Evidence in Arson Cases*, 48 CONN. L. REV. 685, 697–98 (2016) (explaining the rationale behind Rule 404(a)(1)). On the other hand, Rule 406 permits admission of habit evidence for the purpose of showing a person acted on a particular occasion consistent with that habit because of the belief that a habit is a good predictor of behavior. FED. R. EVID. 406; Notes of Advisory Committee on Proposed Rule 406, FED. R. EVID. (noting general consensus that "the uniformity of one's response to habit is far greater than the consistency with which one's conduct conforms to character or disposition.").

4. *See* Notes of Advisory Committee on Proposed Rule 407, FED. R. EVID. (stating that Rule 407 rests in part on "a social policy of encouraging people to take, or at least not discourage them from taking, steps in furtherance of added safety.").

5. *See* FED. R. EVID. 408.

6. *See* FED. R. EVID. 409.

7. *See* FED. R. EVID. 410.

8. *See* FED. R. EVID. 411.

9. *See, e.g.*, United States v. Gonzalez-Garcia, 752 Fed. App'x 208, 208–09 (5th Cir. 2019); United States v. Sheridan, 859 F.3d 579, 584–85 (8th Cir. 2017); United States v. Sadler, 642 Fed. App'x 834, 845 (10th Cir. 2016); United States v. Robinson, 482 F.3d 244, 246 (3d Cir. 2007).

10. *See, e.g.*, Williams v. Oklahoma, 358 U.S. 576, 584 (1959) ("[O]nce the guilt of the accused has been properly established, the sentencing judge, in determining the kind and extent of punishment to be imposed, is not restricted to evidence derived from the examination and cross-examination of witnesses in open court..."); Williams v. New York, 337 U.S. 241, 246–51 (1949) ("[M]odern concepts individualizing punishment have made it all the more necessary that a sentencing judge not be denied an opportunity to obtain pertinent information by a requirement of rigid adherence to restrictive rules of evidence properly applicable to the trial.").

11. *See also* United States v. Paulino, 996 F.2d 1541, 1547 (3d Cir. 1993) ("[T]he introduction of evidence at sentencing is subject to [a] due process standard of reliability.").

12. *See, e.g.*, Williams v. New York, 337 U.S. 241, 250–51 (1949) (holding that consideration of information supplied by witnesses at sentencing who are not subject to cross-examination did not violate Due Process Clause); United States v. Gonzalez-Garcia, 752 Fed. App'x 208, 208–09 (5th Cir. 2019) (holding that due process clause does not require opportunity to cross-examine witnesses at sentencing hearings); United States v. Green, 718 Fed. App'x 141, 142–43 (3rd Cir. 2018) (holding that sentencing court's refusal to allow cross-examination of crime victim did not violate due process clause).

13. *See, e.g.*, United States v. Torres-Landrua, 783 F.3d 58, 64 (1st Cir. 2015) (holding that judges have right, particularly in sentencing hearings, to question and even cross-examine witnesses); United States v. Whitehorse, 2000 WL 219967, at *2 (10th Cir. 2000) (holding that judge's right to ask questions of witnesses to develop facts extends to sentencing hearings); United States v. Mostella, 802 F.2d 358, 361 (9th Cir. 1986) (finding judge permissibly "participate[ed] in the examination of witnesses for the purpose of clarifying the evidence.").

Chapter 13

1. *See* United States v. Aderholt, 87 F.3d 740, 742 (5th Cir. 1996).

2. *See* United States v. Wilder, 15 F.3d 1292, 1296–97 (5th Cir. 1994).

3. *See, e.g.*, United States v. Landron-Class, 696 F.3d 62, 77–78 (1st Cir. 2012); United States v. Massey, 663 F.3d 852, 858 (6th Cir. 2011); United States v. Leiskunas, 656 F.3d 732, 737 (7th Cir. 2011); United States v. Fernandez, 443 F.3d 19, 33 (2d Cir. 2006); United States v. Doe, 398 F.3d 1254, 1260–61 (10th Cir. 2005). *See also* HUTCHISON, ET AL., FEDERAL SENTENCING LAW AND PRACTICE §5K1.1, cmt. 2 n.3 (2012) (noting that although courts may not depart downward for substantial assistance without government motion, "[p]ost-*Booker* ... sentencing courts may weigh a

defendant's assistance or attempts to assist the government as part of the § 3553(a) analysis and vary from the Guidelines if appropriate.").

4. *See* United States v. Palomo, 80 F.3d 138, 139 (5th Cir. 1996).

Chapter 14

1. *See* U.S. SENT'G COMM'N, REP. TO THE CONGRESS: DOWNWARD DEPARTURES FROM THE FEDERAL SENTENCING GUIDELINES 32 fig. 1 (Oct. 2003). *See also* U.S. SENT'G COMM'N SOURCEBOOK 2018, Table 29 (during fiscal year 2018, judges departed upward in only .6% of cases, but departed downward in more than 20% of cases, 10% of which were for substantial assistance).

2. *See* United States v. Fumo, 655 F.3d 288, 317 (3rd Cir. 2011) (reversing and remanding for resentencing when judge failed to articulate whether non-Guidelines sentence resulted from departure or variance).

3. *See, e.g.*, United States v. Nunemacher, 362 F.3d 682, 695 (10th Cir. 20044) ("District courts are supposed to give some rationale *tied to the Guidelines* for the degree of departure *in the specific case*.") (emphasis original); United States v. Scott, 145 F.3d 878, 886 (7th Cir. 1998) ("The law merely requires that district judges link the degree of departure to the structure of the Guidelines and justify the extent of the departure taken."); United States v. Sablan, 90 F.3d 362, 365 (9th Cir. 1996) (holding that in making departure decision, district court has discretion but that does not make court "free to divest itself entirely of the structure of the Guidelines.").

4. *See, e.g.*, United States v. Spring, 108 Fed. App'x 116, 122–23 (4th Cir. 2004) (affirming downward departure on basis that offender would be vulnerable to abuse in prison because of his height (5'6"), weight (90 pounds), and immature appearance).

5. *See* United States v. Washington, 515 F.3d 861, 864 (8th Cir. 2008) (noting government's motion for upward departure based, in part, on §5H1.9); *see also* United States v. Guarin, 898 F.2d 1120, 1122 (6th Cir. 1990) (finding that criminal livelihood, if not adequately reflected in offender's offense level, may also justify departure).

6. *See, e.g.*, Lopez v. United States, 16-20046-Cr-SCOLA, 2017 WL 2912818, at *1 (S.D. Fla. May 2, 2017); United States v. Parker, No. 06-20050, 2007 WL 1544403, at *6 (E.D. Mich. May 25, 2007).

7. *See* United States v. Reed, 774 Fed. App'x 16, 17 (2d Cir. 2018) (stating that for upward departure based on USSG §5K2.21 to apply, uncharged conduct must "relate in some way to the offense of conviction.") (quoting United States v. Kim, 896 F.2d 678, 684 (2d Cir. 1990)).

8. *See* United States v. Sachdev, 279 F.3d 25, 28–29 (1st Cir. 2002) (noting that duress must be serious, offender must subjectively believe threat was made, and court must also objectively find reasonable person in offender's position would perceive threat as serious).

9. *See* United States v. Besler, 86 F.3d 745, 748 (7th Cir. 1996).

10. *See, e.g.*, United States v. Moore, 918 F.3d 368, 371–72 (4th Cir. 2019) (collecting cases).

11. *See, e.g.*, United States v. Sayer, 748 F.3d 425, 436–37 (1st Cir. 2014) (affirming district court's decision not to depart and explaining district court's retention of discretion).

12. Congress has exempted child crimes and sexual offenses from eligibility for such departures. USSG §5K2.20(a)(1).

Chapter 15

1. Although the discussion here will focus on the federal system and the terminology and procedures used in federal court, the underlying advocacy principles are equally applicable to state sentencing schemes, regardless of whether they, too, have adopted advisory guidelines.

2. *See* U.S. SENT'G COMM'N, REP. ON THE CONTINUING IMPACT OF UNITED STATES V. BOOKER ON FEDERAL SENTENCING 69 (2012) (concluding that after *Booker* decision, rate of below-guideline sentences increased).

3. *See* U.S. SENT'G COMM'N, SOURCEBOOK 2018, Table 29 (2019).

4. *See, e.g.*, United States v. Grams, 566 F.3d 683, 686–87 (6th Cir. 2009) (explaining that "the same facts and analyses can, at times, be used to justify both a Guidelines departure and a variance"); United States v. Robinson, 454 F.3d 839, 842 (8th Cir. 2006) (recognizing that "pre-*Booker* departures and post-*Booker* variances are not the same" and that there may be "cases that would not justify a departure under the Guidelines but which are appropriate for a variance" as well as "cases in which a combination of a Guidelines departure and other § 3553(a) factors may produce a lower reasonable sentence than a departure alone").

5. *See* Irizarry v. United States, 553 U.S. 708, 714–16 (2008).

6. *See* United States v. Foy, 617 F.3d 1029, 1035 (8th Cir. 2010) (holding that FED. R. CRIM. P. 32(h), which require judges to give notice to parties in certain circumstances that they are contemplating departing from Guidelines range, does not apply to variances).

7. *Id.* at 712–13.

8. Under some statutes, motive or the purpose of an act may be an element. For example, for a person to be charged with murder in furtherance of a Continuing Criminal Enterprise, the government must prove that a motive or purpose for the murder was to further that criminal enterprise. *See* 21 U.S.C. § 848(e).

9. *See, e.g.*, United States v. Mitchell, 789 Fed. App'x 774, 774 (11th Cir. 2019) (affirming upward variance based on, among other reasons, offender's "frivolous motive" for committing a fraud); United States v. Madsen, 809 F.3d 712, 719–20 (1st

Cir. 2016) (affirming upward variance based in part on offender's profit motive for making false statements in connection with purchasing firearms); United States v. Gomez-Herrera, 523 F.3d 554, 565–66 (5th Cir. 2008) (noting that offender argued, albeit unsuccessfully, for downward variance because one motive for illegal reentry was to see ailing father before he died).

10. Section 3B also contains provisions for enhancements in offense levels for offenders who, in the commission of the offense, abuse a position of trust or use a special skill (USSG §3B1.3), use a minor (USSG §3B1.4), or use body armor in drug trafficking or violent crimes (USSG §3B1.5).

11. *See, e.g.*, United States v. Primus, 713 Fed. App'x 529, 530–31 (8th Cir. 2018) (affirming upward variance, in addition to upward departure under §5K2.8, for extreme conduct when offender injected victim with heroin over prolonged period to control her for forced prostitution).

12. *See, e.g.*, United States v. Christensen, 732 F.3d 1094, 1104–05 (9th Cir. 2013) (affirming upward variance based in part on victim impact); United States v. Schlueter, 634 F.3d 965, 967–68 (7th Cir. 2011) (same); United States v. Siman, 419 Fed. App'x 979, 981–82 (11th Cir. 2011) (same); United States v. Scherrer, 444 F.3d 91, 95 (1st Cir. 2006) (same).

13. *See* Graham v. Florida, 560 U.S. 48, 68 (2010) (noting that "developments in psychology and brain science continue to show fundamental differences between juvenile and adult minds. For example, parts of the brain involved in behavior control continue to mature through late adolescence."). *See also* Emily Buss, *What the Law Should (and Should Not) Learn from Child Development Research*, 38 Hofstra L. Rev. 13, 39 (2009) ("Much of the developmental research suggests that the qualities highlighted by the Court [in *Roper v. Simmons*, 543 U.S. 551 (2005)], described together as psycho-social immaturity, continue to apply to individuals into their twenties, even mid-twenties or beyond.").

14. United States Sentencing Commission, *The Effects of Aging on Recidivism Among Federal Offenders* 3 (2017) (noting that offenders "who were below age 21 at release had the highest rearrest rate at over two-thirds (67.6%). Conversely, those oldest at age of release, over 60 years old, had the lowest recidivism rate (16.0 %).").

15. *Id.*, at 11.

16. *See United States v. Hendrickson*, 25 F. Supp. 3d 1166, 1171–76 (N.D. Iowa 2014) (discussing at length the science and case law supporting the position that addiction is a disease that mitigates offenders' culpability and warrants downward variances). As my former colleague Judge Mark W. Bennett explained in *Hendrickson*, "While '[t]he initial decision to take drugs is mostly voluntary ... when drug abuse takes over, a person's ability to exert self-control can become seriously impaired.' ... Stated plainly, addiction biologically robs drug abusers of their judgment, causing them to act impulsively and ignore the future consequences of their actions." *Hendrickson*, 25 F. Supp.3d at 1172–73 (quoting Nora D. Volkow, *Preface to National Institute on Drug Abuse, Drugs, Brains, and Behavior: The Science of Addiction* 1 (2010), http://www.drugabuse.gov/sites/default/files/sciofaddiction.pdf).

17. *See, e.g.*, United States v. Strahan, 598 Fed. App'x 597, 597 (10th Cir. 2015) (offender sought downward variance based on alleged gambling addiction); United States v. Gonzales, 163 F.Supp.3d 1078, 1089–90 (D.N.M. 2016) (same).

18. *See, e.g.*, United States v. Wade, 890 F.3d 629, 632 (7th Cir. 2018) (offender argued for downward variance on basis of pornography addiction); United States v. Urchak, Criminal No. 08-781 (RMB), 2019 WL 316013, at *1 (D. N.J. Jan. 24, 2019) (offender sought early termination to term of supervised release based on claimed addiction to child pornography).

19. *See, e.g.*, United States v. Chase, 560 F.3d 828, 831 (8th Cir. 2009) (noting that good employment history could warrant downward variance); United States v. Johnson, 554 Fed. App'x 773, 775 (10th Cir. 2014) (affirming upward variance based on poor work history, among other reasons); United States v. Green, 691 F.3d 960, 966 (8th Cir. 2012) (sporadic work history supported upward variance).

20. *See* Kimberly Bahna, *"It's a Family Affair"—The Incarceration of the American Family: Confronting Legal and Social Issues*, 28 U.S.F. L. Rev. 271, 275 (1994) ("Research has shown that the disruption in family ties during incarceration actually increases the criminal behavior of ex-inmates."); Shirley R. Klein et al., *Inmate Family Functioning*, 46 Int'l J. Offender Therapy & Comp. Criminology, 95, 99–100 (2002) ("[A]lthough family ties do not guarantee success after release, the absence of such ties increases the likelihood of failure. The relationship between family ties and lower recidivism has been consistent across study populations, different periods, and different methodological procedures.").

21. *See* United States v. Caldwell, 219 F.3d 1186, 1191 n.5 (10th Cir. 2000).

22. *See* United States v. Cantu, 12 F.3d 1506, 1516 (9th Cir. 1993) ("Desert (blameworthiness) loses some bite because those with reduced ability to reason, or to control their impulses, are less deserving of punishment than those who act of viciousness or greed[.]").

23. *Id.* ("Deterrence has less value ... because people with reduced capacities are less susceptible to a system of punishment and reward.").

24. *See* United States v. Ferguson, 942 F.Supp.2d 1186, 1193 (M.D. Ala. 2013) (noting that inmates with mental health issues are more easily manipulated and victimized in prison).

25. *See, e.g.*, United States v. Cousins, No. 05-04-CR-169, 2007 WL 1454275 (N.D. Ohio May 17, 2007) (varying upward to impose statutory maximum sentence because "[t]he defendant's history of violent conduct, coupled with his obvious unstable mental condition ... strongly suggest that

[he] should never again be pardon [sic], paroled, or released into society.").

26. Citing Abbott, *The Civil War and the Crime Wave of 1865–70*, 1 Soc. Serv. Rev. 212, 232–234 (1927) (discussing movement to pardon or parole prisoners who were Civil War veterans); Rosenbaum, *The Relationship Between War and Crime in the United States*, 30 J.Crim. L. & C. 722, 733–734 (1940) (describing a 1922 study by Wisconsin Board of Control that discussed number of veterans imprisoned in state and considered "the greater leniency that may be shown to ex-service men in court").

27. *See* United States v. Sims, 511 Fed. App'x 429, 431 (6th Cir. 2013) (stating that "[i]n recognizing that veterans have traditionally been afforded leniency, the Supreme Court did not require leniency" in *Porter*).

28. *See, e.g.*, Running v. United States, 81 F.Supp.3d 781, 793 (D S.D. 2015) (court varied downward from advisory Gidelines range in part because of "absence of certain aggravating factors present in many cases involving the production of child pornography").

29. "[A]lthough departure precedent does not bind district courts' variance decisions, … the considerations supporting the denial of a health-based downward departure may also support the denial of a downward variance." United States v. Houston, 476 Fed. App'x 110, 112 (8th Cir. 2012).

30. Indeed, an offender's post-sentencing rehabilitation can even serve as a basis for a downward variance in unusual circumstances when an offender is re-sentenced for some reason. *See* Pepper v. United States, 562 U.S. 476, 490–91 (2011) (holding that district courts may vary downward on account of post-sentencing rehabilitation).

31. *See, e.g.*, United States v. Munoz-Nava, 524 F.3d 1137, 1149 (10th Cir. 2008) (affirming significant downward variance because district court considered, among other things, offender's "behavior while on a year-and-a-half pretrial release," which court "found to be exemplary").

32. Not only does this show some post-offense rehabilitation, it can also prevent a 2-point increase in an offender's security classification level for purposes of placement within the Bureau of Prisons.

33. *See, e.g.*, United States v. Santiago-González, 825 F.3d 41, 50 n.13 (1st Cir. 2016) ("It is well established" that "lack of remorse" is relevant consideration and can support upward variance in sentencing, even if offender accepted responsibility under Guidelines by pleading guilty); United States v. VandeBrake, 679 F.3d 1030, 1037 (8th Cir. 2012) (affirming upward variance for lack of remorse).

34. *See, e.g.*, United States v. Ortiz-Torres, 873 F.3d 346, 348–49 (1st Cir. 2017) (affirming upward variance for lack of remorse when offender executed wounded security guard during robbery).

35. *See, e.g.*, VandeBrake, 679 F.3d at 1034–35 (noting district court's reliance on offender's rationalization that his defrauded customers still got great product for good price as basis for varying upward for lack of remorse).

36. *See, e.g.*, United States v. Beal, 463 F.3d 834, 837 (8th Cir. 2006) ("While we do not suggest that §4A1.3(b)(3)(A) strictly limits the scope of variances post-*Booker*, it remains relevant to consider the Guidelines and the commentary in our assessment of reasonableness…").

37. *See* United States v. Robinson, 454 F.3d 839, 842 (8th Cir. 2006) ("[t]here may well be cases that would not justify a departure under the Guidelines but which are appropriate for a variance."). *See also* United States v. Lanning, 633 F.3d 469, 475 (6th Cir. 2011) (explaining that aspect of offender's criminal history that does not warrant departure under USSG §4A1.3(a) might still form basis for variance under 18 U.S.C. § 3553(a)); United States v. Solis-Bermudez, 501 F.3d 882, 885 (8th Cir. 2007) (same).

38. *See, e.g.*, United States v. Espinoza, 831 F.3d 1096, 1097 (8th Cir. 2016) (affirming upward variance when offender threatened staff at halfway house while on pretrial release).

39. *See, e.g.*, United States v. Shi Chang Huang, 491 Fed. App'x 382, 385 (4th Cir. 2012) (affirming upward variance even when same conduct led court to deny offender reduction for acceptance of responsibility).

40. *See, e.g.*, United States v. Patton, 708 Fed. App'x 488, 492–95 (10th Cir. 2017) (affirming upward variance when offender embezzled money multiple times while on pretrial release).

41. *See, e.g.*, United States v. Thompson, 430 Fed. App'x 805, 809 (11th Cir. 2011) (affirming downward variance to account for time offender served in state custody for conduct connected to offense of conviction because court thought it unlikely Bureau of Prisons would give offender credit for that time).

42. *See, e.g.*, United States v. Corner, 598 F.3d 411, 415 (7th Cir. 2010) (en banc) ("We understand *Kimbrough* and *Spears* to mean that district judges are at liberty to reject any Guideline on policy grounds—though they must act reasonably when using that power."); United States v. Cavera, 550 F.3d 180, 191 (2d Cir. 2008) (en banc) ("[A] district court may vary from the Guidelines range based solely on a policy disagreement with the Guidelines, even where that disagreement applies to a wide class of offenders or offenses."); United States v. Herrera-Zuniga, 571 F.3d 568, 585 (6th Cir. 2009) (collecting cases). *See also* Pepper v. United States, 562 U.S. 476, 501 (2011) ("[A] district court may in appropriate cases impose a non-Guidelines sentence based on a disagreement with the Commission's views.").

43. *See* United States v. Cole, 343 Fed. App'x 109, 115 (6th Cir. 2009) (noting that district court's authority to vary is not limited to crack/powder disparity issue).

44. *See, e.g.*, United States v. Hayes, 948 F.Supp.2d 1009, 1027 (N.D. Iowa 2013) (examining history of methamphetamine Guidelines and concluding that "methamphetamine Guidelines are entitled to less deference than those Guidelines that were based on the Commission's exercise of

institutional expertise and empirical analysis."); United States v. Diaz, No. 11-CR-00821-2 (JG), 2013 WL 322243, at *1 (E.D.N.Y. Jan. 28, 2013) (varying downward on heroin Guidelines based on policy disagreement).

45. *See, e.g.*, United States v. Lopez-Marcias, 661 F.3d 485, 491–92 (10th Cir. 2011) (affirming downward variance based on policy disagreement with USSG §5K3.1, which allowed for downward departure only on motion by government and no more than four levels for so-called fast-track programs in border states for immigration violations).

46. *See, e.g.*, United States v. Henderson, 649 F.3d 955, 960 (9th Cir. 2011) (holding that courts may vary from Guidelines provisions for child pornography offenses). *See also* Ian N. Friedman, *Child Pornography Sentencing: The Road Here and the Road Ahead*, 21 Fed. Sent. R. 83 (2008) (discussing downward variances in child pornography cases because of policy disagreements with Guidelines).

47. See, e.g., United States v. Friedman, 554 F.3d 1301, 1311 (10th Cir. 2009) (applying *Kimbrough's* rationale in context of policy disagreements with career offender guidelines).

48. *See, e.g.*, United States v. Burgos, 761 Fed. App'x 922, 927 (11th Cir. 2019) (affirming upward variance based on policy disagreement with child pornography Guidelines); United States v. VandeBrake, 679 F.3d 1030, 1037 (8th Cir. 2012) (affirming upward variance from antitrust Guidelines based on policy disagreement).

49. *See, e.g.*, United States v. Trejo, 624 Fed. App'x 709, 713–14 (11th Cir. 2015). A district court commits procedural error only when it fails to appreciate its *Kimbrough* discretion to vary from Guidelines based on a categorical policy disagreement with them. United States v. Tutty, 612 F.3d 128, 131 (2d Cir. 2010); United States v. Stone, 575 F.3d 83, 89 (1st Cir. 2009).

50. *See* United States v. Maurice, 69 F.3d 1553, 1557 (11th Cir. 1995) (holding that general objection after sentence was announced is sufficient to preserve supporting arguments made before it was announced when reasons for objection are clear).

Chapter 16

1. For example, the mail fraud statute, 18 U.S.C. § 1341, provides for an increased maximum fine of $1 million if the fraud was connected with a presidentially declared disaster or emergency. The money laundering statute, 18 U.S.C. § 1957, provides for "a fine of not more than $500,000 or twice the value of the property involved in the transaction, whichever is greater."

2. *See* United States v. Perez-Jiminez, 654 F.3d 1136, 1145 (10th Cir. 2011) ("The defendant bears the burden of proving both his present and future inability to pay the fine.") (citing USSG §5E1.2(e)).

3. *See* United States v. Francies, 945 F.2d 851, 852–53 (5th Cir. 1991).

4. *See* McDonald v. City of Chicago, 561 U.S. 742, 765 n.13 (2010) (Alito, J.) (surveying history of incorporation of rights under Fourteenth Amendment and noting that Supreme Court has not decided whether excessive fines clause is incorporated against states).

5. Southern Union Company v. United States, 567 U.S. 343 (2012).

6. *See, e.g.*, United States v. Hernandez-Guevara, 448 Fed. App'x 39, 41–42 (11th Cir. 2011); United States v. Ukomadu, 236 F.3d 333, 340 (6th Cir. 2001); United States v. Ortland, 109 F.3d 539, 549 (9th Cir. 1997).

7. *See* United States v. Soyland, 3 F.3d 1312, 1315 (9th Cir. 1993) (finding offender "failed to carry the burden of showing an inability to pay the fine" when she "refused to provide financial information to the probation officer").

8. *See* United States v. Fuller, 659 Fed. App'x 896, 898 (7th Cir. 2016) (holding that unsworn allocution is not evidence sentencing judge must consider); United States v. Anderson, 632 F.3d 1264, 1270–71 (D.C. Cir. 2011) (same).

Chapter 17

1. *See* Libretti v. United States, 516 U.S. 29, 39 (1995) ("Forfeiture is an element of the sentence imposed following conviction.... Our precedents have ... characterized criminal forfeiture as an aspect of punishment imposed following conviction of a substantive criminal offense.").

2. In contrast, civil forfeiture is an in rem proceeding against the property itself. United States v. Nava, 404 F.3d 1119, 1123 (9th Cir. 2005).

3. *See* Alexander v. United States, 509 U.S. 544, 558–59 (1993).

4. *See* United States v. Bajakajian, 524 U.S. 321, 327–28 (1998).

5. *See, e.g.*, $100,348.00, 354 F.3d at 1122–24 (upholding forfeiture of $10,000 when maximum fine under Sentencing Guidelines could be as little as $5,000).

6. United States v. Fruchter, 411 F.3d 377, 381–83 (2d Cir. 2005).

7. *See, e.g.*, United States v. Nava, 404 F.3d 1119, 1123 (9th Cir. 2005) (holding that preponderance of evidence is burden of proof applicable to forfeiture); United States v. Hasson, 333 F.3d 1264, 1277 (11th Cir. 2003) (same); United States v. Cherry, 330 F.3d 658, 669 (4th Cir. 2003) (same).

8. Organized Crime Control Act of 1970, Pub. L. No. 91-452, § 901, 84 Stat. 922, 941–48 (codified as amended as Racketeer Influenced and Corrupt Organization Act, 18 U.S.C. §§ 1961–1968 (2019)).

9. Comprehensive Drug Abuse Prevention and Control Act, Pub. L. No. 91-513, § 408, 84 Stat. 1236, 1265 (codified as amended at 21 U.S.C. § 848, 853 (2019)).

10. Pub. L. No. 99-570, 100 Stat. 3207-35 (codified as amended at 18 U.S.C. § 982 (2019).

11. Pub. L. 99-570, 100 Stat. 320-7-13, 3207-54.

12. Unless an offender consents to a final order

being entered sooner than the sentencing hearing. FED. R. CRIM. P. 32.2(b)(4)(A).

13. *See* Kaley, 571 U.S. at 323 (noting that one goal of criminal forfeiture is to "recompense victims of a crime").

14. *See* 18 U.S.C. § 981(e)(6) (government may transfer forfeited property "as restoration to any victim of the offense giving rise to the forfeiture"); 21 U.S.C. § 853(i)(1) (stating that government may "restore forfeited property to victims").

15. *See, e.g.*, United States v. Joseph, 743 F.3d 1350, 1354 (11th Cir. 2014); United States v. Martinez, 610 F.3d 1216, 1232 (10th Cir. 2010); United States v. McCracken, 487 F.3d 1125, 1128–29 (8th Cir. 2007); United States v. Bright, 353 F.3d 1114, 1120 (9th Cir. 2004); United States v. Alalade, 204 F.3d 536, 540 (4th Cir. 2000); United States v. Emerson, 128 F.3d 557, 566–67 (7th Cir. 1997).

16. I learned this lesson the hard way when I was a prosecutor. I prosecuted a white-collar offender who stipulated to forfeiture of some real property as part of a plea agreement, admitting that it constituted the proceeds of his fraud scheme. The court duly entered a preliminary order of forfeiture and at sentencing entered a judgment of forfeiture. Then the offender hired a new attorney for appeal and on appeal contested the forfeiture because there was no factual basis in the record establishing a nexus between the crime of conviction and the forfeited real property. The court of appeals agreed and found that the offender's general stipulation that the property constituted criminal proceeds and stipulation to forfeiture was insufficient. The court of appeals remanded the case, and we had to have a multi-day evidentiary hearing to establish the factual nexus so as to allow the forfeiture to go forward. That delayed by several years the final forfeiture of the property and its liquidation so as to use the funds to compensate crime victims. *See* United States v. Beltramea, 785 F.3d 287, 290–91 (8th Cir. 2015).

Chapter 18

1. *See* United States v. Thornbrugh, 764 Fed. App'x 655, 657 (10th Cir. 2019) ("[W]e have repeatedly stated that a sentence of restitution is not criminal punishment."). *But see generally* Cortney E. Lollar, *What is Criminal Restitution*, 100 IOWA L. REV. 93 (2014) (arguing criminal restitution has become a form of criminal punishment because of manner in which courts impose restitution, including for acquitted or uncharged conduct and untethered to offenders' ill-gotten gains).

2. *See* 18 U.S.C. § 3663A (requiring mandatory restitution for certain offenses, including crimes of violence and title 18 property offenses).

3. *See* Paroline v. United States, 572 U.S. 434, 459 (2014) (stating that assessment of victim's losses "cannot be a precise mathematical inquiry and involves the use of discretion and sound judgment").

4. *See, e.g.*, United States v. Newell, 658 F.3d 1, 32 (1st Cir. 2011); United States v. Lessner, 498 F.3d 185, 205–06 (3d Cir. 2007); United States v. Newsome, 322 F.3d 328, 342 (4th Cir. 2003); United States v. Dubose, 146 F.3d 1141, 1147 (9th Cir. 1998).

5. Before the 1980s, the only statute addressing restitution was the Federal Probation Act of 1925 (FPA), which gave judges complete discretion whether to order restitution as part of a criminal sentence. 18 U.S.C. §§ 3651–3656 (1982) (repealed 1984).

6. Pub. L. No. 97-291, 96 Stat. 1248 (1982) (codified as amended at 18 U.S.C. §§ 1512–1515, 3663, 3664 (2019)).

7. Pub.L. 102–521, § 2(a) 106 Stat. 3403 (1992) (codified as amended at 18 U.S.C. § 228 (mandating restitution of child support payments due in all convictions of willful failure to pay past due child support).

8. Pub. L. No. 103–322, 108 Stat. 1796 (1994) (codified as amended at 42 U.S.C. §§ 13925–14045d) (adding mandatory restitution for sexual abuse, sexual exploitation of children, domestic violence, and telemarketing fraud).

9. Pub. L. No. 104–132, 110 Stat. 1214 (1996) (codified as amended at 18 U.S.C. § 3664) (requiring mandatory restitution for certain offenses, including crimes of violence and title 18 property offenses).

10. *See* FED. R. CRIM. P. 32(c)(1)(B) ("If the law permits restitution, the probation officer must conduct an investigation and submit a report [containing] sufficient information for the court to order restitution.").

11. The MVRA provides that "the court shall set a date for the final determination of the victim's losses, not to exceed 90 days after sentencing." 18 U.S.C. § 3664(d)(5). In *Dolan v. United States*, 560 U.S. 605, 608 (2010), the Supreme Court clarified that the 90-day rule applied only to the decision whether to impose restitution, holding that "a sentencing court that misses the 90-day deadline nonetheless retains the power to order restitution ... where ... the sentencing court made clear prior to the deadline's expiration that it would order restitution, leaving open (for more than 90 days) only the amount."

12. A court may, however, order restitution for relevant conduct victims as a condition of supervised release. CITE AUTHORITY

13. *See, e.g.*, United States v. Robertson, 493 F.3d 1322, 1334–35 (11th Cir. 2007).

14. *See* United States v. Bean, 18 F.3d 1367, 1368 (7th Cir. 1994) (holding that voluntary payment of restitution is independent ground for acceptance of responsibility reduction).

15. *See* Gauthier v. United States, No. Civ.A. 98–CV–630 , 1998 WL 808997, at *5 (N.D.N.Y. Nov. 18, 1998) (finding that offender's "failure to make any restitution whatsoever prior to sentencing" among other factors weighed against granting any downward departure for extraordinary acceptance of responsibility).

16. *See, e.g.*, United States v. Whitman, 209 F.3d

619, 622 (6th Cir. 2000) (affirming district court's denial of reduction for acceptance of responsibility when offender failed to make any voluntary restitution before sentencing hearing); United States v. Anderson, 68 F.3d 1050, 1055–56 (8th Cir. 1995) (affirming district court's decision to apply obstruction of justice enhancement and deny acceptance of responsibility reduction when offender failed to provide complete financial information necessary to determine restitution during presentence investigation); United States v. Merritt, 988 F.2d 1298, 1302–05 (2d Cir. 1993) (discussing district court's decision to deny offender acceptance of responsibility adjustment despite guilty plea because of evidence offender secreted assets that could have been used to make restitution); United States v. Stergios, 370 F.Supp.2d 328, 330–31 (D. Maine 2005) (denying reduction for acceptance of responsibility when offender failed "to preserve available assets in order to make restitution as well as [showing a] lack of candor with respect to his assets during the presentence investigation.").

Chapter 19

1. *See* United States v. Smith, 606 F.3d 1270, 1282 (10th Cir. 2010) (stating that conditions of supervised release should "be linked to the offense and be no broader than necessary to rehabilitate the defendant and protect the public.").

2. *See* United States v. Kravchuk, 335 F.3d 1147, 1159 (10th Cir. 2003) (stating that sentencing court is required to give reasons on record for imposition of special conditions of supervised release).

3. *See* United States v. Hahn, 551 F.3d 977, 982–83 (10th Cir. 2008).

4. *See* Addington v. Texas, 441 U.S. 418, 425 (1979) ("This Court repeatedly has recognized that civil commitment for any purpose constitutes a significant deprivation of liberty[.]").

5. *See, e.g.*, United States v. Weber, 451 F.3d 552, 563 (9th Cir. 2006) (finding that imposing condition that offender undergo penile plethysmograph testing affects offender's liberty interests).

6. *See, e.g.*, United States v. Bear, 769 F.3d 1221, 1229 (10th Cir. 2014) (finding that restrictions on offender's contact with his own children are subject to stricter scrutiny).

7. *See, e.g.*, United States v. Williams, 356 F.3d 1045, 1055 (9th Cir. 2004) (holding that condition of supervised release "compelling a person to take antipsychotic medication is an especially grave infringement of liberty" and thus warranted departure from usual rule that district courts need not articulate reasons for imposing supervised release conditions).

8. *See, e.g.*, United States v. Malone, 937 F.33d 1325, 1328 (10th Cir. 2019) (finding that requiring offender to undergo mental health treatment as condition of supervised release implicated liberty interest requiring heightened findings by court at sentencing hearing).

9. *See, e.g.*, United States v. Dean, 940 F.3d 888, 890–91 (5th Cir. 2019) (noting that offender waives objection to condition of supervised release if given notice of it in presentence report and opportunity to object to condition); United States v. Lewis, 823 F.3d 1075, 1083 (7th Cir. 2016) (finding waiver established when "the judge asked specifically about the extent of her explanations of the sentence in general and supervised release in particular" and counsel raised no objections).

10. United States v. Weber, 451 F.3d 552, 559 (9th Cir. 2006).

Chapter 20

1. *See* United States v. Nesbeth, 188 F.Supp.3d 179, 184–86 (E.D.N.Y. 2016) (discussing at length and citing authorities for significant civil collateral consequences that may arise as result of felony conviction). *See also* Sarah Berson, U.S. Dep't of Just., Nat'l Inst. Of Just., *Beyond the Sentence—Understanding Collateral Consequences*, 272 Nat'l Inst. Of Just. J. 24 (2013) (noting that a conviction "brings with it a host of sanctions and disqualifications that can place an unanticipated burden on individuals trying to re-enter society and lead lives as productive citizens.").

2. *See, e.g.*, 7 U.S.C. § 13 (larceny or embezzlement in connection with commodity exchanges); 21 U.S.C. § 844 (simple possession of controlled substances, unless court finds offender lacks ability to pay); 26 U.S.C. § 7201 (attempt to defeat or evade income tax); 26 U.S.C. § 7202 (willful failure to collect or pay tax); 26 U.S.C. § 7203 (willful failure to file income tax return, supply information, or pay tax); 26 U.S.C. § 7206 (fraud and false statements); 26 U.S.C. § 7210 (failure to obey summons); 26 U.S.C. § 7213 (unauthorized disclosure of information); 26 U.S.C. § 7215 (offenses involving collected taxes); 26 U.S.C. § 7216 (disclosure or use of information by preparers of returns); 26 U.S.C. § 7232 (failure to register or false statement by gasoline manufacturer or producer); 42 U.S.C. § 1320c-9 (improper FOIA disclosure); 43 U.S.C. § 942–6 (rights of way for Alaskan wagon roads).

3. *See, e.g.*, United States v. Standiford, 148 F.3d 864, 870 n. 4 (7th Cir. 1998); United States v. Hiland, 909 F.2d 1114, 1141 (8th Cir. 1990).

4. *See* United States v. Stefonek, 179 F.3d 1030, 1037 (7th Cir. 1999) (holding that § 1920 provides exclusive list of "costs of prosecution" that must be assessed against criminal offenders); United States v. Hiland, 909 F.2d 1114, 1142 (8th Cir. 1990) (holding that "[a]bsent explicit statutory or contractual authorization to the contrary, federal district courts may tax as costs only those expenses listed in § 1920.").

5. *See* United States v. Bussell, 504 F.3d 956, 968 (9th Cir. 2007) (noting that court-imposed costs of prosecution of $55,626.09).

6. *See* United States v. Glover, 588 F.2d 876, 879 (2nd Cir. 1978) (explaining that costs of prosecution are appropriate to deprive financially able

offenders of funds which, in fairness, should be remitted to public coffers).

7. *See* 18 U.S.C. § 3621(b) ("The Bureau of Prisons shall designate the place of the prisoner's imprisonment."). *See also* United States v. Williams, 65 F.3d 301, 307 (2d Cir. 1995) ("A sentencing court has no authority to order that a convicted defendant be confined in a particular facility, much less placed in a particular treatment program; those decisions are within the sole discretion of the Bureau of Prisons."); United States v. Voda, 994 F.2d 14, 151–52 (5th Cir. 1993) (observing that "a court may recommend that a sentence imposed under [18 U.S.C. § 3621] be served in a particular prison or jail, but that only the Bureau of Prisons has the actual authority to designate the place of confinement") (citations omitted). Pugliese v. Nelson, 617 F.2d 916, 925 (2d Cir. 1980) ("[J] udicial intervention into the classification of prisoners for monitoring and control purposes would almost inevitably involve the federal courts in the day-to-day operations of our prison system, which are better left to the expertise of prison administration authorities.").

8. *See* Olin v. Wakinekona, 461 U.S. 238, 244–48 (1983).

9. *See* U.S. Dept. of Justice, Federal Bureau of Prisons, Program Statement P5100.08—Inmate Security Designation and Custody Classification, Ch. 3 (Sept. 12, 2006).

10. *See* United States v. Giaimo, 880 F.2d 1561, 1563 (2d Cir. 1989) (holding that Rule 32 does not "give a district court jurisdiction to correct inaccuracies in a [presentence] report after a defendant has been sentenced.").

11. *See, e.g.*, United States v. Ursery, 518 U.S. 267 (1996) (holding that civil forfeiture does not constitute punishment under Double Jeopardy Clause); United States v. Stoller, 78 F.3d 710, 724 (1st Cir. 1996) (holding that indefinite debarment from banking industry does not constitute punishment for purposes of Double Jeopardy Clause); DiCola v. FDA, 77 F.3d 504, 507 (D.C. Cir. 1996) (holding that permanent exclusion from providing services to pharmaceutical industry does not constitute punishment for purposes of Double Jeopardy Clause).

12. *See, e.g.*, United States v. Wing, No. 5:13-CR-87-JMH-HAI-1, 2016 WL 11431968, at *4 (E.D. Kent. Apr. 21, 2016) (refusing to expand holding in *Padilla* to find that defense counsel must advise offenders that conviction may expose offender to future enhanced sentences).

13. *See* Margaret Love, *Collateral Consequences after* Padilla v. Kentucky: *From Punishment to Regulation*, 31 St. Louis U. Pub. L. Rev. 87, 105–110 (2011); Paisly Bender, *Exposing the Hidden Penalties of Pleading Guilty: A Revision of the Collateral Consequences Rule*, 19 Geo. Mason L. Rev. 291, 311–18 (Fall 2011).

14. *See, e.g.*, United States v. Pauley, 511 F.3d 468, 474–75 (4th Cir. 2007) (viewing offender's loss of "teaching certificate and his state pension as a result of his conduct" as appropriate sentencing considerations, "consistent with § 3553(a)'s directive that the sentence reflect the need for 'just punishment and 'adequate deterrence.'"); United States v. Stewart, 590 F.3d 93, 141 (2d Cir. 2009) (affirming significant downward variance from Guidelines range of imprisonment in part because "conviction made it doubtful that the defendant could pursue his career as an academic or translator, and therefore ... the need for further deterrence and protection of the public is lessened because the conviction itself already visits substantial punishment on the defendant.").

15. *See, e.g.*, United States v. Morgan, 635 Fed. App'x 423 (10th Cir. 2015) (unpublished) (holding that district court impermissibly focused on collateral consequences, such as loss of law license and its impact on offender's financial health, because those factors "impermissibly favor criminals ... with privileged backgrounds."); United States. v. Musgrave, 761 F.3d 602, 608 (6th Cir. 2014) (holding that consideration of "four years of legal proceedings, legal fees, the likely loss of [offender's] CPA license, and [his] felony convictions that would follow him for the rest of his life," were impermissible considerations because "these sorts of consequences—particularly ones related to a defendant's humiliation before his community, neighbors, and friends—would tend to support shorter sentences in cases with defendants from privileged backgrounds, who might have more to lose along these lines."); United States v. Kuhlman, 711 F.3d 1321, 1329 (11th Cir. 2013) ("The Sentencing Guidelines authorize no special sentencing discounts on account of economic or social status.").

Chapter 21

1. This may be a product of skepticism, thinking that judges have already made up their minds about the sentence to be imposed and no amount of argument will change that position. I personally find this skepticism misplaced. I believe most judges strive to keep an open mind about the ultimate sentence, even if the judge may have in mind some range within which the judge believes a reasonable sentence would fall. I have personally found myself persuaded by attorneys' arguments, offenders' allocution, victims' statements, and other evidence to arrive at a sentence that was higher or lower than or within the range that I had in mind before the sentencing hearing.

2. If attorneys have any doubt about whether the judge will have read the sentencing memoranda in advance of the hearing, they should research the judge by asking other attorneys about their experiences. It has been my experience both as a practicing attorney and as a judge, however, that judges take sentencing hearings very seriously and have thoroughly prepared for the sentencing hearing, including reading any written sentencing memoranda submitted by the attorneys.

3. *See, e.g.*, United States v. Cavera, 550 F.3d 180, 190 (2d Cir. 2008) (en banc) (stating that

appellate courts determine substantive reasonableness of sentences under "the totality of the circumstances, giving due deference to the sentencing judge's exercise of discretion, and bearing in mind the institutional advantages of district courts.").

4. *See, e.g.*, United States v. Evans, 526 F.3d 155, 162 (4th Cir. 2008) (recognizing that deference to district courts' sentences is required because "sentencing judge is in a superior position to find facts and judge their import under § 3553(a) in the individual case").

5. *See, e.g.*, Elliott v. United States, 332 F.3d 753, 761 (4th Cir. 2003) (stating that because sentencing judge "is in a unique position to evaluate a defendant's acceptance of responsibility," sentencing judge's ruling "is entitled to great deference on review.").

6. ARISTOTLE, RHETORIC, Book I, Part II, Paragraph VII (Trans. W. Rhys Roberts, Mineola, NY; Dover Publications 2004).

7. *See, e.g.*, Chief Justice John G. Roberts Jr., *2016 Year-End Report on the Federal Judiciary* 5 (2016) ("Most district judges agree that sentencing is their most difficult duty."); Hon. Virginia M Kendall, *A Judge Comments*, 41 No. 3 LITIGATION 23, 23 (2015) ("Ask any district court judge about her most difficult job and chances are high she will say sentencing."); Jessica M. Marshall (I Can't Get No) Satisfaction: Using Restorative Justice to Satisfy Victims' Rights, 15 CARDOZO J. CONFLICT RESOL. 569, 569 (2014) ("The responsibility of sentencing defendants is the most difficult task within the criminal justice system."); Mark W. Bennett, *Hard Time: Reflections on Visiting Federal Inmates*, 94 JUDICATURE 304, 304 (2011) ("I have always had a hard time with sentencings. It is an awesome responsibility to take one's liberty away."); Jack B. Weinstein, *Does Religion Have a Role in Criminal Sentencing?*, 23 TOURO L. REV. 539, 539 (2007) ("Sentencing, that is to say punishment, is perhaps the most difficult task of a trial court judge.").

Chapter 22

1. *See* United States v. Christensen, 732 F.3d 1094, 1102, 1106 (9th Cir. 2013) (holding that judge may consider unsworn victim impact statements at sentencing and that offender's due process rights are violated only if court imposes sentence on basis of materially false or unreliable information).

Chapter 23

1. D. Brock Hornby, *Speaking in Sentences*, 14 GREEN BAG 2D 147, 154 (2011).

2. *See* Green v. United States, 365 U.S. 301, 305 (1961).

3. *See* Mitchell v. United States, 526 U.S. 314, 330 (1999) (holding that offenders retain their Fifth Amendment right against self-incrimination at sentencing hearings and judges cannot draw any adverse factual inferences from offenders' silence).

4. *See, e.g.*, United States v. Doyle, 857 F.3d 1115, 1121 (11th Cir. 2017) (holding that it was reversible plain error when sentencing judge failed to afford offender right of allocution); United States v. Murillo-Mora, 703 Fed. App'x 435, 438 (8th Cir. 2017) (per curiam) (holding that failure to give offender the right of allocution is clear error that requires reversal).

5. *See, e.g.*, United States v. Noel, 581 F.3d 490, 501–04 (7th Cir. 2009) (holding that trial judge's failure to personally address offender was plain error); United States v. Robertson, 537 F.3d 859, 861–63 (8th Cir. 2008) (recognizing trial court's duty to address offender personally); United States v. Carney, 88 Fed. App'x 534, 536–37 (3d Cir. 2004) (remanding for failure to address offender personally during sentencing).

6. For an excellent article reflecting my former colleagues' observations of what makes effective and ineffective allocutions, see Mark W. Bennett, *Heartstrings or Heartburn: A Federal Judge's Musings on Defendants' Right and Rite of Allocution*, 35-MAR CHAMPION 26 (2011).

7. *See, e.g.*, United States v. Peel, 668 F.3d 506, 509 (7th Cir. 2012) (noting that offender's "bumptious, defiant" allocution that was "devoid of acknowledgment of wrongdoing" justified longer sentence); United States v. Burgos-Andujar, 275 F.3d 23, 30 (1st Cir. 2001) (allocution in civil disobedience case resulted in longer sentence).

8. *See* Mark W. Bennett & Ira P. Robbins, *Last Words: A Survey and Analysis of Federal Judges' Views on Allocution in Sentencing*, 65 ALA. L. REV. 735, 802 (Appendix Table 28) (2014).

9. *See* Green v. United States, 365 U.S. 301, 304 (1961) (noting that "[t]he most persuasive counsel may not be able to speak for a defendant as the defendant might, with halting eloquence, speak for himself.").

10. *See* Bennett & Robbins, *supra* note 8 in this chapter, at 764 (noting that in authors' survey of federal judges, "96.5% (497) of the judges never warn defendants that allocution can be used to increase a sentence, and only .06% (3) of the judges always provide this warning.").

11. *See* Slagle v. Miller, No. 1:12-cv-839, 2013 WL 950854, at *7 (S.D. Ohio Mar. 12, 2013) (quoting judge's statement to offender at sentencing that, although offender did not have to say anything, if offender did not speak, then judge would assume offender was greedy).

12. *See* D. Brock Hornby, *Speaking in Sentences*, 14 GREEN BAG 2D 147, 155 (2011).

13. *See* Bennett & Robbins, *supra* note 8 in this chapter, at 766–70 (noting authors' and other judges' advice on proper role of defense counsel in helping offenders prepare for allocution).

14. *See* ABA STANDARDS 4-8.1(d) ("Defense counsel should alert the accused to the right of allocution, if any, and to the dangers of making a statement that might tend to prejudice an appeal.").

15. *See, e.g.*, United States v. Whitten, 610 F.3d 168, 199 (2nd Cir. 2010) ("[A]n unsworn, uncrossed

allocution constitutes a limited Fifth Amendment waiver that allows the prosecution to argue for an adverse inference from a defendant's failure to testify as to that to which he has allocuted.").

Chapter 24

1. United States v. Vega, 332 F.3d 849, 852 (5th Cir. 2003) (per curiam).

2. *See, e.g.*, United States v. Cephus, 684 F.3d 703, 709–10 (7th Cir. 2012); United States v. Khoury, 901 F.2d 975, 977–78 (11th Cir. 1990).

3. *Cf.* United States v. Spiropoulos, 976 F.2d 155, 163 (3d Cir. 1992) (holding that judge did not make factual error when describing public official's motive for committing the crime as avarice, explaining that "[we cannot] hold judges to standards of linguistic perfection, especially in the setting of remarks from the bench in the crucible of a highly charged sentencing hearing").

4. *See, e.g.*, United States v. Wintermute, 443 F.3d 993, 1005 (8th Cir. 2006) (holding that judge cannot rely on objected-to facts contained in presentence report in arriving at offender's sentence).

5. *See, e.g.*, United States v. Ward, 626 F.3d 179, 184–85 (3d Cir. 2010) ("[T]he District Court erred by failing to impose a sentence on each count, and that error is plain."); United States v. Moriarty, 429 F.3d 1012, 1025 (11th Cir. 2005) (finding district court's imposition of 20-year general sentence on multiple counts to be plain error when that sentence exceeded 10-year statutory maximum on one count); *see also* United States v. Santopietro, 996 F.2d 17, 20 (2d Cir. 1993) (excusing district court's failure to orally pronounce sentence on each count when written judgment stated sentences imposed on each count to arrive at orally-pronounced total).

6. *See, e.g.*, United States v. Dubray, --- Fed. App'x ---, 2020 WL 2211822 (8th Cir. May 7, 2020) (finding that judge's oral pronouncement that the judge was varying from the advisory Guidelines sentence controlled over the written judgment that indicated the judge departed from the advisory Guidelines sentence).

Chapter 25

1. *See* 18 U.S.C. § 3582(c); United States v. Ross, 245 F.3d 577, 585–86 (6th Cir. 2001).

2. *See* United States v. Cook, 890 F.2d 672, 675 (4th Cir. 1989).

3. *See* United States v. Delgado, 256 F.3d 264, 279 (5th Cir. 2001) (applying Rule 35 to denial of right of allocution).

4. United States v. Steen, 55 F.3d 1022, 1025–26 n.3 (5th Cir. 1995).

5. *See* United States v. Portillo, 363 F.3d 1161, 1164 (11th Cir. 2004).

6. *See* Dillon v. United States, 560 U.S. 817, 826 (2010).

Chapter 27

1. New York Central & Hudson River Railroad v. United States, 212 U.S. 481, 493 (1909).

2. For a thorough and insightful analysis of issues involved in sentencing organizations, I commend the opinion authored by the Honorable William G. Young, United States District Court for the District of Massachusetts. United States v. Orthofix, Inc., 956 F. Supp.2d 316 (D. Mass. 2013).

3. *See* Christopher A. Wray, *Note, Corporate Probation Under the New Organizational Sentencing Guidelines*, 101 YALE L. J. 2017, 2030–31 (1992) (citing 18 U.S.C. § 3553(a)(2, 6, 7).

4. *See* Christopher A. Wray, *Note, Corporate Probation Under the New Organizational Sentencing Guidelines*, 101 YALE L.J. 2017, 2030–31 (1992).

5. *See, e.g.*, Rubashkin v. United States, No. 13-CV-1028-LRR, No. 08-CR-1324-LRR, 2017 WL 384277 (N.D. Iowa Jan. 26, 2017) (forfeiting name of corporation and tradename of its products).

6. *See, e.g.*, United States v. Mongol Nation, 370 F. Supp.3d 1090 (C.D. Cal. 2019) (finding that government's forfeiture of motorcycle organization's trademark violated organization's First Amendment rights).

7. *See also* United States v. Reifler, 446 F.3d 65, 136 (2d Cir. 2006) ("Congress plainly intended that sentencing courts not become embroiled in intricate issues of proof.").

8. *See, e.g.*, United States v. BP Products North America Inc., 610 F.Supp.2d 655, 706 (S.D. Tex.2009) (finding restitution impracticable given number and factually disputed nature of potential restitution claims); (citing in re W.R. Huff Asset Mgt. Co., LLC, 409 F.3d 555, 563–64 (2d Cir. 2005) (finding order of restitution inappropriate because of many victims).

9. *Compare* United States v. Catoggio, 326 F.3d 323, 327–28 (2d Cir. 2003) (finding that victims in RICO securities case were sufficiently identifiable where the government supplied a "1,700-page victim restitution report ... detail[ing] $192 million in actual losses to approximately 10,000 victims" and the government possessed defendant's trading records, which identified the victims and their respective losses) *with* United States v. Ferguson, 584 F.Supp.2d 447, 458 (D. Conn. 2008) (finding restitution inappropriate where defendant's securities fraud victimized 154 institutional holders and the court would need to identify the individuals interested in each and the government did not know the shareholders' identities).

10. *See* Ex. 14, Decl. of Jocelyn Scott, EPA, United States v. DeSimone, et al., No. 5:11-cr-264-DNH, 2013 WL 2309692 (2013) (discussing corporate defendant Mazza & Sons, Inc.).

11. *See, e.g.*, United States v. Haile, 795 F.2d 489, 492 (5th Cir. 1986) ("It might also be true that judicially approved charitable organizations can spend money, and thereby benefit the community, more intelligently than can the U.S. government. Without a statutory footing, however, the courts are not free to make these policy judgments."); Fiore

v. United States, 696 F.2d 205, 209 (2d Cir. 1982) (noting that sentencing courts may not require organization to pay reparations to persons not aggrieved by its crimes, or simply to pay such reparations to community at large).

12. *See* United States v. Haile, 795 F.2d 489, 491 (5th Cir. 1986) (holding that courts cannot impose requirement that organizations make charitable contributions as condition of probation because they would constitute fines under different label); United States v. Missouri Valley. Constr. Co., 741 F.2d 1542, 1544 (8th Cir. 1984) (imposing condition of probation that offender contribute $1,475,000 to University of Nebraska Foundation to endow chair in ethics held unlawful).

Chapter 28

1. *See* United States v. Hammonds, 370 F.3d 1032, 1038 (10th Cir. 2004).

2. *See, e.g.*, United States v. Garner, 969 F.3d 550 (5th Cir. 2020); United States v. Wilson, 939 F.3d 929, 933 (8th Cir. 2019).

3. *See* Morrissey v. Brewer, 408 U.S. 471, 489 (1972).

4. *See, e.g.*, Ash v. Reilly, 431 F.3d 826, 829–30 (D.C. Cir. 2005); *see also* United States v. Carthen, 681 F.3d 94, 100 (2d Cir. 2012); United States v. Hall, 419 F.3d 980, 985–86 (9th Cir. 2005).

5. *See* United States v. Grandlund, 71 F.3d 507, 510 (5th Cir. 1995).

6. *See also* Morrissey, 408 U.S. at 489 (noting that right of confrontation in revocation hearings under Rule 32.1 is not grounded in Sixth Amendment, but is more attenuated right flowing from Due Process Clause); Ash, 431 F.3d at 830 (same).

7. United States v. Stanfield, 360 F.3d 1346, 1359 (D.C. Cir. 2004).

8. *See, e.g.*, United States v. Jordan, 742 F.3d 276, 280 (7th Cir. 2014).

9. Morrissey, 408 U.S. at 489.

10. United States v. Wilmore, 381 F.3d 868, 872 (9th Cir. 2004).

11. *Compare* United States v. Thornhill, 759 F.3d 299, 309–10 (1st Cir. 2014) (holding that judges must still consider Section 3553(a) factors in cases of mandatory revocation under Section 3583(g)) *with* United States v. Carmichael, 777 Fed. App'x 977, 978–79 (11th Cir. 2019) (holding that when revocation of supervised release is mandatory under Section 3583(g), judges need not consider Section 3553(a) factors).

12. *See, e.g.*, United States v. Webb, 738 F.3d 638, 642 (4th Cir. 2013); United States v. Young, 634 F.3d 233, 240–41 (3d Cir. 2011).

13. *See also* United States v. Parks, 823 F.3d 990, 993 (11th Cir. 2016) (explaining that Section 3553(c)(2) applies to sentences imposed upon revocation of supervised release)

14. *See also* United States v. Bennett, 698 F.3d 194, 202 (4th Cir. 2012) (recognizing that breach of trust is "a perfectly appropriate basis—and, in fact, the principal basis on which the Guidelines encourage courts to ground revocation sentences").

15. *See* United States v. Begay, 631 F.3d 1168, 1171–72 (10th Cir. 2011).

16. *See* United States v. Carruth, 528 F.3d 845, 846–47 (11th Cir. 2008) (explaining that right of allocution extended to revocation of supervised release hearings).

17. *See generally* United States v. Johnson, 529 U.S. 53, 59 (2000) ("Congress intended supervised release to assist individuals in their transition to community life. Supervised release fulfills rehabilitative ends, distinct from those served by incarceration.").

Bibliography

Primary Sources

Constitution and Statutes

U.S. Const. amend. VIII
18 U.S.C. § 228
18 U.S.C. § 401
18 U.S.C. § 924
18 U.S.C. § 981
18 U.S.C. § 982
18 U.S.C. § 1111
18 U.S.C. § 1341
18 U.S.C. §§ 1512–1515
18 U.S.C. § 1593
18 U.S.C. § 1920
18 U.S.C. § 1957
18 U.S.C. §§ 1961–1968
18 U.S.C. § 2113
18 U.S.C. § 3013
18 U.S.C. § 3014
18 U.S.C. § 3161
18 U.S.C. § 3510
18 U.S.C. § 3551
18 U.S.C. § 3552
18 U.S.C. § 3553
18 U.S.C. § 3561
18 U.S.C. § 3564
18 U.S.C. § 3571
18 U.S.C. § 3572
18 U.S.C. § 3573
18 U.S.C. § 3582
18 U.S.C. § 3583
18 U.S.C. § 3593
18 U.S.C. § 3621
18 U.S.C. § 3663A
18 U.S.C. § 3664
18 U.S.C. § 3771
21 U.S.C. § 841
21 U.S.C. § 484
21 U.S.C. § 853
34 U.S.C. § 20141
34 U.S.C. § 20142
42 U.S.C. §§ 13925–14045d

Sentencing Commission Publications

U.S. Sent'g Comm'n, Rep. to the Congress: Downward Departures from the Federal Sentencing Guidelines (Oct. 2003).
U.S. Sent'g Comm'n, Rep. on the Continuing Impact of United States v. Booker on Federal Sentencing 69 (2012)
U.S. Sent'g Comm'n Sourcebook 2018
U.S. Sent'g Comm'n, Sourcebook 2019
United States Sentencing Commission, *The Effects of Aging on Recidivism Among Federal Offenders* 3 (2017)

Rules and Codes

Code of Conduct for United States Judges (2019)
Fed. R. Civ. P. 1
Fed. R. Crim. P. 32
Fed. R. Crim. P. 32.1
Fed. R. Crim. P. 32.2
Fed. R. Crim. P. 35
Fed. R. Crim. P. 36
Fed. R. Crim. P. 43
Fed. R. Evid. 104
Fed. R. Evid. 404
Fed. R. Evid. 406
Fed. R. Evid. 407
Fed. R. Evid. 408
Fed. R. Evid. 409
Fed. R. Evid. 410
Fed. R. Evid. 411
Fed. R. Evid. 611
Fed. R. Evid. 1101
Model Rules of Prof'l Conduct (Am. Bar Ass'n 2020)
United States Sentencing Guidelines

Cases

Supreme Court

Addington v. Texas, 441 U.S. 418 (1979)
Alexander v. United States, 509 U.S. 544 (1993)
Apprendi v. New Jersey, 530 U.S. 466 (2000)
Austin v. United States, 509 U.S. 602 (1993)
Browning-Ferris Industries of Vt., Inc. v. Kelco Disposal, Inc., 492 U.S. 257 (1989)
California v. Green, 399 U.S. 149 (1970)
Carter v. Illinois, 329 U.S. 173 (1946)
Dillon v. United States, 560 U.S. 817 (2010)
Dolan v. United States, 560 U.S. 605 (2010)
Ewing v. California, 538 U.S. 11 (2003)

Frank v. United States, 395 U.S. 147 (1969)
Gall v. United States, 552 U.S. 38 (2007)
Graham v. Florida, 560 U.S. 48 (2010)
Green v. United States, 365 U.S. 301 (1961)
Griffin v. Wisconsin, 483 U.S. 868 (1987)
Irizarry v. United States, 553 U.S. 708 (2008)
Johnson v. United States, 529 U.S. 694 (2000)
Kaley v. United States, 571 U.S. 320 (2014)
Kimbrough v. United States, 552 U.S. 85 (2007)
Libretti v. United States, 516 U.S. 29 (1995)
McDonald v. City of Chicago, 561 U.S. 742 (2010)
Mitchell v. United States, 526 U.S. 314 (1999)
Morrissey v. Brewer, 408 U.S. 471 (1972)
Mu'Min v. Virginia, 500 U.S. 415 (1991)
New York Central & Hudson River Railroad v. United States, 212 U.S. 481 (1909)
Olin v. Wakinekona, 461 U.S. 238 (1983)
Padilla v. Kentucky, 559 U.S. 356 (2010)
Paroline v. United States, 572 U.S. 434 (2014)
Pepper v. United States, 562 U.S. 476 (2011)
Peugh v. United States, 569 U.S. 530 (2013)
Porter v. McCollum, 558 US 30 (2009)
Roper v. Simmons, 543 U.S. 551 (2005)
Southern Union Company v. United States, 567 U.S. 343 (2012)
Spears v. United States, 555 U.S. 261 (2009)
Stinson v. United States, 508 U.S. 36 (1993)
Strickland v. Washington, 466 U.S. 668 (1984)
United States v. Bajakajian, 524 U.S. 321 (1998)
United States v. Booker, 543 U.S. 320 (2005)
United States v. Haymond, 139 S. Ct. 2369 (2019)
United States v. Johnson, 529 U.S. 53 (2000)
United States v. Knights, 534 U.S. 112 (2001)
United States v. Munoz-Flores, 495 U.S. 385 (1990)
United States v. Ursery, 518 U.S. 267 (1996)
Wade v. United States, 504 U.S. 181 (1992)
Williams v. New York, 337 U.S. 241 (1949)
Williams v. Oklahoma, 358 U.S. 576 (1959)

Courts of Appeal

Ash v. Reilly, 431 F.3d 826 (D.C. Cir. 2005)
DiCola v. FDA, 77 F.3d 504 (D.C. Cir. 1996)
Elliott v. United States, 332 F.3d 753 (4th Cir. 2003)
Fiore v. United States, 696 F.2d 205 (2d Cir. 1982)
In re W.R. Huff Asset Mgt. Co., LLC, 409 F.3d 555 (2d Cir. 2005)
Null v. Wainwright, 508 F.2d 340 (5th Cir. 1975)
Pugliese v. Nelson, 617 F.2d 916 (2d Cir. 1980)
United States v. Aderholt, 87 F.3d 740 (5th Cir. 1996)
United States v. Alalade, 204 F.3d 536 (4th Cir. 2000)
United States v. Anderson, 632 F.3d 1264 (D.C. Cir. 2011)
United States v. Anderson, 68 F.3d 1050 (8th Cir. 1995)
United States v. Armstrong, 187 F.3d 392 (4th Cir. 1999)
United States v. Beal, 463 F.3d 834 (8th Cir. 2006)
United States v. Bean, 18 F.3d 1367 (7th Cir. 1994)
United States v. Bear, 769 F.3d 1221 (10th Cir. 2014)
United States v. Beecroft, 825 F.3d 991 (9th Cir. 2016)
United States v. Begay, 631 F.3d 1168 (10th Cir. 2011)
United States v. Beltramea, 785 F.3d 287 (8th Cir. 2015)
United States v. Bennett, 698 F.3d 194 (4th Cir. 2012)
United States v. Besler, 86 F.3d 745 (7th Cir. 1996)
United States v. Bieri, 68 F.3d 232 (8th Cir. 1995)
United States v. Book, 889 F.3d 95 (2d Cir. 2018)
United States v. Bowers, 743 F.3d 1182 (8th Cir. 2014)
United States v. Bright, 353 F.3d 1114 (9th Cir. 2004)
United States v. Buchanan, 638 F.3d 448 (4th Cir. 2011)
United States v. Burgos, 761 Fed. App'x 922 (11th Cir. 2019)
United States v. Burgos-Andujar, 275 F.3d 23 (1st Cir. 2001)
United States v. Bussell, 504 F.3d 956 (9th Cir. 2007)
United States v. Caldwell, 219 F.3d 1186 (10th Cir. 2000)
United States v. Cantu, 12 F.3d 1506 (9th Cir. 1993)
United States v. Carmichael, 777 Fed. App'x 977 (11th Cir. 2019)
United States v. Carney, 88 Fed. App'x 534 (3d Cir. 2004)
United States v. Carruth, 528 F.3d 845 (11th Cir. 2008)
United States v. Carthen, 681 F.3d 94 (2d Cir. 2012)
United States v. Catoggio, 326 F.3d 323 (2d Cir. 2003)
United States v. Cavera, 550 F.3d 180 (2d Cir. 2008)
United States v. Cephus, 684 F.3d 703 (7th Cir. 2012)
United States v. Chase, 560 F.3d 828 (8th Cir. 2009)
United States v. Cherry, 330 F.3d 658 (4th Cir. 2003)
United States v. Christensen, 732 F.3d 1094 (9th Cir. 2013)
United States v. Cochrane, 608 F.3d 382 (8th Cir. 2010)
United States v. Cole, 343 Fed. App'x 109 (6th Cir. 2009)
United States v. Cook, 890 F.2d 672 (4th Cir. 1989)
United States v. Corner, 598 F.3d 411 (7th Cir. 2010)
United States v. Delgado, 256 F.3d 264 (5th Cir. 2001)
United States v. Diaz, No. 11-CR-00821-2 (JG), 2013 WL 322243 (E.D.N.Y. Jan. 28, 2013)
United States v. Dean, 940 F.3d 888 (5th Cir. 2019)
United States v. Doe, 398 F.3d 1254 (10th Cir. 2005)
United States v. Doyle, 857 F.3d 1115 (11th Cir. 2017)
United States v. Dubose, 146 F.3d 1141 (9th Cir. 1998)
United States v. Emerson, 128 F.3d 557 (7th Cir. 1997)
United States v. Espinoza, 831 F.3d 1096 (8th Cir. 2016)
United States v. Evans, 526 F.3d 155 (4th Cir. 2008)
United States v. Fernandez, 443 F.3d 19 (2d Cir. 2006)
United States v. Florence, 333 F.3d 1290 (11th Cir. 2003)
United States v. Francies, 945 F.2d 851 (5th Cir. 1991)
United States v. Friedman, 554 F.3d 1301 (10th Cir. 2009)
United States v. Foy, 617 F.3d 1029 (8th Cir. 2010)
United States v. Fruchter, 411 F.3d 377 (2d Cir. 2005)

United States v. Fuller, 659 Fed. App'x 896 (7th Cir. 2016)
United States v. Fumo, 655 F.3d 288 (3rd Cir. 2011)
United States v. Garcia, 580 F.3d 528 (7th Cir. 2009)
United States v. Garner, 969 F.3d 550 (5th Cir. 2020)
United States v. Giaimo, 880 F.2d 1561 (2d Cir. 1989)
United States v. Glover, 588 F.2d 876 (2nd Cir. 1978)
United States v. Gomez-Herrera, 523 F.3d 554 (5th Cir. 2008)
United States v. Gonzalez-Garcia, 752 Fed. App'x 208 (5th Cir. 2019)
United States v. Grams, 566 F.3d 683 (6th Cir. 2009)
United States v. Grandlund, 71 F.3d 507 (5th Cir. 1995)
United States v. Green, 718 Fed. App'x 141 (3rd Cir. 2018)
United States v. Green, 691 F.3d 960 (8th Cir. 2012)
United States v. Guarin, 898 F.2d 1120 (6th Cir. 1990)
United States v. Hahn, 551 F.3d 977 (10th Cir. 2008)
United States v. Haile, 795 F.2d 489 (5th Cir. 1986)
United States v. Hall, 419 F.3d 980 (9th Cir. 2005)
United States v. Hammonds, 370 F.3d 1032 (10th Cir. 2004)
United States v. Hasson, 333 F.3d 1264 (11th Cir. 2003)
United States v. Harper, 946 F.2d 1373 (8th Cir. 1991)
United States v. Hayes, 948 F.Supp.2d 1009 (N.D. Iowa 2013)
United States v. Hazelrigg, 430 F.2d 580 (8th Cir. 1970)
United States v. Hernandez-Guevara, 448 Fed. App'x 39 (11th Cir. 2011)
United States v. Henderson, 649 F.3d 955 (9th Cir. 2011)
United States v. Herrera-Zuniga, 571 F.3d 568 (6th Cir. 2009)
United States v. Hiland, 909 F.2d 1114 (8th Cir. 1990)
United States v. Holloway, 826 F.3d 1237 (10th Cir. 2016)
United States v. Houston, 476 Fed. App'x 110 (8th Cir. 2012)
United States v. Jaimes-Jaimes, 406 F.3d 845 (7th Cir. 2005)
United States v. Jenkins, 772 F.3d 1092 (7th Cir. 2014)
United States v. Johnson, 554 Fed. App'x 773 (10th Cir. 2014)
United States v. Johnson, 529 U.S. 53 (2000)
United States v. Jones, 899 F.2d 1097 (11th Cir. 1990)
United States v. Jordan, 742 F.3d 276 (7th Cir. 2014)
United States v. Jordan, 256 F.3d 922 (9th Cir. 2001)
United States v. Joseph, 743 F.3d 1350 (11th Cir. 2014)
United States v. Khoury, 901 F.2d 975 (11th Cir. 1990)
United States v. Kim, 896 F.2d 678 (2d Cir. 1990)
United States v. Klups, 514 F.3d 532 (6th Cir. 2008)
United States v. Kravchuk, 335 F.3d 1147 (10th Cir. 2003)
United States v. Kuhlman, 711 F.3d 1321 (11th Cir. 2013)
United States v. Landron-Class, 696 F.3d 62 (1st Cir. 2012)
United States v. Lanning, 633 F.3d 469 (6th Cir. 2011)
United States v. Leiskunas, 656 F.3d 732 (7th Cir. 2011)
United States v. Lessner, 498 F.3d 185 (3d Cir. 2007)
United States v. Lewis, 823 F.3d 1075 (7th Cir. 2016)
United States v. Long, 656 F.2d 1162 (5th Cir. 1981)
United States v. Lopez-Marcias, 661 F.3d 485 (10th Cir. 2011)
United States v. Machado, 886 F.3d 1070 (11th Cir. 2018)
United States v. Madsen, 809 F.3d 712 (1st Cir. 2016)
United States v. Malone, 937 F.33d 1325 (10th Cir. 2019)
United States v. Marshall, 411 F.3d 891 (8th Cir. 2005)
United States v. Martinez, 610 F.3d 1216 (10th Cir. 2010)
United States v. Massey, 663 F.3d 852 (6th Cir. 2011)
United States v. Maurice, 69 F.3d 1553 (11th Cir. 1995)
United States v. McCracken, 487 F.3d 1125 (8th Cir. 2007)
United States v. Merritt, 988 F.2d 1298 (2d Cir. 1993)
United States v. Missouri Valley. Constr. Co., 741 F.2d 1542 (8th Cir. 1984)
United States v. Mitchell, 789 Fed. App'x 774 (11th Cir. 2019)
United States v. Moore, 918 F.3d 368 (4th Cir. 2019)
United States v. Morehead, 375 F.3d 677 (8th Cir. 2004)
United States v. Morgan, 635 Fed. App'x 423 (10th Cir. 2015)
United States v. Moriarty, 429 F.3d 1012 (11th Cir. 2005)
United States v. Morrill, 984 F.2d 1136 (11th Cir. 1993)
United States v. Mostella, 802 F.2d 358 (9th Cir. 1986)
United States v. Munoz-Nava, 524 F.3d 1137 (10th Cir. 2008)
United States v. Murillo-Mora, 703 Fed. App'x 435 (8th Cir. 2017)
United States. v. Musgrave, 761 F.3d 602 (6th Cir. 2014)
United States v. Myers, 21 F.3d 826 (8th Cir. 1994)
United States v. Nava, 404 F.3d 1119 (9th Cir. 2005)
United States v. Newell, 658 F.3d 1 (1st Cir. 2011)
United States v. Newman, 659 F.3d 1235 (9th Cir. 2011)
United States v. Newsome, 322 F.3d 328 (4th Cir. 2003)
United States v. Noel, 581 F.3d 490 (7th Cir. 2009)
United States v. Nunemacher, 362 F.3d 682 (10th Cir. 2004)
United States v. Olsen, 519 F.3d 1096 (10th Cir. 2008)
United States v. Ortiz-Torres, 873 F.3d 346 (1st Cir. 2017)
United States v. Ortland, 109 F.3d 539 (9th Cir. 1997)

United States v. Overstreet, 713 F.3d 627 (11th Cir. 2013)
United States v. Palomo, 80 F.3d 138 (5th Cir. 1996)
United States v. Parks, 823 F.3d 990 (11th Cir. 2016)
United States v. Patton, 708 Fed. App'x 488 (10th Cir. 2017)
United States v. Pauley, 511 F.3d 468 (4th Cir. 2007)
United States v. Paulino, 996 F.2d 1541 (3d Cir. 1993)
United States v. Peel, 668 F.3d 506 (7th Cir. 2012)
United States v. Perez-Jiminez, 654 F.3d 1136 (10th Cir. 2011)
United States v. Portillo, 363 F.3d 1161 (11th Cir. 2004)
United States v. Primus, 713 Fed. App'x 529 (8th Cir. 2018)
United States v. Reed, 774 Fed. App'x 16 (2d Cir. 2018)
United States v. Reifler, 446 F.3d 65 (2d Cir. 2006)
United States v. Robertson, 537 F.3d 859 (8th Cir. 2008)
United States v. Robertson, 493 F.3d 1322 (11th Cir. 2007)
United States v. Robinson, 482 F.3d 244 (3d Cir. 2007)
United States v. Robinson, 454 F.3d 839 (8th Cir. 2006)
United States v. Ross, 245 F.3d 577 (6th Cir. 2001)
United States v. Sablan, 90 F.3d 362 (9th Cir. 1996)
United States v. Sachdev, 279 F.3d 25 (1st Cir. 2002)
United States v. Sadler, 642 Fed. App'x 834 (10th Cir. 2016)
United States v. Santiago-González, 825 F.3d 41 (1st Cir. 2016)
United States v. Santopietro, 996 F.2d 17 (2d Cir. 1993)
United States v. Sayer, 748 F.3d 425 (1st Cir. 2014)
United States v. Scherrer, 444 F.3d 91 (1st Cir. 2006)
United States v. Schlueter, 634 F.3d 965 (7th Cir. 2011)
United States v. Scott, 145 F.3d 878 (7th Cir. 1998)
United States v. Scroggins, 880 F.2d 1204 (11th Cir. 1989)
United States v. Sheridan, 859 F.3d 579 (8th Cir. 2017)
United States v. Shi Chang Huang, 491 Fed. App'x 382 (4th Cir. 2012)
United States v. Siman, 419 Fed. App'x 979 (11th Cir. 2011)
United States v. Simmons, 164 F.3d 76 (2d Cir. 1998)
United States v. Simpson, 741 F.3d 539 (5th Cir. 2014)
United States v. Sims, 511 Fed. App'x 429 (6th Cir. 2013)
United States v. Smith, 606 F.3d 1270 (10th Cir. 2010)
United States v. Solis–Bermudez, 501 F.3d 882 (8th Cir. 2007)
United States v. Soyland, 3 F.3d 1312 (9th Cir. 1993)
United States v. Spiropoulos, 976 F.2d 155 (3d Cir. 1992)
United States v. Spring, 108 Fed. App'x 116 (4th Cir. 2004)
United States v. Stanfield, 360 F.3d 1346 (D.C. Cir. 2004)
United States v. Standiford, 148 F.3d 864 (7th Cir. 1998)
United States v. Steen, 55 F.3d 1022 (5th Cir. 1995)
United States v. Stefonek, 179 F.3d 1030 (7th Cir. 1999)
United States v. Stewart, 590 F.3d 93 (2d Cir. 2009)
United States v. Stoller, 78 F.3d 710 (1st Cir. 1996)
United States v. Stone, 575 F.3d 83 (1st Cir. 2009)
United States v. Strahan, 598 Fed. App'x 597 (10th Cir. 2015)
United States v. Stuart, 384 F.3d 1243(11th Cir. 2004)
United States v. Thompson, 430 Fed. App'x 805 (11th Cir. 2011)
United States v. Thornbrugh, 764 Fed. App'x 655 (10th Cir. 2019)
United States v. Thornhill, 759 F.3d 299 (1st Cir. 2014)
United States v. Torres-Landrua, 783 F.3d 58 (1st Cir. 2015)
United States v. Trejo, 624 Fed. App'x 709 (11th Cir. 2015)
United States v. Tutty, 612 F.3d 128 (2d Cir. 2010)
United States v. Ukomadu, 236 F.3d 333 (6th Cir. 2001)
United States v. Valle, 940 F.3d 473 (9th Cir. 2019)
United States v. VandeBrake, 679 F.3d 1030 (8th Cir. 2012)
United States v. Vega, 332 F.3d 849 (5th Cir. 2003)
United States v. Visman, 919 F.2d 1390 (9th Cir. 1990)
United States v. Voda, 994 F.2d 14 (5th Cir. 1993)
United States v. Wade, 890 F.3d 629 (7th Cir. 2018)
United States v. Ward, 626 F.3d 179 (3d Cir. 2010)
United States v. Washington, 515 F.3d 861 (8th Cir. 2008)
United States v. Webb, 738 F.3d 638 (4th Cir. 2013)
United States v. Weber, 451 F.3d 552 (9th Cir. 2006)
United States v. Whitehorse, 2000 WL 219967 (10th Cir. 2000)
United States v. Whitman, 209 F.3d 619 (6th Cir. 2000)
United States v. Wilmore, 381 F.3d 868 (9th Cir. 2004)
United States v. Whitten, 610 F.3d 168 (2nd Cir. 2010)
United States v. Williams, 356 F.3d 1045 (9th Cir. 2004)
United States v. Williams, 65 F.3d 301 (2d Cir. 1995)
United States v. Wilder, 15 F.3d 1292 (5th Cir. 1994)
United States v. Wilson, 939 F.3d 929 (8th Cir. 2019)
United States v. Wintermute, 443 F.3d 993 (8th Cir. 2006)
United States v. Young, 634 F.3d 233 (3d Cir. 2011)

District Courts

Gauthier v. United States, No. Civ.A. 98–CV–630, 1998 WL 808997 (N.D.N.Y. Nov. 18, 1998)
Lopez v. United States, 16–20046-Cr-SCOLA, 2017 WL 2912818 (S.D. Fla. May 2, 2017)

Murphy v. Shaw, A-0906-13T1, 2014 WL 7370131 (N.J. Super. Dec. 30, 2014)
Rubashkin v. United States, No. 08-CR-1324-LRR, 2017 WL 384277 (N.D. Iowa Jan. 26, 2017)
Running v. United States, 81 F.Supp.3d 781 (D S.D. 2015)
Slagle v. Miller, No. 1:12-cv-839, 2013 WL 950854 (S.D. Ohio Mar. 12, 2013)
United States v. BP Products North America Inc., 610 F.Supp.2d 655 (S.D.Tex.2009)
United States v. Cousins, No. 05-04-CR-169, 2007 WL 1454275 (N.D. Ohio May 17, 2007)
United States v. Ferguson, 942 F.Supp.2d 1186 (M.D. Ala. 2013)
United States v. Ferguson, 584 F.Supp.2d 447 (D. Conn. 2008)
United States v. Gonzales, 163 F.Supp.3d 1078 (D.N.M. 2016)
United States v. Hendrickson, 25 F. Supp. 3d 1166 (N.D. Iowa 2014)
United States v. Lawrence, 254 F. Supp. 3d 441 (E.D.N.Y. 2017)
United States v. Mongol Nation, 370 F. Supp.3d 1090 (C.D. Cal. 2019)
United States v. Nesbeth, 188 F.Supp.3d 179 (E.D.N.Y. 2016)
United States v. Orthofix, Inc., 956 F. Supp.2d 316 (D. Mass. 2013)
United States v. Parker, No. 06-20050, 2007 WL 1544403 (E.D. Mich. May 25, 2007)
United States v. Stergios, 370 F.Supp.2d 328 (D. Maine 2005)
United States v. Urchak, Crim. No. 08-781 (RMB), 2019 WL 316013 (D. N.J. Jan. 24, 2019)
United States v. Wilson, 350 F. Supp. 2d 910, 917 (D. Utah 2005)
United States v. Wing, No. 5:13-CR-87-JMH-HAI-1, 2016 WL 11431968 (E.D. Kent. Apr. 21, 2016)

State Courts

People v. Mischley, 417 N.W.2d 537 (Mich. App. 1987)

Secondary Sources

Books

Anthony G. Amsterdam, Trial Manual 5 For the Defense of Criminal Cases (Vol. I 1988)
Aristotle, Rhetoric, Book I, Part II, Paragraph VII (Trans. W. Rhys Roberts, Mineola, NY; Dover Publications 2004)
William W. Berry III, Mitigation in Federal Sentencing in the United States, in Mitigation and Aggravation at Sentencing (Julian V. Roberts ed., 2011)
Arthur W. Campbell, The Law of Sentencing (2009)
Lawrence M. Friedman, American Law in the 20th Century (2002)
Lawrence M. Friedman, A History of American Law (1973)
Catharine M. Goodwin, Jay E. Grenig, & Nathan A. Fishbach, Federal Criminal Restitution (West 2009)
Alan D. Hornstein, Appellate Advocacy in a Nutshell (1998)
Hutchison, et al., Federal Sentencing Law and Practice (2012)
Irving L. Janis, Groupthink (2d ed. 1983)
1 W. LaFave & A. Scott, Substantive Criminal Law (2d ed. 2003)
Steven Lubert & J.C. Lore, Modern Trial Advocacy (5th ed. 2015)
Thomas A. Mauet, Trial Techniques (10th ed. 2017)
John Munkman, The Technique of Advocacy (Butterworth's 2001)
Carl Sandburg, The People, Yes (1937)
John Henry Wigmore, A Treatise on the Anglo-American System of Evidence in Trials at Common Law (2d ed. 1923)

Articles

Abbott, *The Civil War and the Crime Wave of 1865–70*, 1 Soc. Serv. Rev. 212 (1927)
Jeffrey Abramson, *Death-is-Different Jurisprudence and the Role of the Capital Jury*, 2 Ohio St. J. Crim. L. 117 (2004)
Katherine Allen, *The Jury: Modern Day Investigation and Consultation*, 34 Rev. Litig. 529 (2015)
Kimberly Bahna, *"It's a Family Affair"—The Incarceration of the American Family: Confronting Legal and Social Issues*, 28 U.S.F. L. Rev. 271 (1994)
Mary Beth Beazley, *Writing for a Mind at Work: Appellate Advocacy and the Science of Digital Reading*, 54 Duq. L. Rev. 415 (2016)
Paisly Bender, *Exposing the Hidden Penalties of Pleading Guilty: A Revision of the Collateral Consequences Rule*, 19 Geo. Mason L. Rev. 291 (Fall 2011)
Mark W. Bennett, *Heartstrings or Heartburn: A Federal Judge's Musings on Defendants' Right and Rite of Allocution*, 35-MAR Champion 26 (2011)
Mark W. Bennett, *Hard Time: Reflections on Visiting Federal Inmates*, 94 Judicature 304 (2011)
Mark W. Bennett & Ira P. Robbins, *Last Words: A Survey and Analysis of Federal Judges' Views on Allocution in Sentencing*, 65 Ala. L. Rev. 735 (2014)
Eric E. Bergsten, *Experiential Education Through the Vis Moot*, 34 J. L. & Com. 1 (2015)
Sarah Berson, U.S. Dep't of Just., Nat'l Inst. Of Just., *Beyond the Sentence—Understanding Collateral Consequences*, 272 Nat'l Inst. Of Just. J. 24 (2013)
Chrisje Brants, *Wrongful Convictions and Inquisitorial Process: the Case of the Netherlands*, 80 U. Cin. L. Rev. 1069 (2012)
Emily Buss, *What the Law Should (and Should Not) Learn from Child Development Research*, 38 Hofstra L. Rev. 13 (2009)
Joe S. Cecil et al., *Citizen Comprehension of*

Difficult Issues: Lessons from Civil Jury Trials, 40 Am. U. L. Rev. 727 (1991)
Cait Clarke & James Neuhard, *"From Day One": Who's in Control as Problem Solving and Client-Centered Sentencing Take Center Stage*, 29 N.Y.U. Rev. L. & Soc. Change 11 (2004)
Jill M. Cochran, *Courting Death: 30 Years Since Furman, Is the Death Penalty Any Less Discriminatory? Looking at the Problem of Jury Discretion in Capital Sentencing*, 38 Val. U. L. Rev. 1399 (2004)
John P. Cronan, *Is Any of This Making Sense? Reflecting on Guilty Pleas to Aid Criminal Juror Comprehension*, 39 Am. Crim. L. Rev. 1187 (2002)
James D. Dimitri, *Stepping Up to The Podium With Confidence: A Primer For Law Students On Preparing and Delivering An Appellate Oral Argument*, 38 Stetson L. Rev. 75 (2008)
Margareth Etienne, *The Declining Utility of the Right to Counsel in Federal Criminal Courts: An Empirical Study on Diminished Role of Defense Attorney Advocacy Under the Sentencing Guidelines*, 92 Calif. L. Rev. 425 (2004)
Jelani Jefferson Exum, *Why March to a Uniform Beat? Adding Honesty and Proportionality to the Tune of Federal Sentencing*, 15 Tex. J. on C.L. & C.R. 141 (2010)
Ian N. Friedman, *Child Pornography Sentencing: The Road Here and the Road Ahead*, 21 Fed. Sent. R. 83 (2008)
Robert F. Forston, *Sense and Non-Sense: Jury Trial Communication*, 1975 B.Y.U. L. Rev. 601 (1975)
Michael Frost, *Ethos, Pathos & Legal Audience*, 99 Dick. L. Rev. 85 (1994)
John T. Gaubatz, *Moot Court in the Modern Law School*, 31 J. Legal Educ. 87 (1981)
Miriam S. Gohara, *In Defense of the Injured: How Trauma-informed Criminal Defense can Reform Sentencing*, 45 Am. J. Crim. L. 1 (2018)
Miriam S. Gohara, *Grace Notes: A Case for Making Mitigation the Heart of Noncapital Sentencing*, 41 Am. J. Crim. L. 41 (2013)
J. Thomas Greene, *Oral Argument in the District Court*, 26 No. 3 Litig. 3 (2000)
Bruce A. Green & Rebecca Roiphea, *Judicial Activism in Trial Courts*, 74 N.Y.U. Ann. Surv. Am. L. 365 (2018)
Chris Guthrie, et al., *Blinking on the Bench: How judges Decide Cases*, 93 Cornell L. Rev. 1 (2007)
Chris Guthrie, et al., *Can Judges Ignore Inadmissible Information? The Difficulty of Deliberately Disregarding*, 153 U. Pa. L. Rev. 1251 (2005)
Chris Guthrie, et al., *Inside the Judicial Mind*, 86 Cornell L. Rev. 777 (2001)
Jennifer Kruse Hanrahan, 2003 B.Y.U. Educ. & L.J. 299 (2003)
Lisa Hay, *Sentencing: Thinking Like a Judge, Arguing as an Advocate*, 38 Champion 20 (2014).
Thaddeus Hoffmeister, *Investigating Jurors in the Digital Age: One Click at a Time*, 60 U. Kan. L. Rev. 611 (2012)
Paul Holland, *Sharing Stories: Narrative Lawyering in Bench Trials*, 16 Clinical L. Rev. 195 (2009)
D. Brock Hornby, *Speaking in Sentences*, 14 Green Bag 2d 147 (2011)
Hon. Virginia M Kendall, *A Judge Comments*, 41 No. 3 Litigation 23 (2015)
Sara Klco & Francisco Armada, *Tips for Young Lawyers*, 37 No. 3 Trial Advoc. Q. 13 (2018)
Shirley R. Klein et al., *Inmate Family Functioning*, 46 Int'l J. Offender Therapy & Comp. Criminology, 95 (2002)
Joel D. Lieberman & Bruce D. Sales, *What Social Science Teaches Us About the Jury Instruction Process*, 3 Psychol. Pub. Pol'y & L. 589 (1997)
Cortney E. Lollar, *What is Criminal Restitution*, 100 Iowa L. Rev. 93 (2014)
Margaret Love, *Collateral Consequences after* Padilla v. Kentucky: *From Punishment to Regulation*, 31 St. Louis U. Pub. L. Rev. 87 (2011)
Andrew M. Low, *Questions From The Bench*, 27-DEC. Colo. Law. 21 (1998)
Jessica M. Marshall *(I Can't Get No) Satisfaction: Using Restorative Justice to Satisfy Victims' Rights*, 15 Cardozo J. Conflict Resol. 569 (2014)
Sharon Patrick & Jill Miller, *Sentencing Advocates Enhance Reasoned Court Decisions*, 24 Crim. Just. 30 (2009)
Hon. David J. Newblatt, *How to Convince the Judge on Motion Day in Family Court*, 85 Mich. B. J. 16 (2006)
Rachael A. Ream, *Limited Voir Dire*, 23 Crim. Just. 22 (2009)
William J. Rehnquist, *Oral Advocacy: A Disappearing Art*, 35 Mercer L. Rev. 1015 (1984)
William L. Reynolds &; William M. Richman, *Justice and More Judges*, 15 J.L. & Pol. 559 (1999)
Chief Justice John G. Roberts Jr., *2016 Year-End Report on the Federal Judiciary* 5 (2016)
Rosenbaum, *The Relationship Between War and Crime in the United States*, 30 J.Crim. L. & C. 722 (1940)
Samuel V. Schoonmaker IV, Kenneth J. Bartschi, *Effective Family Law Appeals*, 28 Fam. Advoc. 6 (2006)
John N. Sharifi, *Approaching the Bench: Trial Techniques for Defense Counsel in Criminal Bench Trials*, 28 Am. J. Trial Advoc. 687 (2005)
Scott B. Tulman, *Competent and Zealous Representation at Sentencing: Core Ethical Obligations in Criminal Defense Cases*, 2015 WL 7299814 (2015)
Hon. Roger K. Warren, *A Tale of Two Surveys: Judicial and Public Perspective on State Sentencing Reform*, 21 Fed. Sent. R. 276 (2009)
Hon. Justice Thomas D. Waterman, Hon. Judge Mark W. Bennett, & David C. Waterman, *A Fresh Look as Jurors Questioning Witnesses: A Review of Eighth Circuit and Iowa Appellate Precedents and an Empirical Analysis of Federal and State Trial Judges and Trial Lawyers*, 64 Drake L. Rev. 485 (2016)
Jack B. Weinstein, *Does Religion Have a Role in Criminal Sentencing?*, 23 Touro L. Rev. 539 (2007)

Brian Wice, *Oral Argument in Criminal Cases: 10 Tips for Winning the Moot Court Round*, 69 Tex. B. J. 224 (2006)

C.J. Williams & Leonard T. Strand, *Judicial Advocacy: How to Advocate to a Judge*, 43 Am. J. Trial Advoc. 281 (2020)

C.J. Williams & Dasha Ternavska, *A Series of Unfortunate Events: The Admissibility of "Other Fires" Evidence in Arson Cases*, 48 Conn. L. Rev. 685 (2016)

David M. Wilson, *Working Toward a Common Goal: Are You One of Us?*, 48 No. 3 DRI For Def. 14 (2006)

Christopher A. Wray, *Note, Corporate Probation Under the New Organizational Sentencing Guidelines*, 101 Yale L. J. 2017 (1992)

Index